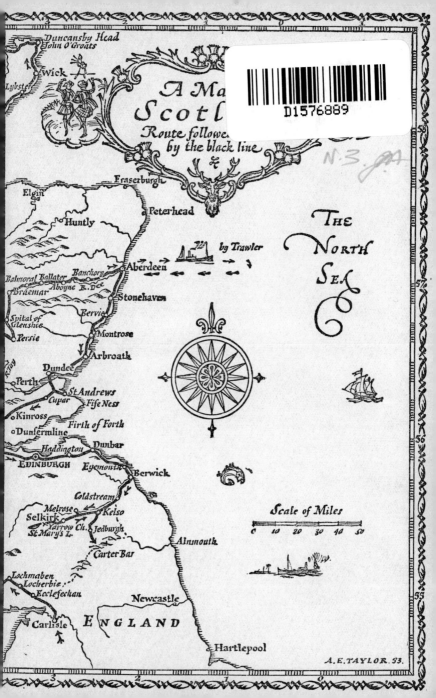

A Map of Scotland

Route followed by the black line

THE NORTH SEA

Duncansby Head
John O'Groats
Wick
Lybster
Fraserburgh
Elgin
Huntly
Peterhead
Aberdeen
by Trawler
Balmoral Ballater Banchory
Braemar Aboyne B. Dee
Spital of Glenshee
Persie
Stonehaven
Bervie
Montrose
Arbroath
Dundee
Perth
St Andrews
Cupar
Fife Ness
Kinross
Dunfermline
Firth of Forth
Haddington
Dunbar
EDINBURGH
Eyemouth
Berwick
Coldstream
Melrose
Selkirk
Kelso
Yarrow Ch. Jedburgh
St Mary's L.
Carter Bar
Alnmouth
Lochmaben
Locherbie
Ecclefechan
Newcastle
Carlisle
ENGLAND
Hartlepool

Scale of Miles
0   10   20   30   40   50

A.E.TAYLOR. 33.

IN SCOTLAND AGAIN

THE BORDER BRIDGE OVER THE SARK

IN SCOTLAND AGAIN

BY

H. V. MORTON

WITH FIFTEEN ILLUSTRATIONS AND A MAP

> Ere ye go through Scotland you shall
> see many good-like men and women, and
> other commodities that will be to your
> contentment.
>
> —JAMES V OF SCOTLAND TO
> MARY OF GUISE

METHUEN & CO. LTD. LONDON
36 Essex Street, Strand, W.C.2

This book was first published October 26th, 1933
Sixteenth edition, 1949
Reprinted, 1952

16.2
CATALOGUE NO. 3447/U

PRINTED IN GREAT BRITAIN

To

C. W. CHAMBERLAIN

INTRODUCTION

THIS companion volume to *In Search of Scotland* is the record of a long and leisurely journey. In the course of it I have shaken up the dust of history and I have tried also to put into words the impression made by Scotland upon the mind of a stranger who, for some reason or other, always feels happy over the Border.

In a sense this book is inspired by people I have never seen. When my first book on Scotland was published four years ago a shower of local pride descended on me from every part of the British Empire in the form of letters from Scotsmen and Scotswomen—some of them very angry—asking why I had missed a certain village, glen, hill or loch! I took this to heart and decided that if ever the chance offered itself I would go back and, in the course of my travels, obey where possible these long-distance directions. I am glad I did so. It would be ungracious not to thank those unknown friends in Canada, Australia, and New Zealand, who will find that their advice, admonition and fierce local pride have not been wasted.

I would like to thank those Scotsmen and Scotswomen nearer home who have given me friendship and a seat at the fire. The more I know of Scotland the more certain I am that of all the countries in the world it is the most kindly, the most polite and the most considerate. The bluffness and the curfness on which the Scot prides himself is a pretence that would not deceive a child, and badly hidden behind this quaint protective mask is a warmth of feeling, a sincerity which is purely Scottish and an emotionalism which is almost Latin. Only the most generous and hospitable of nations could enjoy jokes about its traditional meanness! I enjoy and admire Scotland so much that I should hate to live there in case I ever came to take her for granted.

I would like to thank that delightful writer of Galloway, Mr. Andrew McCormick, who has been good enough to read this book, and also those friends, too numerous to mention by name, who have placed at my disposal such abundant stores of local knowledge. The chapter which describes my experiences in a North Sea trawler appeared at the time in the pages of the *Daily Herald*.

The bibliography includes many books which every writer on Scotland must consult, and I give this list in the hope that it may help to indicate a line of reading to some of those who feel inclined to journey in the pleasant ways of Scottish literature and history.

H. V. M.

LONDON

October, 1933

BIBLIOGRAPHY

THE LOWLANDS AND THE BORDER

Scott's Minstrelsy of the Scottish Border.
The Gallovidian.
Galloway : the Spell of its Hills and Glens, by Andrew McCormick.
Chronicles of Gretna Green, by Peter Orlando Hutchinson.
Raiderland, by S. R. Crockett.
Social Life of Scotland in the Eighteenth Century, by Henry Grey.
The Mediæval Castle in Scotland, by W. Mackay Mackenzie.
Highways and Byways in the Border, by Andrew and J. Lang.
The Border Line, by James Logan Mack.
A History of the House of Douglas, by Sir Herbert Maxwell.
The Making of Scotland, by Sir Herbert Maxwell.
Dumfries and Galloway (County Histories of Scotland), by Sir
    Herbert Maxwell.
Highways and Byways in Galloway and Carrick, by C. H. Dick.
The Story of the Covenant, by T. Ratcliffe Barnet.
Dervorgilla, Lady of Galloway, by Wentworth Huyshe.
The Parish of Urr, by David Frew.
The Buchanite Delusion, by John Cameron.
The Life and Letters of Paul Jones, by Mrs. Reginald de Koven.
Border Byways and Lothian Lore, by T. Ratcliffe Barnett.
Domestic Annals of Scotland, edited by R. Chambers.
Kirkcudbrightshire and Wigtownshire (Cambridge County Geog-
    raphies), by W. Learmonth.
Scottish Symbols, by William M'Millan.
Sir Walter Scott, by John Buchan.
The Life of Walter Scott, by Stephen Gwynn.
Old St. Andrews, by Eric S. Robertson.
History and Poetry of the Scottish Border, by Professor Veitch.
The Gallovidian Encyclopedia, by John Mactaggart.
The Tinkler-Gypsies, by Andrew McCormick.
Montrose, by John Buchan.
John Graham of Claverhouse, by C. S. Terry.
The Secret of Flodden, by W. Mackay Mackenzie.
Lives of the Queens of Scotland, by Agnes Strickland.
The Scottish Regalia, by John J. Reid.

THE HIGHLANDS

The Scottish Gael, by James Logan.
Boswell's Journal of a Tour with Dr. Johnson.
The Rising of 1745, edited by C. Sanford Terry.
Prince Charles Edward, by Andrew Lang.
Pickle the Spy, by Andrew Lang.
The Companions of Pickle, by Andrew Lang.
History of the Rebellion, 1745, by John Home.
Rae's History of the Rebellion.
The Report of the Proceedings and Opinion of the Board of General
    Officers of their Examination into the Conduct, Behaviour and
    Proceedings of Lieutenant-General Sir John Cope.
Glen-Albyn : Tales of the Central Highlands.
The Ogha Mor, by Angus Robertson.
The Highland Clearances, by Alexander MacKenzie.
Inverness (County Histories of Scotland), by J. Cameron Lees.
A Short History of Scotland, by George Malcolm Thomson.
Historic Mysteries, by Andrew Lang.
The King over the Water, by A. Shield and Andrew Lang.
The Prophecies of the Brahan Seer, by Alexander MacKenzie.
Saint Columba of Iona, by Lucy Menzies.
Wild Sports and Natural History of the Highlands, by Charles
    St. John.
Heraldry in Scotland, by J. H. Stevenson.
The Land of the Hills and Glens, by Seton Gordon.
The Piper in Peace and War, by C. A. Malcolm.
Montrose, by John Buchan.
' Mann ' and Manners at the Court of Florence, by Dr. Doran.
London in Jacobite Times, by Dr. Doran.

GUIDE BOOKS

Every motorist should get *Scotland for the Motorist*, by J. Inglis
Ker. Road travellers will also find *The Complete Scotland* (Ward,
Lock & Co.) a useful, concise book with an admirable series of
maps. The best general guide is Muirhead's *Scotland* in the
' Blue Guides ' Series. Mountain climbers cherish the now
out-of-print *Scotland* (2 volumes) in Baddeley's ' Thorough
Guide ' Series. An admirable book for motorists in the eastern
Border is *The Land of Scott* by J. Inglis Ker.

CONTENTS

xi

ILLUSTRATIONS

The illustrations not otherwise acknowledged are from
photographs by Robert M. Adam

IN SCOTLAND AGAIN

IN SCOTLAND AGAIN

CHAPTER ONE

I GO TO SCOTLAND AGAIN.   ON THE WAY I OBSERVE THE DEATH
OF A CASTLE, CROSS THE BORDER AT SARK BAR, INQUIRE INTO
THE ROMANCE OF GRETNA GREEN, VISIT ECCLEFECHAN, SUFFER
A SHOCK AT DUMFRIES AND FIND OUT SOMETHING ABOUT BONNIE
ANNIE LAURIE

§ 1

THE hush of autumn lay like a spell upon the earth.
Trees had borne their fruit and fields their corn.
Apples lay in orchard grass, on every stream sailed a
leaf as red as blood or as yellow as gold, and in cottage
gardens the little daisies of St. Michael told the time of year
as surely as a calendar. Pale stubble, climbing the curve of
the fields, ran upward to a blue sky, and a few late
harvesters moved slowly in the sun as they stacked the
proud pavilions of the year.

Through the warm enchantment of such an afternoon, a
small car moved from the heights of Cumberland towards
the flat green country round Carlisle. There was nothing
about this car to distinguish it from others of the same prolific
family save the expression of the man inside it. It was the
face of one who sees visions. He looked neither to left nor
to right. He cared nothing for the wide moors on which a
giant had spilt his claret, and he gazed without interest at
the girl who, climbing suddenly over a stone wall, stood outlined for a moment against the sky, triumphantly curved and
female, in a pair of khaki shorts.

This traveller was urged onward by two powerful and
primitive emotions : hunger and anticipation. He had not
eaten since daybreak and he had not visited Scotland for
years. Into his mind came one of those stubborn resolutions

quite common to solitary and self-centred men : he swore that he would not eat until he had crossed the Border.

So, as he dipped down over the arched backs of the fells, his mind, seeking relief from the gnawing of his stomach, began to dwell with passionate intentness upon the kind of food that he would so soon be eating. He would arrive in Scotland at that beautiful moment known as ' high tea '. He would sit down in the coffee-room of a country hotel that seemed to be waiting for the arrival of Charles Dickens and his friends. There would be a huge silver urn on a vast mahogany sideboard. A foxed engraving on the wall would show Cromwell in the act of removing the bauble, or perhaps it would be Charles I defending himself in Westminster Hall, for all Scottish hotels are fascinated by the more embarrassing moments in English history. And a little Highland exile with a few freckles round her nose would come to him and ask, in a voice like a wind blowing gently through the glens of Lochaber, what he would like to eat. There would be Findon haddock, fried plaice, eggs, eggs and bacon, and probably steak ; for such is the tremendous foreground of ' high tea '. In the background would be baps and bannocks and scones, white bread and brown bread, gingerbread and currant bread, and apple jelly and jam. And as the traveller contemplated this orgy he conceived the daring idea of ' wishing ' three eggs. Eggs, by the way, are always ' wished ' singly or in pairs. Yes ; he would ride over the Border like a tempest and ' wish ' them in threes :

' Oh, Jeannie,' would sigh the little maid to the cook in the kitchen, ' there's an awfu' man who wishes *three* eggs ! Did ye ever hear the like o' that ? '

And through a lace curtain he would glance across the road and see an ominous pestle and mortar hanging outside a chemist's shop and, when he had eaten and paid his bill, he would be given at least one threepenny bit in his change. So he would know that he was in Scotland again . . .

He raced down from the heights of Cumberland, his eyes, singularly grim and determined, on the north.

§ 2

You will, perhaps, have guessed that this urgent traveller was myself. I was ravenous. And, when I left the hills and came to the Roman road that runs straight as a spear to the city of Carlisle, the Fox and Hounds had opened its doors to a dusty world and I knew that it would take some strength of mind to cross the still-distant Border fasting.

Now as I passed through a stone village which crouched under the Border hills wearing an expression that was both defensive and aggressive, I came to one of those mossy walls that surround the property of a gentleman. On this wall were auctioneer's bills which stated that the property of a gentleman was to be sold ' this day ', lock, stock, and barrel. Those bills leered between the trees and gazed into the road like broker's men. At the main gate two heraldic beasts rampant glared down helplessly at a commissionaire imported from Carlisle, who—strange sight—sat in the carriage drive at a card table piled with catalogues.

The tragedy of this noble house, which is one of the tragedies of this transitional age in which we live, drove all thought of hunger from my mind. I could not have been more down-cast had this house been my own home. All over the country these, the last lovely candles of the eighteenth century, are being blown out by the tax collector.

I drove through a dark, cool wood into a park where, beside a lake, rose up the towers and battlements of a castle in which no man in these days could afford to live or die. Its name had flashed through Border minstrelsy like a drawn sword, and now it stood desolate, its rows of blank windows gazing at the encircling woods. A few motor-cars were drawn up on an unkept lawn and the doors, wide open for the last time, admitted a seedy and ghoulish company.

I have often noticed that the auction-room seems to under-line the worst points in human nature. Even Christie's flings an air of avarice over the nicest people, and I have often been conscious, when bidding for a chair or a picture, advancing carefully and furtively from guinea to guinea, of a rather mean and shameful feeling. This business of winking slyly for other people's possessions is distinctly nasty. And in the great hall, which had known the tragedies and triumphs of an old family, stood men wearing bowler hats and smoking rank pipes. Every shadow seemed to hold the ghost of an outraged footman. And the horror of death and decay, and the humiliation of the scene, appealed so strongly to me that I nearly went away.

But I stayed fascinated, watching people tapping oak panels, turning chairs upside down or running a magnifying-glass over an indignant ancestor. A little Jew stood regarding the vast and intricate stone coat of arms over the fireplace in the ballroom :

'Now, what's the use of that?' he said petulantly in a whining voice. 'You can't sell it—even to an American. I wouldn't give five bob for it.'

And the heraldic beasts supported their shield bravely, with nothing in their proud defiance to suggest that their last fight had been lost.

I wandered through a wilderness of empty rooms, into the great bedroom overlooking the lake, where so many heirs had seen the light of prosperous days, into the library where centuries of squires had at least collected the classics bound in full brown calf, and downstairs into labyrinths of cellars where successive butlers had sampled the best port. It was, like all death-beds, very sad.

Some mischievous spirit of the old house entered into me and I performed a deed so absurd that I am almost ashamed to confess it. There were lifts that rose as high as the third floor of the castle, and on this floor, while meditating gloomily on the pathos of bedrooms to which no one will ever again bring a bride, I heard an auctioneer's voice ascending the lift-shaft :

'Now we come to lot eight hundred and four,' he said, 'a magnificent oak-panelled Otis elevator in perfect working order.'

I heard a murmur of interest from the crowd, and then I heard the auctioneer step into the lift and bang the door. The temptation was irresistible. Swiftly I pressed the button and fled. There was a roar of delighted laughter from below as the auctioneer floated upward out of sight of his audience. Through the crack of a bedroom door I watched him step out on the desolate landing, a truculent-looking man in a morning coat with a clove carnation in his buttonhole. He was dressed for a wedding and not a funeral. So the old house played its last practical joke on the auctioneer who was selling it ; and even my lady's bedroom seemed to smile at me, while the ample nurseries positively rocked with joy.

'It is a curious thing,' said one of the auctioneers, 'that there is a legend that this castle will be burnt down three

DUMFRIES

LOCH TROOL

times. It has been burnt down twice since Norman times, and the third burning is still to come. Nobody will buy it. We are therefore going to blow it up. The local people regard the dynamite which we shall use as the third, and last, fire, and the fulfilment of the prophecy. . . . Now, ladies and gentlemen, lot one thousand and forty-two, a fine cellar door . . .'

After some hesitation an ancient broker said very doubtfully : 'Half a crown.'

I went through the gates to the road again, saddened and uneasy, for these old families, which are being taxed out of existence in life and in death, are part of the roots of an England that I love. They are going, more slowly but as surely as French families went to the guillotine, to make way for an England that no man can see. It is the end of an age that, even at its worst, had good manners.

On the road once more my hunger returned. I entered Carlisle where everybody was eating. I could see girls gorging themselves in tea shops. Outside a public-house stood a large red man worrying a magnificent sandwich, pushing it into his mouth in great gobbets, while he watched a motor-bus cranking up for Dumfries. A herd of cows going north-ward straggled through Carlisle, and one of them looked at me and chewed deliberately. But my mind was set on 'tea' and the 'wishing' of eggs, so I took my hunger along the road that, without beating about the bush, runs straight into Scotland.

§ 3

England and Scotland melt imperceptibly into one another on this western Border. While there is no magnificent summit such as Carter Bar, there is—what shall I call it ?—a slight uneasiness in the air. No land I know, except perhaps the plain of Tuscany, is so haunted by its past as the Scottish Border. The winds blow over it charged with old memories. Here on Solway-side is a happy land of cornfields and woods and gentle green hills ; but it is no less soaked in ancient hatreds and old tragedies than the wilder uplands of the eastern Border, where the wind comes sighing through the heather of Carter Bar with a sound of mourning and where every stone might be a crouching man.

Wild centuries have left their mark along the Border, giving to each comfortable farmstead a rather startled look and to each fat hayrick an air of vague uncertainty. A man never knew what might come out of the Border night ; and to this day I think an air of watchfulness is still present on the border-land, so that one can never see a haystack on either side of the invisible line without remembering the remark of an ancient raider :

' If ye had four legs,' he remarked sorrowfully to a hayrick, as he passed with his stolen cattle, ' ye should not lang stay there ! '

I went on between hawthorn hedges until I came to an arched bridge over the little stream of Sark. At the far end of the bridge was a metal post which held a yellow disc bearing, most dramatically, one word—' Scotland '. I paused there. How happy I was to stand once again on the hospitable doorstep of Scotland ! A few yards and I would be over the threshold. I got out and sat on Sark Bridge, watching with amazement how many people dash over the frontier without a thought. ' Scotland ' declared the metal post ; and in that word were stored up for me all kinds of new adventures and experiences. It was good to be back. . . .

I went on over the bridge, and in the course of a few yards stopped outside a whitewashed toll-house which stands on the right-hand side of the road : the first building in Scotland. I stopped because this toll-house was making itself very noticeable. Unlike all its fellows up and down the country, which stand at cross-roads like the tombstones of the nineteenth century, this toll-house had leapt into a violent life. A hoarding in the garden said :

THIS IS THE HOUSE FAMOUS FOR GRETNA GREEN
RUNAWAY MARRIAGES

Another notice posted over the door announced in large letters :

OVER 10,000 MARRIAGES PERFORMED IN
THIS MARRIAGE ROOM

I went inside and was charged sixpence for a glance into the front room, a stuffy old-fashioned apartment crowded with relics of the days—not so long ago—when the Act forbidding irregular unions in England drove ardent young men, romantic old ones, reprobates, bigamists and all manner of folk who could not look an honest parson in the face, to the Scottish Border.

Why, I wonder, has a singularly cynical and unromantic episode in the history of law-breaking been transformed into a romance ? I suppose people prefer to contemplate star-crossed lovers winning through in spite of every obstacle rather than the unpleasant reality of the old satyr marrying the young girl, or the adventurer in search of a woman's property.

The room was littered with the relics of the time : the dusty stove-pipe hats which successive toll-gate keepers are supposed to have put on when marrying people, old black ties, marriage certificates, and prints showing a young couple urging on the postillions while an apoplectic father comes in sight over the curve of the hill.

What interested me, however, more than the room and its relics, were notices on the wall declaring war on the ' blacksmith's shop ' a few miles off at Gretna Green.

This is all in the true spirit of the past. The rival ' priests ' used to fight like cats for their profitable prey. Now, apparently, those who have come after fight for the profitable tourist. This amused me so much that I determined to go on to Gretna Green and see what the ' blacksmith's shop ' had to say about it. This place, which must be known to thousands of tourists all over the world, exists in a perfect rash of affirmation. It is plastered with placards. The turnstile was clicking merrily as a North Country crowd went in to gaze vacantly at a dreary collection of odds and ends, including an anvil, said to be the very one over which the apocryphal blacksmith used to forge unions. One of the three money collectors told me that eight marriages had been held that very week, and the register was brought out for my inspection. The insinuations of the Sark Toll-House were treated with contempt.

However, some facts about the Gretna marriage trade may be interesting. The first thing to remember is that the road from Carlisle, over Sark Bar to Gretna Green, was not built until 1830. It was called the ' English Road '. Before that time the main road into Scotland ran from Carlisle through

Longtown and entered Scotland slightly north of Gretna Green, running straight up to Kirkpatrick. Thus Gretna Green, although not actually on the main road, used to be the first village in Scotland. When Lord Hardwicke's Act ended the scandal of irregular marriages in 1754, couples who could not for some reason marry in the usual manner used to go to Calais, the Isle of Man, or across the Scottish Border, because Lord Hardwicke's Act, which was passed with great difficulty, applied only to England. Gretna was going strong as a clandestine wedding centre when Pennant toured Scotland in 1771, but no records remain, apparently, to prove by whom these weddings were made or in what building they were held. 'Here', says Pennant, 'the young couple may be instantly united by a fisherman, a joiner or a blacksmith.' As these marriages were a simple affirmation on Scots soil, witnessed by anybody who could write, it is probable that they were held in any beer-house in Gretna Green.

In 1791 a band of weavers settled in the district and formed the village of Springfield, near Gretna Green, and right on the main road. This now became the first village in Scotland and it rapidly took all the marriage trade from Gretna Green. The notorious spot was a small inn known as the King's Head, kept by a man called David Lang. He did so well that he caused the Gretna Green 'priest', Joseph Paisley, a twenty-five-stone mass of fat irrigated by brandy, to desert the Green and start a branch marriage office in Springfield !

By this time the trade was so well organized that the Carlisle hotels had an understanding with the 'priests'. One hotel would send couples to Lang and the other to Paisley. The post boys had reduced the business of flight to a fine art. Jack Ainslie, post boy at the 'Bush' in Carlisle, seems to have developed a deep hatred for parents. The mere suggestion that an anxious father was in pursuit seems to have whipped him into a furious and almost malicious ingenuity, and, so scientific was he in the art of evasion, that he had certain rights-of-way across farms and secret hiding-places in woods and lanes, so that if too hotly pursued he could suddenly draw in and let the pursuing coach go thundering past along the road to Springfield. He was also ever ready to be a witness to a marriage.

But a great change came over the marriage market when the 'English Road' was opened in 1830. This road knocked out Springfield. The coaches now crossed the boundary at Sark Bar and the first house on Scottish soil was Sark Toll Bar. This rapidly fell into the hands of marriage merchants, first Simon Beatie and afterwards an enterprising mason named John Murray, who had been employed on the Glasgow and South-Western Railway. Under these two men the Sark Toll Bar specialized in quantity, while Gretna Hall, a little farther on the road, specialized in quality. These two places and, to a lesser degree, the old inn at Springfield, monopolized the runaway marriage trade until well into the railway era, when emissaries used to haunt the station and tout like hotel porters! But the whole business collapsed when Lord Brougham's Act became law in 1856, since when Scottish law has required a residential qualification for marriage.

When Lord Chancellor Erskine became eccentric and self-indulgent and married his cook at the age of 69, it was to Elliot of Springfield that he went. He arrived with the lady and her four children—surely one of the strangest old lovers in Springfield's history! It has often been said that he arrived disguised as an old woman in order to deceive those of his family who disapproved of the cook, but in an early account of this elopement I have read that his lordship, during the long drive to the Border, amused the children by putting on their mother's bonnet. That was quite enough to start any legend!

The Earl of Westmorland's marriage to Miss Child was another Springfield affair. The earl fell in love with his father-in-law's money—Child was the great London banker—and ran off to the Border. Child came after him like a whirlwind, squandering his money on relays of horses, catching up with the runaways when they were changing teams at High Hesket. Child leapt out, drew a pistol and shot the leading horse of Westmorland's team of four. The post boys cut away the dying horse, ran over to Child's carriage and slit the leather straps on which it hung and then, mounting and putting spurs to their steeds, were off with a team of three. The earl won the race and the girl, but not the bank balance. Child tied up his wealth for children of the marriage, and died within a year of a broken heart.

The most scandalous marriage must be claimed by Gretna Hall. It was the abduction, in 1826, of a fifteen-year-old heiress, Ellen Turner, by an experienced widower named

Edward Gibbon Wakefield. This man invented a cock-and-bull story which no modern schoolgirl would believe for a moment. Her father, he said, was ill and in grave danger and had sent him to bring her to Scotland. During the journey he wrought the poor child into a frightful state of nerves. He told her that her father had been ruined and was flying from creditors, that his uncle had lent her parent the sum of £60,000 and that the only way to save her father was to marry him. This confused girl did at Gretna Hall, and was immediately rushed across to France. But the family followed and rescued her. Wakefield was arrested and was sentenced at Lancaster Assizes to three years' imprisonment for abduction, and the marriage was annulled by a special Act of Parliament.

The strangest feature of the business, to me, is the sequel. If you prowl about the Colonial Office in Whitehall you will see in an honoured position a bust of Edward Gibbon Wakefield, the colonial administrator. After his release from prison he emigrated and made a brilliant career for himself in Australia, New Zealand and Canada. He was, in fact, the apostle of scientific colonisation.

So the rivalry between the various rogues and vagabonds and drunken tradesmen who slept on the Scottish Border, with one ear listening for the sound of a galloping coach team, is still kept up by Sark Toll Bar and Gretna Green. It is rather a pity. I will get up and follow you through the middle of the night to real romance, but I feel—and I am sure that most people will agree with me—that nothing much would be lost if all the dusty top hats, the old cravats, the anvils, the chairs, and the other dreary relics of Sark and Gretna were placed on a bonfire.

And in this mood I left Gretna Green and took the road that runs north, to Kirkpatrick and on to Ecclefechan. I promised myself ' high tea ' in Dumfries.

§ 4

The road ran through quiet fields. On the right hand, where the River Sark winds through the flatness of Solway Moss, the Scottish army, ten thousand strong, broke and fled in the dusk of a November day in 1542, plunging madly in the bog-lands, and dying in the icy depths of Solway Sands as the Warden of the West Marches drove them on. How placid it looked now with the sun over it and the little river lying among green meadows. And the thing that happened on those placid banks broke the heart of James V.

I came to a small precise village with a stream running down the middle of the main street. Ducks dabbled and gobbled in the water and a white cow stood on the bank with the philosophic vagueness of her kind. Children, released from school, were climbing over a tiny bridge, and on each side of the road prim stone houses gazed down with an air of stern but affectionate bigotry. This—no need to ask—was Carlyle's Ecclefechan. It was the ' Entepfuhl ' of *Sartor Resartus*, and that stream running so quietly over its shallow bed was the kindly ' Khubach '. So this was the village that gave to literature the most positive and picturesque personality since Dr. Johnson.

Carlyle lies under a simple stone in the village kirkyard. It would have been easier for him to be buried in Westminster Abbey, but, always a rather difficult man, he chose to return to Ecclefechan.

Facing the stream is a row of houses. One of them is distinguished by a white archway that leads to a yard. It was through this arch that James, Frank, and Tom Carlyle, stone masons, used to cart their loads of granite. To-day the Arched House is a ' birthplace ', and you can pay a shilling and explore the little rooms in which the sage of Chelsea spent his boyhood.

I bought a ticket and was given two threepenny-bits in my change—sure and authentic sign that I had crossed the Border ! And I went inside to drift about in the melancholy atmosphere that pervades all birthplaces.

There are houses in Great Britain to-day which contain fifteen, sixteen, perhaps eighteen, and even twenty, children, but never do they attain to the official dignity of ' birthplaces ', whereas an only child who creates an unusual stir in the world confers the title of ' birthplace ' upon many a mildly astonished cottage. Carlyle's birthplace shares with Shakespeare's house at Stratford, and the Burns cottage at Alloway, the expression with which one is led to believe Napoleon's mother observed the headlong career of her impulsive son. One likes to think that the admirable Madame Bonaparte, never surprised, yet never deceived, by her offspring, regarded a Europe in chaos as a rather large-scale exhibition of her son's naughtiness. It always seems to me that these humble birthplaces are not, as one might think, embarrassed by their fame, or proud of it, but seem to sit back covered in relics, illumined by a mild amusement which seems to say : ' Ah well ; he may have deceived the world, but he couldn't deceive me ! Many's the time he's had a good old spanking on that stool—which all the people come to stare at—and many's the time he's been locked in that closet which they call the Poet's Nook. Nice old nook he thought it the day he threw a stone through Mistress MacDonald's window. . . .'

That, at least, is how ' birthplaces ' affect me ! The hush of reverence which enfolds them, the silence broken only by the emotional cough of the president of a literary society or the ecstatic sigh of a spectacled worshipper, are so incongruous.

And how do we know that ' birthplaces ' are thinking of the famous child ? May they not be remembering the one who made no mark in the world ? How do we know that Shakespeare's birthplace is thinking of William ? It may have preferred Richard ! How do we know that the Alloway cottage is thinking of Robert ? It may be hugging the memory of his younger brother, Gilbert ! And is it not quite likely that the Arched House at Ecclefechan harbours many an unpleasant memory of Tom—for he was a noisy, quarrelsome and irritable child—while it unfeignedly adores the memory of all the great man's brothers and sisters ?

It is not, after all, surprising that ' birthplaces ' should appear mildly cynical when the relics of the famous child come home to roost. Brilliance takes a child away from his family more rapidly than anything. The gulf between cottage and palace is as nothing compared to the distance between an Ecclefechan and a Cheyne Walk. And yet there is something unerringly right and conventional and, in a way, consoling in the fact that now and then the honour that Westminster Abbey can pay is not so precious as the pull of kinship.

In spite of my hunger, for such, alas, is enthusiasm, I went upstairs and examined the personal odds and ends of a great man's life, the things none of us can do without, things insignificant in themselves, yet portentous according to the amount of personality that soaks into them from us.   Carlyle's pen, his inkstand, the knife with which he cut his tobacco, his big felt hat—as painted by Whistler—his big straw hat, a tea caddy, two kitchen-table covers, and the spring safety-pin which he used as a paper-clip.

The impression left by this possibly unfair selection of his personal possessions was one of extreme frugality.   Even his tobacco knife was an ordinary cheap one.   Everything looked quite at home in the Arched House.   And it occurred to me that I was possibly rather sweeping, or perhaps harsh, in my previous thoughts on ' birthplaces '.   Carlyle seems to have taken from his little home, into the dangerous regions of success, a precious and very Scottish sense of austerity and frugality.

So I went away respectfully into the little street where the Kuhbach gurgles through Entepfuhl.   And, as I leaned over the breast-high wall that runs against one side of the stream, I remembered one of the best things written about Carlyle, a few sentences in an essay which Professor G. M. Trevelyan wrote during the War :

' Some old authors,' he wrote, ' when we read them seem to stand at our side, urging us to hold on and do our duty. Among these are Milton and Meredith, but most of all Carlyle.   Whatever the subject—Sartor, the Diamond Necklace, the essay on Scott, or Johnson—it is all the same.   The man speaks through his theme, however apparently remote from the war ; he understands this age of grim necessity and primitive trial of the utmost qualities of men and nations. When you read Carlyle *you feel you will never give in*.'

I went on towards Dumfries, thinking a lot about Carlyle and about the genius of the Scottish Lowlands.   The number of men who emerged from such homes as the Arched House to become great in the world is almost unbelievable.   Take Dumfriesshire alone.   Here is one Lowland county of Scotland with a roll of honour that might satisfy a country.   It is the county not only of Thomas Carlyle, but of the Admirable Crichton, born at Elliock in the parish of Sanquhar ; William

Paterson, projector of the Banks of England and Scotland, born at Skipmire in the parish of Tinwald; Thomas Telford, the great engineer, born at Westerkirk in Eskdalemuir; Dr. James Currie, the biographer of Burns, born at Kirkpatrick-Fleming; Edward Irving, the divine, born at Annan; Allan Cunningham, the poet, born at Blackwood in the parish of Kirkmahoe; Sir John Richardson, the explorer, born at Dumfries; James Hyslop, the author of *The Cameronian Dream*, born at Damhead, and yes, one could go on! But that is surely enough, even for a Lowland county. . . .

With the sun low in the sky I entered Dumfries.

§ 5

O lovers of Scotland, how shall I tell you of the shock which Dumfries inflicted on me?

Miles back on the Cumberland fells I had pictured the room to which I was going: the heavy old sideboard, the early-Victorian chairs, the historical engravings, and the little freckled Highland maid. None of these things is perhaps particularly lovely in itself, but, taken together, they sum up for me the impregnable solidity of the old Border coaching inn and many happy memories of Scotland.

But I walked into a room that might have been anywhere. It was panelled in fumed oak. Pictures of York hung on the walls, with a few bright versions of Canadian rock scenery. A tall and impressive maid, who might have waited with distinction in any embassy, placed before me a printed menu, and then it broke over me, and my heart ached at the knowledge, that the hotel had been brought up to date! Gone was the vast mahogany sideboard, gone the bell-pull that never worked, gone the old pictures and the Victorian lincrusta: one more touch of individuality had vanished from a world whose god is Uniformity.

I was too sad, and a little cowed by the fumed oak that replaced a genuine Victorianism with a hesitant attempt at Tudorism, to 'wish' three eggs. And I noticed, with something like panic, that the wild assortment of baps and bannocks and breads had been replaced by a superior side-table that contained bowls of brown, mean-spirited prunes and a chromatic fruit salad of almost inconceivable loathsomeness. I felt as a man might feel who, braving many perils and dangers to meet again a beloved grandmother, came upon her making merry at a cocktail bar.

I can be as sybaritic as any American widow, and when inhabiting the Ritzes of this world I am a relentless critic of plumbing and of what is known for some mysterious reason as ' service '; but I also appear to be one of the last lovers of the ugly, dark, inconvenient, inefficient and rather amusing old country hotel which is one of our final links with an age of horses. If Dumfries can do this, a town that I should have thought might have been one of the last to stand firm for mahogany and decentralized heat, then, I mourned, we must say good-bye to the little old corners of the world in which a man can forget the idiocies of progress.

How ungenerous disappointment can make a man! Behold, the impressive maid came towards me bearing a tea of supreme beauty and splendour. Two poached eggs sat with a bloated and faintly pink expression upon the half of a golden haddock. They rode above a little lake of milk on which small gold eyes glittered like the gold spots on a trout. And there were jams of Dundee. The orchards of Blairgowrie were blossoming again in jars! Oatcakes were lavished on me. A pot of honey arrived. Then came bread with currants embedded in it.

At this point the woman began to sack other tables. She strode about like a commandeering general. I felt like a pagan conqueror for whose sake a city is ravished. Brown and white breads were showered on the table. An exquisite apple jelly arrived. Then triangular scones, lightly dusted with flour and just faintly astringent with soda, gave a penultimate touch of grandeur to a ' tea ' which achieved its climax in an unforgettable bannock.

'They can sell the mahogany and put a new carpet on the floor,' I thought, ' but this beautiful tea remains an unchanging glory of Scotland! Time cannot alter it nor custom stale . . .'

' Will ye take a little cold ham ? ' interposed the maid.

I turned a slightly bleak eye to her and shook a grateful and contented head.

I went out into the streets of Dumfries. The sun had set, but it was still light. I wondered whether I would go to the Globe Tavern and listen to the rich conversation that is carried on there, night after night, or whether I would run out to the home of Annie Laurie, which I had a vague idea was a few miles beyond Maxwelltown. I got out the car.

I crossed the bridge over the Nith and came to a district at the west end of the bridge called Maxwelltown, but this was a name given in honour of the local lord, the Maxwell family of Terregles, as recently as 1810. I believe that it is generally assumed that 'Annie Laurie' applies to this spot, but it is not so: the 'Maxwelton Braes' lie about eight miles to the west of Dumfries.

I took a long, dusky road, and discovered that the Braes are not visible because they lie several miles away from it, and not a sign could I discover of the house in which Annie Laurie was born. Just as I was giving up and about to turn back to Dumfries, one of those alert and intelligent labourers, so often encountered on Scottish roads, passed on a bicycle. He told me that Annie Laurie's house was another five or six miles along, standing to the right of the road just past the village of Crossford. . . .

I came, in the course of six miles, to the house which, in the absence of corroboration, I assumed to be the one described by the labourer. It stood some way from the road on a slight rise of ground, a small, solid, country house, with a wall separating it from the road and a tree-lined drive curving up to the front door. Lights were shining in the windows. Soon, I supposed, someone would retire to rest in the room where Annie was starved into submission !

'Annie Laurie' is probably the most famous personal love song in the world. English people, many of whom think it was written by Burns, should know that it was penned to Miss Annie Laurie (who, by the way, figures in Burke's Peerage as the daughter of Sir Robert Laurie) by a fiery young soldier, William Douglas, of Fingland, a scion of the Douglases, of Morton Castle.

He retired from the army about 1694, and, settling down at Fingland, fell in love with Annie Laurie. Tradition has it that Annie Laurie did not object to Douglas as a lover, but her parents did so. They chose the old-fashioned method of locking her in a room until she promised to jilt him. This she did. But instead of laying him 'doon to dee', William Douglas eloped with, and married, Miss Elizabeth Clerk, of Glendoich, Lanark, and soon afterwards Annie Laurie married Alexander Fergusson, of Craigdarroch ! These are the lovers whose by no means deathless passion has gone round the world!

But it is not to Douglas that we owe the popularity of the song. Lady John Scott, of Spottiswood, rewrote it and set it to music, giving it instant popularity. It is one of the curiosities of literature that three immortal songs should have been written by three Scotswomen, all of whom concealed their authorship for years. 'The Flowers of the Forest' was written by Jean Elliot, daughter of Sir Gilbert Elliot, of Minto, and 'Auld Robin Gray,' by Lady Anne Barnard, to fit, as she confessed, a naughty old tune!

'Annie Laurie' is hardly ever printed or sung as Lady John Scott wrote it.

To appreciate how, with a touch here and there, she improved the original text, you must read Willie's version:

> Maxwelton banks are bonnie,
> Where early fa's the dew;
> Where me and Annie Laurie
> Made up the promise true;
> Made up the promise true,
> And ne'er forget will I;
> And for bonnie Annie Laurie
> I'll lay me doun and die.

He then described his fair one in terms of natural history:

> She's backit like the peacock;
> She's breistit like the swan,
> She's jimp about the middle;
> Her waist ye weel micht span,
> And she has a rollin' eye;
> And for bonnie Annie Laurie
> I'd lay me doun and die.

I think most people will agree that Lady Scott, in giving Annie Laurie a brow 'like a snaw-drift', a neck like a swan, and a dark-blue instead of a 'rollin'' eye, has left a more presentable picture to posterity!

What a queer thing a song is! What is it but a mood with wings to it? There was nothing remarkable about Annie Laurie and Willie Douglas. Their love affair was humdrum, yet merely because one night Willie, in a sentimental mood, sat down and wrote a song, he immortalized his love for the girl who married someone else!

> And for Bonnie Annie Laurie
> I'd lay doun my head and dee. . . .

Feeling vaguely depressed, I went back to Dumfries as quickly as wheels could take me.

Back again in Dumfries, I was drawn towards that alley where the Globe Tavern stands, the world's most satisfactory memorial to Burns. I would rather see the disappearance of the poet's birthplace at Alloway than the ending of the Globe. Burns would probably smile rather sadly at his birthplace ; but how delighted he would be to know that port and ale are still sold in the Globe, and to exactly the same kind of men with whom he used to drink in that small panelled sanctuary. This is probably one of the few places in Scotland in which Burns would feel instantly at home if he could return from the Shades.

It is the tragic fate of dead poets to fall victims to committees and to be subjected, on the happily rare occasion of their centenaries, to long and arid orations delivered by clergymen or professors, while grocers and manufacturers stand drearily by in scarlet gowns; or they fall a natural prey to dull and adulatory societies which, in life, would have made them violently sick. There is no way, apparently, to protect a poet from his admirers.

The Globe in Dumfries is, however, full every night of ordinary workmen, road-menders and labourers, who drink as much as they can afford to drink, and sing the songs of Burns because they understand them and like them. Reverence, which is such a frightful aspect of all literary societies, is delightfully absent in the Globe. They call him ' auld Rabbie', and remember all the things about him that the Burns societies try so earnestly to forget. I call this the real thing ; and it will be a lasting disgrace to every admirer of Burns, and to every Burns society in the world, if the old Globe Tavern is ever allowed to disappear.

I squeezed my way into the small tap-room, enjoying the hearty rise and fall of the broad Dumfriesshire voices and the robust shouts and bursts of laughter from the larger room outside. I fell into conversation with a red-faced, blue-eyed young man, talking to him about Burns and the Globe like an ignorant and benighted wayfarer. This is the only way to make people talk to you. My morale was considerably shattered when the young man advised me to read my own

book on Scotland. I promised to do so. The inn-keeper in
his shirt sleeves leaned over the bar and said, referring to
myself :
    ' Aye, he was here in this very room, but he didna' make
himself known.'

He said that he would know me at once if I ever came in
again, and he hoped someday to stand me a large drink as
a tribute to my faithful description of his inn on a song night.

I was so touched by this tribute, and by the generous
things that this gathering said about me—for I had always
believed that listeners hear no good of themselves—that I
pulled up my coat collar and hid as well as I could in it.

What a happy, cheerful spot is this tavern in Dumfries.
Its conviviality exists almost like a monument to one who
brought so much conviviality to the task of living. And so,
in a way, it is, because without Burns the Globe would have
no inspiration or tradition. Life goes on there night after
night just as he knew it, and as he would like to think of it.

I felt firmly at home. The warmth and friendliness of
Scotland had met me at the very gates. So I said good
night and left the Globe with the queer feeling that I
was my own ghost. It is a strange experience to be recom-
mended to yourself ; it is also very odd to know that if you
ran yourself down someone would defend you to your face !

As the clock struck ten I retired to a bedroom that contained running water. It was panelled from ceiling to floor
in oak that had been painted white. I looked out of the
window for some time on the broad-paved High Street of
Dumfries. A little group of men expelled from more sociable
surroundings lingered, finishing their arguments round the
rails of a strange and exotic fountain that celebrates, with
superb lack of humour, the arrival of water in Dumfries on
October 21, 1851. It is a queer and improbable erection for
a Scottish town. It rises in tiers like a huge wedding cake.
On the top are three gilded cranes, on a lower tier are four
gilded dolphins, and on the lowest are the gilded figures of
four chubby African boys holding young alligators. Dumfries, living up to this high standard of fantasy, has planted
four cactus plants round the fountain. A more unlikely
memorial to the sobering qualities of water would be difficult
to discover.

The last red 'buses cranked up for Lockerbie and swung

with a blaze of yellow light into English Street. The isolated
outline of the Mid-Steeple was black in the middle of the High
Street and the little round O of its clock-face was as yellow as a
lemon. The footfalls became fainter and fewer. There was
no sound but the voices arguing round the fountain :

'I'll no' believe it till I see it,' shouted one disputant.

There was a deep burble of dissent :

'I'll no' believe it till I see it,' said the stubborn one.

There was a clamp of departing feet and the group broke up.
Still the defiant voice reiterated a lack of faith. There were
now only two men left hotly arguing :

'Guid nicht, Jock.'

'Guid nicht, Tam.'

The voices were shouted across the road but the arguers
paid no attention :

'I'm tellin' ye—I'll no believe it till I see it,' said the man,
as, with an air of tremendous finality, he strode off into the
dark. The yellow clock in the Mid-Steeple struck the hour
and, with a sigh of satisfaction, I drew down the blind.

Yes . . . in Scotland again.

CHAPTER TWO

I ENTER GALLOWAY, AM CHARMED BY THE STRANGE MACS,
MAKE A BUCHANITE PILGRIMAGE, SEE THE PLACE WHERE THE
THAMES EMBANKMENT CAME FROM, GIVE MY OWN VERSION OF A
STORY ABOUT ROBERT THE BRUCE, VISIT THE OLD CASTLE OF
THREAVE AND, IN A TANGLED KIRKYARD, REMEMBER THE SOLEMN
LEAGUE AND COVENANT

§ 1

I SAW Galloway on a clear autumn morning when the rowans were turning red and the woods were wearing the first promise of gold and amber. If I had held to the road it would have taken me to Dalbeattie, but somewhere near a place called, I think, by the lovely name of Beeswing, I turned north.

I am writing on a stone dyke from which I can see the road winding on between grey walls. It is not a main road and nothing comes over it but a farm cart, or a farmer in his ' war memorial ' as they rather dryly call a Ford car in this part of Scotland ! A pretty arched bridge curves itself above a stream in which is a still, deep pool the colour of stout. I cannot keep my eyes from this pool because I am sure that if I wait long enough the speckled half-pounder, who, I swear, is lurking there with his nose to the current, will rise to a fly.

Grey stone walls divide the fields on each side of the road. In one field a herd of ' belties ' is grazing. Should there be a beauty competition for cows, I think the Galloway ' belties ' would win it. They are jet-black beasts with a snow-white band round their middles, which varies in width from a foot to a yard. They give character to the landscape, as the little dung-spattered black cows do to Kerry in Ireland and the polled Angus to other parts of Scotland. The fields slope up towards queer, nibbled-looking hills which grow the greenest grass I have ever seen. They are low, fairy-like hills. If they were in Donegal you would swear that there were

21

leprechauns in them. There is an air of enchantment over them. They look as though they might open and let loose into the world something that has been sleeping for centuries beneath the heather. They have the strange gnawed look of hills whose verdure hides old camps. I feel that perhaps if we could X-ray them we might see swords and helmets lost in some old fight. There might be bones hiding in these hills, the bones of Pict and Roman. Behind the hills are moorlands, high windy places where the claret-coloured heather, full of bees, leans back with its silver-grey stems in the sunlight.

Little platforms of planks are set at intervals along the road. Milk cans stand on them. In the afternoon these cans have vanished mysteriously towards some co-operative creamery. The platforms lend to Galloway an atmosphere of organized efficiency. . . .

There! I was right! I saw him with the tail of my eye! He came out of the brown peat-water, a thin flash of silver, and now a ripple is widening in the pool.

Galloway is a strong land. It is a stubborn land. That is my first thought of it. But just as you are always surprising in strong characters queer nooks and corners of tenderness, so in Galloway the exquisite beauty of woodland and stream and leafy land, and green meadows where the white gulls speak of salt waters, lies against a background of wild moors and wilder hills.

Galloway is composed of two counties, Kirkcudbrightshire and Wigtownshire. They form the outward bulge of south-western Scotland that thrusts itself into the waters of Solway Firth and is visible on a clear day from Ireland and the Isle of Man.

The first thing that the English stranger must learn in Galloway is to pronounce Kirkcudbright as ' Kir-coooo-brie ', and the second thing is that while he should not in conversation talk about the ' county ' or ' shire ' of Kirkcudbright, it is quite in order to talk of the ' county ' or ' shire ' of Wigtown. When referring to Kirkcudbright as a county he should call it ' the Stewartry '. A generation ago it would have been considered as great a solecism to talk about Kirkcudbrightshire as it would be to talk of Cornwall-shire, of

Norfolk-shire or Suffolk-shire, but the post office, it seems, does not recognize ' the Stewartry ' as an official topographical designation, so that unless a man is willing to let his correspondence wander round the county town of Kirkcudbright he is forced to write Kirkcudbrightshire on his letters.

In conversation, however, the old term ' Stewartry ' is employed and the county likes it because it is old, historic, distinguished, and marks it off very sharply from the neighbouring shire of Wigtown, which is equally old, historic and distinguished in its own estimation !

But why, you will ask, should a county be called a Stewartry ? This is the explanation given to me by one of the antiquaries and students of local affairs who abound in Galloway :

' In 1124, when David I became King of Scotland, he introduced many feudal ideas gathered in England. He was brought up in the court of his brother-in-law Henry I. One of these was the easier administration of justice. Therefore he ' shired ' the counties, as the Normans had already done in England. Shire means a division, from an Anglo-Saxon word, *sciran*, to cut or divide, and over these divisions of land was placed a ' shire-reeve ', or sheriff. This office became hereditary. When Archibald the Grim became lord of Galloway he appointed a deputy—a Steward—to collect his rents in eastern Galloway—the modern Kirkcudbrightshire—while western Galloway remained under the jurisdiction of the king's sheriff. So the name Stewartry—a memory of an official appointed in the fourteenth century—has remained until to-day . . .'

Galloway is perhaps the least-known district in Scotland. Although it is more accessible than the Highlands it is, for geographical reasons, infinitely more remote. The Highlands became fashionable in Victorian times, but Galloway remained locked in its native isolation until comparatively recent days. The railway did not come to Galloway—far south of Glasgow!— until after the Inverness and Nairn railway had been opened ! I possess a map of England and Scotland entitled *Bradshaw's Map of Great Britain shewing the Railways Completed and in Progress*. It is dated 1850. This map shows how Galloway remained right off the main line of traffic until late in the century. The main line into Scotland, printed in red, runs straight up from Carlisle to Carstairs and Glasgow, and a thin black line denotes a railway in the building from Carlisle to Dumfries and straight up through Sanquhar to Kilmarnock. But, even so, Galloway remained untouched by it. As late as 1877 a Galloway bard, who signed himself 'O. B.', hailed the branch line from Newton Stewart to Whithorn in terms of the wildest excitement :

> *Oor new clock lichted shows the 'oor.*
> *The parish kirk has got a toor,*
> *And better still, up to our door*
> *Has come the Wigtown Railway.*
>
> *Lord Galloway, gude, worthy man,*
> *The enterprise at first did plan,*
> *An' great and sma' pit to their han'*
> *To help to mak' the Railway.*
>
> *A while it stood at Sorbie Mill,*
> *For want of cash to mount the hill—*
> *But Johnston Stewart, with richt gudewill,*
> *Has brocht us up the Railway. . . .*

The poet then indulges in a vision of the real Galloway welcome that will be given to the railway :

> *Bonfires we'll hae on every hill,*
> *Wi' barrels fu' o' Wigtown yill,*
> *An' stronger drink frae Bladnoch still*
> *Sent doun alang the Railway.*
>
> *Teetotallers, whate'er they may think*
> *Aboot the use o' stronger drink,*
> *Will quaff cauld water till they blink—*
> *Rejoicing ower the Railway.*

He then welcomes the railway on behalf of Galloway's commercial interests :

> *What gudes we noo may hae to spare,*
> *Be't kintra growth or merchant ware,*
> *Is sure to find a sale somewhere—*
> *Thanks to the Wigtown Railway.*
>
> *What gudes we want, be't coarse or fine,*
> *At price accordin' to its kin'*
> *We'll get by cotch or English line,*
> *An' doon the Wigtown Railway. . . .*
>
> *Noo fill us up nae scrimpit sip,*
> *But fill your glasses to the lip—*
> *Three hearty cheers—Hurrah ! Hip ! Hip !*
> *Hurrah ! hurrah ! the Railway !*

And all this excitement about a railway in the fortieth year of Victoria's reign !

Sir Herbert Maxwell, of whom Galloway is so justly proud, remembers a time before the railway came to Galloway. The nearest stations were Dumfries on the east and Ayr on the north. When he set off for school in the south he used to catch a coach that left Portwilliam at 3 a.m. and linked up with the railway at Dumfries, or he would take the *Countess of Galloway*, a paddle-steamer that went to Liverpool. Sometimes the real Countess of Galloway would travel in her namesake, sitting in a private carriage that was securely lashed to the deck.

So Galloway, separated racially and geographically from the rest of Scotland and neglected by the railway until modern times, has always been just off the main line of communication. It has never been indebted too much to the outside world. It has remained a clearly defined little country within a country. I might call it the Yorkshire of Scotland, because it is an epitome of the whole land. If Scotland disappeared, leaving only Galloway, there would still be a miniature Scotland with its Highlands and its Lowlands, its rivers, its valleys and its plains. I might also, for another reason, compare Galloway with East Anglia.

Norfolk and Suffolk, like Kirkcudbrightshire and Wigtownshire, were for centuries separated from the rest of England by fen-lands and rivers, an isolation which explains their rich distinctiveness. The characteristics of a Norfolk man are those of an islander : and it is much the same with Galloway.

How natural it is that an ancient province that once possessed its own king—and has always possessed its own mind—should in the course of centuries of struggle, fighting Scotland one year and England the next, have a keen sense of frontier behind which exists a local patriotism stronger, perhaps, than in any other part of Scotland. A Galloway man in foreign parts is glad to meet another Scotsman, but when he meets another Galloway man they form a Gallovidian Society.

§ 2

The name was McGuffog.

I saw it written up over a shop in a town. I made inquiries about what was, to me, an unknown clan ; but no one seemed to think it at all interesting or remarkable. In another town I saw over a shop an even less credible name—McHarrie.

These are good Galloway names. The meaning of Galloway is the 'Land of the Stranger Gaels'. It comes from Gall, a stranger, and Gaidhel, the Gaels ; and it is interesting to find that these queer Macs—or stranger Gaels—still exist in great numbers in the local telephone directory.

Here is a short selection :

McClumpha	McHaffie
McCrindle	McKeand
McMeeking	McMiken
McSkimming	McCubbin
McCutcheon	McDavid
McFadzean	McWhirter
McQuaker	McHarrie

These names, many of which suggest the queer Macs that occurred in Ireland during the Irishing of the Normans, go right back into Galloway history, and their owners are as justly proud of them as more normal clansmen. But until the visitor becomes accustomed to them, it seems as though some whimsical Barrie has been having a game with the shop fronts !

These Galloway Macs are the very names one might choose for humorous Scottish characters in a novel. (Surely McWhirter is already famous ?)

The Gallovidian has always been a mystery to the historian. He remained a Pict of Galloway when the Southern and the Northern Picts submerged their identity in an alliance with the Irish or Scots. When Kenneth MacAlpine, king of the Dalriadic Scots, defeated the Picts with the help of the Danes in A.D. 844, he claimed all central Scotland as his kingdom, but Galloway remained outside it, the last stronghold of the mysterious Pict.

'The fremit (not a-kin) Scot o' Gallowa' ' is a tag that has stuck to these people through history. The original charter of Melrose Abbey in 1144 is addressed to 'the Normans, English, Scots and Galwegians of the whole realm '. As recently as the sixteenth century Gaelic was spoken in Galloway.

The ancestry of the Galloway men is, therefore, a long and honoured one, and I creep through the little stone towns gazing with awe and respect at the names of the Strange Macs. Who knows what improbable things lie in the race memory of this people ? If the recipe for heather ale exists, it may lie lost in the subconscious mind of someone called McSkimming !

This is a strong country. So much has happened in it ; and it wears the air of remembering everything.

In the Galloway heather the Roman outposts camped, gazing into the world's end, watching the Picts and longing to get back to rest billets in Carlisle. The Vikings beached their ships in the bays of Galloway, and to those shores came the Irish monks to clothe the land with Christ. There was a brief Golden Age, which is well remembered in Galloway, when a woman—Devorgilla, wife of John Balliol—left the world a love story under the broken arches of an abbey.

The Norman storm broke over Galloway until the air was darkened by the bowmen of Wales and Selkirk. The first Scots patriot, Wallace, plotted in Galloway. Men hunted Bruce through Galloway, and from Galloway he took the shaggy little horse that carried him at Bannockburn. After centuries of fighting, the hills of Galloway heard the chanting of psalms and saw the Covenanters assembling on the high moors —it is the greatest and the most solemn memory of this land —and so in time every small kirkyard received its martyr.

Of the crowded memories of Galloway this is the strongest.

§ 3

Wandering the roads and lanes of this heavenly country, I saw that I was only ten miles from the village of Crocketford. The name awakened a number of old memories. Years ago I became so interested in the history of self-deception that I nearly deceived myself into writing a book on the subject. But it is too vast a theme ! It is the subject that a man should reserve for his old age. However, in the notes that I made at the time the village of Crocketford had an honoured place as the last resting-place of those great self-delusionists, the Buchanites, whose eccentric theology ruffled the prevailing solemnity of Scotland towards the close of the eighteenth century.

So to Crocketford I turned my steps—or rather my wheels—and as I went I reviewed what must always remain one of the most astonishing episodes in the long history of fanaticism.

Joanna Southcott in England and Mother Buchan in Scotland, both living at the same period, were obsessed by a conviction of divinity. Mother Buchan discovered an unpleasing Nonconformist minister and proclaimed him as her presumably divine but spiritual 'Man-child', while Joanna Southcott at the age of sixty was convinced that she was about to become the mother of the Messiah. Both these women collected round them a band of earnest fanatics who handed down belief in them almost to our own times.

Elspeth Buchan, or Simpson, to give the lady her maiden name, was the daughter of a man who kept an inn on the Banff and Portsoy road. She was born in 1738. Her childhood was spent, like that of a more famous visionary, in herding cows, and when of marriageable age she wedded an unfortunate working mason, Robert Buchan, who was fated to lend his honoured name to a religious farce that was both laughable and pitiful. She was illiterate, clever, and magnetic. She had a valuable grasp of biblical phraseology and a bewildering gift of prophecy and hocus-pocus, two possessions which, taken with a remarkable personality, were in some way responsible for her success as a divine personage.

It was at the dangerous age of forty-five that Mrs. Buchan seemed to discover her relationship to the Deity. Her discovery was accompanied by the usual symptoms of fasting, visions and delusions. She was a small, stout, good-looking, fresh-complexioned woman and her voice and manner were extraordinarily sincere and persuasive. At this period she met a popular preacher, the Rev. Hugh White of Irvine in Ayrshire. They took each other very seriously. Mr. White recognized Mrs. Buchan, after a period of indecision, as the mystic woman of the Twelfth Chapter of Revelations, and she reciprocated by paying him the blasphemous compliment of kinship with her divinity. He was, by some process of reasoning not clear to us, the 'Man-child' which she had brought forth.

This strange couple set out together—for White was rapidly deposed by the presbytery—to gather disciples. They were accompanied by Mrs. White, who seems to have regarded this astonishing eruption of her placid married life without question. And the converts came in! They gathered, mostly at night, to listen to Friend Mother—as Mrs. Buchan was called—developing her crazy creed. She claimed to be the Spirit of God and pretended to impart the Holy Ghost by a system of breathing.

Burns, in whose country the Buchanites were wandering, came in touch with them and, it is said, tried to rescue a girl named Jean Gardner from their clutches. This Jean, by the way, was established in the poet's affections before Jean Armour came along, and Mr. John Cameron, who has written an admirable summary of Buchanism called *The Buchanite Delusion* (a book that should be reprinted with a good index), makes out a most interesting case for the belief that it was Jean Gardner and not Jean Armour whom Burns mentions in his 'Epistle to Davie'.

The poet, however, had no use for the Buchanites, although he seems to have attended some of their meetings, probably from curiosity and no doubt in company with 'darling Jean':

'Their tenets are a strange jumble of enthusiastic jargon,' wrote Burns to J. Burness in 1784. 'She (Mrs. Buchan) pretends to give them the Holy Ghost by breathing on them, which she does with postures and gestures that are scandalously indecent. They have likewise a community of goods, and live nearly an idle life, carrying on a great farce of pretended devotion in barns and woods, where they lodge and lie together and hold likewise a community of women, as it is another of their tenets that they can commit no mortal sin.'

This is an accurate statement of fact. They were communists. They disbelieved in marriage. They were said also to believe in infanticide, claiming that children were soulless animals. But their great belief, one that ultimately divided the sect, was that Mrs. Buchan would, without the preliminary of physical death, take them all up with her to heaven.

It would seem incredible that such nonsense could have gained adherents, yet when the sect were expelled from Irvine forty-six men and women—many of them grave, respectable tradesmen and farmers—followed Friend Mother and the Rev. 'Man-child' into the wilderness.

The roads of Scotland have rarely seen a more remarkable procession. First went Mother Buchan in a cart, then followed more carts containing the female Buchanites, many of them rosy-cheeked lassies in their teens, and lastly the men.

Mother Buchan addressed the wondering, or scornful, farmers and labourers whenever the procession halted.

' James M'Cleish,' she called to a gardener, ' quit Mr. Copland's garden and come and work in that of the Lord.'

' Thank ye,' replied James M'Cleish, ' but He wasna ower kind to the last gardener He had.'

They settled in various parts of Dumfriesshire, hiring barns and farms, where their mode of life, and especially their communal sleeping arrangements and the stories of their murdered infants, outraged their stern Presbyterian neighbours. They were often attacked, as the following verse shows, a verse worthy of the Great McGonagall but written by the divine Mr. White :

> *The people in Closeburn parish residing*
> *Came often our sermons to hear,*
> *And rudely they questioned our words, tho' most pure !*
> *Our persons they threatened to tear.*
> *They often with batons and cudgels combined,*
> *With billets of wood and with stones ;*
> *But He who has power all men to control*
> *Prevented them breaking our bones.*

One of the most incomprehensible converts at this time was an English farmer from over the Border, who sold up his farm and threw in his lot with the Buchanites.

The great event, however, in the mad history of Buchanism was the Forty Days' Fast which was to be followed by the translation of the entire sect to Paradise. This began in 1786. The whole sect (with the exception of Mrs. Buchan and the Rev. Hugh White !) abstained from food for forty days. They drank water, however, and when, towards the end of the period, some of the fanatics seemed to be on the point of death, the Friend Mother would pass among them and hand out spoonfuls of a preparation of treacle. However, they survived the ordeal, although one girl Buchanite was ever afterwards subject to fits.

In July, 1786, the day of the departure for heaven arrived. The scene of the event was Templand Hill on the Craigenputtock farm, where Carlyle wrote *Sartor Resartus.* Solemn preparations had been made. A wooden platform had been erected on the top of the hill and in the centre a slightly higher one for Mother Buchan. Some days before the event White was seen dressed in clerical gown, bands and gloves, striding about Templand Hill in deep meditation, now and then casting an anxious eye to heaven as if wondering whether the wind was right for their projected flight. On the morning of the translation a ghastly company staggered up the hill. Men and women were emaciated by hunger. They could hardly drag one foot after the other. But they had summoned the energy to shave their heads save for a topknot by which, it was hoped, the angels would haul them into heaven. They had also put on loose slippers which could be kicked away at the moment of taking off!

They arrived before dawn. They climbed up the flimsy wooden scaffold and waited for the sun to rise. Their hymn singing was heard by a startled passing farmer, Mr. Hossack of Thornhill. He saw them standing with their faces to the rising sun and their arms held out.

'While they were shouting, singing, and wildly stretching forth their hands from their frail platform,' says Mr. Paterson, 'and while their glorious Mother—sublimely exalted above the rest, her buxom beauty showing well against the morning sky, and her long hair streaming in the breeze in the ecstasy of the moment—seemed like some divine Hebe about to return to her native sphere amid her quiring worshippers, suddenly a gust of wind swept across the hilltop; the slight erections on which they were frantically swaying about fell to pieces, and vanished in a mass of struggling humanity, including the arch-impostor!'

That was the end of Mrs. Buchan's flight to heaven. This anticlimax to forty days of fasting was too much even for the Buchanites. Half her followers packed up and left in anger and disgust. But Friend Mother dominated those who were still faithful. She blamed the failure on their lack of faith—her invariable excuse when her appointments with Eternity went wrong!

Then—five years later—the next Buchanite sensation occurred. The immortal Mrs. Buchan died! Her infatuated followers could not believe it! She had stated on her deathbed that, although she would appear to die, she was only going to heaven to arrange for their arrival and would be back with them in six days. If, however, their notorious lack of faith prevented her return she would wait in heaven for ten years. Then she would arrive and take them back with her. Should she not arrive in ten years then she would come back in fifty years. After arranging these appointments she died in a calm and saintly manner.

And now began the most extraordinary chapter in this wild and incredible history. Her followers were unwilling to bury her. The most devout disciple was a man named Andrew Innes, who had believed in her from the very start. Nothing could shake his faith. He conceived the idea, which he held until the end of his life, that he was the appointed guardian of Mrs. Buchan's body. He began by hiding the body in the straw of a barn. This caused a terrific sensation. When the followers saw the empty coffin they became delirious with conviction. Friend Mother had ascended to heaven ! But Andrew's trick was discovered and Mrs. Buchan was replaced in her coffin to the sorrow of the entire sect. Here it remained while the Buchanites waited six days for the return of their leader. Alas, she did not return, and they therefore wrapped her in feathers—for their thoughts ran always on flight—and buried her beneath the kitchen hearth in the farm at Auchengibbert.

Even the bones of St. Columba, which were carried about for years, or the body of Christopher Columbus, which crossed the Atlantic twice, had a more restful fate than that reserved for the bones of Mrs. Buchan.

No sooner was she buried under the hearth than Sir Alexander Gordon, Steward-Depute of the Stewartry, began to make inquiries. Strange rumours were flying over the countryside. So strong was the feeling against the ' witch woman ' that men took turns in guarding all the local kirkyards to prevent her burial in consecrated soil. Sir Alexander felt it to be his duty to know where the body rested.

This placed the followers in a quandary. They could not admit that they had buried Mrs. Buchan in the kitchen, therefore a proper burial-place had to be found for her in order to satisfy the authorities. Sir Alexander, in order not to cause a local sensation, as he confessed in after years, agreed to a secret investigation. And the meeting arranged was as eerie as anything imagined by Scott or Crockett.

It was at midnight, and the place was the old kirkyard of Kirkgunzeon. The followers had previously searched round at night for a newly made grave, choosing those kirkyards that were badly guarded by the watching farmers. Such a grave they discovered at Kirkgunzeon. Working in darkness, and with the exhumed body of Mrs. Buchan hidden near them, they dug up the coffin of a man and lowered the coffin containing their leader into the grave. Then they let down the man's coffin and filled in the earth.

When Sir Alexander arrived they went through this laborious proceeding once again. By the light of one lantern the Steward watched them. He ordered the coffin to be opened and, after identifying the woman, went away satisfied. But no sooner had he gone than the cunning Buchanites took up the body and replaced it in the secret grave beneath the kitchen hearth. And there it remained for many years.

Towards the end of the century the leaders of the movement, notably the Rev. Hugh White, broke up and departed, some to America. The others moved into Galloway to the Nine Mile Bar of Crocketford. Popular feeling against them had died away. The remnants of the sect were respected as farmers and weavers. The women were the first to introduce the two-handed spinning wheel into Galloway. And they had made money. Among them was the veteran of the faith, Andrew Innes, now an old man. He alone remained fanatically true to the memory of the woman who had spoken to him with the Voice of God. It is with this man that for the first time pity enters into one's feelings for the Buchanites. No matter how foolish we may know Andrew Innes to have been, or how grotesque the episodes in which he played an unquestioning part, there is something of the sublimity of great tragedy in the spectacle of this old man watching over the remains of his prophetess and believing, when all had ceased to believe, that the time would come when she would remember her promises and show his weary old feet the path to everlasting life.

With the tenacity and the cunning of old age he brought the remains of Mrs. Buchan from Dumfriesshire into Galloway. By this time they were one with Rameses and Amenhotep. She was, on the evidence of those who saw her later, just a brown mummy.

Andrew kept her in a cupboard at the top of the stairs in the New House at Crocketford. Then, for a queer reason that was not clear until later, he built a kind of out-house for the mummy. It was a lean-to shed built on the east gable, opposite the fireplace, and to any casual observer it would seem just a store-shed for a farmer's tools. There was, however, a secret opening near the fireplace that communicated with this shed. Andrew used to sleep in the room with the fire, which he kept burning winter and summer, and for a very odd purpose. Twice a day he would warm a blanket at the fire and push it through the hole into the mortuary chamber. He would then go outside, enter the shed and spread the blanket over Mrs. Buchan's coffin. Why he performed this grotesque ritual is not clear. Possibly he was actuated by some vague idea of warming the relics into life, or of preserving the remains which he firmly believed Mrs. Buchan would require when she returned to take him to heaven.

All the time Andrew was counting the years until, at length, the greatest day in his long life approached—the fiftieth anniversary of Mrs. Buchan's death and the date of her promised return. It was March 29, 1841. Old Andrew made furtive preparations for heaven. He sent for a neighbour and entrusted him with a pile of gold, his life's savings, and at last the day of his expected translation arrived.

Just imagine it. A lonely little stone house beside a road in Galloway. A night in March. The wind howling from the hills. And, in the secrecy of the house beside the road, a poor little bent old man praying beside a coffin with absolute faith that in a few hours he would leap across the awfulness of death into the splendour of Paradise. He removed the lid and watched the shrivelled face of the prophetess for a sign of returning life. Every sound in the night must have made his ancient heart thump in his throat : a horseman going past on the road, the rush of the wind, the call of some creature in the darkness, must have been magnified by this watching man into a portent fearful and tremendous to him. All through that night he watched until his candle guttered and sank with the dawn. He stole out into the pale light of stars and into the chill of the little morning winds a poor, broken old man. Friend Mother had forgotten all about him.

He lingered on for another four years, during which time his sublime faith recovered from the shock. He blamed himself for her failure to keep the appointment ! He was unworthy of so splendid a fate. Then came the time when he, who had lived with death for fifty years and had refused to recognize it, felt it in the room beside him. He knew that his time had come. He called three friends, a joiner, a grocer and a farmer, and ordered them to dig his grave at once in the garden at the back of the house where many other Buchanites were buried. He then instructed them to take the mummy of Mrs. Buchan and bury it in this grave, treading down the earth over it so that his funeral party would not know that she was there. In this way he made sure that if she awakened she would call him in the moment of resurrection.

This was done as he wished ; and so one of the first—and the very last Buchanite—lay in the same grave as the founder of the faith.

I came into Crocketford remembering these things. I came to a neat white village of stone houses lying where three roads meet. A picturesque toll-house stood at the junction of the road to New Galloway. New House, where Andrew Innes kept his vigil, is still standing a little way from the village. It has been enlarged and modernized. I found the memory of the Buchanites still green. Andrew Innes and his infatuation are well remembered, but they think of him as a queer, daft body, a subject more for laughter than for tears. In this I cannot agree. There is something gruesome and morbid about him as of an Edgar Allan Poe character in real life. But loyalty touched him with dignity and his fantastic dream of circumventing death renders him supremely pitiful :

' What has happened to the Buchanite graveyard behind New House ? ' I asked.

' A bathroom has been built out over it,' I was told.

' A bathroom ? '

' Ay, a bathroom. . . . I'm thinkin' it will be verra awkward for some body when the resurrection occurs.'

With this comment on Buchanism as a parting gift from Crocketford, I went on down the sunlit lanes.

§ 4

The man in the Dalbeattie inn was proud of Galloway, but he never mentioned Scotland. He was also tremendously proud of Dalbeattie. He talked to me in that charming, rather aggressive manner adopted by some Scotsmen, as if he were trying to provoke me in the nicest possible manner to contradict him, or as if he desired me to take up some latent challenge underlying his remarks and, by praising Surrey or Devon, cause him to bring up the heavy artillery of his local pride and batter these two counties to the dust. But I am a frightful non-starter. I love listening so much more than talking, and in the process of listening I seem to have acquired a manner that, once strangers become accustomed to it, appears to them a kind of pillow on which they can recline in all the luxury of confidence. That, and a rather unconscious habit of driving a conversation as a drover prods his herds, is the only way I can account for some of the extraordinary things people say to me. I could see this man changing from his first aggressive thought—' Here's another of those damned sniffy Englishmen '—to the unconscious realization that I was an amazingly good audience. He vanquished his third dram and, putting down his glass, said to me :

' I've been in all kinds of places. I was in London for a year. Man, I'm telling you it's no' exaggeration to say that if it hadna been for bonnie Gallowa' I couldna have stuck it. And that's a fact.'

Here he returned for an instant to his previous contentious manner :

' London's no' a beautiful place. Ye'll admit that ? Oh, ye like London ? '

He drew back and observed me as if he had never seen me before :

' Och well, there's no accounting for tastes.'

Then a gleam of aggressive friendship lit his eyes and he gazed at me with sympathy :

' It takes all sorts to make a world,' he said wisely. ' But what I was telling you was this. . . .'

' Have a drink,' I said, knowing that the moment was approaching.

' Och well, a wee one. . . . I was telling you. Have ye ever lived in lodgings in Putney ? Well, ye know what it's like. Many's the day I've got up as sick as a dog—and not wi' drink, mind ye, because in those days I didna touch a drap and I couldna afford it anyway—but just sick for Gallowa'.'

He paused and drained his glass while I waited, knowing that the sentimental poet who hides in every Scotsman was about to leap out stark naked :

'An' I'd remember the stone dykes running up the side of Maidenpap and the green grass on the Mote. D'ye ken what I mean?'

I was delighted with him and slightly ashamed too, for this exposure of love is always rather an embarrassing thing to the listener, when a sudden explosion shuddered on the air and the glasses trembled:

'What's that?'

'They're blasting over in the quarry.'

The explosion blew away the last shred of his poetry. Nothing I could do, nothing I could insinuate, nothing I could provoke even by a mild heretical suggestion that other regions in Scotland were as lovely as Galloway, could bring him back to the point of self-exposure. He had become transformed into a grim realist. He would talk about nothing but granite! A stranger coming upon us would have put him down as an ordinary bore. I felt about him much as the bird photographer must feel when, after disguising himself as a bush or a hillock for a fortnight, he watches his prey leave the nest.

The only interesting thing he said—because I did not know it—was that the Thames Embankment is made of Dalbeattie granite. I think he said also that the lower stages of the Eddystone Lighthouse and the Town Hall of Manchester came out of the local hill. But my hope that I might be privileged to put down in words the longing of a Galloway man exiled in London vanished in a string of industrial statistics. I was quite glad when two men came in and hailed him, and the conversation became general.

I went out into the neat streets of Dalbeattie, which shares with apparently every town in Galloway the appearance of having been recently white-washed, swept and cleaned, and I saw a town built of grey granite. I saw also a high gashed hill. Men, like a swarm of some destructive insects, had eaten it to the bone. Half the hill had gone.

The summit held trees which huddled together in a startled manner as they gazed downward over the split and riven precipice that had once been inviolate. And from that hill, I thought, had come the embankment over which I have leaned so many times in happy moods and despairing moods, watching the brown Thames flow onward to the sea, imparting in its progress little faint slapping kisses to the grey stone of Dalbeattie.

§ 5

The Mote of Urr, which rises in meadows two miles or so
from Dalbeattie, is one of those significant-looking mounds
which old-fashioned antiquaries used to claim as prehistoric
or Roman work.   The modern archaeologist, however, thinks
that they were Saxon or Norman, but he is not yet quite
certain about it.   It seems to me rather curious that, as
carelessness and untidiness are constant factors in human
conduct, objects should not have been dug up round these motes
to settle the problem.   Women have always been losing beads
and the Roman cat was quite as ready as the modern cat to
smash a vase, just as, no doubt, the Saxon serving-maid
possessed hands through which fragile objects slipped as
easily as they do through those of her present-day sister.   But
it seems that the people who lived on and round these motes
were either abnormally careful with their belongings or else
that they owned very few possessions.

It is impossible to gain any idea of the Mote of Urr from a
photograph or from a distant glimpse of it.   You must climb
it.   It is an immense circular, or rather oval, mound that rises
in three tiers, or platforms, which diminish in size as they
ascend.   It is uninteresting except to the antiquary because
it is difficult to imagine what it looked like in the days when
it was one of the greatest fortresses in Galloway.   I imagine
that it must have looked something like the moat of Dinan on
the Bayeux Tapestry.   It is fairly clear from these primitive
drawings that such erections were the forerunners of the stone
keep.   They were merely fortified hills.   There would be
wooden erections on them, sloping gangways would connect
the various platforms and, I suppose, people would build
lean-to houses all round, except, of course, on the ground
level which was circled by a trench filled with water.   The
Norman castle took about a hundred years to cross the Scottish
Border; so we can imagine that if one of the Conqueror's
knights had penetrated in extreme old age to the Mote of
Urr, he would have considered it delightfully quaint and old
fashioned.

The only interesting thing about the Mote of Urr is a local
legend about Robert the Bruce, who wandered, landless and
a fugitive, in Galloway.   The story goes that Bruce came
upon the Mote of Urr one morning, footsore and weary and

there he was surprised by an English knight, Sir Walter Selby, who challenged him to combat. Bruce accepted, and the two men began to fight. Then a most undignified thing happened. An old woman, the wife of a man named Sprotte, whose little hovel was built on the Mote, put down the porridge pot and went out to see what all the noise was about. When Dame Sprotte saw the fugitive king locked in mortal combat she decided, like a decisive Scotswoman, to take part in the fight. So she flung herself on the Englishman; some say she tackled him like a rugger forward, others that she pulled his hair. I think the last is probably more likely. However, Sir Walter, who felt quite capable of engaging the Bruce, surrendered instantly to Mrs. Sprotte. He crashed to the earth and lay there helpless. Bruce, no matter what his enemies said about him, was a gentleman. He refused —probably to the rage of Mrs. Sprotte—to take advantage of the fallen knight. He suggested instead that they should both go and eat Mr. Sprotte's porridge. Once inside the cottage, Mrs. Sprotte proved how difficult a woman can be. She put down the bowl of porridge in front of Bruce with one spoon and flatly refused to get another spoon for the Englishman.

The traditional story is that in thankfulness for his rescue the Bruce promised Dame Sprotte as much land as she could run round. I do not place so low a value on Bruce's sword arm.

Now, my version of the story, based on a knowledge of obstructive old Scotswomen, is that Mrs. Sprotte made herself such a confounded nuisance, glaring at the Englishman, hiding the spoons, making rude growling and snorting noises, that, in order to get rid of her and behave like a gallant gentleman to Sir Walter, Bruce told the old lady to go outside and run about ; and that if ever he gained the crown he would give her the ground she had covered.

Sprotte is not, to my knowledge, an Aberdonian name, but the dame instantly saw the point of this suggestion and rushed wildly round the neighbouring meadows while the Bruce—still with only one spoon—fed Sir Walter with porridge and then took a bit himself ; and so on. It is a charming picture.

It is an historic fact that in after years a grant of twenty Scotch acres was given to the Sprottes of the Mote and that it remained in the family for five hundred years. The condition of the grant was this : that whenever the King of Scotland passed through the Vale of Urr a bowl of porridge was to be presented to him by the Sprottes.

If you can show me a prettier or more water-tight legend than this I shall be surprised. It is a good one to find on the green sides of an old fortified moat that looks as though it is lost in memories of dark and frightful deeds.

§ 6

You will like Castle Douglas if you see it on a fine morning with the sun over it.

Mr. McGuffog stands at the door of his shop, gazing reflectively down the main street as earnestly as imprisoned maidens gaze from the castle-turrets in a fairy tale. He is recalled to reality by a herd of cows which shambles down the centre of the road followed by a herdsman and his dog and, at a decent interval, by a trap containing Mr. McQuaker himself, a farmer with whom Mr. McGuffog gravely agrees about the grandness of the day. The minister is seen in solemn conclave with Mrs. McCubbin, and two alien fishermen in Harris tweed stride masterfully from an hotel and stack their rods in a car. The mournful and ragged genius, the butt of every Scottish town, who has invented something for which somebody else has taken the credit and also the cash, lingers impatiently near the bar of the Douglas Arms ; for it will soon be opening time.

In the old days, when Castle Douglas was a stopping-place on the coach road to Port Partick, the royal mail would come in with a great clatter of hoofs and a sound of bugle : every loiterer in the town would gather round to share in the excitement and taste the thrilling atmosphere of departure.

The Douglas Arms, which was the halting-place for the mails, was kept appropriately by a Mrs. Douglas who was so well known that it is on record that letters were often addressed to Sir William Douglas of Douglas Castle, care of Mrs. Douglas, Douglas Arms, Castle Douglas !

The town has to-day recaptured something of the bustle and excitement of those times. It has developed its trade and the motor coach has brought it back to the King's highway.

On an autumn morning the sunlight slides over the roofs of the solid stone houses and lights up the opposite side of the road, and the placid life of Castle Douglas, in which nothing is too small to be uninteresting, proceeds with a leisurely dignity. The town hides its industry behind a calm exterior. You have to make inquiries before you discover that Castle Douglas makes furniture and soda water. And, characteristic of the fun that Time can have with such places, pleasure boats may be hired on a stretch of beautiful Carlingwark Loch known as the Gallows Plot! Nevertheless, Castle Douglas does not take its name from the House of Douglas, whose Castle of Threave stands a mile or so to the west, but from a later clansman, one Douglas, a business man, who bought the town in 1789.

Not far off, lying on a little island in the Dee, is a square keep of grey stones whose eight-foot-thick walls still bear the marks of cannonade and assault. This was the nest of those wild eagles—the Douglases—whose history is the history of Scotland. I went over to it and found it to be a mere shell. Its walls, from which men-at-arms watched the hills of Galloway, cease raggedly in mid-air, fret-worked against the sky.

Threave Castle was built by Archibald the Grim, the third earl of Douglas, who was the natural son of that mighty Douglas who fell at Otterburn in the light of a new moon, with three spears in his body and a battle-axe in his skull. Archibald the Grim, Lord of Galloway, first enters history in the sudden and unlikely way men did in his day—on the field of Poitiers! He was a dark and ugly lad and was known to his companions as ' Blac Archibalde '. But he wore a splendid suit of armour at Poitiers. He was captured by the English and escaped, thanks to the mental agility of a brother Scot— Sir William Ramsay of Colluthie. They were both prisoners. When Douglas was brought in, Ramsay pretended to fly into a violent passion :

' You treacherous hound,' he shouted, ' how dared you steal my cousin's armour ? Cursed be the hour of your birth, for he sought you all day and for want of his armour was slain by an arrow in camp, as I myself saw. Come ! Pull off my boots.'

As young Archibald, playing the part of a servant, knelt to pull off his compatriot's boots Sir William caught him a blow on the mouth, explaining to the disappointed English that the lad was not a great noble, as they believed, but a rogue and a scullion as they could tell from his face. As in fact Archibald had the reputation of being ' more like a coco (cook-boy) than a noble ' the ruse worked well, and he was set free on the payment of a nominal ransom of forty shillings. This must have delighted every thrifty Scot within hearing, for had Douglas been recognized his ransom would have been enormous !

In later life Archibald found himself Lord of Galloway ' because he took great trouble to purge the country of English blood '. It was assumed, no doubt, that if he could do this he might be capable of dealing with a district as fractious as Galloway ! From this grey square tower in the river he administered the affairs of all lands between the Nith and the Cree.

His household was regal and his little island in the Dee housed an army that was the terror of the surrounding country. I noticed from the doorway a projecting stone and asked the man who had taken me to the island what it was :

' 'Tis the gallows knob,' he said. ' The Earl o' Douglas used to boast that it never lacked a tassel.'

He mentioned a small mound on the west side of the loch which is supposed to have been the pit in which the skeletons were buried after they had rotted on the gallows knob. The legend of Mons Meg is firmly believed in this part of Galloway, and this man repeated it to me. He told me how Threave Castle was the last fortress to hold out for the Douglas when James II confiscated the Douglas estates. The royal army, so the story goes, found that its artillery was not strong enough to batter down the walls of Threave, whereupon a local man, known as Brawny Kim, who carried on the trade of blacksmith at the Three Thorns of Carlingwark, said that he would make a big enough cannon if he were given a sufficient supply of iron bars. Accordingly every householder in Kirkcudbright contributed an iron bar. While Brawny Kim, assisted by his seven sons, was at work on the cannon, another party were busy on the Brennan Hill making granite cannon balls. It is on record that the first shot fired by Kim's cannon was a stone ball the weight of a Carsphairn cow and was fired by a peck of gunpowder ! Legend also says that this first shot passed right through the walls of Threave and carried away the hand

of the Fair Maid of Galloway—Lady Douglas—as she sat
at table lifting the wine cup to her pretty lips.

'And the cannon was called Mons Meg after Kim's wife,
who had a verra powerful voice,' said the man.   'An' ye can
see the gun to-day in Edinburgh Castle.'

I am afraid that historians have shattered this Galloway
legend. It is extremely unlikely that a blacksmith, even
assisted by seven sons, could have made such a cannon as
Mons Meg in the time that James II took in besieging the
Castle of Threave. I believe that Sir Herbert Maxwell has
a number of other weighty reasons in opposition to the legend
but, of course, I did not dare to mention them to my friend
of the boat. I was far from strong enough that day to turn
upon myself the full fury of an outraged Gallovidian!

§ 7

The Galloway Kirk stands roofless among its dead, lost
also in death. No bells have rung for centuries from the
ruined belfry where the wild birds nest; and the ivy clings
to the old stones as if to save them from utter dissolution.
The kirkyard, like most Scottish kirkyards, is a riot of lush
grass. Briars fling their wild arms over headstones and
climb the pedestals of memorial urns. The nobleman, lying
in a walled place apart, sleeps beneath his coat-of-arms;
and all round the worthy villagers lie beneath grey headstones that lean this way and that as if weary of waiting for
the last trumpet. And there is no sound but the bees in
the briar bushes and the softness of wood pigeons in the
trees above.

Grief, once so sharp, speaking out of a past age in the
helpless poignancy of an epitaph, has healed itself, and those
who in the bleakness of sorrow wrote the words which wind
and rain have scarred beyond recognition are themselves
beyond tears. Even the laird's family has died away. No
man has disturbed the nettles in the family tomb for nearly
a hundred years.

In this acre of expended sorrow one stone alone looks as
though men still remembered it. The grass around it is
trampled by the feet of the curious. Those who visit this
stone sometimes scrape away the green moss in order to read
better the words engraved there, and give it an air of life in

surroundings that tell only of death and forgetfulness. This stone says that the men who lie beneath it were 'hanged without law for adhering to the Word of God'. This happened in the 'killing time', when the Covenanters, fighting a war of conscience for fifty years, took the Lord's Supper in the heather of the Galloway muirs.

And the stranger who stands idly in these Galloway kirkyards, each one of which, it seems, holds its Protestant martyr, tries to force his mind backward through time in order to understand this religious war in which Scotsmen who abhorred Popery died like Catholic saints. The Englishman will think that, in spite of Smithfield and its faggots, the Reformation in England was a pale thing compared with Scotland's Reformation. The English made a funny song about the Vicar of Bray, who turned Protestant and then Catholic as it suited him. That song could never have been written or sung in Scotland. And it may seem to a man, as he stands over the graves of Scotsmen who were shot down for their faith, that one of the big differences between the two nations is this : compromise has always been the second nature of the English, while the Scots do not know the meaning of the word. . . .

Some years after Charles I had been crowned at Westminster, the Scottish people felt that His Majesty should visit the land of his ancestors. He accordingly set out in June of the year 1637 with the Duke of Lennox, the Marquis of Hamilton, and Scots and English lords to the number of about five hundred. Edinburgh was in a state of great excitement. The King rode up to the West Port, where a mountain moved at the approach of majesty, while a nymph in sea-green velvet, wearing a headdress of turrets, leaned out, representing Edinburgh, and welcomed a Stuart to his native land.

The provost and the baillies stood by in their furred gowns. A company of the town guard had been fitted out for the occasion with doublets of white satin, black velvet breeches and stockings of fine silk. They carried 'dainty muskets' and also the pikes with which they kept Edinburgh in order, but these were gilded. At the Mercat Cross the god Bacchus drank the King's health and at the Tron nine 'pretty boys' escorted the shepherd Endymion who, like all Edinburgh, was wearing his best clothes, which were of crimson velvet. So with lion-heralds, pursuivants, macers and trumpeters, King Charles I entered his city of Edinburgh without the slightest idea that it was to be anything more than an effusive and rather boring pageant.

The townspeople saw him on many occasions, notably when he sat a fine horse wearing a purple robe richly furred and laced with gold that hung a good way over his horse's tail and was borne by five grooms in a line. But into their appreciation of all this grandeur began to creep a note of awe and dread. The King was crowned in Holyrood. Men began to whisper about the chapel in the abbey there. They said that an altar bearing two wax candles had been placed in it. There was a rich tapestry. There was a crucifix before which the officiating clergy bent the knee.

So the first rumble of the coming storm was heard in the taverns of the Canongate. And Charles bade farewell to his loving citizens and, taking his haughty courage south, rode on unconscious that from that moment his steps were set inevitably towards a snowy morning in January and a scaffold in Whitehall.

In England, Charles and Archbishop Laud put their heads together with the idea of restoring the Bishops to Scotland and of imposing the English liturgy upon the Scot. It was accordingly decreed that a Service Book—which was really the English Book of Common Prayer—should be read in every church in Scotland on Sunday, July 23, 1637. This book roused the worst forebodings of the Scot. Row made an excruciating pun about it. 'Let anyone compare it with the Missale', he said, 'and they shall miss very little.'

On Sunday morning St. Giles' in Edinburgh was packed. It was plain to everyone, except, apparently, the King and his advisers, that something serious was about to happen. This imposed Liturgy was nothing new to Scotland. An attempt had been made in 1549 to force the first Prayer Book of Edward VI down the throat of Scotland and the people had risen in protest. So now the same atmosphere was created as Dean Hannay walked to the reading-desk with a brown leather book in his hand. The very sight of that book caused a riot. They refused to listen to a word of it :

'Rome is entered upon us,' they shouted.

'Baal is entered upon us,' was the cry.

'Darest thou read Mass in my lug?' was flung at the unhappy dean.

But it was not the only thing flung at him. Legend has it that Jenny Geddes, a serving-maid, struck the first blow for the Covenant when, seizing the folding stool on which she was sitting, she flung it violently but with an indifferent sense of direction at the head of the dean. The reading-desk was rushed and the dean was pulled down from his place as the magisterial halbardiers came running to the rescue. So ended Edinburgh's 'blak, doolful Sunday'.

Now since the Reformation it had been Scotland's habit to fight the Roman Church with covenants drawn up and signed by those who pledged themselves to maintain the Presbyterian doctrines. There was a covenant as early as 1557, another in 1581. This document denounced Catholicism in unmeasured terms. It had been signed by James I (and VI) and was re-subscribed in 1590 and 1596.

Now, threatened again, the old covenants were revived and brought up to date. Noblemen, ministers, burgesses and tradesmen, gathered in Edinburgh to sign the document. Some slit their arms and signed in blood. Noblemen travelling about the country carried the National Covenant with them and gathered signatures for it. Hatred for Episcopacy and fear of Popery broke over Scotland like a devouring fire. What insanity possessed Charles and his advisers to force a loathed condition on a stubborn and intractable people who called bishops 'dumb dogs', 'anti-Christian mushrooms' and 'limbs of the Beast'? The great Montrose, who became a Covenanter, forged a terrible sentence out of his passionate indignation. The bishops, he declared, were 'the very quintessence of Popery', and the life of the Gospel 'had been stolen away by enforcing on the Kirk a dead Service Book, the brood of the bowels of the Whore of Babel'.

When Scotsmen talk like this someone is bound to get hurt.

Blue banners appeared in Scotland and on them were written in gold, 'For Religion, King and Kingdomes', and ships put in to the east coast ports and unloaded arms from Poland. A General Assembly of the Kirk met and flung down a challenge to the King by solemnly excommunicating the bishops and abolishing Prelacy. A Scottish force crossed the Border. An alliance was made with France. And now the fat was in the fire.

Charles went north with an ill-trained, reluctant army.

One recruit was such a bad shot that he sent a musket ball through the King's tent. History does not say what happened to him ! So Charles made peace with his Scots. This led to the first coming together of the English and the Scottish peoples. It was a pact known as the Solemn League and Covenant.

Charles was now caught between his English Puritans and his Scottish Covenanters. But to the Scot the League and Covenant was one thing ; to the English it was another. Charles had offended the constitutional sense of England and he had outraged the conscience of Scotland. The English were really fighting for a political principle, the Scots for a religious one. The English wanted military help and the Scots dreamt of a Presbyterian Kingdom of Christ. England plunged into a civil war, Scotland into a religious war, and between the two countries the unbending autocrat galloped across English shires with his long-haired cavaliers. For seven years the war went on. Cromwell's Ironsides sang psalms as they charged in England ; and in Scotland the great Montrose, turned King's man, won six battles with a host of plundering MacDonalds, Camerons and homeless MacGregors. But his host was scattered at Philiphaugh, near Selkirk, when 4,000 cavalry from England cut his army to the bone and thundered with red swords upon the women and children who followed the camp, slaughtering them without compassion.

Charles went down between his Puritans and his Covenanters. The Covenanters handed him to the Puritans and the Puritans handed him to Eternity. But the courage with which he faced death on that snowy January morning in Whitehall was as splendid as the courage of any Covenanter who fell dead in the Galloway heather. The high bearing of the Stuarts upheld him at the last, and when a hush fell over the crowd as the executioner lifted up that Van Dyck head with the cry ' Behold the head of a traitor,' there may have been old men there whose minds went back over sixty-two years to the time when the grandmother of this King met death at Fotheringhay.

But Scotland's crusade for Calvin had but begun. Charles II cynically signed anything that was put before him and repudiated it when it suited him. The wild joy with which Scotland received one of the ' auld Stuarts ' soon turned to dismay when it was seen that Charles II was as determined as his father to establish Episcopacy. The old Covenanting fires blazed up again.

James Sharp, minister of Crail and a hypocritical schemer, went to London as a Presbyterian and returned as the Archbishop of St. Andrews ! It was one of the supreme betrayals in the history of the Kirk. Nine other Presbyterians were seduced by mitres. These men, filled with the bitterness of all turncoats, rounded on their old friends. Over 270 ministers resigned their livings rather than submit to the tribe of Judas. Acts were showered upon Scotland. But, while the religious fervour of the people burned at white heat, the churches remained empty. The Covenanters took to the heather. The exiled ministers were hunted from place to place just as the Roman priests had been hunted in the time of James VI. Whenever it was known that a minister was in the neighbourhood the people would gather from far and near in some fastness of the Galloway hills. Nothing in the history of Scotland is more impressive than the field conventicles, where thousands gathered to take the sacrament under the open sky while armed men lay out on the hillside to give warning of ' Bite-the-Sheep ' Turner and his troops.

The terrible situation lasted for years until the south-west was on the verge of madness. The first signs of the coming rebellion was the murder one dark night of Sharp, the renegade Archbishop of St. Andrews. As his coach was crossing a Fifeshire moor a band of horsemen rose up and seized it.

' Judas be taken ! ' cried one of them.

The horses were cut free, the servants were gagged and bound, and the murderers called the Archbishop out to the lonely moor. The old man sat inside the coach with his daughter, Isobel. Pistols were fired into the coach. Sharp fell back wounded. The horsemen would have ridden off had not the overwrought girl cried out in a loud voice,

' There is life yet ! '

The men returned with daggers. They thrust their arms into the coach and stabbed at Sharp, who rose and struggled up and out of the coach. They fired at the prelate but missed him. Then they drew their swords and hacked him to death.

When they had rifled his pockets they discovered a little box. As they opened it a live bee flew out :

' The devil ! ' cried the horrified assassins. ' His familiar ! '

So perished a man who sold his conscience, if ever he had one to sell, and so began the reign of Terror known as the 'Killing Time'. Now Graham of Claverhouse and his dragoons rode through Galloway hunting down the Covenanters as wild beasts are hunted. At the battle of Drumclog the Covenanters had the best of it : at Bothwell Bridge they were scattered. Hideous tortures were imposed to make men and women say 'God save the King.' There was the thumb-screw and 'the boot'. This was a wooden hoop bound with iron. It was placed round the victim's leg and wedges were driven in between the flesh and the wood until the limb was a shapeless, broken mess.

Among the rocks and heath of Muirkirk, in Ayrshire, was a croft inhabited by a carrier called John Brown. He was a noted Covenanter and he knew that sooner or later an example would be made of him. He lived every day in readiness for death. One day death came to him in the form of three troops of horse led by Claverhouse. Brown was cutting peats near his croft. His wife came out to see what was the matter, a baby in her arms and another child clinging to her skirt :

'Go to your prayer, for you shall immediately die,' said Claverhouse.

The man prayed :

'Take good night of your wife and children,' ordered Claverhouse.

He kissed his wife and children and turned to his murderers.

'I have no more to do but die,' he said,

They shot him :

'What thinkest thou of thy husband now ? ' asked Claverhouse.

'I ever thought muckle good of him,' cried the wife, 'and now more than ever.'

That was the spirit of the Covenant.

Claverhouse and his troopers rode down the hill, leaving a woman and her terrified bairns crying beside a body on which the woman had flung her plaid.

In the year 1684 Margaret Lachlison, aged about 60, Margaret Wilson, a girl of 18, her sister Agnes, aged 13, and a servant girl called Margaret Maxwell, were accused of committing treason by attending field meetings in Galloway. The elderly woman and the two sisters were sentenced to be drowned and the servant girl was sentenced to be flogged through the streets of Wigtown by the public hangman. Gilbert Wilson, the father of the two girls, managed to save the child Agnes by paying a fine of £100, but the sentence on Margaret Wilson and Margaret Lachlison held.

Two stakes were driven into the bed of the Bladnoch while the tide was out. In the old days this river floated ships past Wigtown Church. The tide on its turn would come creeping over the Solway sands, flooding the Bladnoch until it overflowed its banks. The woman and the young girl were tied to these stakes. There was a military guard and at least two of the vile men who had condemned these women to death were present to watch.

Margaret Lachlison was tied to a stake farther out in the water so that the younger woman, watching her death agonies, might repent. The tide came in. The water surged up the narrow channel. Margaret Lachlison struggled and died. As the water lapped the breast of the young girl she began to sing the Twenty-fifth Psalm:

' Margaret, ye are young; if you will pray for the King we will give you your life,' she was told.

' I'll pray for salvation to all the elect, but the damnation of none,' she replied.

She was thrown down in the water and pulled up again:

' O Margaret,' cried the crowd, ' wull ye say it ? '

' Lord, give him repentance, forgiveness and salvation if it be Thy Holy Will,' was her reply.

Robert Grierson of Lag, one of the men who tried the girl, cried out:

' Damned bitch, we do not want such prayers : tender the oaths to her.'

There was no time left. The water was at her chin. She lifted her head:

' No sinful oaths for me,' she cried. ' I am one of Christ's children. Let me go . . .'

A soldier who was standing near lifted his halberd:

' Tak' anither drink, hinny,' he said as he thrust her under the water.

Those two women were the Wigtown Martyrs.

So it is that every kirkyard in Galloway, no matter how ancient and forgotten, contains a stone from which men scrape moss and lichen. High up on the hillside, if you know where to look, you can find the communion stones round which those stubborn doctrinaires gathered to the Lord's Supper in the days of a monarch whose reign has gone down to history as ' merry '.

There has probably been no more passionate outburst of faith in Britain since the First Crusade, and the stranger stands a little awed and puzzled before the evidence of such a faith. Something of the sternness of that time seems to live yet in the grey hills of Galloway when the wind blows and the mists come down over the Merrick. No man can travel alone in Galloway hills without a thought of the Covenant.

' R. L. S.' put the melancholy of the Covenanting country into a few words—one of the loveliest songs of exile ever written :

> Blows the wind to-day, and the sun and the rain are flying ;
>   Blows the wind on the moors to-day and now,
> Where about the graves of the martyrs the whaups are crying,
>   My heart remembers how !
>
> Grey, recumbent tombs of the dead in desert places ;
>   Standing-stones on the vacant, wine-red moor ;
> Hills of sheep, and the howes of the silent, vanished races,
>   And winds austere and pure !
>
> Be it granted to me to behold you again in dying,
>   Hills of home ! and to hear again the call—
> Hear about the graves of the martyrs the peewees crying,
>   And hear no more at all.

CHAPTER THREE

DESCRIBES KIRKCUDBRIGHT AND VARIOUS OTHER THINGS,
INCLUDING MACTAGGART'S MAGNIFICENT ENCYCLOPEDIA, BILLY
MARSHALL, THE GALLOWAY TINKER, AND PAUL JONES. TELLS
HOW I WENT SALMON NETTING ONE DARK NIGHT AND HOW MARY
QUEEN OF SCOTS LEFT SCOTLAND

§ I

I WAS blown into Kirkcudbright in the dead of night by one of the most violent storms I have encountered even in Scotland. The rain fell in sheets. The wind shuddered at windows and doors : it came sweeping round corners with the fury of an invading army.

I saw a town built for such gales : streets of low stone houses crouching in the fury of the night, the weary ruin of a castle, and a wide, muddy estuary at low tide, with the rain sweeping over it like blown smoke. The scene had the quality of one of those early bioscope travel pictures, taken apparently in perpetual rain and concluded in a sudden onset of liverish spots and sheet-lightning.

There was one building that made me stop, even in this storm. It was the old Tolbooth : a long Tudor building with a tower like that of a church. A flight of outside steps leads up to the door. Iron manacles, in which offenders were exhibited in the old days, hang from the walls. Seldom have I seen a more sinister building.

It is the sort of thing you see in unknown villages in the south of France. It looks as though it had walked into Scotland from the pages of Dumas. It suggests moss troopers, hackbuteers, dubskelpers, and all manner of fly-by-nights ; and if you look long enough at the corner where the road swings into darkness you expect d'Artagnan to come galloping round, or Don Quixote, bolt upright on Rosinante, suffering from the pardonable delusion that some fair lady lies chained in Kirkcudbright's derelict prison. . . .

There is one grand virtue in a stormy night. If you are late enough you are at once admitted to that snug little room which exists at the back of every Scottish hotel, where a vast fire is always burning and where a glass of special whisky waits for favoured guests.

The landlord was a young Scotsman who had fought in Gallipoli. We talked of Chocolate Hill and Suvla Bay and then, of course, we became local, and I was told the legend that Burns wrote ' Scots wha hae ' in this hotel.

I took no sides in this contentious question. The same proud claim is put forward, I believe, by the Murray Arms Hotel at Gatehouse of Fleet, while a third tradition insists that Burns composed the greatest of all Scotland's national lyrics as he travelled in a thunderstorm across the moors near Lochanbreck, writing it out afterwards in the Bay Horse at Gatehouse, which is now demolished.

I went to bed in a high, windy room. The storm hurled itself at the windows. In the middle of the night three black ghosts entered and, lighting a candle, I discovered that three blinds were blowing in on me. . . .

In the morning, what a change : I looked out on an irreproachable Scottish town. There was a row of whitewashed houses, a milkman going his rounds, and at the end of the street was the Tolbooth, looking almost friendly in the morning sun.

Kirkcudbright is one of the most picturesque and fascinating Lowland towns I have seen. I think if I wanted to send a stranger to a town which expresses its locality as definitely as county towns in England express their counties, I would send him to the capital of the Stewartry.

The town is good-looking. It is small enough to be interesting and not small enough to be boring. Every one knows every one else's business, his relatives, his virtues and his vices ; so that Kirkcudbright teems with human interest.

It is famous—or notorious—for its colony of artists. These invaders encamped round that far-famed veteran of the ' Glasgow school ', the late Mr. Hornel, who had a large Georgian house overlooking the slimy estuary of the Dee.

I am told that artists have settled in Kirkcudbright in order to catch the subtle colours in the river mud. I cannot believe this. Perhaps I should be here at some other time, in the brilliant light of spring or summer, for I must confess that I have rarely seen a more depressing sight than the Dee at low tide. The mud is the colour of mice. There is, I admit, a sort of silver in it, and when the sun shines it glitters iridescently like bottles that have been buried for a long time in the earth. It is the deepest looking mud I ever hope to see. Though I visited many studios in Kirkcudbright I did not see one canvas that attempted to interpret this mud.

Burns, of course, visited Kirkcudbright and, it is said, left his usual rhyme on a wall. The inn in which he stayed is now a private house and the rhyme is written over a mantel-piece. It is :—

> *When January winds were blawin' cauld*
> *To Kirkcudbright I took my way.*
> *The mirksome night did me enfold*
> *Till earliest day.*
>
> R. BURNS

Not, perhaps, Burns at his best, but interesting.

My favourite spot in Kirkcudbright is a whitewashed wall stacked with lobster pots overlooking the river. There are certain views that never weary and this, in spite of the river slime, is one of them.

There is a whitewashed house at the end of the wall, wash-ing flapping on a line in the yard, and sixteen horse-shoes of various sizes nailed to the wall. A man told me that this was the house of a man once famous in Kirkcudbright, a postman named Houston—' Postie Houston ', they called him.

Most Scottish towns boast a character like him ; an out-standing personality, a prophet and an inventor.

' Postie Houston ', said my friend, ' was, in his way, a genius. Many less interesting and talented men have become famous. He was one-armed, yet he was a grand cricketer and a crack shot.

' He was a marvellous weather prophet. He was always inventing things. He erected a moon-dial on this very wall —a thing that could tell you the time by the moon.

' But the most interesting of all his inspirations was the grandfather-clock invention. He manipulated a grandfather clock so that at the stroke of six the pendulum hit a spring which operated various things in the stable. When this spring was touched a feed of oats slid into the horse's manger, hay followed, and a bucket was filled with water, so that when he was up and dressed his horse was ready to be saddled.

'He invented all sorts of things,' my friend went on ; 'a rat-trap that closed itself when sufficient rats had entered it ; a gate that let you in and closed at the touch of a riding whip, and—a really ambitious and important invention—a system whereby railway carriages would automatically uncouple themselves during a collision. Postie was a great man and he has never been recognized. . . .'

The Tolbooth, which I found so grim at night, is not really so sinister in daylight. It is a distinguished building, and it stands in one of the main streets like a visitor from the Middle Ages. If Kirkcudbright thought as highly of it as I do, some attempt would be made to preserve it or turn it to some purpose.

At the moment it is derelict. It has been used as a factory and a store room. It seems to stand in Kirkcudbright hugging horrible memories, like that of poor Elspeth M'Ewen, an old woman who was burned in a tar-barrel in 1698, the last witch executed in Kirkcudbright. But she was not the last witch to be imprisoned and tried in the Tolbooth. In 1701 a poor old woman was charged with having dealings with the devil, the evidence against her being that a spinning-wheel was seen to revolve in her house without human agency, that a candle was seen to pass into her house with nothing holding it and, worst of all, a strange man, the Devil himself, was seen to enter but was never seen to leave. The poor woman was banished from the Stewartry and sought refuge in Ireland. The same sentence was passed in 1703 on a woman charged with having the ' evil-eye ', and as recently as 1803 Jane Maxwell was tried at Kirkcudbright for ' witchcraft, sorcery, inchantment, conjuration and fortune-telling ', her sentence being twelve months in prison and the degrading obligation to appear once a quarter on market day at Kirkcudbright Cross and stand for a time in the *jougs* or pillory. One wonders how a woman managed to survive such humiliation.

But these are grim memories and Kirkcudbright is not a grim town to-day. It is a town of rare quality, a town that seems to be happy and good-natured : the kind of town that a man is always glad to have seen.

§ 2

The word Kirkcudbright, which looks so uncouth in print and is so soft in speech—Kir-coo-brie—was once spelt Kilcudbrit, a combination of two words *cil* and *Cudbert* the church, or cell, of St. Cuthbert.

This place is one of the many in the Scottish Lowlands and in the north of England in which the monks of Lindisfarne, flying before the Danes, rested awhile with the bones, or rather the miraculously preserved body, of St. Cuthbert. Once a shepherd lad somewhere near Melrose, Cuthbert became one of the most revered saints in Britain. In the half-century before the Norman Conquest Canute, in a mood of exuberant repentance, walked five miles barefoot to pray before Cuthbert's shrine at Durham. The capital of the Stewartry shared the sanctity which followed the incorruptible corpse of Cuthbert wherever it rested, but the Gallovidians celebrated their distinction in a singularly pagan manner, for we learn from the Abbot of Rievaulx that they were in the habit of tying a wretched bull to a stake and baiting it in honour of the saint. What an incredible time the early missionaries must have had in attempting to graft Christianity to the natural paganism of Man!

Kirkcudbright Castle stands with its ivy-covered walls to the main street, a shell within but intact without. I sat in the ruins and made a few notes about the ups and downs of the lords of Kirkcudbright, once the M'Lellans of Bombie. This family obtained the lands of the Franciscan Friary at Kirkcudbright at the Reformation, and built their castle with stone taken from Greyfriars and the old ruins of Castledykes. But it is doubtful whether they ever furnished it, or used more than a few of its rooms, because at this time the rather enigmatic smile of James VI fell upon them and they deserted Kirkcudbright for the dangerous fortunes of a life at court. Sir Thomas M'Lellan took part in the first really serious Scottish invasion of England when, with the great Elizabeth lying dead in Whitehall, King James VI and I rode south to the crash of church bells to become the first Stuart King of England.

When Charles I paid his spectacular visit to Edinburgh he scattered coronation honours among certain of his Scottish courtiers in the hope of winning them to his ill-fated attack on Presbyterianism. Among the exalted was Sir Robert M'Lellan, who became Lord Kirkcudbright. But Charles, as usual, had backed the wrong man. When the Civil Wars broke out Lord Kirkcudbright became a keen Covenanter. He raised a regiment of horse. He was a very popular commander and always marched about Galloway with a barrel of brandy at the head of his squadrons ! In this he showed an admirable grasp of the intimate relation between war and alcohol and we learn, without surprise, that the success of the battle of Philiphaugh was largely due to the dash and gallantry of his regiment. The Kirkcudbright brandy has been immortalized by the ballad-maker :

> *We fight the battles of the Lord,*
> *Let's sing a holy psalm ;*
> *Let ilk man tak to brace his arm*
> *With strength, a guid big dram.*

So Lord Kirkcudbright gallops cheerfully with his barrel across the tragic landscape of Covenanting times, the only really amusing figure on the grim stage. I wish we knew a bit more about him. I would like to think that he gave Oliver Cromwell one over the odds !

But whatever splendour his family achieved seems to have expired with him. The estate was split up on the distaff side. Huge mortgages piled up. Things were so bad in the eighteenth century that the Lord Kirkcudbright of that day kept a thatched ale-house in the town where local worthies on market day called him, I hope respectfully, ' Lord John ', while the heir to the title cleaned the boots and Lady Betty made the beds.

In these days, when all of us know noblemen who keep ale-houses or exploit slightly less dignified methods of living, the fate of Lord John is not very surprising, but in the eighteenth century it must have been embarrassing for all concerned. A later peer became a glover in Edinburgh, and it is good to know that when the Representative Peers of Scotland were elected they always patronized their unfortunate companion.

So Kirkcudbright Castle, which looks as though it has weathered a hundred sieges and has drunk deep of the riot of blood and passion which is history, is really nothing more than a rather pathetic relic of a family that faded out.

§ 3

I climbed the hill towards the churchyard of St. Cuthbert with a man who has steeped himself in the lore of Galloway. He led me through the maze of tombstones to one which bore on its reverse side the peculiar symbols of ram's horns and a pair of crossed spoons.

'Here is one of the most interesting graves in Kirkcudbright,' he said. 'It is the grave of Billy Marshall, the king of the Galloway gipsies, who died in 1792 aged 120 years. They still tell stories about him in the farmhouses all over Galloway. It's a pity that old worthies cannot live in the same world as the railway train, the newspaper, the daily postman and the wireless. My father was full of stories about the strange characters who tramped the western Lowlands when he was a boy, gipsies, tinkers, packmen, and the like, who were known to every household, great and small. They were the villains and heroes of a simpler and, I believe, happier time. Galloway folk used to expend on them the interest which is now squandered on the cinema and the Sunday paper . . .'

'What is Billy Marshall's story?'

'A very interesting one. His people had been gipsies in Galloway in remote times. He used to claim that he was the last Pictish king and a number of educated people seem to have believed this too. Marshall and all his tribe were squat, broad-shouldered dark men. Billy is said to have been born about 1672. When a young man he fought in King William's army at the Battle of the Boyne and it is known that he served in the continental wars of the great Duke of Marlborough. It is supposed that he deserted from the army. They tell a good story about this. Billy is said to have gone to his colonel, a Galloway man and one of the M'Guffogs of Ruscoe, to ask him if he had any message for his native land. As the regiment was in Germany at the time the colonel was surprised and asked if there was any chance of a message being delivered. 'Ay,' said Billy Marshall, 'Keltonhill Fair is just at han', I hae never been absent frae it since my shanks could carry me to it, nor do I intend to let this year be the first!' The colonel probably considered this a good joke but, nevertheless, Billy tramped across Germany and arrived home in time for the fair. . . .

' He then gave up soldiering and settled down to rule the gipsies of the western Lowlands. He was an astonishing person. He was lawfully married seventeen times and in addition to his legal wife maintained an extensive harem. It is said that after his hundredth year he became the father of four children. The ram's horns on the gravestone are a symbol of the old horn spoon industry which Billy and his friends used to carry on.

' The people of Galloway liked the old ruffian because he shared with Robin Hood the reputation of robbing the wealthy and helping the poor. He was up to every kind of trick known to one who lives on his wits, but he never broke a promise or let down any one who had been good to him. He was an ambitious old autocrat and I believe once waged a fearful battle with gipsies who refused to recognize his kingship. Several people died in this battle and many donkeys and ponies were drowned.

' In Billy's time Galloway was overrun with gipsy families. They were Baillies, Millers, Kennedies, MacMillans, Marshalls, Watsons, Wilsons and O'Neills. Many of these famous gipsy families have disappeared or died out. But it will be many a year before the name of Billy Marshall is not recalled round the fire in the winter time.'

I began searching for more information about Billy Marshall. His career is admirably sketched by Mr. Andrew McCormick in *The Tinkler Gypsies*, and I also ran across an account of him written by James Murray M'Culloch of Ardwall in a letter to the editor of *Blackwood's Magazine* for 1817:

' I am one of an old family in the Stewartry of Galloway with whom Billy was intimate for nearly a whole century,' wrote Mr. M'Culloch. ' He visited regularly twice a year my great-grandfather, grandfather, and father, and partook, I daresay, of their hospitality, but he made a graceful and ample return ; for during all the days of Billy's natural life, which the sequel will show not to have been few, the washings could have been safely left out all night without anything from a sheet or a tablecloth down to a dishclout being in any danger. During that long period of time there never was a goose, turkey, duck, or hen, taken away, but what could have been clearly traced to the fox, the brock, or the fumart ; and I have heard an old female domestic of ours declare that she had known Billy Marshall and his gang, again and again, mend all the ' kettles, pans, and crackit pigs in the house, and make twa or three dozen o' horn spoons into the bargain, and never tak a farthing o' the laird's siller '.

The writer describes a meeting with Billy Marshall in the year 1789. The gipsy was then one hundred and seventeen years old. He lived at the hamlet, or clachan, of Palnure. When the writer's carriage stopped near his dwelling, the old man walked to it and after being introduced to Mr. M'Culloch admonished him to ' tak' care of my han', and do naething to dishonour the gude stock o' folk that I was come o' '. He added, says Mr. M'Culloch, ' that I was the fourth generation of us he had been acquaint wi' '.

They gave silver coins to the old king and passed on. Later that night, as they passed Palnure, they heard sounds which proved that Billy Marshall was not too old to take a dram.

' His long reign,' says Mr. M'Culloch, ' if not glorious, was in the main fortunate for himself and his people. Only one great calamity befell him and them during that long space of time in which he held the reins of government. It may have been already suspected that, with Billy Marshall, ambition was a ruling passion, and this bane of human fortune had stimulated in him a desire to extend his dominions from the Brig'-end of Dumfries to the Newton of Ayr at a time when he well knew the Braes of Glenapp and the Water of Doon to be his western precinct. He reached the Newton of Ayr, which I believe is in Kyle, but there he was opposed, and compelled to recross the river by a powerful body of tinkers from Argyle or Dumbarton. He said in his bulletins that they were supported by a strong body of Irish sailors and Kyle colliers. Billy had no artillery, but his cavalry and infantry suffered very severely. He was obliged to leave a great part of his baggage, provisions and camp equipage behind him, consisting of kettles, pots, pans, blankets, crockery, horns, pigs, poultry, &c. A large proportion of shelties, asses and mules were driven into the water and drowned, which occasioned a heavy loss in creels, panniers, hampers, tinkers' tools and cooking utensils, and, although he was as well appointed as to a medical staff as such expeditions usually were, in addition to those who were missing, many died of their wounds.

'However, on reaching Maybole with his broken and dispirited troops he was joined by a faithful ally from the county of Down who, unlike other allies on such occasions, did not forsake him in his adversity. This junction enabled our hero to rally and pursue in his turn. A pitched battle was fought somewhere about the Brig of Doon or Alloway Kirk when both sides, as is usual, claimed a victory, but, however this may have been, it is believed that this disaster, which happened in A.D. 1712, had slaked the thirst of Billy's ambition. He was many years in recovering from the effects of this great political error.'

Billy also gained some notoriety as a 'leveller'. In the eighteenth century fences and walls came into being. Before that time open-field cultivation and wide stretches of unconfined pasture land had been general. When landowners began to build walls and make fences there was a great outcry from shepherds and herdsmen. There was at least one riot in the Stewartry :

> Against the poor the lairds prevail
> With all their wicked works,
> Who will enclose both hill and dale,
> And turn corn-fields to parks.
> The lords and lairds they drive us out
> From mailings where we dwell ;
> The poor man cries, ' Where shall we go ? '
> The rich say, ' Go to hell ! '

That was the voice of the eighteenth-century herdsman. And in Billy Marshall these angry men found a splendid champion. Billy at the head of his 'levellers' would creep out at night throwing down walls and tearing up fences.

Sitting before autumn's first fire in the smoky tap-room of an inn, I remembered my friend's lament for vanished worthies. Men like Marshall were the product of an age that had never heard of mass production. They gave a spice to life because they were supremely themselves as we can never be, subject, as we are, to standardized education, mass emotion and ready-made opinion.

I looked up and saw some queer characters lifting the beer-mugs, old men with faces brown and lined as if carved in hard wood. They looked the part. But over their heads a loud speaker gave them, hot from Falkirk, the latest dance tune crooned in the accents of America.

The old men banged their glasses on the bar in time to jazz.

§ 4

My bedroom in Kirkcudbright is in the roof of the hotel. The window lies in a V-shaped alcove on whose sharp and uncompromising slope I hit my head every morning, because the malicious power that furnished the hotel had placed a Victorian dressing-table half-way inside this alcove, and in such a position that any man in the act of shaving is bound to crack his head. There is nothing else in the room but a few battered articles of the kind sometimes seen spread out in the bright shame of daylight on the cobbles of a street market : a sad, cane-seated chair that suggests generations of orphaned serving-maids peeling off thick black woollen stockings with holes in the heels, a tattered rug that, unlike Man but like all furniture, has actually ascended atticwards in the scale of decay, a fender, a picture of Othello murdering Desdemona, a gas jet over the mantelpiece, and an iron-hard double bed whose frightful experiences in the course of thirty years or so have engendered a hatred of humanity. Not content with offering a rock-like surface to the body, this malevolent structure expresses its aged protests in every kind of rusty wheeze and creak and by dropping several small brass knobs on which one inevitably stands for a painful moment in the early morning.

But every evening at an absurdly early hour I steal up to this awful bed as eagerly as the lovers of its distant youth. I go grasping a blue enamelled candlestick and in my pocket are two extra filched candles, which I dangerously heat and stick on the edge of a cane chair until it resembles some pathetic wayside shrine. And I lie in bed and read John Mactaggart.

Have you ever read John Mactaggart? His *Scottish Gallovidian Encyclopedia* would have delighted Burns and Scott and Hogg. It is the real thing, straight from the byre and the furrow, a book that could have been written only by an inspired peasant in whose heart burned not only great love for his own people but also an acute, detached consciousness of their manifold peculiarities.

Mactaggart writes with that high spirit of youth which, when transferred to print and wedded to an appearance of great learning, suggests the eccentricity of old age. He was born in the parish of Borgue in Kirkcudbright in the year 1791 and he wrote the *Gallovidian Encyclopedia* when he was twenty-five. It is an astonishing collection of Galloway words, phrases and customs. Mactaggart, conscious that he lived in an age when men and manners were changing, went about Galloway collecting words as they flew from the mouths of his countrymen. His introduction to this strange and amusing hotch-potch is not only a piece of honest writing, it is also a piece of prose in which a love of Scotland burns fiercely side by side with a complete contempt for the technique of punctuation. How astonishing it is that the compilers of countless anthologies have never included a paragraph of Mactaggart's ' Introduction '. Listen to this :

' There is nothing I am prouder of than that I am a Scotchman, and, I may add, a Scotch peasant too ; for where on all the earth is there a country that can be compared to Scotland in every noble thing that elevates a nation ? and where is there a class of human beings to be found like her peasantry ? they are not only an honour to the land they live in, but a credit to the whole world, though I add little to their glory. . . . But the divine art of a Burns, or an Ettrick Shepherd, is not by any means the only thing that upraises, or has upraised, the " kintra folks o' Auld Scotland ", they have it in their power to brag of producing learned men and philosophers : they have turned out Euclids and Socrateses. Mungo Park, too, the celebrated traveller, was a peasant ; but, above all, they have the patriot Wullie Wallace, with whom none but a Switzerland Tell can be put on the weigh-beam with ; and, what is all this to their warm, honest hearts, their tender feelings, their simple manners, and their strong independent minds ? He would be a writer of pith indeed, who could praise them too much, and one of matchless impudence who could revile them ; they are, though, in need of neither, for they exist before the eyes of the world, and speak for themselves.'

He goes on to tell how he gathered his ' encyclopedia '.

' Little of this faulty book of mine was composed in the closet,' he explains ; ' it was gathered by my own eyes and ears, concocted in my own slender intellect while at my rural employment, and wrote down on scraps of paper as I found it convenient in the midst of the works of nature, in the open air, beneath the flaring sun, in a quarryhole perhaps. Sometimes again on a " braeside ", and *ablins* whiles in a " thick wud ", or on the back of a " grey stane ", the whole, therefore, has the smell, as it were, of Nature ; her rudeness is about it, and when her *plaid* keeps the shoulders of anything warm, that thing looks contented indeed.'

Mactaggart explains that he had to go about his task in great secrecy, for had he been suspected of book-writing he would have closed up the mouths of his friends !

' By keeping the thing dark,' he says cunningly, ' I came on better ; for none were afraid to talk with me on old matters, because they did not suspect that I was " takin' notes " ; had they thought that, the auld wives and many others would have trembled for me, and keep'd their mouths sealed. As it was, it required me some craft to get the information I wanted ; by putting questions direct nothing is obtained, but to talk in a careless manner about the subjects wanted, as if it was little matter about them, then everything comes bolting out.'

This fills me with sympathetic laughter ! How I would have loved to have gone round with John.

' So God bless my friends,' he concludes, ' and Heaven ever smile on the natives of the South of Scotland ; for a better race of beings is nowhere to be found between the sea and the sun.'

Now let me give you a slight taste of Mactaggart's alphabetical delight. Here is his entry under

'ACKAVITY, ACKWAVITY, or ACKWA.'

'The chief of all spiritous liquors, viz. Whisky, when taken to excess, does not even make such a wreck of the human constitution as others do, such as rum and brandy, and when taken in moderation, as it should be, there is none other half so good. Far be it from me to hold up any thing that may be thought allied to vice; and if whisky be so, as many grave men think, I have little cause to eulogize it, being no great bottle man: nature having given me a frame of body that is a sworn foe to any fluid stronger than Adam's Wine. However, as the majority of men are moulded different, I will say that a *dram of o' gude ackwa* and *cauller-water* refreshes a fainting heart in a sultry *simmer day*; and the same quantity of Farintosh is quite comfortable to take in a cauld wunter morning, while even a *Tumbler or twa o' Toddy* looks social on an evening. So I wont join with M'Neil and others in saying it is the *Scaith o' Scotlan'*. I am more inclined to side with Burns to a certain extent. . . . Many have whisky to be a slow poison, which, perhaps, it may be in a certain degree, particularly if any way adulterated. A person told the celebrated Billy Marshall, the *Tinker*, once, that it was a *slaw pizion*——

'It maun be deils slaw indeed, quoth the Gypsey Chief, for I hae tooted it owre in nogginfus now for mair than a hunner year and am tae fore yet hale and fear.' He died when 120 years of age.

'And once a *Kirkcubrie carter*, having brought some coals to a certain very abstemious medical man, the doctor, according to the custom of the country, presented him with a *dram o' whisky* for by-payment. The carter drank it off in a moment making his *wee finger twirl* above the quickly emptied glass in fine style; when, quoth the Doctor with some emphasis—"That's a nail in thy coffin, Saunders." "Maybe sae (replied the drunkard), I wish it were fu' o' sic tackets."'

I wish I could quote the whole of Mactaggart's remarks on a character known as 'Auld Millhaw' who lived in the parish of Borgue, but it would be too long. This old man

3

was apparently a great railer against the manners of his time and a lover of the days of his youth, and Mactaggart copied down long extracts of his conversation:

'Dear me, but fourscore years mak an unco odds o' the times, and that's about as lang as I can min' ought now. Mony an up and down in the warl has haen Auld Millha, and there's a queer something comes owre him whan he claps his auld bum down on the mossaick by the cheek o' the chaumer door, and begins to think awee and glowre back. . . .'

Here I must ask the English reader to read over again those last six words. There is a vitality and an expressiveness about the vernacular Scots that make one feel at times that writing in ordinary English is like using a worn-out coinage. 'To think awee and glowre back.' You can actually see old Millhaw bending forwards with the firelight on his face. But read this:

'There's no a human cratur drawing the wun o' life now that I ken'd in my young days; they're a' i' the mools lang syne; the last ane wha I min' o' that waded about i' the burns wi' me whan a boy, and neivd beardocks, was Wullie Cockery, and he's gane to his lang hame aboon hauf a dizzen year sin. Wullie was ay but a pieferin useless body a' the days o' him, and ken's about little but how to mak beeskeps, and wattle saughcreels—than he wad hae glaiber'd about the splittin' o' breers for the hale o' a lang forenicht i' the wunter time without wearyin—Wattie Bennoch was gane afore him. Wattie and me had mony a day o't thegether, but he was ane clever cheil, and as sharp as a preen. We gaed awa ance —its langsinsyne now—we a wheen nowt, tae South o' Englan', and as we war gaen by a bit on the road they ca'd (let me think), ay, they ca'd, now when it comes across me, Temple-sorby, out came a meikle bill-dog frae a tannaree, and was beginning to fley our drove, when Wattie drew his gude hazle rung frae neath his coat-tail and hit him a whap wi't aneath the lug till goth he gaed heels owre gowdy without a bough. But some o' the townsfolks gat scent o't, and out they cam bizzin like bees to ding Wattie and me to the deil. I laid on, and sae did he, till some o'us a' hech'd again. We gat out amang them tho' at last wi sair banes; but gin we hadna been a pair o' gye strang rouchtous, we wad hae lain like the thick-nosed colly-tyke that day. . . .'

Listen to Auld Millhaw on the degeneracy of his day—the early nineteenth century :

' I hae seen the days,' he cries, ' whan there war nae carts wi' wheels in a' the parish, nor harrows wi' airn teeth, but carrs and harrows wi' teeth o' whunroots ; and yet we did full weel for a' ; had aye rowth to eat and drink and smoik amang o' the best of things—— Them wi' their thrashing machines, airnpleughs and turnipbarrows, mere falderaloes ripin up a' the bits o' green hoams and forcin' wheat to grow whar Providence never intended it, and a' for the lairds, the tenant bodies are never a bawbee the richer o't ; awa wi' yer nice agriculture, yer game laws and yer Maderia wines . . . awa wi' yer readin' priest, yer Latin dominies, yer rooms spread wi' carpets, yer fallow fiels and yer fenders : and let me hear a cheel skelpin a sermon affloof, anither learnin' the bairns the rule o' three and plain arithmetic ; the bare sleek yird I hae mony a time shook my shanks on—fiels to plow just as my father plow'd, and nae fenders to hinder the aizles frae spangin out, but lads and lassies, bare-fitted and bare-legged wedged thick roun the bonny ingle. . . . Never turn, gentle Borgue, or thou'llt gang a' to the bumwhush ; stick by the creed o' thy forefathers, never laugh at the gude auld law.'

If that is not a magnificent piece of rhetoric and a superb piece of Scots vernacular that breathes truth in every word of it, then I know nothing of such things.

And through Mactaggart's book marches a procession of good, sound, expressive, earthy words : chirkle (to grind the teeth), chitterin' (with cold), clatterbag (a gossip), hirple (to limp), jannerer (a gossiper of no account), whudder (a noise made by the wind on stormy nights), and—wonderful onomatopoetic word—maillies (sheep).

This word, maillies, is a triumph. It expresses in a breath the sound of a flock of sheep, and as an affectionate term applied to animals it is as lovely as mouldiwarp, the old English word for a mole, and flittermouse and—another pretty Scots word—hoolet, an owl. And if you want a descriptive sentence, could you better 'I *whuffed out* the candle'?

Some of the terms employed in derision or contempt were particularly good. A Brilch (now called a bilch), was 'a short thick impudent person', a Clashbag 'a person full of low, mean stories', a Climpie 'a person with a strange lameness', a Clippie 'a person with too neat cut clothes', a Cutty-glies 'a little squat-made female, extremely fond of the male creation', and a Glundy' an ignorant, sour-tempered fellow'.

I think Mactaggart's *Encyclopedia* is one of the great curiosities of Scottish literature. It is remarkable that a young peasant of twenty-five should have had the discernment and the judgement to compile such a treasury of words, phrases and thumb-nail biographies. But the poor fellow came a bad cropper with his book. Its publication in 1824 caused a terrific sensation in Galloway because everyone recognized under the name of 'Star o' Dungyle', a certain Miss H——, the daughter of a local laird about whom John Mactaggart had something to say that was not only out-spoken but, truth or no truth, distinctly libellous. The father of the young lady threatened legal action and in order to avoid this the young author destroyed all available copies of the original edition. This was the libel:

'STAR O' DUNGYLE.—A few years ago the most beautiful woman in Galloway was a Miss H——; her father was a laird. Keltonhill Fair was often by her laid in dust and ashes, for no girl was looked at or admired in all the fair but Miss H——. The celebrated Maggy Lauder never so much attracted the attention of the crowds in Anster Loan, what-ever Tennant may say to the contrary. Many and many Rab the Ranter had she; her features ran exactly in the curve of exquisite beauty, and were always kept in the most en-chanting animation; her eyes, her hair, her lips were the most charming objects man could behold—they set the most callous burning with love! Every movement she made was of the most attracting and engaging nature. The Irishmen from Ballinasloe would have left both their horses and oxen and joined the crowd that followed Miss H——, bawling out, " By Japers, she's the game; O Honey, if I had but thee at the sweet town of Limavadie"; another, " By the long bridge of Belfast. Barney's eyes never saw such a girl. I'd fight for her with my mother of the sloe till all the bones in my body were bettled to mummy "; The sons of John Bull beyond the Tweed got also enamoured of Miss H——, but the good boxer or bruiser were the only persons who could get to speak to her, and she was always fonder of that class than of well-bred rich-dressed gentlemen. In short, for all her beauty and elegance, the low and mean were her associates, and she cared not what length she went with them almost ; would lay in barns with them at night, put on beggar weeds, and bade farewell to virtue altogether, and bore to some of them bastard children : yet for all this whenever she appeared in proper array all in Galloway was charmed with the lovely Miss H——. Beauty of the very first order, in defiance of vice, brought her always crowds of admirers who obeyed every nod of her head, every wave of her hand : her sway was truly despotic in the world of gallantry. A strong blacksmith who could not get her entirely to himself, got so mortified that he would off and perish in the wilderness of Canada for her sake ; away he went to the banks of Loch Huron, but was not there long before a letter followed him from Miss H—— inviting him to return again to Galloway and she would assuredly marry him. Back over the Atlantic the son of Vulcan came, true to her mandate ; but alas ! how he must have been deceived when the dear Miss H—— disdained to look or speak to him ? Thus she wielded the sceptre of love ! He afterwards became a gamekeeper, and she really married an old cattle dealer who had weeped about her many years ; to him she acted the part of not a bad wife —had a family—is yet living ; but, like the celebrated Mary of Buttermere, the Beauty of Cumberland, her beauty hath entirely fled her ; she will be remembered in Galloway not only by the songs of her Laureates, but by hundreds of others, years unseen yet ; her popular name was " Star o' Dungyle ".'

It looks to me very much as though John had been jilted by ' the Star '. He must have had some bitter motive for such an attack. He went to Canada for three years, but after the publication of the *Encyclopedia*, so that we cannot picture him as the exiled blacksmith. In Canada, by the way, he was clerk of works to the Rideau Canal, but his health was not good and he returned in 1828 and died at the tragic age—for a writer of his originality—of thirty-nine.

The best story about Mactaggart's *Gallovidian Encyclopedia* concerns the elder Mactaggart, from whom all knowledge of the work had been concealed. He first became aware of it when he saw it in a bookseller's window in Kirkcudbright. When he reached home he greeted his son with :

' John, yer ain family kent ye were a fool, but noo the hale world'll ken ! '

§ 5

Kirkcudbright is the only place I know where a villainous form of salmon poaching is a legal operation ! There is a stretch of the Dee belonging to the manor of St. Mary's Isle in which the flinging of a shoulder-net for salmon has been a custom since ancient times. The local legend is that this right—now granted by the Crown—descends from the Franciscan monks of the thirteenth century.

One night I was invited to accompany the salmon netters on a night's fishing. I was lucky, because salmon fishing in the Dee ends earlier than in many Scottish waters and this was one of their final flings.

It was about ten o'clock and the night was pitch dark. I could hear the Dee in spate roaring over a cataract called the Doachs half a mile away. This river is formed by ten or twelve rills, which rise on the slopes of Corserine Hill. While it is young it is called the Sauch Burn, then it becomes Cooran Lane. After it has received the surplus waters of Loch Dee it is known as the ' dark stream ', or Dee, a name given to it because the mosses in which it has its origin darken its water. It is said that salmon in the Dee are darker than the fish in any other river in the south of Scotland.

Half a mile or so outside Kirkcudbright a steep road leads to the Doachs. I blundered down in the darkness and discovered three shadowy figures waiting for me in the lee of a building that seemed to be an old mill. The river roared like an angry beast. One of the men put his mouth to my ear and shouted at the top of his voice that there was too much water in the river, and we might not therefore get a fish. I looked out over the Doachs, and saw the water steaming and boiling over the rocks. It seemed impossible that any fish could live in such rapids.

'Come along,' shouted my friend. 'We must cross the river.'

Cross the river ? How ? I knew that there was no bridge ; but there was no time for questions, for the shadowy men had set off, shouldering their nets, and the only thing to do was to follow.

I discovered to my horror—for I have a hatred of narrow planks—that this furious torrent (which this night looked to me wider than any river I have ever seen !) is crossed by a series of temporary planks about a foot wide, guarded on one side by a rope that serves not as a support but merely as a guide. It swung about when touched.

The planks went in one way for perhaps fifty yards, then they changed direction and criss-crossed above the rapids. The water in parts swirled over the planking until the flimsy woodwork trembled and shivered. I was glad that it was dark.

There was something sinister and distinctly perilous in our delicate, crouching progress through the night with our wicked shoulder net. I felt that a man with a gun would pop up from somewhere and arrest us.

I dropped down with relief on an island in the Doachs about the size of a small sitting-room. We were in the centre of the river. All round us were white tufts where the water cascaded over submerged rocks.

The net-thrower prepared to fish. A grooved wooden implement was strapped on his right shoulder. He took a twenty-foot pole, at the end of which was a big net. He swung it in the air, poised it above him in the manner of a javelin thrower and cast it from him into the torrent. There was so little room on the island that we had to lie flat in the wet grass to escape the swing of the pole.

It was exciting to lie there in the roaring tumult and see the fisher silhouetted against the white rapids, rhythmically poising, flinging, then placing the great pole on the wooden shoulder groove and bringing in the net with a quick hand-over-hand movement.

' There's nae fish the nicht ! ' he said, coming over to me and bellowing. ' D'ye wish to cast the net ? '

I did.

With great effort I managed to lift the pole into what I considered a flinging position, but, unable to cast the weighty thing, I let it drop into the river, and at the very instant it touched the water I felt that I had caught a whale, the net gave a jump that lifted me from my feet and sent me crashing into my companions. But they were waiting for me. They caught me—and the pole. Had they not done so I would have been lifted up and flung far into the water.

When I looked at the fishers I could tell by their open mouths that they were having what was evidently a loud laugh.

Casting the net demands not only great muscular strength but a skill that comes only with practice. The fishers told me that in one or, at the most, two casts they can tell whether there is a fish in the pool or not. They told me stories of pulling in the net full to the brim with salmon.

They then tried a pool on the other side of the rock at the foot of a waterfall. The pole was poised and out it shot, the net falling neatly as a knife into the water ; then, so quickly that I could not follow what happened, it was withdrawn, and inside it were four feet of silver desperation.

The salmon went mad ! It leaped high and crashed down to earth ! I could hear the noise of its struggle above the thunder of the Doachs. A man leaped on it and hit it with a mallet.

I was aware of a faint feeling of revulsion. I thought sympathetically of the patient fishermen in all parts of Scotland who were paying hundreds of pounds for the pleasure of standing to their waists in water and gallantly casting hour after hour, day after day. And here we were in the night clubbing salmon to death with a hammer !

It was immoral. . . .

The fishermen held a consultation, and eventually shouted that fishing was over for the night. There were no more fish in the pool.

A thin, determined rain was falling. The planks were wet and slimy. Going back was worse than arriving, because I knew all the dangerous bits. Ahead walked the net-thrower with his twenty-foot pole on his shoulder. Behind walked the man who carried the salmon.

We weighed the fish in a shed. He turned the scale at eighteen pounds.

'What are you going to do with him ? ' I asked.

'London,' they replied.

What an appetite London has ; and from what strange places, and in what queer ways, its appetite is satisfied !

§ 6

Paul Jones, the Galloway gardener's boy who founded the American Navy, has been compared by his admirers with Nelson and by his detractors with Captain Kidd.

I prefer to think of him as one of the most remarkable and puzzling Scotsmen in history and one of the most effective rebels who ever opposed British arms. What a tower of strength he would have been in the '45 !

' Was he a pirate ? ' I asked a man in Kirkcudbright.

' Well,' he replied, after examining every stone in the Tolbooth, ' I wouldna say that. He pu' the wund up the country sae weel that maybe in revenge posterity hasna been verra kind to him.'

And that, I think, puts the whole thing in a nutshell.

' Did ye ever hear the story of how Paul Jones pu' the wund up Kirkcaldy, where they make the linoleum ? Ye never did ? It's a true story and it's been pu' in a buik . . .'

This is the story.

About the time that Paul Jones, the first accredited American admiral, was attacking His Majesty's ships and harrying the coast towns of the north, the rumour spread that he had rounded the Firth of Forth and was laying off Kirkcaldy. The townspeople were terrified. The pamphleteers had done their work well and Paul Jones was dreaded by young and old.

Now in Kirkcaldy was an eccentric old Presbyterian minister who had a singular trick of addressing the Deity in a familiar and hectoring manner. It was sometimes difficult to discover whether he was praying or addressing a singularly stubborn member of his flock. But he was a good, God-fearing old man, like all his type.

When the townspeople rushed to the shore to catch sight of the dreaded frigate, the old minister was seen pushing his way through the crowd with an arm-chair. He set this at the edge of the incoming tide and began to pray :

' Neu, deed Laird, dinna ye think it's shame on ye to send the vile pireet to rub out folk o' Kircawdy ; for ye ken they're a' puir eneugh a'ready, and hae naething to spare. As the wun blaws, he'll be here the noo', and wha kens what he may do ? Muckle's the mischief he has dune a'ready. Ony packet gear they hae gathered thegither he will gang wi' the heal o't ; and burn their hooses, tak' their vary claes and tirl them to the sark ; and, waes me ! wha kens but the bluidy villain micht tak their lives ! The puir weemen are maist freightened oot o' their wuts, and the bairns skirling after them. I canna thol't ! I hae been lang a faithful servant to ye, Laird, but—gin ye dinna turn the wun aboot, and blow the scoundrel oot o' the gate, I'll nay stur a fit, but wull just sit until the tide drowns me. Sae tak' ye're wull o't . . .'

And, it is good to relate, the ' wun blew aboot ', and Paul Jones was driven out to sea.

In a charming house on St. Mary's Isle, Kirkcudbright, Sir Charles and Lady Hope-Dunbar keep the historic teapot (with the 152-year-old tea leaves in it), the silver jug, salt cellars, and the rest of the plate which Paul Jones carried off during his famous raid in April, 1778.

Now and then wistful Americans arrive and ask to be shown the plate and say, " Well, well, you don't say . . ." and then ask to be shown the exact spot on which Paul Jones landed from the *Ranger*. This is far down on the isle, beyond the Japanese garden, where cultivation expires on a narrow neck of land that thrusts itself into Kirkcudbright Bay.

Early on an April morning in 1778 a three-masted frigate disguised as a merchantman slipped into this bay. This was the vessel fitted out by the Americans to attack British commerce. It was commanded by Paul Jones. He landed with about forty men. While they went up with orders to kidnap the Earl of Selkirk, whose house, now rebuilt, stood among dense trees a little way inland, Paul Jones paced up and down thinking—of what ?

It must have been a curious adventure, even for him. He had been a gardener's boy on this estate. It seems clear that he also believed himself to be the earl's illegitimate son, though why it is difficult to say. His plan was to capture the earl and hold him as a hostage for the treatment of American prisoners of war.

However, the earl was from home and the raiders returned with the silver plate, which they had demanded from the countess. Then the *Ranger* put out to sea again.

The story is continued in the Charter Chest of St. Mary's

Isle, in which are all the letters that passed between Paul Jones and the earl and countess about the theft of the plate.

Surely no " pirate " has ever taken anything so much to heart ! Paul Jones wrote about this regrettable episode like a rather pained curate whose school treat got out of hand and did damage to a garden !

' It cannot be too much lamented ', he wrote to the countess, ' that in the profession of arms, the officer of fine feelings and of real sensibility should be under the necessity of winking at any action of persons under his command which his heart cannot approve.'

Then follow pages of flamboyant regret, and the promise that when the spoons and forks and jugs should be put up for sale he would purchase them and return them with his respects to their rightful owners ! An incredible letter from a ' pirate ' !

Paul Jones kept his word. Six years later he wrote to the Earl of Selkirk—still in the same pained and apologetic vein—telling him that he was forwarding the plate to London.

He also sent a letter to the countess regretting that he was only permitted by his agents to pay carriage as far as London, because ' I could have wished to have ended this delicate business by delivering the plate to you at St. Mary's Isle in Scotland '. And hear him on the American War :

' Tho' I have drawn my sword in the present generous struggle for the right of man, yet I am not in arms as an American, nor am I in pursuit of riches. My fortune is liberal enough, having no wife nor family, and having lived long enough to know that riches cannot ensure happiness. I profess myself a citizen of the world, totally unfettered by the little, mean distinctions of climate or of country which diminish the benevolence of the heart and set bounds to philanthropy. Before this war began I had at an early time of life withdrawn from sea service in favour of " calm contemplation and poetic ease ". I have sacrificed not only my favourite scheme of life, but the softer affections of the heart and my prospects of domestic happiness, and I am ready to sacrifice my life also with cheerfulness, if that forfeiture could restore peace and good will among mankind. . . .'

Strange sentiment for a ' bluidy villain ' !

It seems to me that the truth about Paul Jones has not yet

been told. His complex character has evaded all his biographers, even those who wish him well.

There was a fine fantastic flavour in him. After successfully defying the British Navy with a squadron of five French and American ships, we catch glimpses of this Scottish gardener's son bowing above the hands of ladies in foreign Courts, hailed everywhere, except in Britain, as the greatest naval hero in history.

It seems in tune with his strange life that Catherine the Great of Russia should have summoned him to her aid in her war with the Turk. And his crazy dash to Russia, where the Empress ' waited him from day to day ', is in keeping with his character—and hers ! He was in Sweden at the time. Ice blocked the Gulf of Bothnia. He decided on a mad enterprise that had never before been attemped : to cut through the ice to the southward and enter the Baltic Sea.

He set off in the dawn from Gresholm in a thirty-foot boat and with a smaller boat to drag over the ice. His crew had no idea of the peril they were in. When, however, they understood the mad enterprise, Paul Jones had to cover them with a pistol and urge them on with threats.

All day he steered south along the coast of Sweden, picking his way between the ice floes, and at night he sat, pistol in hand, facing his terrified crew and steering for the open sea. He hit a storm, and for four days and nights he steered by the light of a travelling lamp fixed over the compass. He finally crossed the Gulf of Finland and landed at Revel.

Shortly afterwards he became a Russian rear-admiral. Four years after he died in poverty, slandered and deserted, in Paris.

What, then, is the truth about Paul Jones ?

There are some men, I think, who, in spite of their courage or abilities, are dogged all their lives by envy, slander and misfortune. He was one of them. He seems to have been a man with a deep-seated grudge. This may have caused him to turn rebel as it may have caused him to raid St. Mary's Isle with the idea of capturing the man whom he believed to be his father. There may have been some idea of ' getting his own back ' when he raided the scenes of his childhood.

He was a brooding creature, one of those men who even in success brood on imaginary failure, and no doubt the fact that he was always being ' let down ' developed this habit, deepening his melancholy and his sense of injustice. There is a modern term for this attitude: persecution complex.

He shared with Nelson many of the traits of genius. He was wildly ambitious and he had a childish love of honours. Action stimulated him; inaction flung him into ill-health and melancholy. Both men were reckless in love, both adored not wealth but fame.

Few men have been more vilely caricatured than Paul Jones; and he writhed under it. He wanted, above everything, to be popular and praised: and he was detested and slandered.

It is curious that rebels with nothing of his character or ability have in the generosity of time become national heroes. Perhaps his great fault was that he was a Scotsman who never expressed any affection for his native land.

But whether you regard him as a ' pirate '—though I fail to see how the first accredited officer to fly the Stars and Stripes in Europe can be a ' pirate '—or whether you regard him as a ruffian, the fact remains that he was a magnificent sailor and, to my way of thinking, one of the most interesting men on Galloway's roll of fame.

§ 7

Dundrennan Abbey lifts its broken arches a few miles from the waters of Solway Firth. Old gravestones lie in the grass, bitten by the wind and rain, or stand up-ended against mossy walls with the faint figures of dead men carved on them. Dundrennan village, a single row of cottages, runs along a slight hill at the back of the Abbey, from which on clear days you can see, across twenty miles of water, the blue hills of Cumberland lying fold on fold. So near they seem on bright days that you can pick out white farms and little bright green fields.

You ask for the key at a cottage and you walk down a steep path and enter the ruins of the great church which Fergus, King of Galloway, erected to the glory of God in 1142. It was colonized by monks from Rievaulx, in Yorkshire. The caretaker will not worry you with the usual patter, so you may wander where you like.

I think you should sit for a long time in that lovely chapter house, now open to the sky, and remember the greatest memory of this abbey—the last night that Mary Stuart spent in Scotland . . .

Eleven days after young Willie Douglas stole the key of Lochleven Castle and rowed the Queen from eleven months of captivity, her nobles gathered round her to fight the Battle of Langside.

It is the unlucky morning of May 13, 1568. Mary, Queen of Scots, sitting on a palfrey, overlooks the village of Langside, a few miles from Glasgow. In three-quarters of an hour she is flying for her life. Her army is routed. Search parties are after her. She is guided by Lord Herries to the wilds of Galloway. She sees this bleak land for the second time, and she sees it through her tears.

The first day she rides sixty miles. As the horses are spent they are turned loose and the fugitives take to the heather. They move only by night. They hide in glens and caves. Mary's head is shaved and she wears a dark wig. When she passes over a bridge her followers destroy it ; and so, painfully, the broken Queen comes out of the Galloway highlands to the soft country of the Solway shore.

A more hopeful race than the Stuarts never existed. Even as she flies like a gipsy over the mountains this young woman of twenty-six is full of new hopes. She will go to her cousin Elizabeth, and together they will make plans. Mary has always longed to meet Elizabeth. In failure and despair her heart has always turned to her successful cousin of England.

She pauses at a cottage, dog-weary and on foot. There is no food but water and oatmeal. Mary calls the poor cottage woman, thanks her for the hospitality, and asks what favour she may confer on her. (The Stuarts were ever most regal in misfortune.) The woman says that she always longed to own her cottage, and the Queen says that it shall be hers.

Historians have wondered how, in the broken state of her fortunes and during her last hours in Scotland, she was able to confer this favour. It seems probable that Lord Herries, the principal landowner of that district, who was present, would redeem his Queen's promise.

At Dundrennan the monks meet her. History says that she spent the last night in their abbey, but legend says that a lodging was found for her outside the abbey precincts. The story goes that the poor Queen, lonely, weary, and a prey to the horrors that continually afflicted her, ached for human companionship. Her women had scattered after the Battle of Langside. She had sent them flying in different directions to puzzle her pursuers. Now she was alone with the night before her. She noticed a little boy, and asked that he might be allowed to sleep with her. So the Queen of Scots slept her last night in Scotland holding in her arms an unknown child.

Perhaps her last council meeting was held in the ruined chapter house of Dundrennan. We can imagine how her travel-stained followers beg her to remain concealed in her own country. And we can imagine her, rather strange with her shaven head under a dark wig, being stubbornly deaf to them as this new dream of friendship with Elizabeth burns in her eager mind. Not far from the abbey, at a place called Port Mary, is a big stone washed by the tide. They say it was from this stone that in the morning the Queen embarked in a fishing boat for England.

Men kneel as the Queen of Scots says good-bye to Scotland. The Lord Abbot blesses her and the monks pray for her. She will come again with a victorious army from England!

But some hint of her fate, some foreknowledge of the nineteen years of captivity ahead of her, and of the block at Fotheringay, seems to have been given to the Archbishop of St. Andrews, who, as the boat is casting off, plunges waist-deep into the water and, seizing the gunwale with both hands, begs and implores the Queen to stay in Scotland.

But sails fill with wind. It is a wild day. They work against wind and tide for four hours, and then ahead of them are the blue mountains of Cumberland. And the Queen steps ashore. . . .

On a good day the coast road from Dundrennan to Balcary Point is, I think, one of the most beautiful in Galloway. Inland, the green, fretted Galloway hills fade to higher moorlands stained with heather, and over the water the mountains of England lift themselves in long soft lines as blue as smoke.

But, no matter how lovely the day and how sweet the salt wind, a man cannot see a fishing boat going to England without a small, perhaps unreasonable, ache in the heart.

CHAPTER FOUR

IN WHICH I DIVE INTO GALLOWAY, HEARD ABOUT DEVORGILLA
THE GOOD, FALL IN LOVE WITH THE TOWN OF NEWTON STEWART,
CLIMB THE MIGHTY MERRICK, SEE WIGTOWN OF THE MARTYRS
AND THE ' WHITE CHURCH ' OF ST. NINIAN AND, WHEN EXPLORING
THE MULL, DISCOVER A POOL FULL OF PET CODFISH

§ I

I WOULD like to gather together a crowd of people who are tired of cities and take them through Galloway. There would be bright days when we would walk that lovely coast road from Gatehouse of Fleet to Newton Stewart. We would take all the by-roads, get lost, sit on stone walls and tell stories, admire the ' belties ', lean over bridges and watch brown burn water flowing.

At Newton Stewart we would cross the bridge over the Cree and envy the people who live in houses which go straight down to the water, as they do in Venice. It would be grand to lie in bed and fish ! We would find the little inn where the pretty girl says shyly that the water isna verra guid, but the beer's fine.

One day we would gird our loins and take that terrible mountain road used by the smugglers. It goes north into Ayrshire, getting bleaker and wilder every mile. Grouse start up from the heather under your feet, and you can see lonely hawks cruising out of the clouds. We would stand beside mountain lochs, like Macaterick or Lochrecar, and feel a solitude that is balm to a hurt mind. And we would come into apparently dead villages that lie in the heather with the sweet reek of peat over them.

We would go to Threave Castle and remember the days when the wild Douglases thundered through this land with a thousand armed men behind them.

And there would be grey days, too, with a thin rain falling and grey walls shining and hills grey as cobwebs. The kirk-yards of Galloway would be dripping, and the grey stones leaning in the long grass. We would give ourselves over to

melancholy and read the flat stones that lie above the Covenanters, the deep-cut, wordy epitaphs, full of water as if
somebody still wept for them.

There would be dewy mornings when we would rise early
and see the shadows of the white farms lying the wrong way
round on the grass, our footprints black in the cold silver of
the meadows, and we would admire the sunlight stealing
through the slender birch woods and the light shining on the
blood-red clusters of the mountain ash. We would walk over
roads silent between their grey stone dykes and return to a
vast breakfast of bacon, or perhaps the last pink grilse of
the year.

We would walk in the rain too, the rain that sweeps over
Galloway, turning the grass a brighter green and the walls
a deeper grey, and sometimes, with a plate of cheese beside
us and a mug of ale, we would take John Mactaggart carefully from the protective pocket of a waterproof and stretching our legs before an inn fire, read bits like this from his
Encyclopedia :

' I, being only six years of age . . . ran about and hunted
butterflies, built little houses on brae sides and adorned them
with bleached periwinkle shells brought to me from the shore ;
I also waded in a burn that ran by beside the house and
neived beardocks. I had no companion but a hoolet ; this
was brought to me, when young, from the auld castle ; I fed
it with mice, but it found the way to an old sooty truff laft,
and there caught plenty of mice for itself ; one day it came
down from its reeky habitation to wash itself, having need
enough of that, and while doing so by a tub by the door, a
cock came the way and sank his deadly spurs into the skull
of my poor hoolet. I mourned about this many a day. At
last I was thought fit to go with my sisters to school, and
then again began my woes. Nothing could I learn. I was
begun to the Latin long before I knew anything almost of
English, as the order ran in those days " one could not be
put to the Latin too young ". Of a truth then I was put
young enough to it, but could learn nothing about it. I
was lashed upstairs and downstairs and was saved, I believe,
from dying an unnatural death by my parents flitting from
Lennox Plunton to the farm of Torrs in the parish of Kirkcudbright. A country school lay just beside us, we had only

a hill to go over to it. The master taught the scholars no Latin. This was a great thing to me : he was quite an easy, soothing teacher, a good counter and could read and write pretty well. If I have any learning or genius about me, to this man am I indebted for their improvement. Had he been a dominie who gave out tasks, who obliged the scholars to learn this, and then that, who made a slave of the mind when in its tender state, and who valued the feelings nothing, then I, Mac, would never have been heard of. I should have crawled about, a mean artificial worm of man's formation, without one spark of fire about me. Whenever a fox-hunt, a shipwreck, a *bonspiel*, or such thing, happened in the neighbourhood, the school was flung open to all who wished to run and see ; and I, for one, seldom stayed behind. Indeed I was looked on as rather a careless boy of my book, speiled heuchs for gull's eggs, and trees for young craws, went a fishing frequently, attended all raffles, tea-drinkings, fairs, and what not. Whenever there were any curious sights to be seen, there was I ; nothing would have kept them from me : but as I got older I met with fewer novelties.'

I call that good, honest writing. There is something of every man's boyhood in it :

' I, now in my thirteenth year,' continues John, ' took a huff at schools and schoolmasters altogether, leaving them both with disgust. At this my parents were displeased ; however, they let me take my own mind of it, and as I had now to work at little jobs about the farm, I soon relished this life not very well either ; so I would learn a trade : a mill-wright was thought a good one, and a ship carpenter, but I would go and bind myself to neither. That of a book printer pleased me best of any. I wrote to the firm of Oliver and Boyd, Edinburgh, stating the matter and my wish to become an apprentice. My letter was never answered. I wrote again to Fairbairn and Co. in the same city, and to Mr. Jackson, Dumfries, but never received any answer from either, which caused me to grow very dull. It was about this time that I began to feel a melancholy working in on me which I will never get rid of. I may here mention though that ever since that night on which my mother told me that there would come a day on which I should die and be covered up with cold mould in a grave, I have been rather haunted with thought. It gives the young mind a dreadful shock on first being made acquainted with this awful truth. Finding, therefore, myself worsted in getting to be a printer, I consoled myself with my lot, and became extremely bookish inclined ; and, as the old song goes :

> *I bought and borrowed everywhere,*
> *I studied night and day,*
> *Ne'er missed what Dean nor Doctor wrote*
> *That happen'd in my way.*

'A friend who lived in the neighbourhood had an *Encyclopedia Britannica* ; this I was given whenever I wanted a volume, and I must own that I have received no small benefit from this kindness. I gathered ten times more out of that book than I did at the College of Edinburgh, a place to which I started on foot, staff in hand, when in my nineteenth year. Before this time I had taken a ramble through England, had been often in love, had wrote poetry and the devil knows what. . . .'

Poor John Mactaggart ! The cold mould that he feared so greatly was shortly to cover him, leaving nothing but this notebook of local peculiarity and eccentricity which he had so remarkably gathered together.

And so, with our legs in the fender and the Galloway rain beating against the windows, we would wonder how Scottish literature might have been enriched if the Edinburgh publishers had answered the letter from the unknown young man with the hard, gritty Galloway name. My affection for him deepens the more I read his *Encyclopedia*. He is spiritually a descendant of Burns and I cannot help feeling, as I read these juvenile prose efforts of his, that, had his luck and his health been better, John Mactaggart might have filled the gap in Scottish literature that still waits for the writer of vernacular prose. He was a keen and humorous observer of his fellow men and he had the gift of putting down his impressions in a terse and vivid manner, which owes very little to art and everything to personality. Who, for instance, could better his description of an old fireside game called 'Wadds and Wears' :

'One of the most celebrated amusements of the ingle-ring,'

he says. 'To begin with then, one in the ring speaks as follows :

> I hae been awa at the wadds and wears
> These seven lang years :
> And's come hame a puir broken ploughman :
> What will ye gie me to help me to my trade ?

'He may either say he's a " puir broken ploughman ", or any other trade ; but since he has chosen that trade some of the articles of that trade must always be given or offered in order to recruit him. But the article he most wants he tells privately to one of the party who is not allowed, of course, to offer him anything as he knows the thing which will throw the " offerer " in a *wadd*, is a very serious matter, as shall afterwards be explained. Now, the one on the left hand of the poor ploughman, makes the first offer by way of answer to what above was said ; " I'll gie ye the *coutter* to help ye to your trade." The ploughman answers, " I don't thank ye for your *coutter*, I hae ane already." Then another offers him another article belonging to the ploughman's business, such as the *moolbred*, but this also is refused ; another, perhaps, gives the *sock*, another the *stilts*, another the *spattle*, another the *naigs*, another the *naig-graith*, and so on ; until one gives the *soam*, which was the article he most wanted ; and was the thing secretly told to one, and is the thing that throws the giver into a *wadd*, out of which he is relieved in the following manner :

'The ploughman says to the one in the wadd, " Whether will ye hae three questions and two commands, or three commands and two questions, to answer or gang on wi', sae that ye may win out o' the *wadd* ? " For the one so fixed has always the choice which of these alternatives to take. Suppose he takes the first, two commands and three questions, then a specimen of these may run so :

' " I command ye to kiss the *crook*," says the ploughman, which must be completely obeyed by the one in the *wadd*— his naked lips must salute the *sooty* implement.

'Secondly, saith the ploughman, I command ye to stand up in that neuk, and say :

> Here stan I, as stiff's a stake,
> Wha'ill kiss me for pity's sake ?

'Which must also be done ; in a corner of the house must

he stand and repeat that couplet, till some tender-hearted lass relieves him. Now for the questions, which are most deeply laid, or so *touching* to him, that he finds much difficulty to answer them.

'Firstly then, "Suppose ye were in a bed with *Maggie Lowden* and *Jennie Logan*, your two great sweet-hearts, what ane o'm wad ye ding owre the bed side, and what ane wad ye turn to and *clap* and *cuddle* ? " He makes answer by choosing *Maggie Lowden*, perhaps, to the great mirth of the party.

'Secondly, then, "Suppose ye were stanin stark naked on the *tap o' Cairnhattie*, whether wad ye cry on *Peggie Kirtle* or *Nell o' Killimingie* to come wi' yer *claise* ? "

'He answers again in a similar manner.

'Lastly, then, "Suppose ye were in a boat wi' *Tibbie Tait, Mary Kairnie, Sallie Snadrap*, and *Kate o' Minnieive*, and it was to coup wi' ye, what ane o' em wad ye *sink* ? what ane wad ye *soom* ? wha wad ye bring to lan' ? and what wad ye marry ? ' Then he answers again, to the fun of the company, perhaps in this way, ' I wad sink *Mary Kairnie*, soom *Tibbie Tait*, bring *Sallie Snadrap* aneath my oxter to lan', and marry sweet *Kattie o' Minnieive*."

'And so ends that bout at the *wadds and the wears*, to give place to Hey Willie Wine and How Willie Wine, or the Dambrod and Legendary stories.'

And with that glimpse of merry Galloway let us close up John Mactaggart and go out, for the rain has stopped, the sun is shining once again and the birds are singing.

§ 2

In the gardens of a country house which run down to the Galloway coast a man talked to me of Devorgilla as if he had met her at dinner last week ; also as if he had once been in love with her.

Scotland is a land of romantic loyalties. Perhaps they are part of the national warmth of heart. There is nothing mean or half-hearted about Scottish loyalties, although sometimes they are strangely unreasonable. But then there is no such thing as reason in true love. Galloway has a number of its own loyalties. This province took a long time to make up its mind about Robert Bruce, because he conflicted with an old loyalty, and for other reasons it refused to follow either the Old Chevalier or Bonnie Prince Charlie ; so the old kingdom of the Southern Picts goes diving far back into its history for its heroes.

My friend talked about the stormy days of King Alan and John Balliol as if they were recent history. He was proud because the Galloway men were privileged to form the van in battle, and he delighted in the memory of a King of Galloway who threatened the King of Norway with a navy. But when he mentioned Devorgilla he used words, and a voice, which might have made his wife jealous.

' Devorgilla is still a lovely memory in Galloway,' he said, ' although she died over six centuries ago. And really, when you think of it, how few people are remembered only for their virtue and their piety ; how few widows for their fidelity ! This long-dead lady has influenced all my life . . .'

I knew what he meant. He is a Balliol man ; and Devorgilla—not her husband—is the real founder of Balliol College, Oxford.

' All my happiest years have been spent in Devorgilla's country,' said my friend, ' and it was Devorgilla who drew me to Balliol. Surely every Galloway visitor to Oxford must be thrilled when he stands at the great gate of the college in the Broad and sees on the college shield above it the Crowned Lion of Galloway impaled with the Orle of Balliol . . .'

We went into his library and dug out books that spoke of Devorgilla and her century. She was born about 1210 at Kenmure in Galloway, where to-day a ruined castle overlooks the head of the loch and marks the site of the stronghold of her father, Alan, last of the Kings of Galloway. He was Constable of Scotland and probably the most powerful noble in the two kingdoms. His wife, the mother of Devorgilla, was Margaret, daughter of David, Earl of Huntingdon, brother of William the Lion.

Devorgilla married John Balliol when she was twenty. It was the union of two great houses. Balliol, one of the wealthiest barons of his time, owned not only half Galloway but twenty knights fees in England, besides an ancestral home in Picardy and the title of Lord of Bailleul-en-Vimeu, Dompierre, Hélicourt and Hornoy. Death added to their possessions, when, a year after his daughter's marriage, Alan of Galloway died. Devorgilla brought to the already astounding landscape of the Balliol possessions the over-lordship of Eastern Galloway and the castles of Lochfergus, Kenmure and Botel. Within the first four or five years of her married life more estates were piled up when relatives, departing with a generous gesture, left to her enormous portions of the map of England, including a castle that was to loom largely in the history of Scotland—Fotheringhay. So these two between them owned vast tracks of mountains, woods and meadows, and would have had to travel nearly five hundred miles from their northern-most possessions in Scotland to their French estates on the Somme.

They took their brilliant place in an important century.

' It was a century of great world movements,' says Wentworth Huyshe in his admirable book *Devorgilla, Lady of Galloway* ; ' it witnessed the dawn of liberty in England ; the culmination of the Power of the Holy See, under Pope Innocent III ; the rise of Gothic architecture. Salisbury Cathedral, the crowning glory of the Early English style, was founded and completed, Westminster Abbey rebuilt, and the choir of Lincoln erected by St. Hugh within the lifetime of Devorgilla. It witnessed the culmination of Saracenic architecture in the Alhambra of Granada, begun by Mohammed in 1273 ; the foundation of the Universities of Oxford and Cambridge, and of the House of Commons by Simon de Montfort. It was the age of St. Francis and St. Dominic, and saw the establishment of their Orders throughout Europe. As a child Devorgilla doubtless heard of the death of both saints, St. Dominic in 1221 and St. Francis in 1224, and in her later years must have seen the great Dominican monastery of Blackfriars grow stone by stone on the lands granted by the Corporation of London, hard by the City wall between Lud Gate and the river. Devorgilla had just come of age at the time of the death of St. Anthony of Padua. The whole life of St. Thomas Aquinas lay within the compass of her own. Later on in her widowed life when the past was for her one long memory of her lost husband, and her days, drawing to a close, were devoted to good deeds, James de Voragine wrote his " Golden Legend ", a work in which we may be sure she took special delight, and a copy of which she probably presented to the library of her monks of the Abbey of the Sweet Heart.

' It was a century of great wars and political upheavals.

The Christian chivalry of Europe waged incessant war with the Saracens for the Holy Places. Louis IX, St. Louis, noblest and holiest of monarchs—won and lost Damietta and at last perished, plague-stricken, at Tunis. Prince Edward, afterwards Edward I, " Hammer of the Scots ", captured Nazareth and was saved from the poisoned dagger of the Saracenic assassin by the devotion of his noble wife Eleanor of Castile. In Spain also the struggle of Cross against Crescent continued without cessation ; the Moors met severe defeat at Navas de Tolosa in Andalusia in 1212, and lost Cordova in 1236. It was a century of great battles which decided the course of European history for many generations. The English navy—or, to be more accurate, an English army on ships—triumphed over the French at Damme off the coast of Flanders in 1213, but Philip Augustus had his revenge in the following year at Bouvines, where the united armies of King John and the Emperor Otto were disastrously routed. In both these battles William Longuespee, son of Fair Rosamund, was one of the leaders. His beautiful effigy in Salisbury Cathedral is a type of the knightly arms and dress of the period. Eastern Europe was threatened with peril from Turk and Tartar, but already a barrier to their aggression was rising in the House of Hapsburg, whose founder Rudolf was crowned at Aix with the Imperial diadem of Charlemagne. Not many years before that event the Holy See triumphed over the House of Hohenstaufen when Charles of Anjou, brother of St. Louis, broke the power of Manfred. Two years afterwards Conradin perished on the scaffold at Naples, throwing his glove amongst the crowd before the axe fell which sheared off his young head. A few more years of tyranny and oppression in south Italy and Sicily, and then the career of Charles of Anjou was checked by the " Sicilian Vespers ", that terrible massacre of the French garrisons who had so long held at their mercy the lives of the men and the honour of the women in Sicily—a deed, done on Easter Monday, 1282, when the bells were ringing for Vespers, which will be remembered as long as men love liberty.'

Devorgilla and her husband took part in many of the great events of their time. It is probable that she travelled south to London with her husband when he was appointed one of twelve commissioners deputed to confer on the Gascony war debts. In Scotland at the Castle of Botel—which is now called Buittle—or in England at Barnard Castle, the Balliols ruled with the state and power of petty sovereigns. The deed by which Balliol is now chiefly remembered—the foundation of Balliol College—grew from what at the time must have seemed one of the least-significant acts in the life of a busy and powerful baron.

The neighbouring landowner at Barnard Castle was Walter Chirkham, Bishop Palatine of Durham. He was a small, arrogant, hot-tempered man. In 1255 he excommunicated some of the Balliol retainers during a dispute on boundaries. No doubt they trespassed on Durham property. Balliol's retort was in tune with the age. He laid an ambush for Walter Chirkham, insulted the angry little man and captured a part of his retinue. The Bishop appealed to the King. The King issued a writ against Balliol, demanding instant reparation. Then Balliol was forced to acknowledge what he had no doubt forgotten in the heat of temper : that it was a very dangerous thing for any baron, no matter how powerful, to offend a spiritual baron ! Anointed kings had repented in sackcloth for this same sin ! So the people of Durham were treated to the interesting sight of John Balliol, clothed in the unhappy garb of a penitent, kneeling in expiation of his sin at the door of the cathedral before little Walter Chirkham, who grasped a whip. But the fiery bishop was not content with giving Balliol a good hiding : he insisted that in order to make the penitence complete a substantial act of charity should be performed. Therefore John hired a small house in the suburbs of Oxford, near the Church of St. Mary Magdalene, and this he opened as a hostel for sixteen poor students, allowing each one of them a gift of 8d. a day. So Balliol College emerges in history, the price of a great baron's penitence.

But the credit of consolidating the gift and giving the college a constitution belongs not to John but to Devorgilla. After Balliol's death in 1268 Devorgilla devoted herself to acts of charity and one of these was the establishment of Balliol College :

' Great indeed would have been the surprise of that stout old obscurantist, her husband, to learn that he and she would be chiefly known to posterity as the benefactors of a few poor scholars,' writes H. W. C. Davis in his history of the college. 'In his eyes it would be of far greater moment that he had once held the Regency of Scotland, and that he had been foremost in opposition to the usurper Montfort. With his wife it was different. The scholars of Balliol occupied a large place in her thoughts ; she spent her money and her energies in their service ; she treated them as trusted friends. Though she ruled by hereditary right over one of the most uncouth and lawless districts in southern Scotland, she had been educated at the court of her grandfather, David, Earl of Huntingdon, and there was little enough of the fierce Galwegian in her composition. Her widowhood was passed in the company of the religious and her chief occupation seems to have been the planning of good works which should perpetuate her husband's memory.'

His memory was with her day and night.

She caused John Balliol's heart to be embalmed and enclosed in a casket of silver and ivory. The box, it is said, never left her side during the twenty-one years she survived him.

When she sat at meals the little casket containing Balliol's heart was with her. She paid it reverence as if her lord were present. Food was set before it, course after course, and when Devorgilla rose from the table this food was taken out and distributed among the poor.

She built a magnificent tomb for her lord's heart. Soon the lovely red sandstone walls of an abbey rose on Solwayside in the shelter of the great hill of Criffel. From its red tower men could look over the water to the blue mountains of Cumberland. She called this church 'The Abbey of the Sweet Heart'.

And we can imagine this great lady attending to the affairs of her estates, approving the design of a bridge, signing the charter of Balliol College in her distant castle of Buittle, or making a journey in a litter accompanied by armed men, monks, and serving-women, going slowly southward towards her English manors, from guest-house to guest-house ; and all the time at her side the heart of John Balliol in its silver casket.

When she died the monks made a grave for her before the high altar of Sweetheart Abbey. She died in an English shire. The funeral cortège came slowly northward into Galloway ;

and at last, to solemn chanting and in the light of tapers of unbleached wax, they placed her in the good earth of Galloway, which she loved above all other earth. On her breast was the casket of silver and ivory. . . .

This story seems to civilize a wild age. It is one of Scotland's few happy love tales.

In the chapel of Balliol College on stated Sundays the ' bidding prayer ' is recited—' We thank God for John Balliol and Devorgilla.' And a man sitting among the ruins of Sweetheart Abbey—a robin singing his high elegy from a ragged arch—will wish to repeat this prayer, because a love story purged of all passion, pure as the snow that comes over the Merrick in the winter time, comes to us out of an age of war and murder.

§ 3

He was standing in the middle of the road, speaking in a loud voice to a tree, the garden wall of a cottage and a rain-tub. He wore like a breastplate an evangelical poster which announced in startling letters that ' the Coming of the Lord Draweth Nigh '. His coat was neat and black, his trousers were the striped trousers of a city clerk, and his shoes, very different from the thick boots of the Galloway countryman, were slender and once elegant black shoes made for the streets. He was altogether an odd and unexpected sight in this Galloway lane, his face tanned by the sun, his neat shoes powdered with the dust of the roads.

The fact that he was addressing the empty air did not apparently affect or surprise him. His manners were those of the platform. He shook his fingers in the air, clenched his fists, swept an arm round the landscape and indulged in all the comic motions which humanity makes when attempting to impress humanity. But he received nothing for his pains but the waving of the leaves, the stolid indifference of the garden wall and the blank disinterest of the rain-tub.

I sidled to a big oak tree growing beside the road and watched him. It was really extraordinary that he should be so independent of an audience. It was something quite new in oratory. I had seen the same sort of thing at Hyde Park Corner, and in any street where an orator was attempting to gather a crowd, but here in the lane no amount of speaking would attract people to him. I watched with interest how he crouched down before a bush in the garden as if it were a fascinated front-seat member of his congregation, and how he delivered a peroration for the benefit of a flight of passing corbies. Every now and then he would turn round as if giving an immense throng assembled at his back the benefit of his address.

This dealt with Armageddon and the second coming of Christ. It was the usual highfalutin' affair flavoured with quotations from Revelations, and scattered every other minute with statistics about bomb-bearing aeroplanes and poison gas which I thought very much to the point.

All this was delivered in an educated English voice faintly flavoured with a touch of the North Country. I wondered who he was. A clerk suffering from religious mania ? A man down on his luck tramping the roads for some end-of-the-world society ? He puzzled me.

His voice suddenly ceased. He wiped his brow. Then he stood to attention and sang these words in the empty lane to a kind of marching hymn tune :

> He's coming back again,
> He's coming back again,
> He went away, but not to stay,
> He's coming back again.

He sang this at least six times until I found myself also humming the idiotic verse. When his hymn was ended he gave a hitch to the banner round his neck and, as if he were striding triumphantly from the platform of the Albert Hall, turned about and walked rapidly down the lane.

I was about to follow him to ask him why he was doing this when I was surprised to hear a loud cough quite near me. I looked round the immense oak trunk and there, hidden from me all the time, sat one of those old men found nowhere but in Scotland.

He was sitting on a little stool placed so near the tree that he could lean back against the trunk. He wore an old cloth cap and a suit of threadbare tweed. He was small and plump. A beard of that stubborn shade of brown that will turn grey but will never become a uniform white climbed all over his face and had outposts in the form of two thin hedges of hair high up on his cheek-bones. Behind steel spectacles a pair of stern little blue eyes looked up at me, but he never changed his position, which was a judicial pose, knees far apart, hands crossed over the handle of a walking-stick. The same kind of hair grew on the backs of his hands ; and on one finger was a wedding ring about half an inch wide.

He was, I suppose, an ancient grandfather and all over him was printed an indefinite air of prosperity. He was not, like so many old villagers in England, a pathetic relic of another day : he was a perfectly complacent, self-satisfied, determined old man who looked as though he had said to himself, ' I'll retire when I'm saxty-five,' and had done so. I looked into his blue eyes and realized that for him life had no mysteries. It was all clear to him and he was satisfied. The world was running to plan and he knew what the plan was :

' Who was that man ? ' I asked, nodding in the direction of the vanishing evangelist.

' He's a gaun buddy.'

' I beg your pardon.'

' He's a gaun buddy,' said the old man. ' He's a bit cranky.'

' I see. Where does he come from ? '

' I've never set eyes on him before the day.'

The old man then wiped me from the Universe by gazing straight out over his folded hands.

' Good day,' he said with extreme reluctance as I went off down the road.

About a mile farther on I saw the evangelist again. Ten small children stood in a ring round him. Two little boys had climbed up into the branches of a tree to listen to him. He made exactly the same speech that he had made to the tree, the wall, and the rain-tub. The little ones listened very solemnly to it. Now and then two little girls would place red heads together and giggle for a moment, but they were stiffened instantly into respectfulness when the eye of the speaker found them.

I was sure he was not ' a bit cranky.' I was sure that he knew what he was doing, but why he was doing it I did not know. He was as content with his audience of small children as with an enormous crowd. Then he sang the ' coming back again ' hymn and he inveigled the small people to join in with him. His robust English voice was followed a fraction of a second later by a shy sighing treble sound of small voices. When he marched off this time most of the children ran away ;

a few followed, and when they fell out the sturdy small figures of two extremely small boys were seen marching in time with the evangelist. He had found two disciples! They were hatless little fellows with torn trousers, and they marched with their faces lifted towards him because he talked to them on godly matters as he strode forward.

It was a silly idea perhaps, but I wondered, as I watched their sturdy little backs and their little brown legs keeping time, if a dash of Covenanting blood was driving them along the road with this unaccountable stranger.

When they came to a drive leading to a large house, lying back among trees, an elderly lady was standing there talking to a child. She was a prim Scottish grandmother:

'Are you right with the Lord, madam?' shouted the evangelist in the matter-of-fact voice that a tradesman uses when he says: 'Do you want any fish to-day?'

The old lady turned and walked rapidly down the drive.

Turning a corner, the man and his two tiny followers entered Newton Stewart. Possibly because I was afraid of becoming involved in his mission, I hesitated to go up and question him. I have regretted it ever since.

And no one to whom I mentioned him had ever seen him before or knew a thing about him.

§ 4

Newton Stewart, which strangely enough is not in the Stewartry but just over the border in Wigtownshire, is one of the bonniest little towns in the whole of Galloway. You enter it over a fine old bridge across the River Cree. The old houses on the west bank drop straight down to the water exactly as houses do in Venice and beside the canals of Bruges.

The bridge crosses roughly in the line of the ancient Black Ford of Cree, across which in the old days immense herds of Galloway cattle were driven on their way to the great fairs at Carlisle and farther south. There is a little garden which you can see by peeping over the east end of the bridge, and it still looks as though flattened by the thousands of hooves which at this point were shod with leather to protect them during the long march to the south.

Across the bridge lies Newton Stewart, a clean, swept and garnished little town which even on weekdays has an atmosphere of the Sabbath about it. It reminds me of those small-scale models which you sometimes see on an architect's table, abnormally neat and tidy and clear-cut. Someone in Newton Stewart has set an inhuman standard of cleanliness and integrity to which the town faithfully adheres. At least that is my impression. I would hate in any way to offend the community. In that case I am sure the disapproving windows of Newton Stewart and the prim houses flush with the street would haunt me to the end of my days.

The town has no thrilling history but it has something much better : one of the grandest views in Galloway. From a road at the back of Newton Stewart you look across a green belt of lowland verdure to the wilderness of the hills. Before you lie the long, gentle slopes of Craignelder and Cairnsmore of Fleet, one against the other. When the sun is on them you can see the heather like spilt wine ; on dull days they loom, more remotely, as blue shadows against the sky. They have countless moods, so that a man who has lived with them all his life might on some days feel that he had never seen them before. When the sun touches them in the morning and sinks behind them at night, when the snow melts and the spring steals over them, and when autumn stains them with purple and brown and gold, they give their generous beauty to Galloway and a stranger knows that something of them is locked away in the hearts of all men and women who have been born in this place.

Just as the visitor who wishes to know Galloway should settle himself in Kirkcudbright for the south-east, and in Dalry or New Galloway for the north, so he should make himself at home in Newton Stewart and from that place explore the adjacent parts of the Stewartry and Wigtownshire and the long hammer-head of the Mull.

The banks of the Cree delighted Burns as they must delight any one who walks along them. I walked out one evening to Minnigaff. It was the end of a hot autumn day. The sun was setting and, through a thick screen of trees, I could see the Cree stained with the yellows of the sunset, shining as it sang on the last few miles of its journey to the bay. I came to the bend of the road where the tower of Minnigaff Church shows above its trees, and down a dark woody path to the left I came to a swing bridge over the river. Below was a natural swimming-pool formed by the river, which at this spot had carved its way through rock. In the shallow places the peaty Cree water was stained the colour of stout, and in the deep places it had the oily polish of jet.

Two young men, poised on a rock, straightened their white bodies for a dive. They cut the cold pool like seals and for an instant I could see them, olive green in the peat water, curving upwards to the surface. I wondered, as I watched them, if they realized that their swim in the Cree at the end of a hot autumn day is the kind of thing that remains in a man's memory after many more important things have become dim.

The swimmers rose with wet hair in their eyes, shook their heads and spluttered, spitting the brown peat water from their mouths, and then with long, overarm strokes, white flesh shouldering the brown water, they struck off together up the pool. The swifts darted low down over the water. Against the lemon-coloured sky a bat flittered, was gone and was back again, performing its strange soft flight ; and the swimmers shouted and splashed in a placid pool where the reflected sky fell about them like showers of liquid gold. If one or both of you, I thought, are fated to go far away and make your lives, for instance, in Canada or Australia, how dear to you this moment will become, a moment of which you now think but little. All the time, although you are unaware of it, your brains are storing up every fraction of these moments, so that you will always remember the colour of this evening and the coolness of this water, and perhaps even the flight of the bat and the screaming of the swifts, and you will still remember it although the names and faces of women you have known will have become like ghosts in your minds. You may wonder why it seemed so ordinary at the time. It is this bright pattern of simple memories that gives us roots on earth and without them we are lost creatures drifting with unanchored hearts.

The little kirkyard of Minnigaff stands side by side with the ghost of the old kirk and kirkyard. The old kirk is a riot of tangled briars. Ivy has covered every inch of the roofless building. The headstones nod together and the tall grass seeks to hide them as if ashamed of man's pathetic hankering for immortality.

The gravedigger came up to me and we began to talk. Although every gravedigger I have met has been a pleasant fellow, I can never quite conquer a faint shudder when I encounter men of this calling. Their sheds, into which one stumbles sometimes by mistake, are so ghastly, with clay-caked spades lying about in corners among a confusion of decayed wreaths ; and the way in which even the kindest gravedigger casts a professional eye over the graveyard sends a thin shiver down the spine. They have a habit, which chills me, of referring to the dead as ' them '.

This gravedigger was, I was glad to note, not too pro-fessional, and we walked quietly round the old kirkyard until we came to a red sandstone slab on the reverse side of which was an elaborate coat-of-arms.

It pictured a raven with an arrow through its neck, and below were two ravens transfixed through the throat by a single arrow :

' When King Robert the Bruce was hiding in the hills over there,' said the gravedigger, waving in the direction of the Galloway Highlands, ' he came to the house of the auld wife of Craigencalzie. She had been married three times and had three sons who were ready to fight for the King. One son was called Murdoch, another was called McLurg and the third was called McKie. So the King set them a test with the bow and arrow. The first lad shot a raven that was sitting on the craig. The second one shot two flying ravens with one arrow. But the third missed. And these families have ever since put the ravens on their grave-stones.'

He gave the stone a slap :

' And here's one of them,' he said.

' Yes, but what happened to the third boy—the one who missed.'

' Nothing at all,' replied the gravedigger. ' He joined up with the others.'

I left the kirkyard with the feeling that there is something wrong with this story. The moral seems to be missing.

§ 5

Take the road that runs with the Penkiln Burn singing in a deep cleft of green to one side of it and you will come

4

to McKeand's mill, and beside the mill is a small old bridge. The water comes rushing down past the mill-race and under the bridge, where it falls into a series of pretty peat-brown rock pools. This is Queen Mary's Bridge, although until the other day antiquaries swore that the Queen of Scots had never set foot on it. Popular tradition, which is embedded in the minds of generations, is sometimes more accurate than antiquaries, who are only embedded in libraries. And so it has proved in this instance.

Mary came a second time to Galloway after the Battle of Langside in 1568. She came, a broken, hunted fugitive, half dead with fatigue, for she had not drawn rein since she spurred from the stricken field at Glasgow. It is known that she entered Galloway from Dumfries and made straight for the Abbey of Dundrennan on the south seacoast, stopping the first night at Corra, north of Dalbeattie.

How, therefore, could she possibly have crossed Queen Mary's Bridge at Cumloden, thirty-six miles off her direct route ?

For years the historian and the antiquary laughed at the name of the bridge, believing that the local people had indulged in the common trick of linking a famous name with an old landmark. The only official recognition was that of the Ordnance Survey, who as map-makers are interested in names, not legends. However, in the last few years evidence has been discovered which proves beyond any doubt that local tradition is correct and that Mary Queen of Scots did cross this little bridge, but not during her flight from Langside.

She paid a previous visit in 1563 when, as a gay, young unmarried queen, the storms were gathering but had not broken over her. This visit was performed in state and the authority for the belief that she crossed the Cumloden bridge has been found in the expense rolls of this journey written in old French. They are in the Edinburgh archives and have only recently been fully examined. It is interesting, I think, that the man who got on the track of this and who was the means of taking Queen Mary's Bridge out of legend into history is Mr. Andrew McCormick, the charming Galloway writer, whose house at Newton Stewart stands only a short walk from the bridge. In making the graceful bow which scholarship always makes to tradition when scholarship has been at fault, Sir Herbert Maxwell wrote as follows in the *Scottish Historical Review* for October 1920 :

'Examination of the Queen's itinerary in 1563 strengthens the tradition connecting her name with the old bridge at Cumloden. She was travelling, not as a fugitive as when she escaped to Galloway from Langside five years later, but in considerable state. The passage of herself and suite, with eighteen horses and six baggage mules, would in itself have sufficed to command the admiration from the populace ; but when, as was doubtless the case, her personal retinue was swelled by the escort of the barons and lairds through whose lands she passed, each with his armed following, the spectacle was one to create a lasting impression, greatly enhanced in effect by the beauty and grace of the young Sovereign.

'On Friday, 13th August, the Queen left Clary, three miles south of Newton Stewart, on her way to Kenmure. If, as is probable, she forded the Cree just above the confluence of the Penkiln, she and her train must have ridden over the bridge at Cumloden and taken the direct road (at that time only a pack-horse track) through the pass of Talnotry, across the Dee at Clatterinshaws and so down by the Knocknarling glen to New Galloway. As the glittering cavalcade filed over the narrow arch at Cumloden Mill, the spectacle may well have impressed the spectators in such manner as to cause them to associate the Queen's name with the bridge, and to pass the name down to their children. . . .'

So in the shade of the Penkiln glen you can sit on Queen Mary's Bridge with the knowledge that she came that way in the days before her heart was broken. Her eyes looked into that tunnel of the green where the dark waters come down from the hills, and perhaps the birds sang to her from the brake as they sing to-day.

While I was wondering what she wore that day and if the sunlight dappled her face for a moment as she passed from the light of the road into the shadow of the leaves, three young men came and leant over the bridge. They had filled their pockets with pebbles. Each one took three stones and dropped them slowly and deliberately straight down towards the burn. I thought at first that they were trying to stir a fish that they had seen, but when I looked over the parapet I saw that they were trying to put their pebbles into a stone hollow low down near the water level. It was formed by one of the stones of the bridge and the receptacle was already piled high with pebbles. Very solemnly each young man dropped three stones. Then, failing to get three into the hollow, they all had another attempt. One lad succeeded and appeared very pleased with himself:

' Why do you do that ? ' I asked.

' It's just a wishing well,' said one shyly, trying to make a joke of it.

' Three stones in and you get your wish ? ' I asked.

' That's the way of it,' they said.

I wonder if that stone, which can be a ' well ' only in winter when the burn is in spate, has any connection with Mary Stuart ! Surely her presence on the bridge may have given it a kind of sanctity in the eyes of the local people, or at least a virtue that marked it off from other bridges that they knew. It is just the sort of joke that life plays now and then—a wishing-well in memory of a queen whose wishes never came true.

§ 6

The Merrick is the highest hill in the south of Scotland, and is generally to be observed dozing in a white cloud like an old man asleep under a handkerchief. Sometimes, when he awakes with his head in the light of the sun, foolish people like myself think to outwit the old gentleman and so, grasping our sticks, we set off in his direction with great dispatch and vigour, but, lo, in the twinkling of an eye the Merrick whistles towards the Atlantic and up comes a cloud which he promptly assumes. It is irritating ; but you cannot, unfortunately, be angry with a mountain.

However, one morning the sky was blue from edge to edge ; but, not content with this, I sought the Air Ministry's report, which stated that an anticyclone stretched across the Atlantic. On the strength of this I decided that the Merrick was practically defenceless, and went towards him in a mood of glee that was tempered by respect.

Now the Merrick, which is 2,784 feet in height, does not sound very difficult, but he is actually a preposterous pro-

tuberance—as Johnson would certainly have called him—
because he lies so far from any town or habitation and to
reach him by the easiest way you have to climb another
mountain first—Benyellary !

At Bargrennan I turned right and entered the glorious
five miles of Glen Trool. A little winding road runs through
a green wood, and in time you see on your right hand, far
below and shining through the green leaves, the narrow silver
waters of Loch Trool. Before you is a wide hill-scape. The
Merrick and his massive outriders lie to the west, the Rhinns
of Kells shoulder each other to the north-east ; and you gaze
with awe at untold miles of bald hill-side, stone dykes running up straight as knives, patches of heather and dark
corries where the glens run half-way and then give up like a
company of frightened fairies.

As I was going along this shady little road a black rabbit
ran across my path. There was not one white hair on him.
This, I thought to myself, is the most amazing luck ! If a
black cat is lucky, what of a black rabbit ?

Round the corner another rabbit bolted into the fern. He
was snow white ! Did this cancel the good luck and, as it
were, wipe out the black rabbit ? While I was wondering
what to make of it a black and white rabbit bolted out ;
and at the sight of him I began to feel rather upset. Glen
Trool was becoming slightly fantastic ! I was almost prepared to meet the Walrus and the Carpenter.

In a mile or so I met a young country lad and I asked
him if he had ever seen any black or white rabbits in Glen
Trool. He looked at me with massive solemnity and after
prolonged thought said:

' Ay.'

' Where do they come from ? ' I asked him.

' They're wild,' he said.

' But were they ever tame ? '

' Ay,' he said.

Scottish witnesses must be the cross-examining barrister's
dream of heaven. Never can they depart into the unpathed
regions of irrelevance. How often in English law courts have
I heard judge and council implore witnesses almost on bended
knees to answer ' yes ' or ' no '. After five minutes I managed
to excavate the information that some time ago a man who
kept tame rabbits near Glen Trool either set them free

or carelessly allowed them to escape, so that they have affected the pigmentation of the local rabbits, or else, perhaps, forming a black and white aristocracy, as in Rome, have bred among themselves.

Where the road reaches its highest point is a magnificent view of the loch lying below, trees creeping down the flank of the opposite hills, little islands of tall dark firs near the shore, and on a piece of high ground overlooking Loch Trool an immense boulder poised upon a plinth, and on it these words :

In Loyal Rememberance
of
Robert the Bruce
King of Scots

whose victory in this glen over an English force in March 1307 opened the campaign of Independence which he brought to a decisive close at Bannockburn on 24th June 1314.

I recently met a man who, when the subject of conversation turned to Scotland, asked me :

' By the way, who won Bannockburn ? Did we, or did the Scots ? '

As the English rarely read history—except that of race-horses and criminals—I was surprised only by the fact that he wanted to know.

' It's like this,' he explained, ' I was with a Scotsman the other night and the name of Bannockburn cropped up. He said something about Bruce beating us at Bannockburn and I said " Oh, really " ; and he seemed rather annoyed. I wondered whether I'd said anything wrong.'

The ' oh really ' of the English must be to people of other nationalities one of the most irritating sounds on earth. Although the English sense of nationality is so strong, no Englishman thinks about Alfred the Great as Scotsmen think of Bruce or as the Welsh think of Arthur. Alfred is not the hero who drove the Danes into the sea : he is the rather silly ass who burnt the cakes.

I once saw with amusement two Scotsmen nearly come to blows beneath the large and hideous memorial to Wallace near Dryburgh, because one had mistaken the other to have said that Wallace was no credit to Scotland. What he really did say was that the statue was no credit to Scotland. The row! Then the apologies and the laughter! Now such a thing could not possibly happen in England. Anyone can insult a public monument in England. Our sense of the present is so strong, perhaps, that it has obliterated our sense of the past. Yet no nation cherishes more carefully her relics of the past and habits of the past. It is rather puzzling; and I suppose the whole question boils down to the fact that our nationality has never been seriously threatened by invasion, so that our real heroes are not nationalists like Wallace and Bruce but jolly old pirates like Francis Drake. The only king we revere as a national hero is Richard the Lionheart, who could not speak English and spent his whole life out of the country!

The Bruce Monument in Glen Trool is perfectly placed, for it was in this glen and on the surrounding hills that Bruce wandered as a fugitive, a lonely, hunted king without a kingdom, in the days after his famous episode with the spider, which is said to have occurred in a cave in Rachryne Isle.

Bruce put up a magnificent fight against that aged warrior Edward I, the 'Hammer of the Scot', and when he died in arms on the way to the north, King Robert carried on the war with his son, Edward II. Bruce in Galloway and Prince Charlie in the Highlands are the two most romantic men in the history of Scotland. (Montrose was, perhaps, too complicated to be purely romantic.)

Bruce had been hiding, first in Rachryne Isle and then in Arran, when he descended on the Galloway shores. He had his spies on the mainland, who had arranged that when the time was ripe a fire would be lit which the King would see from his cave on the east side of the island. It was early spring. The farmers were about to burn the heather. At the sight of the first blaze Bruce launched his galleys, believing it to be the signal. He landed in a grey March morning with three hundred wild and shaggy Highlanders. They were hungry and desperate. They raided a hamlet and then made for the hills. Bruce's plight was now desperate. He had landed by mistake in the one district in all Scotland which detested his cause: the land of Comyn and Balliol. Scots and English were closing round him. It would seem impossible that any man could escape from the hedge of steel that fenced him in the hills. The viceroy, Aymer de Valence, waited on the border of Ayrshire with 700 archers. The Nithsdale passes were watched by 70 horse and 200 archers. Sir Geoffrey de Moubray with three captains and a force of 300 men was sent to search the solitudes of Glen Trool. And through Ayrshire marched 800 Highlanders under John of Lorn.

It was from John of Lorn that Bruce made his most marvellous escape. This man had brought with him a bloodhound that had belonged to Bruce and was devoted to his master. He let the dog loose on the hills. The chase became so hot that Bruce and a companion were actually seen. Five Highlanders were told off to run after them and slay them. Three attacked Bruce and two attacked the companion. The five Highlanders were slain and, with the main body almost in sight, the fugitives sped exhausted over the crags, coming at length to a stream through a wood. They travelled in the water for some time and, crossing to the other bank, destroyed the scent.

Now and again in his wanderings the future King of Scots met a humble friend in the Galloway hills. The most famous was the widow with the three sons, who lived on the hill called to this day Craigencalzie, the crag of the *cailleach* or old woman. Her story, you will remember, had been baldly outlined to me by the sexton of Minnigaff. John Barbour, archdeacon of Aberdeen and a contemporary of Chaucer, is the authority for the wanderings of Bruce. His epic poem is a mine of picturesque information. He states that this widow had only two sons, but Galloway tradition is absolutely adamant on three.

The story goes that when the Bruce, half dead with fatigue, presented himself at the widow's bothy and begged for refreshment the woman said that all wanderers were welcome for the sake of one. When he asked who that one might be, she mentioned his own name. Then the King declared himself. The widow's three sons returned. Their mother made them do obeisance to the King and the lads offered to become his men. Bruce, wishing to see their quality as marksmen, bade them bring out their bows and shoot for him. M'Kie saw two ravens on a crag. He let fly and killed them with the same arrow. Murdoch performed a more difficult shot. He saw a raven on the wing. He drew his bow to the ear and let fly. The bird dropped dead. M'Lurg, the

youngest lad, missed his mark but, nevertheless, seems to have
joined with his brothers.

It is said that when Bruce was in power he remembered
the woman who had aided him in one of the most critical
moments of his life and asked how he could reward her.   Her
reply was :

'Just give me the wee bit hassock o' land between Palnure
and Penkiln.'

This ' wee bit hassock ' was five miles long and three miles
broad.   It was divided among the three sons.   This was
the origin of the families of M'Kie of Larg, Murdoch of Cumloden and M'Lurg of Kirouchtrie.   The actual descendants of
Murdoch owned their lands until the end of the eighteenth
century and you can see their tombs in the kirkyards of the
neighbourhood, always distinguished, in the language of the
herald, by : ' *Argent*, two ravens hanging paleways, *sable*,
with an arrow through both their heads fessways, *proper*.'

The turning-points in the fortunes of the Bruce were his
magnificent gallantry in risking the battle of Loudon Hill
and the death of that great soldier, his arch-enemy, Edward I
of England.   His victory over the superior English force
at Loudon Hill was the first event in a chain of victories that
led to Bannockburn.   So Glen Trool and its surrounding
fastnesses can justly be called the cradle of Scottish Independence.

It is interesting, by the way, to realize that Bruce, like
Wallace, was not by ancestry a Scotsman.   The name le
Waleys means a Welshman and the family of Wallace was an
old British, or Welsh, family of Strathclyde.   Bruce, on the
other hand, possessed Norman blood and the origin of the name
is to be found in the Castle of Brus, or Brix, whose site can still
be seen near Cherbourg.   An ancestor of the Bruce, Robert
de Brus, contributed 200 men to the Conqueror's invasion of
England in 1066.   His reward was 40,000 acres in Yorkshire.
The son of this Bruce, also a Robert, became friendly with
David I of Scotland, whom he met at the court of Henry I.
It was from David that this Bruce received a present of land
bordering on Nithsdale.   So the Bruces crossed the Border.

In contemplating Bruce I had almost forgotten about the
Merrick, or rather, if you like, in contemplating Bruce

I had tried to forget about the Merrick! But I could no longer avoid him. He stood up like a challenge, his green hair in a cloudless sky.

Now the way I had been told to climb the Merrick was to go over the top of the adjacent Benyellary. The road to this hill follows the Buchan Burn up a gentle rocky path. The burn spilt itself from boulder to boulder to my right, running beneath a screen of leaves. Slender rowan trees stood on the banks, holding their scarlet berries in the sun.

The path mounted and fell towards a bleak panorama of moorland where huge, broad-based hills rose into the sky. Had it been a dull day the sight would have been terrible. I could see the Merrick lying far off ahead, but as I advanced he sank down behind Benyellary and I saw him no more for a long, long time. In the Culsharg Valley, and at the base of Benyellary, was a small shepherd's cottage. On my way I passed the time of day with the shepherd who was working in the fields. A litter of beautiful little black and white collie pups was being sunned on a rug in the porch of the cottage under the watchful eye of a black and white mother. She barked furiously at me, thinking that I represented danger to the puppies, and the shepherd, to quieten her, gave a command which caused her to desert her young and go streaking off across the moor, where she lay down, the tip of her black nose just visible over a tussock. He told me the best way to climb the Merrick—the way he goes in the lambing time—was to follow a burn that runs very much to the left of Benyellary and, when almost on the summit, turn right and go over the top of Benyellary :

' Then ', he said, " ye'll see the Merrick right ahead o' ye and there'll be no more climbing for ye : ye can walk to it across a shoulder as flat as a road.'

In talking about the Merrick he told me that two golden eagles nest on the Lum o' the Black Gitter. He had seen them but he had never known them to attack his lambs. He did not believe that an eagle would attack a lamb.

I continued the climb, following the steep burn, plodding upward through a soggy mire of peat and lovely red and yellow sphagnum moss, towards a ridge that seemed to become more remote every minute. I was tempted to disregard the shepherd's advice and strike off over the steep open mountain-side to the right, because it seemed pointless to go all round the mountain to reach the top of it ; but then wisdom came to my rescue and I thought of the hundreds of times the shepherd had tramped Benyellary in winter and summer. He knew ; and I must obey !

Almost at the top, I lay down in the heather with bursting lungs and looked round on as wild a hill-scape as you will see in Scotland. It was too hot for a long view. But the Kells range opposite was magnificent and to the south I could see the low, green country and a gleam of blue Wigtown Bay. The lowland lochs caught the sun and glittered like little bits of broken glass.

I crossed the ridge and kept to the side of a grey stone dyke that runs straight up the flank of Benyellary. On the top of the hill I found a cairn and immediately north of me—the Merrick. He looked magnificent. If I had been at my last gasp I would have been forced to go on to him. He pushed a green shoulder into a blue sky and the path to him was a narrow shoulder of soft grass, almost flat, that ran straight towards him for two or three miles.

I lay down on the scrubby grass on the top of Benyellary and caught my breath for a while. I always take something to read when I climb a mountain and this time I had stolen the only readable looking material in the hotel lounge, which happened to be the *Scots Magazine* for September 1930 !

It is a tribute to the permanent quality of the *Scots Magazine* that I found it as readable as if it had been the current number. An article by R. J. B. Sellar on the humour of Highland sport made me laugh.

The head keeper of a Highland estate was discussing with the ghillies the distinguished company who would be out shooting in the morning :

' There's a Juke ', he said, ' and a Markis and an Earl, as weel as a Brigadier-General and a Canon.'

All the men were suitably impressed save one, who remarked :

' Ou, weel, they should manage to bag a brace or twa wi' the cannon.'

I liked the story of the pompous London sportsman who chafed under what he considered to be his ghillie's utter lack of respect. He could not make the man address him as ' sir '. At last, exasperated beyond endurance, he broke out with :

' Look here, my man, where are your manners ? You

don't know whom you are addressing, apparently. Do you realize that I've shot at Balmoral Castle, Mar Lodge, Moy Hall and Bolton Abbey?'

'Ay, ay,' said the ghillie calmly, 'and missed them a', nae doot.'

I came across another beauty:

The same kind of ass was allotted during a shoot one of those great tall, thin, bearded figures of doom and dourness who achieve a certain immortality every autumn in the unchanging pages of *Punch*:

'And what is your name, my man?' said the sportsman.

'It's Thomas Robertson Bogie Macdonald,' said the man.

'Dear me, dear me,' replied the Londoner, 'that's much too long to remember. For the future I shall call you " Old Tom ".'

After a while the ghillie, who had shown no annoyance, asked with innocence:

'And what might your name be, sir?'

'Well, if you must know, it's Nicholas Fitzpaine Mainwaring.'

'Guidsakes,' said the ghillie, 'that's an awfu' moothfu'. I'll just ca' ye " Auld Nick " for the future.'

Here is one that surely must have appeared in *Punch*:

A tenant, a frightful shot, annoyed his ghillies by wearing tweeds of a singularly outrageous pattern. One day they picked up a dead grouse that showed no sign of having been shot.

'That's strange,' said the man. 'I wonder how it died.'

'Man, sir,' replied a ghillie, 'I'm thinkin' it must hae laughed itsel' to daith.'

And I enjoyed this one:

An Englishman went out alone with a gun, but, as he did not know the country and possessed no hunting instincts, he did not see a single grouse. Presently he noticed a schoolboy coming along a path.

'I say, boy,' he said, 'is there anything to shoot hereabouts?'

'Ay,' said the laddie in a bitter voice, 'the schulemester'll be comin' ower the hill in twa-three meenits.'

I put the magazine away and went on over the shoulder. It was like walking on the South Downs, but on each side was a terrible drop to distant valleys. Looking to the north-west I could see Ailsa Craig lying in a blue heat mist. I

could see a line of white across its base that might have been
sand or the breaking of waves.   The last mile to the Merrick
is a gentle uphill walk.   From the cairn at the top I looked
across a mighty valley to the narrow waters of Loch Doon.
But the best view of all was eastward, where the chain of
lochs—Loch Enoch, Loch Neldricken, and Loch Valley—lie in
utter solitude with their wind-swept waters curling over on
shores of silver sand.   On top of the Merrick you realize the
astonishing remoteness of Galloway.   Here, far south of
Glasgow, is a wilderness deeper than that of the better-known
Highlands.   Yet a man can breakfast in London and have
tea within sight of the Merrick !   He can leave Euston at
10 a.m. and be in Newton Stewart shortly after 6 p.m. !   It
seems impossible that in a few hours anyone could pass from
London into such a solitude.

No wonder the most extravagant scares and rumours grew
up in these hills during the War.   There were stories of
strange lights.   There were tales of German hydroplanes
landing on the lonely lochs.   And so reasonable did they
seem—and so reasonable do they seem to you when you sit
on top of the Merrick and gaze down into the desolate valleys—
that it is impossible to laugh at the Glen Trool patrol that
for months combed these valleys and mountains for enemy
aircraft.   There were stories of strange signal lights seen in
these hills, and of a German petrol dump placed there for the
use of hydroplanes that had a secret base on one of the lochs.

Captain Dinwiddie, who now presides over an excellent
bookshop in Dumfries, was for some time in charge of this
patrol and he can tell you how real was the alarm and how
strange the stories.   When he took charge, an ancient postman,
who used to deliver letters now and then to the handful of
people in Glen Trool, remarked :

' Ah weel, there'll be no more lichts seen in the glen the
noo, I'm thinkin', for I hear they've got a teetotal officer up
at the lodge.'

It is easy now to laugh at the cord that was once stretched
across the Caldons meadow to cut the wings of German
aeroplanes, and at the inspecting general officer who, entering
a shepherd's hut, pounced on the primitive apparatus for
the making of candle dips as a sinister signalling machine,
but when you look down into a wilderness as remote as the
Galloway fastnesses—and when you remember what war

nerves were like—it is easy to understand the stories that
spread through Galloway.

I looked down over the Lum o' the Black Gitter in the
hope of seeing the eagles ; but all I saw was a terrifying
drop and all I heard was the eerie whistle of the wind that,
even on a hot day, blows round the cairn.

Gradually, and rather footsore, I dropped again to the
valley where Mr. Johnstone, the shepherd of Culsharg, made
me a cup of tea and showed me a flint arrow-head that he
had dug up in the moss :

'There are a lot of arts', he said, 'that have been lost ;
and no man living the day could make a thing like this.'

And he held up the tiny chipped stone in his large fingers.

§ 7

There was no one on the road that runs from New Galloway
to Newton Stewart, so that I had to climb the hill to find out
why men had placed an obelisk on the top of it. The climb
was easy, a bit wet and peaty in parts, but it was worth it
because Murray's Monument commemorates one of the greatest
stories not only of Galloway but of Scotland . . .

Less than a century and a half ago a man climbing these
hills might have heard a young shepherd boy talking to
himself, and the God-fearing climber might well have fled
the hill in the belief that the boy was bewitched for he spoke
neither in Scots nor English. With a book on his knee, he
would recite the Lord's Prayer in Hebrew. If the eaves-
dropper remained long enough he might have heard Greek,
Latin, Arabic or Anglo-Saxon. This lad was Alexander
Murray, a shepherd and son of a shepherd, who, with no
encouragement and the most meagre aids to knowledge but
urged onward by the genius within him, became one of the
greatest masters of Oriental language and dialect.

Genius has no rules. If it is great enough it will fight its
way out of a man as it fought its way out of young Alexander
Murray while he watched his sheep on the hill.

He was born in an old 'biggin' at Dunkitterick in the
parish of Minnigaff in the autumn of 1775. He was a delicate
child and precocious from the beginning. At the age of six
he begged to be taught to read. In the winter evenings his
father would painfully trace out the letters of the alphabet

on a wool-card, a charred heather stem serving as his pen. Young Alexander sucked up knowledge as the parched earth absorbs rain. His eager mind, it would seem, knew from the start exactly what it wanted ; but how to find it in a clay ' biggin ' or on a wild hillside in Galloway ? If the will is strong enough there is always the way.

There is something almost terrifying in Murray's determination to learn, something akin to the processes of Nature where events move instinctively towards their fulfilment. And his first triumph was a chance copy of Salmon's *System of Geography*. In this book was printed the Lord's Prayer in the various languages of the world. So the seed was set.

When Murray was ten years of age he could read Cæsar, Ovid, and Homer. He had taught himself the Hebrew alphabet from the headings prefaced to the 119th Psalm! The pride of his life was a Greek Testament. When the lad was about twelve his father moved nearer to Minnigaff and Alexander was sent to school there. The parish schoolmaster was astonished by the boy. In a few weeks a good working knowledge of French and German was added to his accomplishments. Then came a copy of the Psalms in Hebrew. In a few months Alexander Murray could read Hebrew, although he had never heard one word of this language pronounced ! A copy of the Arabic alphabet came his way. He began to learn Abyssinian from a few stray passages in the *Ancient Universal History* ! Before he was sixteen he was studying Anglo-Saxon and Welsh.

Then he encountered one of those characters whose function in life is to help on genius and receive no laurels. This was a smuggler named M'Harg, a good-natured, generous fellow who was tremendously impressed by the learning of young Murray. He went to Edinburgh with a sack of smuggled tea and so enthusiastically did he sing the praises of the young Galloway prodigy that curiosity was roused and, at length, young Murray was asked to visit the capital.

One morning in November 1793 the genius and the smuggler set off together. M'Harg carried on his shoulder a sack whose contents one can only imagine and young Murray bore— beloved burden of the ambitious Scot—a sack of oatmeal. Murray was a capable-looking youth with black hair, deep-set hazel eyes, a determined jaw and, that pointer to fame, a large, straight nose. So they passed along the road together, and those who saw them would have seen not one of the greatest sons of Galloway and his strange friend but a middle-aged pedlar and a country lad in a coat of hodden grey.

Murray was examined by three professors of Edinburgh University. Whatever he lacked in finesse he made up in the scope of his studies. The professors were astonished by him. Murray found himself the holder of a town council bursary.

In the short life that remained to him the shepherd boy from Galloway won a European reputation. He became one of the greatest linguists of his time. He mastered Chinese, Sanskrit, Hindustani, Persian and Icelandic. He specialized in the Abyssinian dialects. When the Governor of Tygri, in Abyssinia, wrote a letter to George III, the only man in Britain who could read it was Alexander Murray.

At this time Murray, who, like many a humble Scottish lad, had heard the call of the ministry, was in charge of the parish of Urr in Galloway. There he found a wife. There he studied. There he preached dreary and long-winded sermons. Then Dr. Moodie, Professor of Oriental Languages in Edinburgh University, died. This was the professor who had examined Murray when he tramped from Galloway to Edinburgh with his sack of meal. The young scholar was elected in his place.

One wonders what Murray might have done had he been blessed with health and spared to enjoy the old age in which so many university professors seem so happily embedded, but, alas, he broke down in health and died of tuberculosis in his thirty-seventh year. He left behind him more than knowledge. He takes his place high up in Scotland's splendid roll of fame, an example to all those who, with nothing to help them but their own courage and determination, find their footsteps faltering on the road to achievement.

I climbed down from the Murray Monument to the road that goes to Newton Stewart, thinking that a father with a lazy and indolent son might do a lot worse than climb this hill with his boy and tell the story of the young shepherd. I suppose, however, that a modern boy would shatter the sententiousness of his parent with :

" Very interesting, dad, but, of course, the fellow was a genius."

I am afraid there is no retort to this.

§ 8

In the tangled kirkyards of Galloway one is continually
thinking of ' Old Mortality ', whose work is pointed out on
many a gravestone, notably at Girthon, Minnigaff, and Kirk-
michael.   The old man himself is supposed to lie beneath the
stone in the kirkyard of Caerlaverock put up in a reverent
but humourless moment by a firm of publishers.

Robert Paterson, to give ' Old Mortality ' his real name, was
one of those characters whom Scott made and who seemed
made for Scott.   He was born at Haggisha near Hawick in the
year 1715, and he married a woman called Elizabeth Gray,
who had been cook to Sir Thomas Kirkpatrick of Closeburn,
Dumfriesshire.   Through the influence of this man, Paterson
obtained a lease of a freestone quarry at Gatelawbrigg in the
parish of Morton, and there he followed the gloomy trade of
stone mason.   He was a violent Presbyterian and an anti-
Jacobite.   When the '45 Rebellion took place he was a man of
thirty and he let every one know that he considered the
House of Stuart both ' bloody ' and ' wicked '.   Unfortunately
for him, his quarry lay in the direct path of Charles Edward's
army as they came back from England.   Paterson's anti-
Jacobitism infuriated the Highlanders, who plundered his
house and carried him off with them.

We next hear of him as a follower of Richard Cameron, the
Covenanting martyr, who was slain in 1680 and whose severed
head and hands were fixed to the Nether Bowgate of Edinburgh.   While quite a young man, Paterson conceived the
idea which ultimately made him famous.   He cleaned and
restored the gravestones of Covenanting heroes and where a
grave lacked a stone he would supply one made in his own yard
with an inscription composed by himself.   This self-imposed
task became a mania.   In 1758, when a man of fifty-seven,
he deserted his wife and five children.   Mrs. Paterson sent
her son Walter, a boy of twelve, to find his father and to beg
him to return home.   The lad discovered his parent working
on a gravestone in the old kirkyard of Kirkchrist on the Dee,
opposite Kirkcudbright, but Paterson was deaf to his son's
pleading.   For forty-three years Paterson travelled about
Scotland, haunting the kirkyards and seeking out the graves
of the martyrs.   His melancholy figure mounted on a white
pony became one of the familiar sights of the lowland country-

side. His poor wife was forced to support her family and, with considerable courage and success, opened a small school.

It was when Scott, a young advocate of twenty-two, visited Galloway in connection with a case in which he was concerned, that he is supposed first to have heard of Robert Paterson. The lawsuit, by the way, was the trial of the Rev. Mr. M'Naught, minister of Girthon, charged before the General Assembly of the Kirk with habitual drunkenness, the singing of lewd and profane songs, dancing and toying at a penny wedding with a 'sweetie wife'—a woman who sold gingerbread and such things.

It was while Scott was sitting in a parlour, being entertained by a Galloway lady, that the old stonemason called at the door. Scott naturally asked who he was and the lady, in a moment of happy inspiration, said 'Old Mortality'—a reference to Paterson's melancholy employment. Paterson was then seventy-eight, and Scott, apparently, did not speak to him. It seems, however, that Scott and 'Old Mortality' did meet once and in the same year, but on the east coast of Scotland. Lockhart states that this meeting took place at Dunnottar, when 'Old Mortality' was cleaning the headstones of the Covenanters who died in the dungeons of Dunnottar Castle.

This strange character lingered on into the first year of the nineteenth century, dying at last a veteran of eighty-six. One of his sons went to America and settled in Baltimore. It has often by some strange error been stated that he was the father of Elizabeth Paterson of Baltimore, who married Jerome Bonaparte, afterwards King of Westphalia. This is not so. The father of Madame Bonaparte was a William Paterson who had emigrated from County Donegal. . . .

So deeply has Old Paterson engraved his personality on Galloway that often, when you enter a kirkyard, it seems that you should see his aged form pulling the green carpet of moss from a stone, and the sound of his chisel seems to be echoed whenever a blackbird flies with his bright chink of alarm from briar to tree.

§ 9

Wigtown is a quiet, rather solemn, town on a hill overlooking a bay. It is, like all Galloway towns, as neat and swept as a town can be. Its centre is a large space, almost a square, in which cattle were once herded for safety at night when the town gates were shut. The harbour, which was once alive, is now dead. This, I think, explains the quiet of Wigtown. The death of a harbour always withdraws a seaport from the world and spreads through its streets an air of bereavement. As a mother will in silence mourn a child, so places like Wigtown mourn their vanished ships.

The mind of Wigtown seems to be cast back into other times. Perhaps so much happened to it during its youth that nothing can surprise or interest it now.

The average visitor goes to Wigtown for one thing only: to see the tombs of the Wigtown Martyrs. These are to be discovered behind a low iron railing in the churchyard. A large horizontal stone bears this inscription:

Here lyes Margrat Willson Doughter to Gilbert
Willson in Glenvernoch who was Dround Anno 1685
Aged 18

> *Let earth and stone still witness beare*
> *There lyes a Virgine Martyre here*
> *Murther'd for owning Christ supreame*
> *Head of His Church, and no more crime*
> *But not abjuring Presbytery,*
> *And her not owning Prelacy*
> *They her condem'd by unjust Law ;*
> *Of Heaven nor Hell they stood no Aw.*
> *Within the sea ty'd to a stake ;*
> *She suffered for Christ Jesus' sake ;*
> *The actors of this cruel crime*
> *Was Lagg, Strachan, Winram and Grahame.*
> *Neither young yeares nor yet old age*
> *Could stop the fury of their rage.*

There are in the same enclosure two other stones, one to the memory of Margaret Lachlane who was drowned in company with poor young Margaret Wilson, and three men who were hanged ' without sentence of Law '—as the stone puts it—in 1685. Another curious inscription—nothing to do with Covenanting martyrs, however—bids farewell to John Cowan ' of honest fame ':

> *Of stature small and leg lame,*
> *Content he was with portion small,*
> *Keeped shop in Wigtown and that's all.*

The road runs south through flat green country for about fourteen miles to a tiny peninsula where the ruins of a grey church stand beside the sea. This is a church on the site of the

Candida Casa—the White House—whose name shines like a bright light through the mists of centuries. St. Ninian was one of the most significant men who ever set foot in Scotland, but strangely enough his memory is not cherished as it might be. It was on this little isle of Whithorn that he built a church which is said to have been the first stone church erected to the glory of God in Great Britain. I suppose the worship of Christ took place first along the Roman Wall. All new religions flew straight to the north and spread among the queer jumble of nationalities which guarded the western frontier of the Roman Empire. Little statues of Isis have been found along the Wall, the bull of Mithras was also very popular ; and it is easy to believe that the new faith found converts among the polytheistic colonial auxiliaries of Rome. St. David, the patron saint of Wales, belonged to a Christian family, and St. Ninian probably came from exactly the same sort of family : cultured people of British birth who had assimilated the intellectual atmosphere of the Roman world. He is supposed to have been born in the year A.D. 362, the time of Julian the Apostate. The storms that were to wreck the Empire were already blowing. Only another half-century remained of Roman rule in Britain—a country that had been Roman for a period of time as long as that which separates us to-day from the age of Henry VIII.

When St. Ninian journeyed to Rome he travelled over the well-worn military roads, passing through an ordered Roman world to the distant historic seat of the Roman power. He returned to a land that was so soon to be subjected to the wildest anarchy. He had come back as a holy man and a missionary, and he decided to build his church north of the Wall, in a country that had resisted Rome. He went to the little isle of Whithorn, where his ' white house ', or stone church, rose above the waters. This was in the year 396—167 years before St. Columba, who is often spoken of as the first Christian missionary to Britain, stepped ashore at Iona ! St. Ninian's mass bell rang out over the Solway waters for more than thirty years. News must have come to the holy man at Whithorn that the whole structure of the world as he knew it had collapsed. Rome herself was in peril. The Great Wall of Hadrian was rocking. The Picts of Galloway and the Scots were waiting their chance to storm it and plunder the rich lands of the south. And on these very rocks at

Whithorn St. Ninian must have gone down on his knees and prayed for the Christian world when he heard that the legions that had guarded Britain for over four hundred years had been ordered to the rescue of Rome.

I stood before this little roofless church on Whithorn thinking that it is one of the most appealing buildings in the whole of Scotland. In its beginning it shone like a solitary candle in the darkness of its time. It is with reverence and something like awe that one realizes that it is possible to see and to touch the stones of the successor of Candida Casa.

§ 10

The Mull of Galloway is, in a sense, the Land's End of Scotland.

It is the extremity of a long slender strip about thirty miles in length that, but for the narrow neck of land between Glenluce and Stranraer, would be a little island off the coast of Wigtownshire. It has, like all out-of-the-way places, an island atmosphere. It reminds me very much of the Lleyn Peninsula in Wales.

I went there on a lovely windy morning, with the salt waters breaking over the splendid Sands of Luce. I found myself in a soft, gentle land of woods and broad fields continually swept by sea winds. The Rhinns of Galloway, as this peninsula is termed, have a character of their own ; and I imagine that ways of speech and habits, long vanished from what one thinks of as ' the mainland ', are to be found here among the secluded little lanes and the lonely white farms.

On the way down through the Rhinns I came on the west side of the peninsula to a tiny place called Port Logan. There is a white turreted building on the shore approached by a long drive, and near this building is a pond of pet codfish. It is characteristic of Scotland's generosity, and of the unsophisticated Rhinns, that this sight, which in any other country I know would command an entrance fee of sixpence or a shilling, is free to all comers. You just sign your name in the visitors' book, and are taken by a young fisherman to a beautiful deep pool hewn out of the rock in such a way that every tide fills it without giving the fish their liberty. The young man keeps a basket of shelled mussels always ready with which to feed the fish.

The pond is the property of the laird, M'Douall of Logan, whose family, says Sir Herbert Maxwell, is the only family of Pictish origin in Galloway which has kept its lands to the present day. Colonel Andrew M'Douall made the fish-pond in the year 1800 with the idea of providing his larder with a supply of fresh cod and other sea fish. Somehow or other the idea, happily for the fish, was not always observed, with the result that for years successive generations of cod fish have become tame and hand-fed. This pond is unique and, I am told, naturalists have come from all parts of the world to see it.

We passed through a door, and at the bottom of a flight of stone steps was a pond about 50 feet across. As soon as the door banged the water was cut with the powerful green forms of cod fish, some of them ten pounds in weight :

' They hear me coming,' commented the fisherman.

He went down to the water's edge and held a mussel in his hand. Five or six fish put their heads out of the water and nosed for the morsel like dogs. It was an extraordinary sight. Some of them cruised round, but one, the canniest, just waited with his head out of the water ! There was the opening of a mouth that looked like an empty white-kid hand-bag, a sudden snap and then a splash ! He had been fed.

One enormous fish seemed to enjoy thrusting himself out of the water. The fisherman scratched his back !

' How long have they been in the pool ? ' I asked.

' Some of them three years,' he told me. ' But many are quite new. They get tame in about three months. We catch them in nets in the sea and then put them in the pond.'

I noticed a fish that was blind in one eye. He told me that it had been blinded in the net when it was caught. It has been suggested also that in rushing for the same morsel of food some of the fish have blinded each other with their sharp teeth.

' Three months ago ', said the fisherman, offering a mussel to a villainous-looking white hand-bag, ' yon fush was in the sea, but he's as tame as a kitten . . .'

He drew back his hand swiftly as the snap occurred. Feeding codfish by hand is not everybody's fun !

The Mull itself is a small steep promontory whose tall cliffs drop sheer to the sea. I had no idea that such fine rock scenery was to be found at the Mull. There is a lighthouse on the point and the lighthouse-keeper, an Arran man, told me that on clear days he can see Ireland, the Isle of Man, the Cumberland hills, the Paps of Jura and the Merrick.

While we were talking, a small sailing boat came slanting towards Portankill :

' There's yon Frenchman again,' said my friend.

' What's a Frenchman doing here ? '

' He's a poacher. Lobsters.'

How France loves lobsters ! Imagine the journey from France up the west coast of England to the Mull of Galloway and all for the love of a lobster ! I met the same kind of poachers once in the most desolate part of the Connemara coast.

' The men down in the village asked me to take his number,' said the lighthouse man, ' but the mist was down and my glass magnifies the mist, ye ken, so I didna spot him.'

He walked swiftly away, apparently to take the Frenchman's number like any policeman with an erring motor-car. . . .

It was on this wild headland that tradition says the famous episode of the heather ale took place. The story goes that the Picts possessed the secret of making a delicious wine from the heather flower. James Logan in *The Scottish Gael* says that he had heard of a pleasant drink made in his time in the Highlands chiefly from heather, honey and sugar. But the Pictish ale is traditionally supposed to have required no additional ingredients. After the slaughter of the Picts in the time of Kenneth MacAlpine it is said that the last brewers of Pictish ale were a father and son. They were condemned to death, but were promised pardon and liberty if they would tell the Scots how to make the famous drink. After long persuasion the old man agreed to tell the secret if first his son was flung to death from the Mull of Galloway. This was promptly and gladly done. As soon as the old man knew that his son was dead he invited the Scots to kill him also because now, he said, he alone knew the recipe and would never reveal it. He perished and with him heather ale. I think a better and alternative story is that the old man said that he would give the secret only to a member of his own tribe, a traitor Pict who had gone over to the enemy. This was agreed. But when the old man encountered the traitor he flung himself upon him, and together they fell to death on the sharp rocks of the Mull.

It is curious that a similar legend about heather ale exists in the Island of Eigg. Miss M. E. M. Donaldson, in her book *Wanderings in the Western Highlands and Islands*, states that two or three hundred years ago a Norwegian is said to have worked a still in the locality of the Sgurr of Eigg, in which he made a drink like Benedictine from heather flowers. He guarded the recipe with great secrecy. The islanders, however, were determined to find it out. ' The man replied,' writes Miss Donaldson, " ' If you will kill my son I will tell you," ' and when they returned to him, saying his son was killed, he said, ' " Now you can kill me, for I will never tell you : I feared that my son might do so under threats." '

This is exactly the same story, but in another part of the country. May it not be an echo of the older story ?

It is impossible not to sympathize with the Scots on the question of heather ale. I have frequently discerned in the minds of some Scotsmen a tenacious belief that perhaps something sublimely beautiful and beyond imagination was lost on the legendary occasion. One can only conclude that in the process of trying to re-invent heather ale they stumbled upon the drink known all over the world to-day as ' Scotch '. It seems, one must admit, a fairly adequate compensation.

CHAPTER FIVE

DESCRIBES HOW I MEET THE TARTAN WEAVERS OF KILBAR-
CHAN, PASS THROUGH GLASGOW, VISIT THE DUCAL TOWN OF
INVERARAY, GO NORTH TO OBAN, TAKE SHIP TO MULL, WANDER
AN ENCHANTED ISLAND, HEAR ALL ABOUT THE TOBERMORY GAL-
LEON AND SET FOOT ON THE HOLY ISLAND OF IONA

§ I

'IT'S three o'clock,' says the boots, placing a lit candle on the chair beside my bed, 'and here's your hot water.'

I jump up at once, for I have to be off over dark moors to Ardrossan and the boat to Arran. The stars burn above the little Galloway town. Still lamplight falls over white-washed walls. It is very quiet. One of Scotland's sternest habits, I meditate, is this trick of pulling a man out of bed before it is day. In the Highlands you have to wait at cold little mountain junctions for cold little trains, and in the west you wait in starlight on cold little jetties for cold little ships.

This is one of the last thrills left in travel. When I no longer feel it I shall know that I am too old to travel and I shall stay at home. The hour of five a.m.—a furtive and sinister hour—imparts to all one's actions an air of adven-turous urgency. Everyone is asleep. Houses are fast shut-tered against the dangers of night. And in a little pool of candlelight you cut your chin, and in a little china bowl you make a pretence at washing, conscious that this is no ordinary journey. At this hour strapped luggage looks more im-portant than at any other time. The boy hidden inside you, who holds whatever of youth is left to you, comes whisper-ing down the corridors of memory to remind you that this is how all spies, musketeers, cavaliers, Jacobites, all heroes, and all dark, muddy villains, set out on their adventures. And here in Galloway, I reflect, the scene is just the same. The boots who brought in the candle was the same boots who roused some sleeping agent of the '45 to the same vision of

a town under the same pale stars. There would be a tired
horse in the stable instead of a reluctant car. That is all.

I go downstairs gently, not to rouse the sleepers, and I
drink a cup of tea brewed for me by the boots. The hotel
cat is asleep on a couch. The lounge is scattered with empty
glasses. An air of death and farewell presides over it, mingled
with the stale incense of past hilarity and the rank fumes of
tobacco. The disposition of empty glasses is extraordinarily
significant. Neither you nor I could create quite the same
effect by dotting empty glasses about a room. Who, attempting to reproduce an hotel lounge in the early morning, would
think of placing an empty glass upon the head of Sir Walter
Scott? These things happen only in real life.

The boots waves me off over a dark road. The time between night and day has a beautiful but eerie quality of its
own. Common things seem unreal. You feel that you are
seeing them for the first time. The country is hushed and
grey. All colour is sucked out of it. The mountains lie withdrawn in still clouds and the wind is not strong enough to
move them. The hill burns are louder than by day, and
over a wood one last star is burning. Grey trees move
uneasily in little stray winds, and you feel that the stealthy
life of the night is over.

Gradually, like a slow tide flowing, colour comes back into
the world. The grey grass becomes dark-green, and in the
east is a promise of light.

I went north through Galloway into Ayrshire, and found
myself in Ardrossan hours before the Arran boat was due.

I saw a long, dead street. I went to the docks, where lights
shone on the masts of ships. The water in the harbour was
still as glass. The Belfast boat that docks at the unearthly
hour of 4 a.m. was the only scene of life. It was surrounded
by the hearty smell of boiled haddock and kippers.

I looked through portholes into a cosy dining-saloon, where
a few weary men and women were reluctantly eating, looking
their worst and aware of it.

I felt terribly hungry.

I stole aboard, trying to look like a passenger from Belfast,
and there I ate an enormous breakfast.

Then bars of light streaked the sky to the east : an uncertain sun lifted himself over the roofs of Ardrossan, and some one said that it was going to rain like blazes.

The Arran boat, which is called *Atalanta*, came sidling up to the jetty, bringing to the mainland a cargo of holiday-makers. There were sturdy girls loaded like pack mules, bearing on their shoulders, in haversacks, all the complicated contrivances associated with the simple life. There were cyclists shivering in khaki shorts, and several young men wearing the kilt. They all looked unbelievably healthy.

When the *Atalanta* set out on her backward voyage I caught my breath in astonishment. Far out to sea and framed in the mouth of the harbour was the Isle of Arran. The sun was shining, and in spite of the rather unfortunate sunrise the day was going to be fine. Arran lay ahead like some magic island that had been towed into the Firth of Clyde from the Golden Age. A great ridge of mountains rose sheer from the sea and the morning mists lay heavy on them, lying across them in a straight white line from which the top of Goatfell lifted itself to the sun.

The island was the colour of dark-blue grapes, and I have never in all my travels in Scotland seen anything that looked more beautiful. I remembered the remark of Jessie King, who paints in Arran :

'The Devil made Skye,' she said, 'and God made Arran to rebuke him for the Coolins.'

Even as I looked, big banks of cloud came swinging from the west, and in fifteen minutes this magic island was blotted out.

When I landed at Lamlash it was pouring, for Arran, like Skye and the Western Isles, has its own supply of weather.

§ 2

The Isle of Arran is the top of a submerged mountain range that lies beneath the Firth of Clyde, and the highest peak is a big brute called Goatfell. This mountain broods over Arran like a threat or, perhaps, a challenge. It is generally in daily conference with heaven, but there come rare times when, shining baldly against the sky, it seems deceptively near. Goatfell is 2,866 feet high, or eight times as high as the cross of St. Paul's. This, like most similar comparisons, means little, because it would be easier to climb St. Paul's eight times than to climb Goatfell once.

Now every morning soon after breakfast people emerge from the cottages, in which they have been surviving the rigours of the simple life, queerly dressed for the conquest of Goatfell. The men wear khaki shorts and shirts open at the neck, and the girls wear either the kilt or khaki shorts. Only very slim girls should wear khaki shorts.

They look up at the sky, read barometers, and go about asking the islanders :

' Is it a good day for Goatfell ? '

Generally the islanders say ' No ', and advise the climbers to remain earthbound. But now and then a golden day comes sailing in from the Atlantic ; old Goatfell rises up, pin-sharp and grey with the cloud shadows moving over him, and the climbers grasp their sticks and set off.

On such a day I climbed Goatfell.

Give me sunlight, a mountain, a blue sea, the dry smell of heather, and hill streams brown with peat, and you can have all the motor-cars in the world, all the hotels, all the golf courses.

There is a great moment in the climbing of a mountain, before you get your second wind, when, with a heart beating as fast as a running dog's and the sound of it in your ears, you scorn to lie down and rest, urging yourself upward by picking on some distant landmark and saying to yourself :

' When I have reached that big rock that looks like a dead giant I will rest ; but not until then. . . .'

Every upward step becomes a beautiful agony. And the weak man in your character pleads, begs, and makes excuses to be allowed to lie down before you reach the rock, but the strong, determined woman in your character says :

' No ! Where is your self-respect ? Do you call yourself a man ? Onward and upward, my lad . . .'

Then ; what a moment when you reach the rock : the same feeling as that when you touched the tape and won a race as a boy ! You drop into the heather like a shot stag. Unsuspected muscles ache all over you. The soggy mountain grass is cold and lovely on the palms of your hands. And if there is a mountain torrent—as there is all the way up

Goatfell from Corrie—what heavenly torture to lie and listen to it and promise yourself a drink of iced water !

No drink is ever so good as water from a stream that comes cascading down a mountain from pool to pool. You can scoop it up in your hands, or you can put your mouth to the place where the cold stream splashes downward from a pool, or you can lie flat on the earth and put your mouth into the pool and drink.

Then on you go ; and the wind becomes colder. You know that you are now high up. You enter a moving mist and come again into sunlight. You look back to see the mist sailing away, blotting out miles of distant earth. You have passed through a cloud.

I worked round the southern shoulder of Goatfell and found myself in a barren world of heather and tumbled boulders. They looked as though they had been flung by giants in some Ossianic battle. The wind had ice in it, but the sun was brilliant. The path became steep. It lost itself in mighty ledges of rock, showed again to the left or right and mounted almost perpendicularly to the summit.

Two girls were resting. They had opened their knapsacks and were eating sandwiches. They were perched on a great boulder, looking down to the sea and the distant mainland of Scotland. They called to me in the manly, imperious voices of girls who have been brought up with brothers :

' You've jolly well got to hurry ! ' they cried. ' The clouds are coming, but you'll just do it ! '

So I sprang upward, trying to hurry, and in half an hour I arrived on the summit of Goatfell more exhausted than when I climbed the higher Ben Nevis.

Some people who climb mountains find themselves becoming God-like. They develop what is called a superiority complex. I always feel humble, inferior, and, subconsciously perhaps, a bit startled. It is like being one of the last men left on earth. And the people whom you meet on mountain-tops seem queerly interesting. They possess the importance of all survivors.

About six men and girls stood on the edge of a dreadful abyss, gazing down to an earth so far off that roads were thinner than cotton thread and big lakes were spoons full of silver.

They looked as though they were waiting for the end of

the world. And something not unlike the end of the world was advancing. A few miles away a storm was sailing in from the Atlantic. Massed battalions of clouds were moving slowly, some of them lower than we were, their ragged edges streaming out underneath and pushing long fingers of mist into the lower air.

There is something frightening in the advance of clouds to the top of a mountain : something hostile and sinister. . . .

But what a view ! I consider the view from Goatfell on a clear day finer than that from Ben Nevis. From the Ben you look over miles of mountain-tops ; from Goatfell you see land and water.

I looked to the south-west and, far off on the very edge of the sea, I saw Ireland. It looked like a dark blue ridge on the horizon. At my feet was the Firth of Clyde, blue on this glorious day as the Bay of Naples, and, across fifteen miles of sunlit water, was the mainland of Scotland. I could see Ardrossan dead opposite. I could even see the tiny cranes on the dockside.

Ayr lay in a fume of grey smoke, then the coast rose to the uplands of Galloway, remote and faintly blue, where the Merrick lifts himself above his wild neighbours.

But to the north and north-east, incredibly lovely, lay the fretted coast-line of the Firth and of Argyle, a county so indented that its coast measures over 2,000 miles, a greater distance than from Ireland to Newfoundland. I looked away to the great mountains, far off over the blue sea : Ben Cruachan to the north ; the Paps of Jura to the north-west ; Ben Lomond to the north-east.

I have never seen a more perfect blend of sea, mountain, and coast scenery. It would be worth waiting a whole year for a day like this and the view from Goatfell; but westward lay the advancing storm.

The clouds moved towards the Saddle, a grim ridge of mountains, fretted and barbaric like the Coolins in Skye. The clouds were dark in parts, but miles of them were like grey wool, puffing themselves out, advancing, retreating into themselves, rolling a little, but coming on like Fate to engulf us.

Now they were so near that we could see miles of the glen through the rents that the wind blew in them. These cloud-holes framed sharp little pictures of the distant sunlit earth. The advance guard came to us as a thin quick mist.

'Let's get out of this before they settle and hang about,' said some one. 'It's a bad path in a mist.'

So like fugitives we grasped our sticks and retreated from the clouds.

The sunlight was brilliant in the glen. I looked back at Goatfell. He was hidden in cloud.

I saw a herd of deer. I sat on a rock for a long time, watching them, and thinking they seemed very tame. I think they knew I was there, for they stiffened and seemed about to run off, but the stags, after standing looking towards me, continued to graze, so that the hinds with their fawns, who get their nervous reactions from the masculine fringe of the herd, were soothed and unalarmed.

The stag is a lovely balanced thing. I like the arch of his neck when he lifts his head, and the pretty movement of his thin legs.

There was the sound of a shot. One of the stags pitched head-first into the heather, tried to lift his head, kicked his hind legs in the air, and then lay still. And the herd streaked off and left him like so many flashes of brown light.

An hour after, when my anger had left me, I came across him as I plodded down the glen. He was tied to the back of a white pony, his tongue was hanging out, and his pretty legs were sticking out like the legs of a chair. There was blood on his nose ; and the obedient pony jogged him down the glen.

§ 3

On the magnificent shore road that runs right round Arran, and at a point of it not far from Lamlash, I rested on a stone wall that enclosed the most triumphant colony of thistles I have ever seen. Agriculturally it was a deplorable spectacle but æsthetically a satisfactory one, because the thistle with its reddish-purple tuft and its hedge of green bayonets is a sturdy and attractive plant.

It occurred to me that unless one knew that the thistle is the national emblem of Scotland one would never associate this plant with the country. I have, as a matter of fact, seen more thistles in Ireland than I have seen in either England or Scotland. It is the heather that one associates with Scotland, heather in its full symphony of colour or heather blown and water-logged, each little bell faded and brown at the edges.

Why did the thistle become the emblem of Scotland?

Its history is more difficult to trace than that of our other national emblems: the rose, the leek, and the shamrock. Every one knows that the rose of England is the badge of the Yorkists and the Lancastrians. The shamrock, it is said, was employed by St. Patrick to illustrate the mystery of the Holy Trinity, and the leek is believed to have been worn as a distinguishing badge by Welsh soldiers during the battle of Meigen in the seventh century. But it is rather difficult to trace the entry of the thistle into Scottish heraldry.

In the first place, what variety of thistle is the traditional Scottish thistle? Is it the common cotton thistle or the golden thistle, the musk thistle or the milk thistle? I must confess that I do not know. Some of these varieties are by no means as frequent in Scotland as in England. The milk thistle is, for instance, said to grow only in very few localities, including the Rock of Dumbarton, on which, says legend, it was planted by Mary Queen of Scots. Why Mary should have sown thistles at Dumbarton and why Bonnie Prince Charlie should have sown the convolvulus on the Isle of Eriskay are questions that must trouble, no matter how much they may charm, the inquiring mind!

I have an idea that the thistle is a much older badge than the meticulous historians will allow. It must have been recognized as a Scottish emblem a long time before it printed itself on a flag. There is a legend that the plant was adopted in the dim ages when the Vikings were ravaging the western coast. The story goes that one night, when the Danes were creeping towards the Scottish camp, an unfortunate pirate stepped on a thistle and let forth such a howl of agony that the sleeping Scots awakened and rushed to arms. So the thistle is believed to have done for Scotland what the Roman geese did for the Capitol.

This story appears several times in Scottish folk-lore. One version of it applies to the Battle of Largs and another to the wars of Robert the Bruce.

When I was in Spain recently I had an interesting illustration of the vitality of such legends. In the cloisters of

THE TAME SEA FISH AT THE MULL OF GALLOWAY

BRODICK IN THE ISLE OF ARRAN

Barcelona Cathedral are six or seven enormously fat geese. Their presence in such a place interested me, but no one could explain it. It took me over a week to track down the legend that in remote times the cackling of geese had saved the city of Barcelona from assault, and that as a token of gratitude it was decreed that geese must always be kept in the cathedral cloisters. If to-day six or seven very solid geese owe their daily bread and immunity from anxiety to the cackle of ancestors who died many centuries ago, surely it is quite possible that the legend of the thistle may be true and that the bare foot of a distant Dane imprinted it on the banner of Scotland ?

We must, however, leave these hazy regions of legend and come right down into historic times before we can obtain an heraldic thistle that would, for instance, satisfy a solicitor. This, the first officially recorded thistle, is to be found during the reign of James III, when in an inventory drawn up in 1488 is this item : ' a covering of varied purple tartan embroidered with thistles and a unicorn '.

The thistle must have been well established in the following reign, when William Dunbar greeted the marriage of the King of Scots with Margaret Tudor with the poem : ' The Thistle and the Rose '.

§ 4

Less than a hundred years ago the Gaelic was spoken in Arran, the runrig system was in operation, there were no fences or walls, panniers slung over the backs of ponies and sledges were the usual methods of haulage, the people used to wear skin moccasins like those still worn by the islanders of Aran off the west coast of Galway, and on many a windless day men could see a thin spire of smoke rising from the hills, marking an illicit still.

Superficially, I suppose, Arran has changed. The old ' black houses ' have gone and there are ugly white houses. There are good roads. There are a few motor-cars. There are post offices, and throughout the season various west-coast steamers, which carry on the work of Highland communication begun by General Wade, come slipping into Lamlash Bay from the Outer Isles or, performing a less ambitious voyage, deposit on the shores of Arran the annual quota of discerning strangers.

Essentially, however, Arran remains unchanged. Modern transport has linked her to the mainland, but spiritually she belongs to the Western Isles. In the winter time, when the storms come howling over Kilbrannan Sound from the Atlantic Ocean, it would not surprise me to hear that the Gaelic awakens over the firesides of Arran.

This island has had a narrow escape. It might have become so easily a blot on the map of Scotland. If the firm hand of the Hamiltons had been relaxed, and if the island had fallen into the clutches of speculators whose idea of beauty is a swing-boat and a full till, then we would have said good-bye to the Isle of Arran. We should have known it only as a place to avoid. So many harsh things are said now and then in Scotland about landowners that I think it only fair to suggest that all those who love the beauty of Scotland owe gratitude to the owners of Arran for their policy of undevelopment. Many a hungry eye must have been cast on Arran's fair shores.

One of the chief glories of the island is Glen Sannox. Here are three miles of the wildest Highland scenery that can be imagined. The hills rise up on each side of the glen, bare, steep and terrible. At first you compare this glen with Glencoe, but your second thought will be more accurate: Glen Sligachan in Skye. It has the same desolate grandeur, the same eerie quality, the same air of the world's end. I am afraid I may not have expressed this very clearly. In Glencoe one has the knowledge, grand and terrific as it is, that its awesomeness is not permanent. One knows, just as the traveller in a dark tunnel is aware that the end of the tunnel is not far off, that Glencoe will end in the softness of Ballachulish. But in Glen Sligachan it is different. There is something almost hypnotic in this glen. One goes through it conscious of the terrifying Coolins and with the feeling that the end of it should be some queer unearthly blue land washed by a light not of sun or moon and inhabited by strange fabulous birds and beasts. Little Glen Sannox in Arran is the only other glen I know which possesses this same eerie quality. It might have been taken up out of Valhalla and planted in Arran.

I went out from Corrie in the evening with a man who was line-fishing for mackerel. There was not a breath of wind. We crossed the shingle that is dotted with vast boulders deposited, possibly from Scandinavia, in the age of ice, and we rowed a little boat out over a sea that was glass calm. Every time we lifted the oars a chain of quicksilver dripped back into the sea. The sun had set and an afterglow burned in the sky.

I pulled near the shore while my companion flung a line into the silver water. To our left rose up the outline of Arran, growing darker and blacker and, it seemed, higher minute by minute as the light went out of the sky. Colours lost their softness and hardened into black. The outlines of hills grew pin-sharp against the sky ; and we could hear dogs barking in the fields and children singing on the shore. There was a sudden convulsive movement in the stern and the fisherman began to pull hand over hand. Something mad and silver shattered the calmness of the water, sliding along the top of it, struggling and splashing. He took the mackerel from the hook and threw it into the boat : a lovely silver thing that shimmered with purple and blue and gold. Dusk fell. An enormous yellow moon, wild and improbable like a moon of legend, rose up over the sea, and in the light of this moon the fisherman pulled up fish after fish, each one silver, like a child of the moonlight. Neither of us spoke. There was no sound but the creak of the rowlocks and the soft swish of the boat over the moonlit sea.

In this enchantment of the night we slipped over smooth water to the island where the moonlight was falling like green rain. There was the scrunch of our keel on the pebbles and then silence.

Early in the morning I went down to the little pier and took the boat to the mainland.

§ 5

When I landed at Ardrossan I wondered whether I would take the long coast road to Glasgow through Greenock and up the Clyde, or whether I would dive at the black city in the regular and more direct way through Paisley. I took the second road, urged on angrily by a desire to get into Glasgow before the shops closed because, as usual, I had left nearly all my socks behind. Some day, perhaps, in the beautiful but obscure future science will make it possible for a man to travel unharassed by the hellish necessity of holding a periodic inquest on his belongings, of cramming collars, shirts, ties, socks, golf stockings, suits, pyjamas, and shoes into bags which shrink maliciously day by day. There is something about me that makes expanding suitcases contract, and even those most sensible of all bags, called for some good reason, no doubt, after Mr. Gladstone, show a mulish tendency to hold less every time they are filled. But this is sheer temper. What is really annoying about strewing trousers and socks over a strange country is the fact that it is due to one's own crass stupidity and carelessness. It is a strange fact, however, that you never lose anything in a bad hotel. It is only in good hotels, where well-trained servants cherish one's garments and fondly hide them away like magpies in all kinds of impossible places, that one suffers this annoyance. All wardrobes should have plate-glass doors. Forgive me. . . .

When I was approaching Paisley I remembered a promise made long ago to a ripe and knowledgeable Scotsman :

' If ever you are near Paisley,' he said, ' get away from it quickly and go to Kilbarchan. Although it is only a few miles from Glasgow no one knows about it, and it is one of the most interesting places in the country. Promise to go there.'

So I turned off at Johnstone and came in time to a place where the Paisley tramcars end. There was a long, steepish hill and on the top of it was the village of Kilbarchan, the last place left in Scotland where a colony of hand-loom weavers make clan tartans.

I gave one glance at streets which climb and descend hills flanked on each side by solid-stone whitewashed houses whose front doors are flush with the road, and I knew that something from the eighteenth century had managed to survive the twentieth. Kilbarchan is an astonishing place. The deliberate ending of the tramcar at the foot of its hill is pleasingly symbolic. Everything that has made Glasgow, Paisley, and all the satellite towns of Lanarkshire, stops short at Kilbarchan's hill. Here is a little lowland town with its feet in the eighteenth century. Its survival is all the more remarkable because it stands in the heart of one of the largest industrial centres in Great Britain. How Kilbarchan has resisted the cheap allurements of this age I really do not know.

In a niche in the church steeple stands the most famous inhabitant of Kilbarchan. He is the *lares* and likewise the *penates* of the place. His name is Habbie Simpson, the piper of Kilbarchan, of whom Robert Sempill of Beltrees wrote a poem in 1600, the first of those homely elegies which attained their glory in Burns. Habbie is carved in wood and he stands with his pipes on his shoulder, a fitting patron saint for a town that lives in the past.

I looked through a window which, like most of the windows in Kilbarchan, was low and flush with the street. Inside sat an old woman at a hand loom. I heard the clack-clack of the flying shuttle. The evening sun fell through the window and lit up a piece of red dress tartan which the woman was making. I watched her for a long time. She would consult a ticket which hung on the loom in front of her, change a shuttle loaded with red wool for one loaded with green, and then— clack-clack, clack-clack, clack-clack—and a thin green line would grow on the edge of the red cloth.

I entered and talked to her. She looked at me over the rim of her spectacles and went on making the tartan, answering me as she worked. She told me that in Kilbarchan is the last colony of hand-loom tartan weavers in Scotland. Each one is over fifty years of age, most of them are women and one old man is over eighty.

' And when we're deid ', she said, ' there'll be nane to come efter us, for the young ones wilna learn the loom ! '

Fifty years ago, she told me, there were eight hundred looms working in Kilbarchan, making clan tartans as fast as they could. To-day there are only twenty looms and no apprentices to follow on, because the young girl and the young man of to-day want more money and don't like hard work.

I sought out Mr. John Borland, who knows all about the tartan weavers of Kilbarchan. He is nearly seventy, but has the bright blue eyes of a man of thirty. He was wearing a tweed jacket, with the red-piped trousers and waistcoat of a postman. Yes ; it was true ! The hand-made tartan would end with the twenty weavers. There were still ' big bugs ' —Hielanmen—who insisted that their kilts should be made by hand, as the tartan was made for their forefathers. And they would not wear chemically dyed tartan either. It had to be vegetable dye, as it was in the old days, and it had to be woven by hand as it was in old times, tough, hand-woven tartan that would never wear out.

So said John Borland.

My visit to the last twenty tartan weavers of Kilbarchan was one of the most delightful experiences I have had in Scotland.

I would enter a small house. Looms filled the front rooms. Although it was dusk the shuttles were clacking like mad, for, as one old lady put it, ' nae weaver wastes daylight '. In some a white-haired woman—for most of the weavers are women between fifty and seventy—sat at a spinning wheel and handed the wool straight from the wheel to her companion at the loom.

The good nature, the good humour, the easy courtesy, the simplicity, and the lovableness of these old people went to my heart. They knew nothing except that they were weaving tartan for a cloth merchant. He would send down the material and the instructions for the sett. They simply had to follow out the regulation pattern : so many threads of red, so many green, then so many white, and so on. A quick worker could make from seven to ten yards in a day. Miss Bella Borland, one of the quickest, can do ten. The pay per yard is $11\frac{1}{2}d.$ or 1s.

This seemed miserably inadequate to my mind, when hand-made tartan is probably 15s. or 20s. a yard, possibly more, but the weavers refused to feel under-paid.

' It's the best Botany wool,' they explained, ' and it's verra expensive. We havena ony responsibility but to weave it. . . .'

They took pride in bringing for my inspection fine lengths of tartan—Munro, MacKenzie, MacLean of Duart, the gaudy yellow Buchanan, and that most difficult of all tartans to weave, the Ogilvie.

I met ' Sandy ' Grey, who is over eighty years of age. He started weaving tartan seventy years ago. He stood in Shuttle Street (what a name !), and told me how Kilbarchan sounded in his youth when eight hundred looms were working from daylight to dark.

I also met the ' baby ' of Kilbarchan, William Meikle, who is fifty ! In a few years' time loom after loom will become silent and a great and historic industry will be dead.

' Aye, it's a tragedy,' said William Meikle, ' for there's no other trade like weaving where a man can make his ain money in his ain hame and sit at the loom watching the flowers in his garden. . . .'

The strange thing about William Meikle is that he has learnt this difficult art of tartan weaving since the war. When he came out of the army—he served with the Argyll and Sutherland Highlanders—he decided to go back to the trade of his fathers. To-day he is the only man in Scotland—probably in the world—who can weave two clan tartans at once.

These are travelling rugs.

On one side is the husband's tartan, on the other the wife's. I watched him at work on a rug of Grant tartan, the reverse side of which was a MacLean. It was an extraordinarily complicated process :

' How on earth do you do it ? ' I asked.

' Well, my eye's on the MacLean and my mind's on the Grant.'

This is probably the most difficult hand-loom job a man could tackle.

' Kilbarchan's a strange place,' said William Meikle. ' A girl from the next town who marries a Kilbarchan man is an incomer all the days of her life. And if a Kilbarchan girl goes away to be married they never call her by her husband's name if she comes back on a visit. She may be Mrs. Blake, but we say, " Oh, there's Janet Muir back again. . . ." '

I heard from the lips of William Meikle a diatribe on cities that would have delighted anyone who believes that the strength of a nation is not in its great cosmopolitan centres, but in its small towns and villages.

' The cities just suck all the good out of little places,' said William Meikle. ' I mind the day when we could call on twenty performers at a concert here, all local people, singers and reciters and such. But now I doubt if we could find one. The young boys and girls think only of going to dances and pictures in Paisley or Glasgow. And it's so easy, with the trams at the bottom of the hill. Kilbarchan's not good enough for the young people. They work outside, they play outside, and they come home just to sleep. I think we were better in the old days, when we were proud of belonging to our own little town. . . .'

And William Meikle banged his fist on the table.

The irrepressible friendliness of Kilbarchan vanquished me. I was powerless to move on to Glasgow. I was taken to see Kilbarchan's pride and joy, the fire-engine. It is as good as anything in the South Kensington Museum. It was bought in London over a century ago. And it still works, encouraged, no doubt, by the feeling that those who man its stubborn obsolescence are its contemporaries! It can be drawn by horse or hand and, I was told, that when all hands are at the pump the old veteran can shoot a jet of water as high as Habbie Simpson.

By this time I was surrounded by an eager crowd of old men. What jokes and laughter and cackling and toothless mirth, what nudging in the ribs, what sudden appearances in overheated cottage sitting-rooms, where grandchildren with tousled heads gazed out from beds built into the wall; what generous invitations to tea and what introductions to buxom and sharp-tongued old ladies! I began to feel that I belonged to Kilbarchan. And I thought how impossible it would be for an inquisitive stranger to appear in any English village and receive such a welcome:

' Man, ye canna be an Englishman wi' a name like Morton,' I was told in one house, perhaps the greatest compliment that has ever been paid to me! And in another I was taken away from the warm, scone-smelling kitchen to a sepulchral apartment full of unhappy chairs, antimacassars, and enormously enlarged photographs of stern old men with goatee beards and cut-throat collars, and equally granite-like old ladies with hair parted down the centre and black dresses that hooked right up to the chin, and in this solemn and unfrequented place, a veritable annexe to the tomb, I admired dim representations of my ancient host garbed as an athlete in the days of his distant youth.

The scene changed to the warm fireside of the village inn, where we sat round a deal table. I had no idea such rich characters still existed in the world. There was a delightful little man who wore a baggy morning coat with a black yachting-cap. He nodded gravely to everyone and combed a straggling white moustache with the stem of his pipe. He was, I learnt, the local oracle on all matters relating to affairs beyond the confines of Kilbarchan, for he had been to sea, a fact perpetuated by the yachting-cap. There were lean craggy men with white beards and piercing blue eyes, there

were big, slow farmer-like old men given to devastating ' ays '
and ' ay-he's ' and among this assembly the face of William
Meikle looked absurdly juvenile.

Old John Borland gave us his political convictions. He
told us that never had a Conservative speech ended in Kilbarchan, though many a one had started there. He unfolded
a flaming Radicalism that would have horrified the Iron Duke.
While he talked I seemed to hear the angry mutter of the
Reform Bill mobs. Everyone nodded in agreement. I
thought that if you bottle Radicalism long enough it becomes
mellow and fruity Toryism. Then with a change of drink
John Borland changed the conversation and informed me that
he was a hundred and twenty years old :

' Ay, och ay, I'm older than any Irishman ever born,' he
said. ' I was thirty years weaver and lamp-lighter—that's
saxty—I was thirty years rural postman and thirty years
captain of the fire brigade—that's anither saxty ! '

He brought his hand down smack on the table and cried
in a loud voice :

' A hundred and twenty, that's ma age, as ye can see for
yersel' ! '

There was a great roar of laughter and a young man in an
apron appeared to fill up the mugs and glasses.

The talk became wild and disconnected. It began to sound
much funnier than it was. The quiet little old man in the
yachting-cap had something which he badly wished to tell me,
but every time he leaned forward and pulled my sleeve some
one cut in, leaving him combing his moustache and mutter-
ing on the edge of the conversation. William became heavily
sociological, John became incoherently Scottish. Good nature
seemed to bathe the assembly. Everybody oozed kindliness
and good fellowship. I had the feeling that the party had
reached that stage which so often culminated in the old days
in somebody getting up and sticking a knife in somebody
else. Fortunately the law stepped in and decreed our departure. There was a hearty volley of farewells outside and
then I found myself walking along with the old man in the
cut-away coat and the yachting-cap. He was still seething
with an urgent communication. When we reached the top
of a slight hill he paused and faced me. Now at last I was
going to hear. But he was very deliberate. He fixed me
with a shining eye. Then he lifted his yachting-cap and held

it in the air. His hair was as white as his moustache. He
began to beat time with his walking-stick and sang in a high
thin voice :

> *Maxwelton braes are bonnie,*
> *Where early fa's the dew,*
> *And it's there that Annie Laurie*
> *Gie'd me her promise true. . . .*

He paused, looked down the road, and gave a wave of that
cap which brings the tang of the ocean to Kilbarchan, and
resumed in a slightly lower key :

> *Gie'd me her promise true ;*
> *That ne'er forgot sall be ;*
> *And for Bonnie Annie Laurie*
> *I'd lay doon my head . . .*

Here he paused dramatically and taking a step towards me
whispered with almost inaudible emotion : ' . . . *and dee.*'

I did not quite know what to say to him, but I was
touched.

'D'ye ken yon ? ' he asked.

'I know it well.'

'Guid nicht,' he cried suddenly, thrusting out his hand.

Then he turned and, leaning heavily on his stick, clumped
down the hill :

'Ay, he's o'er eighty,' said some one, 'an' he's been a great
traveller aboot the world.'

'He sang 'Annie Laurie' to me.'

'Did he so ? That's a verra great compliment. . . .'

Then down the moonlit hill we met a tall, gaunt man with
a fine calm face, a straight nose, and a close silver beard. It
was a face half saint and half poet. I felt that I had met
Marcus Aurelius in a homespun coat. He carried a bundle
of books under his arm. This was Daniel Borland coming
from his night school. I longed for the genius of an Orpen,
to paint him as he stood there touched by the moonlight, the
very embodiment of Scotland's thirst and hunger for knowledge. Someone whispered that he was a botanist, an
ornithologist and a great scholar. 'He has the Latin,' I
was told.

From the bottom of the hill Kilbarchan has an air of hiding

in the darkness and as I left it I went carefully, for ' I must not,' I smiled to myself, ' run over Rabbie's ghost.'

In the darkness I entered Glasgow.

§ 6

There is a bagpipe factory in Glasgow which I have always wanted to visit. It exports pipes to every part of the world. There are more bagpipes in Canada, India, and New Zealand —to mention only three of the markets—than in all Scotland.

The bagpipe is one of the oldest musical instruments in the world. Its Asiatic origin possibly explains why it is the only instrument of the West which genuinely delights the Oriental. In the Sahara, not far from Sidi Okba, I once came on a coal-black Nubian strutting over a sandhill, playing bagpipes from which fluttered a few rags of Royal Stewart tartan. I have heard Spanish bagpipes ; also the classic instrument with its sheepskin bag which is still played by shepherds in remote parts of Italy.

Bagpipes of a kind were played in ancient Egypt, Greece, and Rome. (Nero once promised to appear in the arena as a bagpipe player.) They were popular in England during the Middle Ages. Both Chaucer and Shakespeare mention them. But to-day the old Lowland (or Northumbrian) bagpipe, which was played by an arm bellows, is seldom heard ; the sweet, quick, organ-like Irish pipes are not common, and the survivor of a numerous and ancient family is the Piob-mhòr, or great Highland bagpipe.

I would go miles to hear it among hills and open country, and I would go miles to avoid hearing it in the Albert Hall !

There is nothing on earth like it for lightening the feet of marching men ; and the Piob-mhòr expresses perfectly two primitive emotions : sorrow and rage.

The first thing which you learn in the bagpipe factory of North Wallace Street is that practically the only Scottish ingredient in the modern bagpipe is the wind that fills the bag ! The wood for blow-pipe, chanter, bass and tenor drones, is blackwood from Africa or cocuswood from the West Indies. The reeds are of Spanish cane. The ivory mounts are from Africa. The bag is made of Australian sheepskin. The tartan that covers it, however, is made in Scotland, but the five yards of silk clan ribbon that flutter from the pipes come, of all unlikely places, from Switzerland !

I expressed a sentimental regret that the raw material of the bagpipe could not be drawn from Scotland.

'That is impossible,' I was told.   'The modern bagpipe is an infinitely finer instrument than the bagpipe of the old days.   It bears the same relation to them that a piano bears to a spinet.   It is necessary to get the very best raw material, and most of it is found abroad.'

I was shown the first stage in the manufacture of a set of pipes. The African blackwood, after being cut and bored in the rough, is allowed to season, sometimes for years. It then goes to a workshop, where men, assisted by cunning machines, form the several parts of the pipes. Extreme care is necessary in piercing the holes in the chanter and in boring a drone.

A bagpipe factory gives one the impression of a number of men making a great number of small things. There are fourteen main wooden parts in a set of pipes, which, when fitted, form the big bass drone, the two tenor drones, the chanter, and the blow pipe. There are thirty-one tubes, mounts, and projecting mounts.

In another shop a saddler sits sewing the pipe bags. He has before him a pile of specially selected sheep skins. In sewing the bag it is necessary that the thread used should be thicker than the needle in order that the bag shall be air-tight. This is very skilful work, and an error in this stage of manufacture is ruinous.

The parts of a set of pipes are tested at every stage of their making, and, finally, a man assembles them and plays them.

But perhaps most interesting of all was the room in which bagpipes were packed ready for export.

'Those two sets are going to the Scots Guards,' I was told. 'Those twelve sets are for infantry regiments in India. That set is going to Morocco ; that set—a most expensive one—is for the private piper of an Indian prince. . . .'

Every year Glasgow sends out pipes to native rulers. I remembered the amusing story which Frank Adam tells in his *Clans, Septs and Regiments of the Scottish Highlands.* When the British occupation of Egypt began, a pasha so admired the pipe bands of the Scottish regiments that he desired to introduce bagpipes into the Egyptian army. One of the Highland pipers was called in to advise him. Could the Egyptian be taught to play the bagpipes ?

'Weel, he micht learn, or he micht no',' said the piper.

' But let me tell ye, it needs wind and muckle strength to fill the bag o' the pipes an' keep blawin'. Sae if yin of thae Egyptian chaps took the job on, he'd need to be bandaged a' ow're like yin o' thae mummies, or maybe he'd burst himsel'.'

The pasha took this very literally, and the Egyptian army never had its pipe bands !

' This set,' said my guide, ' is going to a Scotsman away out in the Australian bush. We are always getting orders from isolated exiles.'

There is a certain pathos about this pipe factory ! Can you not see the Scots Australian pacing mournfully—too far away perhaps even to belong to a Caledonian society, if that is possible—trying to pull the straths and the glens out of time and distance ?

A side-line in the pipe factory, or rather a special branch of it, is the manufacture of the multitudinous brooches, dirks and buckles which make Highland dress such a regrettable expense. Here men fix great amber-coloured cairngorms into buckles and into the hafts of skean-dhus. Another disillusion !

' Where do the cairngorms come from ? '

' The real ones from Scotland and the imitation from Austria ! '

We saw a man repairing a skean-dhu which seemed to have been used in a series of violent clan battles. Its leather scabbard was out at heel and tattered. The blade itself was stained red as with blood. The metal was notched :

' How did this happen ? '

' It comes from America.'

' That hardly explains it ! '

' Well, you see, it belongs to a commercial traveller, who goes round in Highland dress while his pal plays the pipes to get a crowd. . . .'

I left the pipe factory still mystified by this skean-dhu. It must have been blunted on the hard-headed farmers of the Middle West !

§ 7

I went to the offices of a Clyde shipyard to meet a friend, and I was shown into the waiting-room. It was a dignified, solid, polished mahogany room from which all knowledge of world chaos had been carefully concealed. The room was living in the bright prosperity of the Edwardian Age when a man in a silk hat might drop in on the spur of the moment to order a couple of liners. At least that is how it impressed me. It impressed me also as a fragment of a world that has vanished. Nothing in our world is quite so solid and assured as the waiting-room of a Clyde shipyard. Even the clubs of Pall Mall, to which this room bears a distinct resemblance, have subtly changed with the times, but here beside the Clyde, now so tragically silent, this rich, confident room lingers on in a condition of suspended animation.

Vast glass cases occupy one side of the room, and in them stand six-foot scale models of liners and warships. The compelling atmosphere of the room insists that the visitor should walk round inspecting them, admiring them and behaving as though the act of ordering a ship is an ordinary everyday affair—as indeed it was in the good old days.

In the middle of the room is a great polished table with gigantic padded chairs set round it. Pots that hold about half a pint of ink stand on the shining expanse, and one feels that round the table have gathered members of foreign governments writing cheques for millions of pounds.

What a stupendous age it was, the age before the War. This room, built for the reception of Admiralty officials and the directors of shipping companies, reflected the grandeur of it, turning the mind to a day when Britain's confidence and pride were supreme. I felt that it should be preserved in some museum: models, table, chairs and everything. Figures in silk hats and frock coats might be set round the table in attitudes of earnest discussion, so that our impoverished descendants may know what it looked like when Britannia ruled the waves.

On the walls were framed photographs which pictured the distinguished children of the shipyard forging ahead on the high seas, looking rather new and innocent but supremely competent and adequate. Who, I wondered, names destroyers ? Somewhere in the Admiralty is an unknown poet. Their names are as right and apt as the names of hounds: *Spindrift, Sardonyx, Morning Star, Paragon, Unity, Swift, Mischief, Mindful* . . . wonderful, perfect names.

The door of the waiting-room opened and my friend came in :

' How are you ? '

' Oh, not too bad. No work.'

' Will things ever get better ? '

' Ask me something else.'

Then I took him by the arm and led him out into the silent place where the empty slipways go down to the Clyde, in order that the magnificent room might hear nothing of our troubles, and go on dreaming of the old ships and the old times and—the old cheques.

§ 8

When I am old I hope I shall be sufficiently placid to sit back contentedly and remember the many early morning journeys I have made in my life. Possibly because I was always sent early to bed as a child, I used often to be up and out at sunrise, wandering the still dewy world with a feeling that it belonged in some exclusive way to me ; and this may explain why now in manhood, I derive more pleasure from one sunny early morning than from a month of afternoons.

I have come to the conclusion that the only completely magic age in life is between the ages of ten and fourteen, a time when the senses are vividly aware of beauty yet un-awakened to evil. It is the only time in life when, for a brief period, heaven is on earth and we, in the astounding self-sufficiency of youth, are in the centre of it and there-fore very near to God. I often watch children in the early teens and wonder if the world to them is as exquisite as it was to me, and if, in the amazing secrecy in which the mind unfolds itself, they can claim as many lovely dreams as those which once belonged to me.

A faint echo of this old magic meets me now and then round the bend of a road, the scent of fennel always awakens it, or the sight of a bee in a snapdragon or a nest full of young birds with their bare necks stretched out, the grey down on their heads. Just as some notes can be pitched high enough to break a glass, so these associations vibrating in the mind shatter cynicism and re-create for a fraction of a second a shining, sensuous world, a million times more lovely than the world has ever been, but, in less time than a shadow flies across the grass, the second passes and a man is left where he was before with realities around him.

So in the early mornings, which age is ever more reluctant to face as if afraid of them, a man may encounter a strange almost frightening happiness ; or so it is with me. And so it was when the sun rose in the hush of the morning, and I took the road that runs into the Highlands along the west bank of Loch Lomond.

I followed the north bank of the Clyde, passing through the miles of ugly streets that lead to Dumbarton. I passed through Bowling where to the left, standing near the water, is an obelisk to the memory of Henry Bell, the designer of the *Comet*. Poor Bell was one of Scotland's great army of inventors. Even if he cannot be called the inventor of the steamship—which was invented, at least on paper, in the eighteenth century—he was certainly the first man to launch a practical steamboat on any European river. Fulton, who I believe was Bell's pupil and got his ideas from Bell, antici- pated him by running a steamboat on the Hudson five years before the *Comet* began to run from Glasgow to Greenock. The three-horse-power engine that inaugurated an age of steam navigation is, by the way, in the Victoria and Albert Museum.

The Rock of Dumbarton, with the early morning sun falling on its steep slopes, lay anchored dramatically in the middle of the river. This is one of the most picturesque rocks in Scotland and, as I looked at it, I made a resolution to set foot on it some day and find out if there still exists on the dramatic hump any memory of that day in 1548 when a French fleet lay in the Clyde and a girl of six, Mary of Scotland, went aboard and set sail for France.

I left the green uplands of the Old Kilpatrick hills to my right and was soon at the lower end of Loch Lomond, where the house boats cluster and the rowing boats are moored. What a morning it was ! The lake was smooth at the edges, placid and still as ice, and only far out, fifty yards or so from the shore, was the water stirred into slow ripples by the soft wind of morning. Mists were stealing from the hills. Ben Lomond himself stood up grand in the sunlight gazing northward to Ben Nevis, and half-way down his green flanks was a lost cloud lying like a smoke ring. It melted and stirred uneasily in the warmth of the day.

The rowans were red at the lake-side and the fern was

turning brown. Slender birch trees stood with their pretty piebald trunks almost in the water. Two wild duck flew low down over the lake, cutting the water with their feet as they flew, making a line that widened into enormous ripples behind them. In the neat white houses of Luss men and women were awakening; and I smelt wood smoke.

What a large part of Loch Lomond's beauty is due to its islands, those beautiful green tangled islands that lie like jewels on its surface. A lake without islands has the melancholy of the sea about it. It is like a piece of imprisoned ocean. But islands in a lake bring to it beauty and romance, for there is never an island, no matter how small, without its story.

There is, first of all, Inchmurrin, the grassy isle, an island packed with memories. The gaunt ruin of Lennox Castle crowns one of its lake-side hills. It was to this castle that the old Countess of Lennox retired to live with her grandchildren after the execution of her husband, her two sons, and her father, at Stirling, by James I in 1425.

James VI visited Inchmurrin in 1617, when he made his one and only return visit to Scotland after his accession to the English throne. That was the time when, during his progress through the principal towns, William Drummond wrote *Forth Feasting*, and welcomed the unpleasant James as ' A king of wonder, wonder unto kings! ' But James seems to have found time, when not infuriating the Presbyterians with his Church observances, to go hunting. There is a record that Lord Lennox wrote from Glasgow on July 23, 1617, warning the custodian of Inchmurrin to prepare food for ' a good nombre of sharpe stomaches '.

Off the east bank is Inchcailloch, ' the Isle of Old Women ', which takes its name from the nunnery that once stood there. This isle is sacred to the MacGregors and in the tangled brambles and among the green trees is their ancient burial-ground. It was on the halidom of him ' who sleeps beneath the grey stone of Inchcailloch ' that members of this vigorous clan used to take their oaths. Then there is Inchfad, the ' long isle ', Inchcruim, the ' round isle ', Inchmoan, the ' peat isle ', Inchconnachan, the ' dog isle ', and Inchclonaig, the ' marsh isle ', whose yew trees, it is said, were planted by Robert the Bruce for his archers.

I know of few sights that are more ominous than the north

end of Loch Lomond where the loch narrows and ends at
Ardlui. The perfect view of this mighty vista is from the
Isle of Inchmurrin. You see the strong outlines of the
Lomond-side hills piled up on both sides of the loch, but in
the remote distance are wilder, more terrible hills lying above
Crianlarich. They are like something held in leash. There
is an opening, a cleft, where the road runs through Glen
Falloch, and it seems to you, when you stand on an island
in Loch Lomond, that this road should be guarded. That
cleft in the hills to the north is like an open gate. And it is
a gate : the gate to the Highlands. If I lived on Loch Lomond
it would take me some time to accept this view with equa-
nimity, especially at night when I had locked the door and
prepared for bed. No matter how well my own door was
locked, I should feel that Loch Lomond's door was on the
latch, and that through it all the Highlands might come pouring with no more warning than the sudden skirling of a pipe.

I turned off to the left at Tarbet and entered a glorious
two-mile-long glen, a narrow strip of land that separates the
fresh water of Loch Lomond from the salt water of Loch Long.
Then I plunged into the wild mountain pass of Glencroe. At
the entrance to the right hand rose a tremendous giant, the
Cobbler, and facing him on the left hand was the Brack. The
road rose steeply through the wilderness and there was no
sound but the murmur of the beautiful dark mountain stream
that runs through the valley. The immense flanks of the
hills rose to the sky, dark brown and littered with rocks,
streaked here and there on their summits by a white fall of
water, and as I climbed on the solitude grew deeper, the
wilderness became harsher and, turning, I looked back on a
stern Highland pass that seemed to me almost equal in
grandeur to the pass with a similar name—Glencoe. The road
wound upward to a summit called, with superb rightness,
' Rest and be Thankful '. Then it relented and dropped
gently down through Glen Kinglass to a strip of green country
lying beside a salt-water loch. And in a short time I entered
the town of Inveraray, where I broke my rule and ate porridge,
which is the only thing in Scotland that I dislike. I followed
it with two of the most seductive kippers I have ever encountered. The waiter swore that they came out of Loch
Fyne, but he could not explain why herring caught in Loch
Fyne should be larger and fatter than those caught elsewhere.

§ 9

Inveraray lies on the edge of Loch Fyne like a relic of the feudal age. It is the seat—one almost writes royal seat—of the Campbells of Argyll and above the thick trees on the loch-side rise the four flanking turrets of the Castle from which, when the Duke is at home, flies the Standard of Argyll.

The little town lies on a pretty curve of land that thrusts itself into the waters of the loch. Neat whitewashed buildings expose demure faces to the loch and to the smooth, green hills that lie against each other, closing in the view on all sides. There is one main street, a wide, hilly street lined with modest houses and shops, including one or two full of those tartan odds and ends which the visitors from pleasure steamers presumably buy in order to prove that they have been far from home. But there is over Inveraray a respectful hush as if someone had just coughed deferentially. There is much the same hush over Balmoral and, to a lesser degree, over Sandringham.

It is in Inveraray that the delighted visitor will probably see his first kilt, for the adherents of the House of Campbell all wear the green tartan with the thin yellow and white cross stripe that the MacDonalds loathe. The most astonishing thing about Inveraray is that the shop fronts so rarely bear the name Campbell. There is McLaren, Dewar, Malcolm, Macintyre, Macnaughton, Robertson, Munro, and even Rose, which strikes me as remarkable in a town that is the historic home of the ancestor of MacCaillean Mor. You can hardly go anywhere in the world without meeting a Campbell, and I should have thought that every shop-window in Inveraray would have shrieked the name. Perhaps this can be explained. The fact that the Campbells are always coming infers that they are also going, so possibly they have left the shops of Inveraray to other clans and have advanced to what they consider, with true Campbell perspicacity, more lucrative regions!

But nothing can rival the air of reverence which spreads through Inveraray when the Galley of Lorne flies from the turrets of the Castle. His Grace is in residence! The head of the clan may at any moment become visible. It is not a servile atmosphere. It is acceptance of authority based on centuries of clan leadership. One realizes that the history of Inveraray is the history of Campbell. But I find it rather difficult to explain why this small town should appear more important when the Duke is there than, for instance, Warwick when the descendant of the Kingmaker is in his far grander castle, or when the Duke of Devonshire is at Chatsworth. Possibly it is because the history of England is the history of kings, while that of Scotland is the history of great nobles. If a door were suddenly flung open and a voice cried 'Campbell of Argyll', you would have a much greater thrill than if the same voice announced 'the Duke of Norfolk'.

The Campbell loyalty in Inveraray finds amusing and unconscious expression in the town guide-book, from which I take the following gem :

'In the Main Street is situated the snug and comfortable old-world hostelry, the *George Hotel*, where the visitor will find a courteous welcome and prompt attention to all and every requirement. It was in the " George " that Lord Malcolm of Poltalloch stayed when he contested Argyllshire against Lord Colin Campbell. It can be understood that his supporters in the Town were few when the Poll was declared —showing Poltalloch second. In the general enthusiasm which followed, Poltalloch and his few loyal supporters suffered somewhat both in dignity and property. When Lord Malcolm drove away from the " George ", it was amid a thunder of ironical applause, and the windows of both hotel and carriage, as well as of houses of supporters resident in the Square, suffered under a shower of missiles.'

I do not know—and it does not matter much—whether this happened yesterday or centuries ago, but no one who has been to Inveraray can read about it without a deep respect for the reckless courage of Lord Malcolm of Poltalloch.

I wandered about Inveraray, admiring the calm loch, the gentle hills, the placid main street ; exploring the old court house and the gaol and the building, once a law court and now estate offices, in which a Campbell jury condemned Stewart of Appin to death. Then I went for a walk through a wood and up a hill. In all Scotland there are no finer trees than those round Inveraray. Oaks as immense as those in Windsor Great Park, beech and ash as splendid as any in the New Forest, and firs and limes by the thousand, stood in close belts of dark woodland ; and it was with delight that I caught sight of the loch shining through the trees and, far below, the little French-looking town white on the loch's edge.

I lay down in the fern and read Boswell's *Journal of a Tour to the Hebrides with Dr. Johnson*. It was in Inveraray that the Doctor first tasted whisky. He arrived with his devoted companion in October :

' We got at night to Inveraray,' writes Boswell, ' where we found an excellent inn. Even here, Dr. Johnson would not change his wet clothes.

' The prospect of good accommodation cheered us much. We supped well ; and after supper, Dr. Johnson, whom I had not seen taste any fermented liquor during all our travels, called for a gill of whisky. " Come," (said he) " let me know what it is that makes a Scotchman happy." He drank it all but a drop which I begged leave to pour into my glass, that I might say we had drunk whisky together.'

While at Inveraray the travellers accepted an invitation to dine with the Duke and Duchess of Argyll. ' What I admire here,' said Dr. Johnson when viewing the castle, ' is the total defiance of expense.' The dinner went off very successfully, except that Boswell was consistently snubbed by the Duchess, who disliked him. This duchess, by the way, who had married the Duke on the death of her first husband, the Duke of Hamilton, was one of the famous Gunning ' Goddesses '. The Doctor, however, was in great form and issued his usual pontifical opinions, to his adoring shadow's great delight. ' I never saw him so gentle and complaisant as this day,' remarks Boswell.

I was interested to observe that the same reverence with which Inveraray infects the stranger seems to pervade the ingenuous prose of Boswell. Evidently he, and to some extent the mighty Doctor, approached the head of Clan Campbell on tiptoe.

Down the hill again to the town and the little empty main street. It looked as if waiting for the Duke to march past behind his pipers, with banners flying and claymores white in the sun. I went into the post office to send some telegrams. While I was waiting for change I wandered to the door. The only figure in the high street was a man on a bicycle who came free-wheeling down the hill at considerable speed. He wore a kilt. It was the first time I had ever seen a kilted cyclist.

'Who is that ? ' I asked the girl in the post office.
'Oh,' she said, ' that's his Grace.'

§ 10

On the pine tree near the bridge was nailed this notice :
'To the Cattle Show ', and a little hand pointed vaguely
over the bridge in the direction of a range of hills.

I followed a straggling crowd along the lane, thinking that
a Highland crowd, when dressed for a kirk or a cattle show,
seems to fulfil all that was meant by the word ' respectable '
in the days of good Queen Victoria. Elderly women were
walking down the lane wearing sombre costumes and black
gloves. The little boys looked as though they were forbidden
to whistle on Sundays. The girls achieved an international
smartness due to the mass production of cheap clothes and
the standardization of female fashion.

But the tragedy of any social occasion in the country is
the bowler hat. In Scotland, as in England, this ludicrous
black inverted pudding-basin offends Nature. In Ireland
all men rightly despise their hats, and the bowlers you see
have been kicked about, left in the rain, taken to drunken
parties, and generally de-bowlerized, with the happy result
that in their incredible decline they assume a certain pathetic
grandeur.

Alas, the countrymen of England and Scotland take care
of their bowlers ! So, against a background of blue hills,
blood-red rowanberries and yellowing leaves, these priggish
lids moved solemnly down the lane ; and under each a tousled
Highland head.

Farmer Campbell had devoted his field to the occasion,
and he stood at the gate collecting the money. He was a
big yellow Highlander of the kind that sprouts tufts of hair
high on the cheekbones and on the nose. He collected two
shillings from every motorist who churned up his field. He had
the manner of an offensive brigand and the voice of a woman.

' Ye'll pay two shillings if ye go in for two minutes or two
hours . . .' he said to a motorist who had declined to pay.

If Farmer Campbell had been invisible this sentence would
have sounded like a love lyric, but the expression of his
bleak eyes and his threatening presence made it seem like a
declaration of war. The motorist quickly paid up !

A Highland cattle show is too good to be true. It is sincere and of the soil.

The farmers, their wives and families, had come in from miles around. They had crossed great hills. They had arrived in every kind of car and trap. A pipe band in full regalia sent its reckless challenge to the hills. Cows mooed. Sheep bleated. Dogs barked. Dotted about the field were cattle-pens. The crowd surrounded these pens and gazed at cattle with the peculiar intensity of countrymen on such occasions. And the cattle gazed back with a similar expression, amazed, it seemed, to recognize their masters in stiff Sabbath garments.

' Well, well, if that isn't Mrs. MacDonald,' the cows seemed to be thinking, as the transfigured lady placed a black glove on the hurdles and paused a moment in critical interest.

And then from the fringe of bowler hats rose a deep, satisfied murmur :

' Ay,' said the farmers.

' Ay—ay-he.'

' A verra fine peast . . .'

' Ay—ay-he.'

And the cows looked back, thinking :

' Oh, Archie Campbell, man, why are ye wearing yon hat ? '

I joined the crowd at the sheep-dog trials. A shepherd in his best clothes—natty blue suit and bowler hat—stood with his back to us, whistling short and long notes. Two hundred yards away a little black-and-white sheep dog obeyed his whistles. There is no more marvellous example of co-operation between man and beast.

The dog had to find three sheep which were out of sight over a rise of ground. He sat in the grass, panting with eagerness and watching the shepherd, his sharp ears cocked. He looked like a black fox. The shepherd gave the signal, and off went the dog. He appeared driving the sheep before him.

A long whistle. He lay down, and the wretched sheep bunched together and watched him.

Three whistles. He slipped through the grass like a ferret and began to drive the sheep.

One long and one short. He ran on the outside of the sheep and turned them.

Two short whistles. He drove straight ahead.

It was exactly like watching a ship steered by wireless.

The dog understood this language of whistles as easily as we understand words. Now and then, if he did not hear a whistle clearly, he paused and cocked his head to listen, then, with something almost like a nod of understanding, he streaked off to obey the order.

He had to drive his sheep on the left of a hurdle. He then had to manœuvre them down the centre of the field and make them circle a hurdle on the right. The shepherd singled one of the sheep. The little collie sat up watching. He knew exactly what he had to do. He flattened himself in the grass and seemed to mesmerize the sheep. They stood trembling and looking towards him. He crept a bit nearer. He was like a ferret mesmerizing a rabbit. The sheep wanted to get away. They made flustered little movements of flight, but were unable to take their eyes from the dog. Then, quick as a flash, he darted in and separated one sheep from the others. He took the frightened creature far out into the field and, by running in circles round it, frustrated every attempt made by it to regain its companions. He seemed to read the sheep's mind and to anticipate every move it made.

His final test was to pen the sheep. He was wonderful. He never barked. He never nipped the sheep. He was a miracle of skill.

The men never wearied of watching the sheep dogs. The women did. They wandered off to several tents which were full of hand-knitted stockings, honey, cakes, and jellies.

This show summed up the life of these people, and that was why it was important.

Two earnest young reporters, one a Lowlander and the other an Argyllshire boy, went earnestly round the tents, noting down every stocking, cake, comb of honey, jelly, and the name of its maker.

'Where's Mrs. Macpherson's apple jelly?' asked the Highlander.

'I havena seen it,' replied the Lowlander.

'Man, we must find it!'

And the two boys searched the tent for an item of news which would be read with greater interest throughout Argyllshire than the news of a government crisis.

Outside in the field the cows and the sheep regarded their masters with slow, reflective eyes, the pipe band got its second wind and skirled like mad, the twenty-fifth sheep dog gave its exhibition of genius, and the hills changed colour with the setting sun.

It was rather like being taken into some one's home. And what a good, healthy, clean home it is, lying on the side of a mountain, with its sheep on the hillside and its cows on the flatland, its milk, its butter, its honeycombs, its worsted stockings, and its Sabbath clothes.

§ 11

The shop windows of Oban are, in the season, as hysterical as Walter Scott's welcome to George IV. They blaze with clan tartan, they shine with cairngorms, they glitter with skean dhus, and there are in Oban probably more comic postcards about Scotsmen (printed in England) than in any other town of this size in the world.

Oban, like Stratford-on-Avon, has a dual personality. One Oban turns with agreeable eagerness to the tourist ; the other is a possibly less tartan Oban reserved for winter, the fireside and friends. I have never seen this Oban, but I have no doubt that it is a good-looking, friendly one.

I think that Oban is one of the most beautiful coast towns in Scotland. On a bright day there is something Mediterranean about it. The gentle western hills slope gracefully to the water ; the buildings fringe the waterside, and on the hills are villas. I have heard men criticize the Roman arena which broods over Oban. This miniature Colosseum, which a local banker in a classical moment erected as a family memorial, gives a distinct and alien character to the place. It is quite pointless and out-of-place, but then so are the majority of memorials !

There cannot be anywhere in the world a more model seaport. All the untidy aspects of shipping are absent from Oban. It is the kind of seaport that a millionaire might create if he wanted one of his own. Even the south pier, where the purely commercial ships tie up, looks on a busy day as if it had been arranged by a committee of the Royal Academy. The herring girls knit stockings and jumpers as they sit on boxes waiting for their ' shift ' to move on into the packing yards.

In these yards barrels of herrings are swiftly packed for America and, I believe, Russia. The girls stand at long troughs, the sleeves rolled over their sturdy arms, and slit-slit-slit-splash, in three automatic movements they gut the silver shoals.

Tied up to the jetty are the little, tough-looking trawlers, dirty from days at sea ; a picturesque huddle of masts and funnels and high fo'c'sles, and through open hatchways you can see the herrings lying, silver and red-eyed, in crushed ice.

And Oban, more so than any town on the west coast of Scotland, is a place of happy memories.

It is from Oban that thousands of people set out to visit the enchanted Western Isles which lie out in the Atlantic and do not seem to belong to this world. It is to Oban that the little steamers bring back travellers from the west. After weeks spent out of the world in lovely places, Oban, with its hectic shop windows, seems a kind of metropolis.

There is in Oban, too, a promise of the west, just as the unearthly winds of Connemara blow through the grey streets of Galway, in Ireland. There is a touch of the Gaelic in the air. And in the evening as a western sunset burns in the sky and you look towards the mountains of Mull, you feel that you stand on the frontier of a new land.

I took the road north-east from Oban and came to the ruins of a great castle which stands on a promontory where Loch Linnhe enters Loch Etive. This was the famous stronghold of Dunstaffnage. It is from this old ruin that the Captain of Dunstaffnage takes his ancient title. A guide book that should know better states that the Duke of Argyll, as chief of the Clan Campbell, is the hereditary keeper of Dunstaffnage. This is not so. In 1910 the Duke claimed the title, but Angus John Campbell, the present holder and the twentieth Captain of Dunstaffnage, made good his claim in the Court of Session that his ancestors had held the title since 1436.

It has been a magnificent castle : now it is merely a shell with nine-foot-thick walls from which is one of the finest views on the west coast.

Stand, as I did, in the afternoon of one of those summer days that swing in from the Atlantic in October, and you will never forget the crumbling ramparts of Dunstaffnage. You look eastward up Loch Etive towards the twin peaks of Ben Cruachan ; westward over the narrow sea are the blue mountains of Mull and Morven ; to the north is Loch Nell with its fringe of saffron weed.

Round you are woods stained with autumn colours ; the rowans turning crimson, the chestnuts bright gold above the deep russet of dead bracken, and at the back the hills wear the last heather of the year.

Lying neglected beside a wall in this castle is a magnificent cannon, which should be rescued and placed in a museum.

' It came from the Spanish Armada,' said the young man who opened the gates of Dunstaffnage to me. ' It was taken out of Tobermory Bay, but no one thinks anything of it.'

It is possible with difficulty to read the name of its maker : Asuerus Koster, of Amsterdam.

The greatest memory of Dunstaffnage is that of the Coronation Stone, which is to-day in Westminster Abbey beneath that famous chair on which so many schoolboys have carved their names. This stone was the ancient Coronation stone of the Irish kings. It was said to have been Jacob's pillow on the plains of Luz.

When the Scots came over from Ireland to settle in Caledonia they brought this stone with them, first to Iona and then to Dunstaffnage, which became the capital of the Dalriadic kingdom. Afterwards, when Scone became the capital, the Stone of Destiny went there, and remained from 850 until the year 1297, when Edward I removed it to Westminster Abbey.

There is another memory in this castle. In 1746 a boat came over from the Western Isles bringing Flora Macdonald as a state prisoner to Dunstaffnage. She was on her way to London to be tried for helping Prince Charles Edward to escape after Culloden. She was kept there for ten days. . . .

Among the trees at the back is one of those ruined kirkyards so frequent in Scotland, where the shrubs and the weeds push apart the gravestones. The gravestones nod together, the green mould grows on the walls, the spiders spin shrouds from tomb to tomb, and there is no sound but the whisper of autumn leaves and the high little song of a robin rising and falling on the still air.

These graveyards are melancholy things. If I had nothing else to do I would like to go round Scotland, as Old Mortality did in the Covenanting Country, tidying them up and weeding a bit here and there.

§ 12

I met him in the boat that slips out in the evening from Oban into the Sound of Mull. Our fellow passengers were farmers and drovers returning to their islands from a cattle sale. There was a varied cargo, including a calf in a sack. It looked like the conjurer's pretty assistant who permits herself to be tied up in view of the audience.

The little man interested me, because he was not the sort of man whom you would expect to meet on the road to the Hebrides.

He looked as though some mighty wind had taken him up from Queen Victoria Street or Cheapside and dropped him neatly in this boat. He was the perfect little Londoner. When he walked the deck I seemed to hear the clicking of a garden gate, and when he stood against the rail the great hills behind him seemed to lose their gaunt outlines and form into something like St. Paul's Cathedral.

I was rather frightened by him because he looked talkative and the kind of man who knows all about dahlias or postage stamps. . . .

We steamed out past Kerrera towards Mull. A few gulls followed us and the setting sun was in our eyes. All round us were the grape-blue hills hushed in peace, and above the hum of the engines I could hear the crew making jokes in Gaelic.

So we set our course for that world beyond the world—the Western Isles.

' That's nice,' said the little man, knocking his pipe out on the rail.

I found that he was looking at the sunset which burned in the third movement of its symphony behind Duart Castle. The sea was a blinding sheet of silver that moved and shivered as if with millions of small fish. Beyond was the hypnotic peace of lonely places, a peace that was calling me on to wild hills and desolate valleys so that I wanted to stand in silence.

' I said that's rather nice,' repeated the little man.

I was about to employ a curt snub, when I looked down at the little man and liked him.

' D'you live here, in Scotland ? ' he asked.

' No.'

' I don't, either,' he said simply.

' You're from London ? '

' How d'you know that ? ' he asked.

' Oh, instinct, a guess, that's all.'

' D'you know Brixton ? You do ? Well ; that's interesting. Glad to meet you. Funny to think of the Number Three 'buses going up past the town hall, up to Tulse Hill —d'you know Tulse Hill ?—and Herne Hill and the Croxted Road. D'you know that part ? Thurloe Park Road and Dulwich. Nice part. I always say it's the nicest part of London ; but it's funny to think of it all the same, isn't it ? '

' I suppose it is.'

And the sunset burnt itself out in gold and red above Ben More.

I wondered, and I wondered again, why this dear little fellow was losing himself on the road to the isles ; but I was too lazy to tackle him and find out.

The peace of the isles, which is like no other peace on earth, was falling over me like a mist and drenching me. I was content to babble about London and to look out at the hills, thinking that no solitude and no simplicity like this exist east of the Balkan States.

A bell rang. The engines stopped. The ship drifted. Down below we saw a long boat and three islanders in it, jet black against the silver of the sea. Five farmers got into it and a few herdsmen. One was drunk and fell down. Everybody laughed. They held bulky brown paper parcels. A new bicycle was carefully lowered. A mail bag was flung in, a little one hardly bigger than a woman's handbag. There was a slim parcel containing the morning newspapers. The bell rang.

The ship moved off ; and we saw the long boat rowing to the near-by shore, where a few scattered lights shone on the mountain-side.

The little community had experienced its daily contact with the outside world. It had received its letters, its newspapers, a new bicycle for Jeanie and its mysterious brown paper packages from Oban.

The moon was rising and the *Lochinvar* went on through the silent Sound with a light at her masthead.

In twenty minutes or so the engine-room bell rang again, the boat sidled up to a little jetty and made fast. Here we landed the calf.

There was a tin shed and a life-belt hanging on it, and

behind dark hills shouldered the sky. The entire population was on the jetty; old men leaning on sticks, hatless young maids, great clumsy youths, all gazing eagerly at the boat which was the one sensation of the day. They looked at the little man and myself and took in every detail about us, whispering and wondering.

There were shouted conversations between the islanders in the boat and those on the jetty. They all knew one another. Then the engines threshed the water and we moved off to 'Good-byes' and Gaelic farewells and waving hands, leaving them in the silence and the shadow of their hills.

'You wouldn't think this could go on twenty-four hours from London, would you?' said the little man. 'Think of Piccadilly Circus now, not that I go up west much these days, but—think of it!'

I was getting rather tired of this sort of thing, but still I liked the little man. He was full of wonder. He had something to say which he could not express, and I was too lazy to help him to say it. At the same time, I wished that he would get it off his chest.

'It's cold. Come down in the cabin and have a drink.'

'I don't drink,' said the little man.

'Well, have some tea.'

'That would be very nice.'

We sat on plush seats in the little cabin. The artificial flowers trembled in their vases as the ship went over the still waters. On a panel let into the wall *Lochinvar* was escaping on horseback with a fair maiden.

'Are you on holiday?'

'Yes; it's a funny place to come for a holiday all alone. My family think I'm potty. They like Eastbourne. But, you know, I find that London gets on my nerves a bit. I think every one ought to get away from London. It isn't natural, is it? If I had money I'd go right round the world.'

'Why do you come to a place like this?'

'I like being alone. I like to stand in these boats—I came here last year, only earlier—and think that London's going on just the same and I'm right out of it. Of course, I'm always glad to get back. But would anyone believe London is only a day's journey away from—this?'

He waved his hand towards the portholes and we saw a mountain slide past.

'Then you find that getting right away gives you—what ? Balance ? '

' That's it. I go down to an office every day, and I suppose if all goes well I shall do so until I drop or get too old. But I never get worried or fed up when I miss a train or have to stand all the way from Brixton in a tram, because I think of—all this. You know. Quiet ! Mind, I don't like too much of it. If I were here alone too long I'd get restless and fed up, but three or four days just put me right.'

He said a lot more on these lines. I thought he was very sound. He was in search of detachment. He had found the antidote that most Londoners need so badly.

We came slowly into Tobermory Bay.

A half moon was bright in the sky. We could see a fringe of houses, white in the moonlight, curving round the harbour, and nothing but sleeping hills and silence as deep as the ocean.

The farmers and the herdsmen were stamping about the deck and looking towards the lights of home. They were adventurers. They had been to Scotland for the day. They had sold their cattle. They had bought all the things their wives had ordered them to buy. They had had a few drinks and felt full of virtue.

We landed on the jetty. There was a crowd of perhaps fifty people present, standing in the light of oil flares watching every face as it came down the gang plank. Then we walked through the deserted street beside the harbour. There was no sound but that of a river tumbling over rocks somewhere near. We were right out of the world, " over the hills and far away."

The little man looked at me :

' By Jove ! ' he said, ' it's difficult to . . .'

' It's incredible,' I said quickly.

§ 13

I have spent two days wandering about the Isle of Mull, and during that time I have met on the roads perhaps ten people. The great hills rise up over the island, clothed with green almost to their summits, and above them, and never for long invisible, is Ben More, the presiding giant of Mull. He is an extinct volcano. From his lofty crater poured out the molten masses that have cooled into the weird and massive columns in the south of Mull.

The roads dip down in silence through dark valleys, they rise up to wild moorlands where the heather is dying, they wind round lovely sheets of water cupped in a hollow of the hills ; and all this land is as it left the hand of God.

You are never far from salt water. You climb a hill, or you turn a bend in the road, and there before you is the Sound of Mull with the mountains of Morven rising to the north, and over the calm waters, distant and small as a floating willow leaf, is the steamer that goes to Scotland once a day.

Mull is a solemn, beautiful place ; an island to which a man should go for what the Catholics call examination of conscience. There is nothing pagan about it as there is about Skye. If something should appear from behind the great boulders that lie in the valleys and on the hills of Skye it would be a Norse god, armed and bloodthirsty ; but if Mull is haunted I feel that a man might meet an Irish saint, his sandals brushing through the dying heather.

Iona has made the Sign of the Cross over Mull.

You come across the ruins of houses, because Mull is full of deserted clachans. There may be only a few stones piled together, or a space of beaten earth on which the thorns grow, to tell you that fifty or a hundred years ago a little Highland village stood there.

Mull suffered bitterly during that disgraceful chapter in Scottish history, the evictions, when families were turned from their homes and the thatch burnt over them.

The result is that Mull is the deserted home of a great family of MacLeans (and Maclaines) who all over the world, particularly in Canada and New Zealand, retain some memory of this island although they may never have set foot in it.

This clan is one of the most ancient and interesting in the Highlands, and in loyalty and pride is second to no other clan. The whole of Mull is strewn with memories of its war-like deeds ; in fact there can be hardly a square mile of Mull which tradition does not claim as the scene of some reckless act of gallantry or cunning.

I cannot help smiling at the little circular which I have just seen announcing an annual gathering of the Clan MacLean in a Glasgow restaurant. How tame it seems in Mull, where every mention of the name MacLean accompanies the whistle of a sword, to read that ' the gathering will take the form of

TOBERMORY

LOCH SHIEL

an " at home " and there will be modern and Highland
dancing ! ' Alas, alas. . . .

Then again, I learn that ' members of the clan may bring
as many guests as they please '. That sounds more like
the real thing ! There have been occasions in the history
of the clan when as many guests as possible were treated
to a rather uncomfortable evening ! Although the MacLeans
never violated the sacred laws of hospitality, they often invited as many enemies as possible to their ' at homes ' ; and
these were wise if they just eased their daggers before they
sat down to dinner.

The Castle of Duart, which you see jet-black in the sunset
on a point of land as you approach Mull, was for two centuries an abandoned ruin. The gallant MacLeans wrecked
their fortune in the Stuart cause. In 1691 they were dispossessed, and the last chief who made his home in Mull was
Sir Alan MacLean, the twenty-second of his line, who entertained Dr. Johnson on the little isle of Inchkenneth when the
weighty Londoner made his astonishing journey through the
Western Isles.

But the romance of the MacLeans is a modern story.
Nearly eighty years ago a young boy was on a yachting
cruise with his father round the islands. He visited Duart
and stood among its tumbled stones. That boy was the
present chief of the clan, Sir Fitzroy Donald MacLean, the
twenty-sixth MacLean of Duart, now in his ninety-sixth year.

He swore at that time that some day he would return and
mend the family fortunes and bring the old ruin back to
life. It took him sixty years to fulfil his vow. His career
as a soldier took him all over the world. He joined the 13th
Hussars in 1852, and received his commission from the Duke
of Wellington. He took part in the battle of Alma and the
siege of Sebastopol. There his dream of the Clan MacLean
came near to ending, for he was wounded and the doctor
gave him only ten hours to live.

In the year 1912 Sir Fitzroy MacLean came again to Duart.
He was a man of seventy-seven. But he had kept his vow.
He had bought the old ruin. He had rebuilt it, and he had
sent out the fiery cross to the clan in all parts of the world
bidding them, if they could, to come to Duart and see their
chief take possession of the rock.

And they came. They gathered from America, Canada,

6

Australia, Germany, Holland ; and on an August day in 1912 they stood before the castle, where a messenger asked the ancient question :

' Is it your wish that the chief know of your desire to see him ? '

A great cry went up. MacLean of Ardgour raised his staff and rapped loudly on the castle gate. Duart opened the gate himself, an old man of seventy-seven, whose dream had come true after sixty years. Pipers played ' The Chief's Salute ' ; the MacLean banner flew from the ramparts of Duart for the first time in two centuries.

The MacLean had come home.

This is one of the happiest stories in the Highlands. No man can look at the firm fine castle on its base of rock without a thrill of pleasure.

It does not often happen that a man can realize his ambition at the age of seventy-seven, and it is as rare for a man to hold to a dream for sixty years.

There is in all this something in keeping with the heroic legends of the Clan MacLean. It is, perhaps, the finest story of all.

§ 14

I wish some one would find the treasure chest of the Tobermory galleon and go away bulging with gold. Then at least we might know the truth about this mystery.

If they even found gold in small quantities—say £5 worth —then it would be encouraging. But no ; nearly every year the same eager treasure hunters arrive in Tobermory with their innocent, hopeful faces and their divers and dredgers. And Tobermory, which has seen this display of hope since 1640, when, in fact, Tobermory was nothing but a few scattered huts, smiles in its beard. The Spanish galleon is Tobermory's typically long Scottish joke !

The latest treasure hunters have fished up the usual bits of hard wood and a few odds and ends, but the mighty treasure chest of the Spanish Armada, which has been thought to contain gold valued at anything (and everything) from £500,000 to £30,000,000, has eluded their enthusiasm.

The wreck lies in deep water and beneath silted sand only a few yards from Tobermory Pier. While the treasure hunters are at home finding shareholders, the Tobermory River at the back pours itself into the harbour and covers the ancient timbers with new mud and sand.

When the Spanish Armada was defeated in 1588 many of the great galleons were blown by storm to various parts of our coast, thus complicating an ethnological problem which has given much fun to the learned in Galway and Cornwall. Several of these ships were wrecked off the Scottish coast.

There is one lying to-day all ready for treasure hunters in Loch Don, opposite Oban. Another lies close to the entrance to the Sound of Mull at a spot called Rhu-na-Rhidire.

But no one troubles about these two galleons, because it is believed that the pay chest of the Spanish Armada went down in a big galleon called the *Florida*, which was blown up by the wild and terrible MacLeans in Tobermory Bay. The reason why they blew it up shall be told in a moment.

Now is this ship the *Florida*, and, if so, was the pay chest aboard her when she sank ? It is hardly credible that any self-respecting Highlanders would permit a ship to sink with a treasure chest in her !

The *Florida* was an Italian ship fitted out by Tuscany. She appears in Spanish records sometimes as *Galeon del Duque de Florencia* (the galleon of the Duke of Florence), or *Almiranta de Florencia* (the flagship of Florence), and sometimes as the *San Francisco* (the *St. Francis*).

The Armada was a saintly navy. There were three ships named *San Francisco*, eight *La Concepcion*, eleven ships named *Nuestra Senora*, and at least eight *San Juan*.

Which *San Francisco* is supposed to lie in Tobermory Bay ?

If it is a *San Francisco* that lies in the bay, what proof is there that she carried the pay chest ? If it is not the *San Francisco*, but a ship called *San Juan*, as some people have suggested, what proof is there that she carried the pay chest ?

I do wish the treasure hunters would have a wonderful stroke of luck and settle this problem.

The argument of those who believe that millions in gold lie still in the strong room of this wreck seems supported by the fact that when Charles II, who had a nose for ready money, heard that the Duke of Argyll had got a diving-bell from Sweden and intended to seek the treasure, he sent a man-of-war to Tobermory to stop the operations !

Then followed a long lawsuit, in which the Duke defeated

the Crown and established his sole right to carry on the campaign of hope ; a right which the present Duke still maintains.

The best thing that has come from the wreck is in the gardens of the Duke of Argyll's seat, Inveraray Castle. This is a beautiful bronze cannon about ten feet long, which the second Duke dredged up in 1740. It bears the monogram of Benvenuto Cellini and the arms of Francis I of France.

Spanish records state that several such guns were on board a ship provided by the State of Tuscany, hence the belief that this ship is the *Florencia* or *Florida*.

Another piece of evidence was collected in later years.

A piece of plate bearing a coat of arms, evidently a silver dish used by the commander, was found. The then Duke of Argyll approached the Spanish and Portuguese authorities, and discovered that the arms were those of the Fareiga or Periera family, which is the name local legend attributes to the foreign soldier in command of the Spanish ship.

That is about all the positive evidence which every year lures the optimists to Tobermory. But I cannot feel sorry for them. It is a wonderful place for a holiday.

'Why was the galleon blown up ? ' I asked an old man who is full of local stories.

'There was a woman on board,' he said. 'She was the daughter of the King of Spain, and she sailed with the Spanish Armada because in a dream she had seen the face of the man she would marry. Her father said, " You shall sail in that ship and find the man of your heart." The ship came into Tobermory Bay and the MacLeans went down to see her. As soon as the princess saw the face of Duart, she recognized the man of her dream.

'Now the wife of Duart heard of it. And she saw him going on board the big ship day after day to see the Spanish princess. So what did she do but confer with all the famous witches, the witch of Islay and the witch of Tiree and the famous Doiteag Mhuileach, but not one of them could do anything ! Then came Gormshuil Mhor of Lochaber and sank the ship as she rode at anchor. That's the story. . . .'

It is a story typical of the embroidery that has covered an historical fact. There are, probably, many others of the same kind in Mull. I have heard a version which says that the jealous wife smuggled gunpowder aboard the galleon in a ball of wool.

What really happened seems to be this. The galleon was driven into Tobermory by the storm, but was still capable of making her way back to Spain. She had men and munitions, but required water and food.

When the clansmen came down to the ship The MacLean promised to revictual the galleon if the captain would lend him a hundred soldiers to ravage the islands of Rum and Muck. When this little war was over The MacLean and his mercenaries returned to the galleon, but he refused to permit the Spaniards to go aboard until he had received payment for the food in pieces of eight. This the captain agreed to give.

The Highland chief sent one of his clan, Donald Glas, to collect the money. He was held captive. The ship was prepared for sea. Just before she made off for Spain the imprisoned Highlander found his way to the powder magazine and blew her sky high.

That story is, I suppose, as good as any.

'They have bad luck year after year,' said a Tobermory man to me. 'They bring up old wood and sometimes a bit of rusty metal. It hurts you to see them working so hard and all for nothing.'

He lowered his voice:

'Do you know,' he said, 'I've been minded more than once to go out at night in a boat and drop a few things for them to fish up, just to cheer them up?'

'I've got a Spanish dagger,' I told him.

'Have you so?' he said, brightening.

But it would be no good. They want gold in enormous quantities and—they deserve it.

§ 15

'If you have to wait for a week,' said a friend in Mull, 'go to Iona when the sun is shining.'

And in the morning, behold one of those warm days, like a day of June that has been lost at sea, which the Atlantic now and then sends over the Western Isles in autumn. Mull was a heaven. The hills rode against a sky not only blue and cloudless, but rimmed with that brown colour which in these heroic islands looks like the dust of chariot wheels.

So I set off for Iona.

What a name it is! Iona and Lindisfarne and Tintagel are to me three of the most splendid names in Great Britain. Iona is the sweetest. It has the west wind in it, not the wind that runs through trees, but the wind that goes over rocks beside the sea. There is also, I think, the sound of bells in it, not church bells but the little bronze bells like sheep bells which St. Patrick and the Irish saints rang in the morning of faith.

In the history of Christianity there is no more lovely chapter than the coming of the Word from Ireland to Scotland and from Scotland to the north of England. There was no sound in these islands but the breaking of boughs as the Saxon war bands forced their way through the overgrown Roman cities, and no sound on the sea coasts but the cries of the Ancient Britons as they beached their coracles on the saffron weed of western lochs.

And in this time the Irish monks set out to clothe the land with Christ. They tramped the wild roads of Europe. They founded churches in Cologne, in Namur, in Liège, in Strasbourg, in Switzerland ; and they crossed the Alps and saw Rome.

Columcille, or St. Columba, set out in the year 563 to take the Christian faith over the sea.

In the name of his island, Iona, you can hear the wild sea wind, the chanting of the first Christians, and the sound of a bronze bell.

I crossed the Isle of Mull by Glen More and the coast road by Loch Scridain, then the land became less wild, less mountainous, but astonishingly Irish, with black peat seams in the fields and white cabins shining on the low hills. I came to Fionphort, where the rocks go down to the sea, and there before me, across a mile of water, was Iona.

There are some things which you never forget and never wish to repeat, because you feel that they could never happen again in exactly the same way. I looked at Iona and knew it to be one of the most beautiful sights in Scotland. It seems as if Nature has here created a special scene for the coming of Christ to the north. The approach to Iona is like nothing else in these islands.

Great masses of red granite streaked with white quartz and felspar are piled up on the Mull coast. They slope down to miles of pure white sand. This sand is formed by the shells of land snails. It lies for miles beneath the Sound of Iona. When the sun shines you look down at bright green water moving over its white bed. Here and there are streaks of deep purple formed by drift weed. Never, except around the Balearic Islands, off the coast of Spain, have I seen such clear sea water. And the sun shines over the cliffs of red granite and the white sands, and across the green water is the small hilly isle of Iona, its green fields shining in the sunlight, its miniature mountains faintly blue and scarred by tiny corries full of shadow, at their feet the cathedral and the ruins of the Celtic monastery.

I sat in the little ferry boat and looked down to the bed of the sound. The water was so limpid that every ridge on the sea bed was visible, and the sun's light rippled below over the white sands in successive waves. I could see the beds of weed at the bottom of the sea, and once we passed over a shoal of small silver fish.

As we crossed the sound my boatman told me that the population of Iona is a little over two hundred. And these two hundred, he said, had become prohibitionists by common vote. The inn was shut down years ago because there was not sufficient custom.

'They're better without it,' he said. 'But if they want a drink they can row over the sound and walk six miles to Bunessan. But nobody in Iona ever does want a drink except in the winter.'

Iona is unlike any other island in the world. Even if we did not know its sacred story we would feel that there is something unearthly about it. The hills are the queer, fairy-like hills of the kind seen in Connemara : miniature mountain ranges that lift weird fretted ridges against the sky. You cannot walk a yard over this saintly soil without meeting some memorial of olden times.

When the sick world recovers again there will be a scheme, I am told, for the creation of a Gaelic College on Iona. It is one of Time's perfect ironies that the land of Columbus may send a mission to the island of Columba. That distinguished Gaelic scholar, Mr. Angus Robertson, is the wizard behind this vision, and those who believe that the Celt has a message for this blundering world welcome this scheme as the re-kindling of Iona's lamp.

The cathedral has been almost too lovingly restored. It

is for an older Iona—an Iona of which not one visible trace remains—that the mind hungers ; and it is possible to find this, I think, on the hills and beside the lonely little rock-bound bays of the island rather than in the fragment of a dog-toothed arch or the shell of a chapel.

There are believed to be sixty kings buried on Iona : forty-eight are said to be Scottish, eight are Norwegian, and four are Irish. They were buried in three great chapels, which have now vanished. The long lines of their tombstones are ranged in rows. They are green with age and defaced by the winds of centuries. Macbeth lies here, and so does his royal victim, Duncan.

As one looks at these tombs it is not difficult to imagine the coming of the dead kings to the sacred isle.

They were landed at a little bay a few hundred yards from the royal burial-ground. Their funeral boats would come slowly over the Sound of Iona to the plucking of harp strings. The Irish monks, their heads shaven from ear to ear across the crown, would meet them on the white sands. There would be chanting and incense, and the bodies would be carried over that paved road, now partly hidden, but still known as ' the Street of the Dead '.

It is to St. Columba that the mind returns always in Iona. He left Ireland, so it is said, either willingly or as an exile for his share in the Battle of Culdremne in 561, or, as one story goes, because he quarrelled over a copy of a sacred book ; and he went in search of a place from which he could no longer see his native land.

There is a legend that he landed on one of the outer isles, or on the Mull of Kintyre, but when he mounted a hill he could still see Ireland, so the long boat again put out to sea. It came to rest in Iona.

No man of ancient times has impressed his personality more vividly on future generations, especially in Ireland. Stories of Columcille, or Columba, as we call him, have been handed down from mouth to mouth for thirteen centuries. I have heard countrymen in Donegal who cannot read English talk about Columcille as though they had met him at a fair last week.

He was big, dark, and bearded, of immense physique, tire-less and commanding, with a voice that could be heard reciting the Psalms over phenomenal distances. There are stories that prove that he had a temper and also a sense of humour. He was probably a typical Irishman.

My favourite legend is the grimly amusing story of the foundation of St. Oran's Chapel. Columba, it is said, received a heavenly message that a human victim must be buried alive in the foundations. As soon as this was known a saintly monk, Oran, offered himself, or, as other versions of the story have it, was chosen by lot. He was buried alive.

Three days afterwards Columba, who was deeply attached to Oran, dug open his grave in order to take a last look at his friend. He found Oran quite fit and well. Oran said: ' There is no wonder in death, and hell is not as it is reported.'

This unorthodoxy so horrified Columba that he hastily took a spade and reburied his friend with the words:

' Earth, earth, fill the mouth of Oran that he may gossip no more ! '

St. Columba died in 597, shortly after St. Augustine had reluctantly landed in Kent with orders to convert the Anglo-Saxons. His body was buried in Iona, and a century after translated to Ireland. His remains then disappeared. Some say that they were returned to Iona and buried secretly, but it is more probable that they were scattered, a bone here and there, over Celtic Christendom.

Iona is a solemn, haunted place. Its influence has been enormous on the faith of the early world. It has been called the Rome of Ireland. And when you stand on its hills and look west over the Atlantic where the outermost isles ride like ships at anchor, when you see the vivid Atlantic sunsets staining the granite hills and the white sands, you feel that this is a place apart: a little sanctuary for ever dedicated to God.

CHAPTER SIX

HOW I LEAVE MULL, REVIEW THE APPIN MURDER, CROSS THE FERRY, JOURNEY INTO MOIDART, SEE BONNIE PRINCE CHARLIE'S MONUMENT (WITH SOME REFLECTIONS ON THE '45) AND ATTEND THE GAELIC MOD

§ 1

RAIN fell all day with the nagging persistence of toothache. There were moments when it would torment with a pretence at ending, only to resume with renewed vigour. The sky fell. The earth gushed water. Boulders shone like brown glass. Mists hung out of heaven to wrap the world in a grey wetness. Burns spouted. Rivers rose to the bridges. Pools overflowed. New and unexpected streams were born out of a responsive earth. The wind joined in, hurling the rain upwards in sudden mad gusts, so that in the magnificent sincerity of the storm the very laws of gravity were defied and, in other words, it was made perfectly clear why Scotland invented whisky.

Now and then over the roads of Mull would come the figure of some ancient dripping man with the rain beads on his beard, on his shaggy eyebrows, and on the ridges of fox-coloured hair which Highlanders grow on the cheek-bones. And he would pause to say, after grim deliberation, with the air of one who has convinced himself of a mighty truth :

' Ay-he, it's wet the dee.'

The recognized reply as, standing in a young river, you lean against the storm, is to shout :

' Ay, it is so ! '

And the old man will splash on, apparently confirmed in his opinion.

Scotland is two absolutely different countries : Scotland in sunlight and Scotland in rain. One is the most beautiful country in the world and the other is the most awesome. A thing hidden is terrifying. The thought of the hills of Mull concealed in the grey mists strikes some primitive chord of terror in the mind. It is to these grey fearful days that one can trace the moody, poetic, sensitive temperament of the Gael.

All day and all night the rain fell, and in the morning a little steamer tied up at the pier of Tobermory, with a ring of solemn storm-blown faces, pale from an awful buffeting from the Outer Isles, gazing over the rails. It was the Oban steamer—the ' mainland ' steamer, as one thinks of it in Mull. I fought my way to it head down against the wind, and we slipped off over leaden waters touched with white. We found Oban a deserted town swept by slanting arrows of water, and over a road like the bed of a stream I set off to Fort William.

§ 2

I can tell you nothing of this road. The mist was low and, as I have suggested, the day was wet. For twenty miles or so there was a sombre gleam to my left, where the grey waters of Loch Linnhe lapped a shore fringed with saffron weed. When I passed through Duror I kept my eyes open for a white house. I saw it near Kentallen, where a narrow road turns to the left and runs through the woods to Ardsheal. The house, which stands nearly opposite the church, is an ordinary whitewashed cottage with a painted corrugated iron roof. It was in this house that James of the Glen lived when the Appin Murder, of which he was wrongfully accused and for which he was hanged, took place on the hillside not far away.

The Appin Murder and the Gowrie Conspiracy are Scotland's two great mysteries. Although the Appin Murder took place over a century and a half ago, it is still the one undying topic of conversation in the Appin country. There are certain circumstances which mark it out from any other Scottish murder, and a strange touch is given to the affair by the legend—which I believe to be true—that the name of the real murderer is handed down from father to son among the Stewarts of Appin. I have met several people in Scotland who claim to know the secret of the Appin Stewarts, but I never know whether to believe them or not. Andrew Lang seems to have started the mysterious business of saying, ' I know who killed the Red Fox, but my lips are sealed. I know but cannot tell.' A more recent claimant to the secret is the Rev. Ratcliffe Barnet, whose delightful books must charm all lovers of Scotland.

If ever I meet Mr. Barnet I shall try and wring the secret from him, not with any hope of success but for the amusement of observing the air of hush-hush assumed by all who claim to know the solution of this 150-year-old crime when tackled about it :

'As I was wandering in a place of Appin,' writes Mr. Barnett in *The Road to Rannoch*, 'I met an old man with the Gaelic tradition in his soul, and the Celt's long memory that never forgets—and, at long last, he told me the secret. I now know the name of the man who killed the Red Fox. I know the house where until recently there lay the *gunne dubh a mhi-fhortain*—the black gun of the misfortune. I know also, why and where the fatal gun will never now be found. But, strangest of all, I, too, when asked for the secret, can only smile like the men of Lochaber and the men of Appin, and say, "I may not tell." '

One concludes that the real murderer was someone connected with a family still living in the district, perhaps someone connected with the head of the clan, perhaps a woman, perhaps one of James Stewart's sons. But whoever it was for whom James Stewart went to the scaffold, what possible reason can there be for making a mystery of it to-day ?

I am, however, so interested in the Appin Mystery that I climbed the hill track by Kentallen in an attempt to find the cairn of stones which marks the spot where the murder took place. There is the mark of an old road up the hill, but the stones are not, as I had been told, on the side of this road, but much higher on the hill lying among bracken. It was a dreary spot on a wet day and I was glad to leave it and go on to the little inn at Ballachulish.

The rain stopped and I climbed the slight hill at the back known as the Gallows Hill, on which stands a monument 'Erected in 1911 to the memory of James Stewart of Acharn, or James of the Glens, executed on this spot Nov. 8, 1752, for a crime of which he was not guilty.'

By this time the English reader will be asking whom James Stewart was supposed to have killed. This is the story.

On the afternoon of May 14 in the year 1752, Colin Campbell

of Glenure—the Red Fox—crossed the Ballachulish ferry in company with three men, a sheriff's officer called Kennedy, a young Edinburgh lawyer named Stewart and a servant named MacKenzie.

Campbell was the factor and rent collector on several Highland estates which had been forfeited because their owners had been ' out ' with Bonnie Prince Charlie in the Rebellion of 1745. Campbell, like others of his clan, had fought on the English side, therefore he was continually collecting rents from Jacobites who regarded him as a traitor and an enemy. It was only six years after Culloden. Cumberland's cruelties had rubbed salt into the wounds of Scottish Gaeldom. Rebels had been hanged, drawn and quartered. The kilt was an illegal garb, the pipes were a forbidden instrument, and the Highlander was forced to hide his gun in the thatch of his roof. And the situation was inflamed by rumours, disturbing to the Hanoverian authorities, that Prince Charles was plotting another descent on the Highlands with the backing of Frederick the Great. So, as Campbell rode through the glens visiting the dour and suppressed tenantry, he must have roused the bitterest of feelings : he was a ' traitor Campbell ' set in authority by the new masters. He knew perfectly well what feelings he roused. He knew well that he was collecting rents from people who were paying two rents : one to him and another, a voluntary rent, to the old dispossessed clan chieftains who had gone into exile in France. Campbell knew well, no doubt, that many a Highlander, probably in his cups, had threatened to take a shot at him.

On this day in May he knew without question that he travelled through a hostile country-side, because he was bound on one of the most unpleasant of all tasks in a Gaelic district : the eviction of certain tenants in Appin. Now this eviction had been challenged by a respected and upright man, James Stewart—James of the Glen—a man who had fought for Charles Edward at Culloden and was said to be a natural brother of the clan chieftain. James, on at least one occasion, had been heard to say hard things about Campbell. James had two sons and a daughter. One son was grown up ; the other was a young lad. He had also staying with him a young man, the son of an old friend who, on his death-bed, had entrusted his children to Stewart. This was Allan Breck, known as ' Allan the Pock-marked '. He was a wastrel and an adventurer. He joined the English army, was taken prisoner at Prestonpans and afterwards fought with the Jacobites. He was present at Culloden and after that battle fled to France. But he was in the habit of appearing secretly in Appin now and then, acting as a go-between for his clan chieftain and probably also as a recruiting officer for Scottish forces in the French army in which he had enlisted. His official police description after the murder was ' 5 feet 10 inches high, his face much marked with the Small Pox, black bushy hair which he usually put up in a bag, a little inknee'd, round shouldered, and is about 30 years of age, wears a blew coat, Britches, and Vest, a Hatt and Feather, but his Cloathes he may have changed '.

Allan Breck was forced to lead a furtive existence in Scotland during his flying visits, because he was liable to arrest as a deserter from the English army.

Now the one topic of conversation in the district on Thursday, May 14, was the injustice of the forthcoming evictions. Stewarts were to be turned out for Campbells, and Colin Campbell of Glenure was the man who would do the deed. It was about 5 p.m. when he and his three companions crossed the ferry and began to ride on the old hill road that would take them to Kentallen. Suddenly, as they were passing through a wood at Leitir Mhor, a shot rang out and Campbell cried : ' Oh, I am dead ! ' His three companions at once ran up the hill-side in search of the assassin. When they returned Campbell, still sitting his horse, made an attempt to open his shirt and then swayed in the saddle and fell to the ground. Two bullets had entered his back near the spinal cord and had come out through the stomach. He died on the spot.

The servant MacKenzie was sent to find help while the lawyer and the sheriff's officer remained beside the dead body of Campbell. MacKenzie galloped to Achindarroch, where he was sent on to Acharn. Here he saw James Stewart, who was sowing oats or, as one account says, talking to Robert Stewart of the old mill at Duror and his son, Duncan. When James Stewart heard the approaching hoofs he said in the Gaelic :

' Whoever the rider may be, the horse is not his own.'

When Mackenzie galloped up and told the little group about the murder, James turned to Robert Stewart and said quietly :

' Ah Rob, whoever is the culprit, I shall be the victim.'

How truly he spoke. Suspicion turned on Allan Breck.

He was missing. And the very next day poor James of the Glen was arrested as his accessory in order—so the Stewarts said and so many people say to this day—that a Stewart life might pay for a Campbell's. The wretched man was taken to Inveraray, the capital of the Campbell country, and there, before a jury of fifteen that included eleven Campbells presided over by the head of Clan Campbell, the Duke of Argyle, as Lord Justice General of Scotland, he was condemned to death.

Anyone reading the full account of the trial must come to the conclusion that James Stewart was condemned to death on evidence that to-day—and perhaps even in his time if the trial had been held before an impartial jury in Edinburgh— would have gained the good Scottish verdict of ' Not proven '. How high ran the feeling of partisanship may be gathered from the speech in which the Duke of Argyle condemned James to death. His Grace addressed him as the member of a rebel clan rather than as the accessory to a murder.

' In the year 1745 ' said the Duke, addressing the prisoner, ' the restless spirits of the disaffected Highlanders again prompted them to raise a third Rebellion, in which you and your clan formed a regiment in that impious service, and in which you persevered to the last. The Divine Providence at first permitted you to obtain some advantages, which have possibly been to give you time to repent of your crimes. But who can dive into the secrets of the Almighty ? At last Heaven raised up a great Prince, the son of our gracious king, who, with courage equal to that of his ancestors, and conduct superior to his years, did, at one blow, put an end to all your wicked attempts.'

After this description of Butcher Cumberland it is not surprising to know that the Duke concluded in these words :

' If you had been successful in that rebellion you had now been triumphant with your confederates, trampling upon the laws of your country, the liberties of your fellow subjects and on the Protestant religion. You might have been giving the law where now you have received the judgement of it ; and we, who are this day your judges, might have been tried before one of your mock courts of judicature, and then you might have been satiated with the blood of any name or clan to which you had an aversion. . . . You may yet, during the short time you have to live, be of great service to your friends and neighbours by warning them against those principles and practices which have brought you to this untimely end ; and may the Lord have mercy upon your soul.'

James of the Glen listened with composure to this outrageous political speech and then, when sentence of death had been passed, said :

' My lords, I tamely submit to my hard sentence. I forgive the jury and the witnesses who have sworn several things falsely against me, and I declare before the great God and this auditory, that I had *no previous knowledge of the murder of Colin Campbell of Glenure, and am as innocent of it as a child unborn.* I am not afraid to die, but what grieves me is my character, that after-ages should think me capable of such a horrid and barbarous murder.'

James was taken under military escort to the little knoll above Ballachulish Ferry on a windy November day. He was given the usual privilege of a last speech. He spoke for a long time. In a closely reasoned and calm address he outlined the case against him, declaring before God his complete innocence and mentioning the bribery and lying of witnesses that had helped to bring him to his doom. With a touch of what at any other moment might have been grim humour, he said that it was apparently not only Campbell's death he had to answer for but the sins of his fathers in the Jacobite Rebellions. Then his speech drew to a close and his sorrowing clansmen heard these words above the wind from the loch :

' My dearest friends and relations, I frankly forgive all these evidences and jury. I earnestly recommend and entreat you, for God's sake, that you bear no grudge, hatred or malice to those people, both evidence and jury, who have been the means of this, my fatal end. Rather pity them, and pray for them, as they have my blood to answer for. And though you hear my prosecutors load my character with the greatest calumny, bear it patiently, and satisfy yourselves with your own conviction of my innocence. And may this, my hard fate, put an end to all discords among you, and may you all be united by brotherly love and charity. . . .'

At five o'clock that afternoon the dead body of James Stewart hung in chains from the gallows. Red-coats guarded it in order to prevent the Stewarts carrying it off for decent burial. For three years it was guarded ! In January 1755 it fell from the chains ; but it was not allowed burial. The bones were wired together and the skeleton was rehung. Later in the year it fell again and this time into the hands of the clan. It is believed that the bones were carefully gathered and buried in secret among the Stewarts of Ardsheal in the little kirkyard of Keil.

But who shot the Red Fox?

That is the question that has been asked ever since James Stewart swung for a crime of which he knew nothing. It is believed that Allan Breck, who was undoubtedly concerned in the murder, did not fire the shot but was accompanied by another man. It was this other man who fired the shot that killed Campbell. But who was this other man?

The legend handed down from father to son in Appin until this very day is that when Stewart was hanged this man lay gagged and bound in a certain house in the neighbourhood. His friends were forced to restrain him from confession which, they pointed out, could not save Stewart's life and would only cause him to share the gallows. But so violent did this man become that he was forcibly restrained from action by members of the clan.

' I found during a recent visit to the district,' wrote Mr. David N. Mackay in *The Trial of James Stewart*, ' that only a very few of the inhabitants of Appin and Ballachulish have ever seen any printed account of the trial of James Stewart, and that not a few learned with surprise that any such record existed. This fact is not altogether to be regretted, as it justifies the belief that such tales as survive have been repeated from father to son, and are not the fanciful creations of persons whose knowledge was derived from print. . . . But what has tradition to say as to the identity of the murderer? As the net result of many conversations with friends and acquaintances in the country between Glencoe and Oban, I am satisfied that, if wide currency among well-informed persons can be held to put the seal of truth upon tradition, the following assertions are true :

' First, that James Stewart had no part whatever in the planning or accomplishment of the assassination.

' Second, that Allan Breck, though he was an accessory, did *not* fire the fatal shot ;

' Third, that several young men were concerned along with Allan Breck in the plot against Glenure ;

' And, fourth, that the whole facts were known to several

persons prior to the execution of James Stewart, and that at least one of those persons had to be bound with ropes by his family to prevent his going to the scaffold on the fatal morning to make the facts known.

'As to the identity of the plotters and the murderer various mutually destructive tales are told. Many persons who believe themselves to be possessed of *the* secret are the victims of idle rumour. The real truth is known, I believe, to a few members of the Stewart clan, and to them only.'

The net result of the mystery seems to be this : that Allan Breck ran away as the best means of drawing suspicion upon himself and saving his friend and guardian, James Stewart, and that James Stewart—who certainly did not, apparently, know who the murderer was—was permitted to die in order to save the lives of some members of his family or clan.

Many years after, when a girl named Janet MacInnes was herding cattle on the hill behind Ballachulish House, she found a rusty old gun in the hollow of an elder tree She took it to old Mr. Stewart of Ballachulish, who said : ' That is the gun of the misfortune.' This grim relic was until recently kept in a private house in the neighbourhood. It was known as *An t-slinneanach*—the shoulder-blade—because it was a heavy piece that could only be carried on the shoulder.

The following note appears in the appendix to *Rob Roy* :

'About 1789 a friend of mine, when residing in Paris, was invited to see some procession likely to interest him from the windows of an apartment occupied by a Benedictine priest. He found sitting by the fire a tall, thin, raw-boned, grim-looking old man, with the *petit croix* of St. Louis. His visage was strongly marked by the irregular projections of the cheek-bones and chin. His eyes were grey. His grizzled hair exhibited marks of having been red, and his complexion was weather-beaten and remarkably freckled. Such civilities in French passed between the old man and my friend, in the course of which they talked of the streets and squares of Paris, till at length the old soldier, for such he seemed, and such he was, said with a sigh in a sharp Highland accent : " Deil ane o' them a' is worth the Hie Street of Edinburgh." On inquiry this admirer of Auld Reekie, which he was never to see again, proved to be Allan Breck Stewart. He lived decently on his little pension and had in no subsequent period of his life shown anything of the savage mood in which he was generally believed to have assassinated the enemy and oppressor, as he supposed him, of his family and clan.'

I would only comment that the official police description of Allan Breck at the time of the Appin Murder gave him black hair and not red, and may not Sir Walter Scott's informant have mistaken Breck's marks of small-pox for freckles ? However, with this glimpse of him, old and apparently rather soured and perhaps haunted, we will leave the mystery of Appin and pass on over the ferry.

§ 3

The profession of ferryman is peculiar. He is, like the lift attendant, always travelling but never arriving. The moment his craft touches the bank there comes a cry from the opposite shore, and back he goes with the divine patience of his kind.

But to the ferryman is added the mighty significance of mythology. There is no calling, except, perhaps, that of gravedigger, which strikes a more thoughtful and sombre chord in the mind. Where is the traveller who can hail the ferryman with no thought of Charon ; where is the man who can pay his toll in shillings and not add to them an awful, invisible obolus ?

Scotland is the perfect country for such gloomy voyages, when the mists are down over the loch and the ferry moves towards a ghostly opposite shore. The Highlander who directs the ferry, wrapped in gloom and a gleaming oilskin, helps the dreadful illusion with his monosyllabic grunts, his grim ' ay-hes ', his grudging ' maybes ', his sporadic ' yesses ', his devastating ' noes '.

In England a man can travel for months without meeting a ferry which is not more trouble than a few extra miles in a car. In fact the only inevitable English ferry I can recall off-hand is the one from the Lincolnshire coast at New Holland to Hull. Scotland, however, so full of jagged peninsulas and wide firths, contains at least twelve ferries which a man must know if he would save himself long and painful detours ; and one of them is the short cut to Fort William—the Ballachulish ferry over Loch Leven.

Imagine dark mountains rising from a tidal loch, ridges of trees marching the hills like regiments, the mountains piling up in the distance towards the gloomy fastnesses of Glencoe and Lochaber, the whole scene mirrored in sleety-grey water ruffled at the edges by a fresh wind and swirling in a central channel with an incoming tide. A thin rain is falling, making the opposite shore seem twice as distant.

The ferry is a flat, experienced-looking, beetle-like boat which has in its middle-age acquired, perhaps to its indignation, an engine. It is worked by a man and a boy, both of whom are bi-lingual. They speak to each other in sparkling cascades of Gaelic and then turn to you and express themselves in slow, deliberate English.

When it becomes evident to the ferry that you intend to introduce a motor-car to it, the ferryman shouts sternly:
" Noo stey whaur ye are ! "

This is excellent but unnecessary advice, because a too sudden passion for the ferry might easily end in Loch Leven ; but there is nothing like caution ! They then swing a heavy wooden turntable towards the shore, fix several pieces of wood to form a gangway, and ' Come alang, noo ! ' they order, as you drive with a mighty bump on to the little craft.

The ferry puffed itself out into Loch Leven, firing on most of its cylinders. It encountered the current, said ' Sorry,' and dashed off down-stream with it. Then, hitting smooth water, it curved prettily round to its destination on the Fort William bank.

While we were on the way the ferryman fixed an Ancient Mariner's eye on me, and I knew what was about to happen. The mysterious stranger who on all days and at all times lurks behind every ferryman (and has lurked there probably since the first ferry was run) was about to appear and ask for a lift ! I was right !

Could I, asked the ferryman in a whisper, give a lift into Fort William to an excellent fellow, a commercial traveller, one who had carelessly missed the train from Ballachulish and would not, therefore, see Fort William that night unless I came nobly to the rescue ? I was more than anxious to meet a man who had the stamina even to contemplate such a journey by train. It is about eight miles by road and about eighty-five, via Oban and Crianlarich, by rail !

I was then introduced to a bright little Scotsman who sat in the ferry's entrails, wearing a bowler hat and an expression of patient hopefulness. He carried a brown bag, and looked so good at his job that it would not have surprised me had he suddenly opened this and sold me a pair of corsets or the kind of tobacco I never smoke.

Off we went together down the road to Fort William, with Loch Linnhe shining on our left.

The stranger was one of the unrecognized heroes of this world—the commercial traveller who has to ' travel ' the Highlands by train. The motor-omnibuses have not helped him much because they run mainly on the chief roads, and his business takes him into small places.

He told me, with some bitterness and emphasis, what he thought about life, commercial travel, hard goods, soft goods, farmers and Skyemen, not one word of which was printable.

I have caught the Scottish habit of listening to a man's accent and spotting his county.

' You're Renfrewshire and your father was a Highlander ! ' I said, blunt as a Scot.

' And hoo did ye guess ? ' said the stranger.

I told him. And I was right !

He told me a fascinating story. It came after a discussion on the difficulty of travelling in certain parts of the Highlands. The hardships he endured when the last train had gone were, he said, nothing compared with the awful things that happened to the Scottish troops when the Napoleonic wars were ended.

He told me that the Highlanders were paid off at Dover and had to walk back to their homes. So the veterans of Waterloo tightened their kilts and set off. In many parts of the Highlands the farmers and crofters put out food for the men. There was an old farmer in his father's birthplace who every night placed basins of porridge just high enough to be out of the way of dogs. He did this for two years ! The amazing trek back to the Highlands lasted that time !

' Imagine it,' said the man, ' every nicht for twa years and in the morn' no' a drap o' porridge in ony o' the bowls. . . .'

So they passed on like ghosts in the night, with thin brogues and ragged kilts, and, to complete their tragedy, many of them found when they got home that the little crofts which they had left years before had been burned down in the ' clearances '.

The stranger left me at Fort William, but his story of a kilted army pushing forward by ones and twos to their remote homes, stealing up hungrily in the darkness to take food placed for them on window-sills and in outhouses and plodding onward over the mountains, will remain with me for a long time.

§ 4

In Fort William I saw people putting up banners of welcome across the main street. Uncomfortable chairs of the kind associated with public meetings were being carried into halls. The Gaelic Mod—the Eisteddfod of the Scottish Gael —was due to begin in a day or so. I decided to stay and find out how the Mod differs from the Eisteddfod.

The morning, however, was so clear that I got up early and took the road to Arisaig. I wanted to see Prince Charlie's Monument at Glenfinnan. What a road this is! For about eight miles it runs along the north bank of Loch Eil into an enchanted country of great hills and salt-water lochs, of desolate moors and dark woodland. White farms and small stone country houses are tucked away out of the wind, and every one of them stands with its roots in romance, because this is the place where the Young Chevalier landed without money, without men, armed only with justice and the fatal Stuart charm.

On the right hand I noticed, standing among trees, Fassifern House, the residence of John Cameron, Lochiel's brother, where Prince Charles spent a night four days after the raising of the Standard. And at the end of Loch Eil I ran down a perfect mountain road to the head of Loch Shiel. Fir trees march to the water in dark companies. The hills rise up on every side, folded one against the other in every shade of brown and blue, and the narrow loch twists in its fretted channel, never straight for very long, its seaward extremity obscured by the bens of Sunart. On a sunny morning this loch and its hills form as grand a picture of western solitude as the eye can see, but once the sun goes in and clouds roll landwards from the Atlantic, cutting off hill-tops in their progress and flinging shadows on the loch water, you have a gloomy, melancholy vista of land as rugged and untamed as when it left the workshop of the Creator.

Separated from the road by a morass is a tower like a lighthouse with a circular wall all round it. On the top of the tower is a statue of Prince Charlie in Highland dress, stand-

ing with his back to the loch and his face to the north. This
monument, which was erected in 1815 by Macdonald of
Glenaladale, the grandson of the Macdonald who was one
of the Prince's first adherents, stands on the exact spot on
which Charles Stuart was standing when the banner of the
'45 Rebellion was unfurled. Before it was erected a cairn
of stones had marked the site and in 1815, when the founda-
tion-stone of this column was laid down, there were some
old men present who, as small children, had seen Bonnie
Prince Charlie at Glenfinnan and had heard his speech to
the clansmen on this spot seventy years before.

I shipped a shoeful of water as I crossed the bog-land to
the monument. The gulls perched on the walls rose and
flew away to settle on the loch. I walked round in the quag-
mire as best I could, admiring the situation of this monument,
which is the only sign of man's handiwork in a bleak wilderness. The storms of more than a century have done their
worst and the column is badly in need of restoration. It is
neither a beautiful nor a worthy memorial to Prince Charles
Edward. He is skied unhappily, a dwarfed figure in Highland dress on the top of an eighty-foot lighthouse. The
lower part of the tower was designed as a little shooting box,
but it has never, I think, been used, and from it a stairway
runs inside the column to the top.

Monuments, even of conquering heroes, are the most depressing sights in the world unless someone paints them and keeps
them in order and, as I sat on the mossy wall that runs round
the monument in Glenfinnan, I thought that it was as sad
as Charlie's grave in the crypt of St. Peter's in Rome. A
haze of almost impenetrable romance has been cast round the
Rebellion of '45 so that everything that happened in those
not so distant times seems to shine with an epic splendour.
I have seen grim Presbyterians, who would refuse to bend the
knee to an altar, thrown into a state of romantic emotionalism
by thoughts of Bonnie Prince Charlie. The more one knows
about the rebellion and the deeper one delves into the plotting,
the lying, the jealousy, the self-seeking and the indifferent
leadership, the more one doubts the romance ; and yet—and
yet. In spite of all, two things remain : the heroism of the
young Prince who came to claim his own, and the superb
fidelity of the Highland clans. Such is the very essence of
romance. Many a prince has landed with an army at his

back to give battle to his rival, but where else, except in fiction or in poetry, has he come empty-handed, armed only with his pride and his sense of justice and his belief in the loyalty of his people? And I, while I sat on the wall that runs round an ugly decaying tower in Glenfinnan, fell into the reverie to which every man must surrender in this place.

In the small hours of January 9, 1744, just before dawn, a coach passes out of Rome under the Porta Capena and lurches along the road that in a few hundred yards or so branches into the Via Latina and the Via Appia. This coach takes the right-hand path and goes on over the straight ghostliness of the Appian Way, where the tombs and the cypresses stand etched against the stars. It is cold and frosty, with a bite in the dawn wind that tells the travellers, even if they did not already know it, that there is snow in the north on the Tuscan Hills.

Inside the coach are a young man and his tutor. Servants ride behind, gazing sleepily into the cold morning and watching for pot-holes in the rough road as they follow, burdened with the paraphernalia of a shooting party. The young man is a great sportsman and he is going to shoot wild duck at Cisterna on the edge of the Pontine marshes.

As the coach goes slowly over the road that has seen so much history, the young man, who is a very wilful and impetuous young man, plots with his tutor. He arranges that he will suddenly feel the cold and call for a horse. The tutor will pretend to dissuade him; but he will insist. A horse will be provided. He will ride off; but not to Cisterna. He will double back to Albano and ride north through Tuscany and—take boat to France. All this is necessary because this young man is well known and his smallest actions are noted and discussed. Meanwhile, it is arranged, the coach shall continue to Cisterna as if nothing had happened.

As he lies back in the moving darkness of the coach this young man thinks of his father, to whom he has just said good-bye. He does not know that he will never see this father again; but so it is.

'I trust, by the aid of God,' this young man had said in farewell, 'that I shall soon be able to lay three crowns at your Majesty's feet.'

And the father, who was blessed by great lucidity of mind, had looked at his boy sadly and said:

'Be careful of yourself, my dear boy, for I would not lose you for all the crowns in the world.'

Now in the darkness of the Appian Way, farewells over, the young man is keyed to the intense pleasure of action. He stops the coach. The servants ride up. He makes a fuss about the cold. His tutor objects. The young man insists. He mounts and rides off, followed by two faithful servants. He rides for a few miles until the hoofs can no longer be heard in the cold air. Then he dismounts, takes off his wig and coat and puts on the disguise of a Spanish courier with a big black hat that hides his face. He rides to a lonely country house, the house of Cardinal Acquaviva —fateful name—where fresh horses are mysteriously waiting; passports are silently handed to him and off he gallops into the greyness of the morning.

He rides north towards Massa. The snow lies thickly on the roads. The hills are white with it. That night he sleeps in his clothes. He reaches Massa. Another night in his clothes. He pushes on to Genoa. Still he sleeps in his clothes. For five nights he lies down dog-weary as he leapt from the saddle. He reaches Genoa. He pushes on to Savona. Here after a week's waiting he finds a small ship and, for the first time since leaving Rome, he rests as the vessel carries him innocently through a British fleet and lands him at Antibes. Now the long journey across France faces him. He takes post to Paris, arriving safely just a month after his mysterious flight from Rome.

How impossible for him to remain unknown. While he was riding disguised through Italy and France many important people were concerned about him. Mr. Horace Mann, the British minister at the Court of Florence, had written on 22 January—nineteen days before the young man arrived in Paris !—to his friend Horace Walpole in London:

'The Pretender's eldest son is departed from Rome,' he writes, 'the notice of which has been sent to me by two Expresses from thence; he is said to travel in the habit and with the arms of a Neapolitan courier. I can't doubt of the truth of this information, therefore have not hesitated to despatch it to England, where, I suppose, it will make a great noise. He is said to be going on board the Brest fleet, and so make a descent on Scotland.'

In this melodramatic way—a night escape, a disguise, a secret journey—began the slow train of events which, piling melodrama on drama, and adding a touch of the operatic now and then, were to culminate in Culloden and the wanderings of Bonnie Prince Charlie.

For a year and six months Charles hides in Paris, an ace in the sleeve of Louis XV. All Europe wonders when the young man will be played. The Hessian dragoons and the red-coats of George II face the armies of Louis XV and Frederick the Great on the Continent : the sound of gunfire rolls even to the white coast towns of the South Americas where British men-o'-war hunt the Spanish treasure ships. In London a young man, who afterwards became Bishop Hurd, writes to a parson friend : ' Nothing is talked of here but an invasion from the French. The Chevalier is in Paris and we are to expect him here in a short time. Whatever there may be in this news, it seems to have consternated the Ministry. The Tower is trebly guarded, and so is St. James's and the soldiers have orders to be ready for action at an hour's warning.' The fear of invasion from the French runs down the social scale, agitating even the serving woman of Mrs. Donnellan in Fulham, who writes to a friend in the country : ' I really do believe in my heart, Master do not care if the French comes and eats us all up alive. For my part I dare not go to the Thames, for fear they should be coming ; and if I see one of our own boats laden with carrots, I am ready to drop down thinking it one of the French.'

And in lonely country houses English Catholics rise to drink the health of ' the King over the Water ' while the candlelight draws twisted, cynical smiles from the faces of cavalier ancestors painted by Lely and Vandyck.

In Paris, Charles Edward Stuart waits for the French armada that is getting ready to land him at Dover. Count Maurice of Saxe, a soldier who seems incapable of failure, is working out a plan to capture Dover and Chatham and march swiftly on London. Spies cross the Channel. Some go to Marshal Saxe ; some to the young Prince. These spies tell different stories. Marshal Saxe is told that a foreign fleet, instead of provoking a Jacobite rising, will unite Jacobites

and Hanoverians against the French. The Prince is told
another tale :

' I have the most encouraging accounts possible from the
King's friends in England,' he writes to a friend. ' They are
such as would almost, without the assistance of troops, deter-
mine me to go amongst them, and relieve his Majesty's subjects, or perish with them . . .' But Marshal Saxe, having
his own information, smiles grimly and turns to his maps of
Kent and his charts of sandbanks in the Thames.

In the first few days of March, while a gale rages in the
Channel, 7,000 French troops embark on transports at Dunkirk.
A French squadron scouting off Spithead sends back news
that the coast is clear and begs the expeditionary force to set
sail at once. The Prince watches the armada, his heart beating, three crowns, in his imagination, already in his hands ;
the romantic hands that long to place them at his father's
feet. What a perfect Stuart ! He did not dream of placing
them on his father's head, which is the right and normal
place for a crown, but at his feet !

Meanwhile the French ships, scouting off the English coast,
sight the British fleet coming round the South Foreland.
A fight seems inevitable, but the tide changes and the rival
fleets weigh anchor at two leagues distance from each other.
Then a Hanoverian wind blows from the north-east. It
reaches gale force. The channel is a fury of wind and wave.
The French decide on flight. The gale blows them down
channel, four leagues an hour they go under mizzen sails
alone, to hurl them back, shattered and broken, on the shores
of France. This same Protestant wind takes eleven of the
Dunkirk transports and drives them ashore. Lives are lost.
Tents that were to be pitched in English meadows, shot that
was to be fired on London—lost, ruined ! And the troops
march out of Dunkirk ; Marshal Saxe is recalled by Louis
to take command in Flanders—the ' English Invasion ' is
indefinitely postponed. So the Catholic Prince of Wales
stands broken-hearted on the French coast. But not for long.
Charles is a young man of action. Inaction is death and
decay to him. Into his mind comes the wild dream of invading Britain all by himself. Louis has let him down. Very
well ; he has a paper in his pocket appointing him regent
for His Catholic Majesty, King James VIII. He has Divine
Right on his side. Why not ?

This is March 1744. In April the Prince, during one of his many disguises, writes to his father : ' I am obliged very often not to stir out of my room for fear of somebody noting my face. I often think you would laugh very heartily if you saw me going about with a single servant buying fish and other things and squabbling for a penny, more or less. I hope your Majesty will be thoroughly persuaded that no constraint or trouble whatsoever, either of mind or body, will ever stop me in going on with my duty, in doing anything that I think can tend to your service or your Glory.'

And poor James Stuart, so weary of ambition, so tired of plotting and deceit, so philosophic, writes back urging his stormy petrel to ' avoid precipitate and dangerous measures ' and ' rash and ill-conceived projects ' that would end only in his boy's ruin and the ruin of all who joined with him.

In the June of 1744 a young man who calls himself the Chevalier Douglas goes to live in a pretty little house in a suburb of Paris called Montmartre. He has a garden and a lovely view. He lives like a hermit and the pretty girls in Montmartre wonder who he really is. Men come to this house with white dust on their riding-boots. They whisper and talk. Some say ' yes,' some say ' no.' And they bow to the Chevalier Douglas and ride back to the coast and take ship to Leith.

This is the most interesting period in the life of Charles Edward Stuart. It was easier to land on the shores of Scotland alone and call on the clans for support than it was to live in disguise in a little suburban villa in Montmartre and decide to take the fantastic risk. He could have lived an easy life. He could have shrugged his shoulders. Was it his fault that the invasion had failed ? He could have cut a gay figure in a gay world. But this strange young man, who possesses the pride of Charles I and the personality of Charles II, is made for great adventures. He burns with the hot temper of the dispossessed heir. He has youth, faith, courage and ambition. And it seems to him, as he speaks with his spies and drinks the heady wine of opposition, that the glittering prize is for the striving.

It is about this time that Lady Clifford, sister of the Duchess of Gordon, writes from Paris to James in Rome : ' Don't you see plainly that till the Prince has proper people about him, he may go on years and ages in the same fruitless way

he has passed days and months, since he has been in France.'
The people with him, she says, are ' unknown, low-born of
no credit or weight, and so useless '. And she is quite right.
His staff are a handful of Irish adventurers and his advisers
are self-seeking or timid agents.

So the year grows old. In the January of '45 he writes
to his father : ' I own one must have a great stock of patience
to bear all the ill usage I have from the French Court, and
the *tracasseries* of our own people.' In March he writes : ' I
wish you would pawn all my jewels, for on *this* side of the
water I should wear them with a very sore heart.' He adds
that he would even pawn his shirt for money. In June comes
the bombshell. He writes : ' I believe your Majesty little
expected a courier at this time, and much less from me, to
tell you a thing that will be a great surprise to you. I have
been, above six months ago, invited by our friends to go to
Scotland, and to carry what money and arms I could conveniently get ; this being, they are fully persuaded, the only
way of restoring you to the Crown, and them to their liberties.'
He then in imagination sees the kind, sad face of his father
reading these words, and he starts to excuse his rashness :
' A horse that is to be sold,' he writes, ' if spurred does not
skip, or show some sign of life, nobody would come to have
him even for nothing ; just so my friends would care very
little to have me if after such usage, which all the world is
sensible of, I could not show that I have life in me.' Once
again the sad face of his father comes between Prince Charlie
and the paper and his ingenuous pen makes this shrewd
cut. ' Your Majesty cannot disprove a son's following the
example of his father. You yourself did the like in the year
'15.'

No wonder stern kirk-going Presbyterians can shed tears
for this gloriously mad-headed young man ! What a young
Don Quixote setting out on his adventures, what a brave,
pleading knight errant—' You yourself did the like in the
year '15.'

So he goes secretly to Nantes. His crew of ' useless, low-
born people ' take different routes to the same town. When
they meet in the street they do not recognise one another.
(Alexander Dumas is anticipated in the streets of Nantes !)
But they go down to the quayside to look at a ship called
the *Doutelle*, a small, fast 18-gun brig that had been fitted

up as a French privateer. In Nantes also, attempting to appear quite unofficial, is a French man-o'-war, the *Elizabeth*, carrying 68 guns. While mysterious cargo is being shipped in the *Doutelle*, Charles makes a great show of stag-hunting at the Duc de Bouillon's country seat. By day he is Charles, Prince of Wales; by night he slips down to the quay side at Nantes under a different name. And he writes numerous letters. In one to Edgar James, his father's secretary, he exposes his plans, writing in the spirit of any young man off on a holiday: he says that he has purchased 1,500 guns, 1,000 broadswords . . . '. . . Powder, Balls, Flints, Dirks, Brandy, &c., and some hundreds more of fusils and broadswords, of which I cannot at present tell the exact number . . . 20 small field pieces, two of which a mule can carry, and my casette is 4,000 *louis d'or*; all these things will go in the Frigate which carries myself, she has 20 guns and is an excellent sailor. It will appear strange to you how I got these things without the knowledge of the French Court. I employed one Rutledge and one Walch, who are subjects, the first got the grant of a man-of-war from the French King to cruise on the Coast of Scotland, and is luckily obliged to go as far north as I do . . . Walch understands his business and is an excellent Seaman; he has offered to go with me, the vessel being his own. . . . Adieu, friend, I hope it will not be long before you hear comfortable news. *PS.* I intend to land at, or about the Isle of Mull.'

In the evening of a June day in 1745 a young man who has allowed a soft brown beard to grow on his chin embarks in the *Doutelle* as she lies at the mouth of the Loire. He has seven companions with him. It is agreed that Charles is a young abbé who is seeing the world. That is the disguise this time! He wears a simple black coat, a plain shirt, a cambric stock, black stockings, black shoes with brass buckles and a plain black hat with a string guard attached to one of his coat buttons. The brig sails off to anchor lower down the river, where she waits a week for the French man-o'-war to come up with her. During this time the young clergyman writes to his father's secretary: 'I am, thank God, in perfect health, but have been a little sea-sick, and expect to be more so; but it does not keep me much a-bed, for I find the more I struggle against it the better.'

They put to sea. On the fourth day a British man-o'-war

opens fire on the *Elizabeth*. A furious battle goes on for six hours. The young clergyman in the *Doutelle* forgets himself and rages and storms, begging, praying, ordering that the guns of the small brig be brought into action. The commander of the *Doutelle* tells his war-like abbé to restrain his feelings or else, exerting the authority of a captain, he will order him to his cabin. The fight goes on until night, when the dark sea is lit up by the flash of broadsides. At ten o'clock the firing ends. Both ships are wounded. The British ship veers off. The French ship is so badly hammered that she must limp back to Brest. And so the young man in the black coat watches the greater part of his stores depart. Shall the *Doutelle* follow? No! The young clergyman says ' No.' He will go to Scotland if he goes alone. And so the small brig continues on her course. She sails in complete darkness. The only light aboard her is the compass light, and this is so screened that not one ray escapes on the sea. There is some alarm when two British men-o'-war are sighted, but a mist comes down and the little *Doutelle* glides onward towards a rocky island. High in the air above hovers a golden eagle. One of the seven men turns to the young clergyman with these words : ' The king of birds is come to welcome your royal highness upon your arrival in Scotland.'

The *Doutelle's* anchor goes down into the water. They launch the long boat. They step ashore. They can smell peat burning. The storm clouds break and the rain falls. They catch a few plaice and cook them in the white ash of a peat fire. And so Prince Charles Edward Stuart sets foot on the land of his ancestors just eighteen months after he had slipped away from Rome on a cold night, disguised as a Spanish courier. The '45 is ready to begin.

From this point Charles pursues his wilful path in the fierce glare of history. During these eighteen months that led him to Scotland we see him only darkly through a line or two in a letter, a sentence in a memoir, a Foreign Office minute, or a note in a journal of the day. Once in Scotland, however, he steps into the light. We know how he wooed and won Lochiel. We know how he cast off the clerical garments and, in a kilt, toasted his father's health in Gaelic. And we know how on the morning of August 19, 1745, he came in a rowing-boat up Loch Shiel and stepped ashore on this marshy foreshore of Glenfinnan. He expected to find the shore filled with men. There were only a few MacDonalds. The gulls were wheeling overhead as they are wheeling now over his monument ; and once again that light heart sank as he paced the shore, waiting for two long hours. Then—the sound of the pipes ; and down from the hills came Lochiel and the Camerons. Charles bade the standard to be unfurled. The old Marquis of Tullibardine, enfeebled by age and infirmity, tottered out supported on each side by two Highlanders. A banner of red silk with a white spot in the centre flew out in the mountain wind. The Marquis of Tullibardine, still held up by his attendants, read in a feeble voice a proclamation signed by James the Eighth at Rome denouncing the claims of the German usurper and exhorting all loyal subjects to join the standard of their legitimate King. Then Charles spoke. He had come, he said, because he knew that they were prepared to live or die with him and, for his part, he was resolved to conquer or die leading them. In his audience was one unwilling spectator, an English soldier, Captain Sweetenham, who had been taken prisoner at Spean Bridge during the first action of the '45. Charles treated him with great civility and released him on parole, saying : ' Go to your general, say what you have seen, and add that I am coming to give him battle.'

What dramatist could have done this better than Charles ? And as I sit on the wall which runs round the monument in Glenfinnan I wonder how we may analyse the feelings which Prince Charles inspires. First, he was a Stuart armed with every bit of the fatal family charm ; he was also a romantic anachronism. When Don Quixote put on his armour and sallied forth on Rosinante he was old and half-witted and everybody laughed at him ; but Bonnie Prince Charlie, fired by exactly the same old-fashioned passion for knight errantry, was young and handsome and—a Stuart. His methods were a delicious breath of old romance in a world that was nearly ready for the railway engine, for James Watt was already a boy of nine when Charles unfurled the Standard in Glenfinnan. Charles was like a boy playing a romantic game which the English Jacobites were too old to understand. They belonged to a world that had moved away from romance. Most of the Scottish noblemen who had

PRINCE CHARLIE MONUMENT IN GLENFINNAN

JOHN O'GROATS FROM THE BEACH

followed the Old Chevalier in the revolt of 1715 were either old or dead ; and so Charles had been forced to play this game with a few Irish soldiers of fortune.   But in the High-lands, which did not belong to the modern world, he touched hands with the age to which he spiritually belonged.   He was not the anachronism in the Highlands that he would have been in the cynical London of Horace Walpole and Lady Mary Wortley Montagu.   To the English Jacobites the Stuarts were already a sentiment, but to the clansmen they were still a religion.   So when fate led him to the Highlands he found the one place in Great Britain which was old-fashioned enough not to regard him as out of date.   As he stepped ashore at Eriskay he stepped into the Middle Ages and, by a strange irony of fate, it was the landing of this medieval Prince in search of his fortune that was to shatter the medieval isolation of the Highlands and open a way for the intrusion of the modern world.

What a narrow squeak it was !   Even the year 1745 was rather late for a knight-errant.   Even Lochiel was almost too modern to play the old game.   Yet, after all, what Catholic, living in the atmosphere of an older, braver, less selfish world, could refuse to follow the knight to the gallant suicide, on the sleet-driven moor of Culloden, of the last remaining vestige of the Middle Ages ?

§ 5

The road from Kinlochaylort to Arisaig runs sometimes beside the water, then it mounts and twists among the hills ; but every yard of it is beautiful with the almost supernatural beauty of the west.   I can compare it only to the west coast of Ireland, where the hills have as many moods as a petulant girl.

From high places on the way to Arisaig you look out to-wards the strange little islands which dot the sea ; the hills of Eigg rise up sharply like a wall ; southward you see the abrupt ridges of the mountains in Mull ; and below you is the salt water of Loch Ailort.

One of the most beautiful sights in the Western Highlands is the bright saffron weed which fringes the salt-water lochs. In the old days men made a dye from it and there are three distinct kinds of weed, each of them, I imagine, rich in iodine.

7

This is the same weed which girls in the west of Ireland carry in great dripping creels to the potato patches.

But how impossible to find words to paint the silence, the loneliness! Perhaps nothing impresses one with the wildness of this place more than the stone beside the road erected to the memory of Susan McCallum, 'seventeen years landlady of the Kinlochaylort Inn'.

Comfortable, easy landscapes have no such memorials! To beat up through rain and against the wind and read that stone is to feel a reverence and respect for the woman who for seventeen years gave fire, food and shelter.

I gazed down on Loch Nan Uamh, a wide arm of the sea lying girdled in golden weed, and I saw in imagination the *Doutelle* sailing in under the hills to drop anchor. What a memorial it would be to reconstruct this frigate on one of the little islands near the shore, so that men coming over the hill would see it with the same gasp of astonishment which its presence must have caused in 1745!

For hours I met no human being. I turned a corner suddenly and saw, within twenty yards of me, an enormous bird sitting on a tree stump. He got up and, opening his tremendous wings, flew up over the hill. A buzzard.

Near the stream at Boisdale I discovered a man lying on his stomach shaving himself, using a rock pool as a mirror. He was a young man, and as soon as he opened his mouth I knew that he was from Galloway. Beside him was a large basket covered with black oilskin. He was a packman.

His basket was full of the wretched little things whose absence holds up civilization: tape, safety-pins, studs, buttons, hairpins. He was a strange young man. I have always found that tramps and packmen are either bores or philosophers. There seems to be no middle way with them.

The packman wiped the soap from his face with his hand and plunged the shaving-brush into the pool, turning it milky white for a minute, then he sat down and looked up at the hills and spat, and said it was no life for a man, tramping round like a beast with a basket on his back.

'What's your ambition?' I asked him.

'To get off the road,' he said bitterly, 'but I canna! Could I get a pound a week and ma keep I'd chuck this basket in the loch.'

Then he said a number of things. He had been in the Navy, and he wanted to write a book.

' I go about obsairving,' he said with a smile. ' All's fush that comes to ma net. Och, you'd no' believe the things I've seen and the people I've met ; all kinds, gaolbirds and burglars—all on the road, all trapesing along scraping a living somehow, frightened to gang awa' back to cities some o' them. . . . Do you believe me when I say I've been living wi' a millionaire for a week ? Weel, I have that ! He's one o' these. . . .'

Here he lifted an arm and quaffed an invisible tankard of beer.

' Always a wee bit the worse for drink. He comes into the bar at —— lookin' for somebody to drink wi', and he spots me ! I can spin a story and—weel, he insists that I stay wi' him, which I did for a week and, O mon, the drink we pu' doon, the drink ! Losh, ma heid's just burstin' ! But could I only get a shorthand-typist to tak doon the things I've seen and the people I've met—what a buik ! Ye wouldna believe it ! '

' Why do you see beggars, tramps and gipsies in the Highlands and seldom in the Lowlands ? '

' Weel, the Heilan' man wulna let ye starve, and ye can mak sairtain o' a bed, if it's only a sack in an auld barn. But when it comes to selling him a safety razor—och, he's the verra de'il himself, and the wurst o' all Heilan' men for money is the Skyeman . . .'

He told me that he had tramped the Highlands for seven years and there was not a house or a barn he hadn't slept in within two hundred miles. He hated all Catholics. He became quite heated and theological :

' I'm frae Galloway,' he shouted, ' and I'd dee for the Faith our fathers fought for . . .'

He got up and with an expression of loathing took up his basket, spat in Boisdale burn and, with a wave of his hand, trudged off into the glory of the hills, a sour, discontented man.

I went on all through that afternoon, and when I came to a hill above Toigal I saw lying below me the mouth of the Morar River and a large bay of silver sand. I sat fascinated by the Falls of Morar, which, I think, are the finest falls I have seen in Scotland. The river was in spate. It came, moving slowly and heavily like a sheet of glass, down from the divine loch at the back ; and then it just flung itself into the air and fell snow white in long wind-blown streamers.

It was getting dark as I came into that outpost of the world —Mallaig. Here is a harbour, and in the harbour a queer, stormy-looking fleet of small ships with high fo'c'sles. They smell of all the more sea-sick foods : pea soup, mutton, bacon. These are the ships that almost convince the Outer Isles that there is somewhere a place called Britain. They go out to Portree in Skye, they go nosing heavily over to Harris where the tweed comes from, and to Stornoway, in Lewis, where the late Lord Leverhulme tried to modernise the Gael.

They lie at anchor with their lights twinkling against the stormy sky, and there is about them an air of adventure unknown to the Cunard Company.

In the morning I returned over the same road to Fort William.

§ 6

Fort William was transformed. I had left it an ordinary quiet Highland town, but now I looked at it with amazement. Its streets were full of kilted men. Grants walked with Frazers, MacLeans with MacKinnons, Mackenzies with Mackintoshs ; in fact, a casual scrutiny seemed to suggest that every clan feud had been healed except, of course, that of MacDonald and Campbell.

The hotel lounge, so recently an abode of peace, was full of Highlanders. The bar was also full. Every one was talking about the Mod, about choirs, about recitations. Men came in swinging their tartan kilts. Everybody knew everybody else. It was a cheerful gathering of the clans.

The kilt dignifies every occasion. Even a fat man groping in a sporran to find a shilling to pay for his tea cannot appear ridiculous. While the Welsh Eisteddfod brings to mind hundreds of men in their best blue serge suits, the Gaelic Mod will always remind me of clan tartan. I did not, as a complete alien, feel so strange in this assembly as a couple of Lowland Scotsmen in the hotel, who exhibited signs of acute distress. They were very plainly in enemy country !

Am I right, I wonder, in the suspicion that something in the Lowland blood shrank from this display of Highland splendour ?

In England we make no distinction between the Highlander and the Lowlander : they are both Scotsmen. It is a point of view inaugurated by Sir Walter Scott and it has done Scotland a power of good. But in Fort William during the Mod I began to feel that the Highland Line was standing up across Scotland like a wall, and that we in Fort William were one side of it and the rest of the world on the other. I also felt that it was a great privilege to be on our side of it. The two Lowland Scots smiled at the great gusts of laughter from the bar, at the shouts of ' Slainte ' and the high-pitched Gaelic voices : but I do not think they really liked it. They felt out of it. They were in Scotland, yet not in their Scotland. After all, it is not yet two centuries since a Lowlander, if forced by any urgency of business to venture into the Highlands, first made his will. It is not yet two centuries since the skirl of the pipes and the sight of Prince Charlie's ragged clansmen struck acute terror into the Lowland heart.

I have, therefore, every sympathy with the two harmless Scots who came up to Fort William to sell tin buckets, or something, and discovered themselves in the middle of an aggressive Highland gathering in which every man walked about with the name of his tribe wrapped round his middle.

A number of the more earnest Gaels had, I learnt, arrived from London only that morning. They were mostly middle-aged men in beautifully cut Highland garments, huge cairngorms shining in the hafts of the skean dhus and their black brogues laced with leather thongs.

' Are they playing like children at a fancy dress party,' I wondered, ' or is this real ? No doubt these men were to be found in London yesterday wearing trousers and behaving like normal ordinary Londoners, with nothing about them save perhaps a Gaelic softness in the speech to distinguish them from their fellows. Now look at them swaggering in their clan tartans . . .'

When I entered the bar a ring of heated Highland faces presented itself. Voices were loud in argument and in story. All the arguments were abstract and all the stories about people who were dead ! This Mod, I said to myself, is more interesting than the Eisteddfod of the Welsh because it is a social reunion as well as an artistic one. In Wales they do not waste time filling the bars with laughter and with argument: it would ruin their wind. But here at the Mod, so it seemed to me, the meeting of the clans was just as important as the music which was the official reason for the meeting.

§ 7

What is the Mod, and how did it begin?

The word means 'gathering'. It is the annual assembly of An Comunn Gaidhealach, a society founded in 1891 to preserve and develop the speech, music, folk-art and industry of the Scottish Gael. In other words, the Mod is to the Highlands exactly what the Eisteddfod is to Wales: an annual feast of song at which people who speak two languages —English and their mother tongue—assemble to warm their hands at the fire of a common racial culture.

One of the miracles of this world is that Gaelic should have survived as a spoken language. When Prince Charles Edward roused the clans in the 1745 Rebellion, the Highlands could speak very little English. There are many amusing manuscripts in the British Museum which prove what terror the 'gibberish' of the Highlander inspired in the minds of Lowland Scots and English. They could not have been more startled had a tribe of Zulus broken out of the hills.

One manuscript, a letter from the daughter of a Mr. Hewit of Carlisle, describes how she and her mother were alone in the house when a Highlander entered the room with a drawn sword in his hand. The women screamed. The Highlander addressed them in soothing words, none of which they understood. He then, as a sign that he meant no harm, sheathed his sword, drew his dirk out of his stocking and placed it, together with his pistol, on the table. This only made the women scream louder. They thought that this generous disarmament was merely a preparation! The Highlander then tried a little humour. He began to dance round the room, giving out a few merry 'hoochs'. This display of animal spirits seemed to the terrified women to be a kind of war dance:

'Then the agsaparated devil got 'is wapons to put ous

derackly to death,' wrote Miss Hewit, who seems to have been as deficient in English as in Gaelic! But the poor Highlander had no such intentions. He merely cursed the silly women and walked out.

But this, less than two hundred years ago, was the general effect of Highland clansmen on the country.

After the defeat of Prince Charles at Culloden the Government tried to stamp out every Gaelic thing. The methods employed by the barbaric Duke of Cumberland were those that might have been used against a tribe of savages. When that good and kindly man, President Forbes, ventured to oppose the barbarities of the Hanoverian troops and mentioned the outraged 'laws of the country', Cumberland turned to him and roared 'Laws of the Country! I'll make a brigade give laws, by God.' The Gaelic tongue, the kilt, the bagpipe, were alike forbidden as the signs of a rebel. A man in a kilt could be shot at sight.

In a district ravaged by fire and sword, its clan chieftains either dead or in exile, its ancient customs under a fierce and relentless ban, its very language either sneered at as a barbarism or suspected as a political offence, it is surely a miracle that any Highland thing survived the ghastly years of the proscriptions.

And to-day how times have changed. Members of the Royal Family wear the Stuart tartan when they visit the Highlands—the very tartan that was once such a red rag to Cumberland—and in Scotland to-day thousands of people are learning the Gaelic tongue. Moreover, the Lowland descendants of those worthy folk who were frightened out of their lives by the clans in the '45 take great pride to-day in a few words of Gaelic. A tongue that the eighteenth century considered barbaric has become the passport to a magic region of song and legend. It is the fashion to-day, a result probably of our urbanisation, for earnest young men and women to excavate the unwilling memories of old countrymen and countrywomen in search of odd scraps of folk-lore and wisdom. As proud as peacocks, they return to the town with them to write books or to set their excavations to music. Since the Gaelic revival the Highlands have been heavily subjected to these literary excavators. Old men have been made to sing songs to them and old women have been made to recite poems, so that almost any crofter in the

Western Isles can tell a Gaelic enthusiast at sight. It is all part of the obsequies of bygone age.

An Comunn Gaidhealach has attempted to arrest the death of Gaelic. It has done one great thing for the language : it has placed it on a pinnacle. Young people no longer regard it as a sign of age and the mark of a dying generation. It is also mainly responsible for the clause in the 1918 Education Act which empowers local authorities in Gaelic-speaking districts to teach the old language in the schools.

The association has knit together the archipelago of scattered western islands with the Gaelic-speaking mainland, and given a common parliament to the artistic instincts of lovers and speakers of the ancient tongue.

§ 8

After two days at the Mod I began to suffer from mental indigestion ! Too much happens simultaneously.

In the first hall which I entered one morning, judges were listening to original Gaelic poetry. I do not think I have ever seen a more vivid illustration of the difference between Celt and Saxon. The poets were all farmers or crofters or humble men from the small islands in the Hebrides.

Can you imagine a Sussex yokel standing up in a general parliament of the Muses and delivering his own verse ! Scratch the Gael and you discover a poet. He may not always be a very good poet, but he is always a sincere one.

One old man with silver hair and huge hobnailed boots stood up and delivered in Gaelic, with complete unself-consciousness, a poem about his marriage. He told how marriage had brightened the world for him, how his life had altered, and how everything around him was illuminated by his happiness.

A huge farmer followed with a poem on the coming of spring, and a third, a sensitive young Gael from the romantic isle of Eriskay, delivered an ode to the Western Atlantic. He spoke of the ocean's quiet moods and stormy moods, and he ended with a verse which said that, in spite of the dead men who lie beneath the seas and the ships which lie broken there, he could never find it in his heart to hate the sea.

The most surprising poem was from a very intense young man in a blue serge suit. He delivered a tremendous oration. He marched from strength to strength. He forgot himself. He shot out his arms and his eyes blazed with conviction.

I thought that he was delivering a great patriotic essay; and so he was!

One of the judges told me that his poem dealt with Easdale, a tiny slate-quarrying island off the coast of Argyll! His poem described the splendour and beauty of the isle. 'Who,' asked the poet, 'could cut slate like the men of Easdale?'

If patriotism begins at home, this competitor was surely one of the greatest patriots in Scotland.

In the next hall I was in time to hear a competition in 'Puirt-a-beul' or 'Mouth Tunes.'

A mixed choir stood on the platform and sang Gaelic verses which reproduced with amazing fidelity the rhythm and sound of pipes playing a reel. The effect was gained by repeating tongue-twisting lines with incredible speed and changing from Strathspey time into quick reel time. The singing of these mouth-tunes struck me as the most interesting feature of the Mod programme.

It is difficult to explain the peculiar charm of these tunes. It is impossible to keep still while they are being sung. You must tap the floor in time to them. They are the perfect dance tunes. Here is a Strathspey that I heard a young man sing at a private concert and which I considered particularly good. It is called 'Brochan Lom, Tana Lom' and was sung to the tune of 'Orange and Blue'.

> *Brochan lom tana lom, brochan lom sùghain,*
> *Brochan lom tana lom, brochan lom sùghain,*
> *Brochan lom tana lom, brochan lom sùghain,*
> *Brochan lom tana lom, brochan lom sùghain.*

> *Brochan tana tana tana, brochan tana sùghain,*
> *Brochan tana tana tana, brochan tana sùghain,*
> *Brochan tana tana tana, brochan tana sùghain,*
> *Brochan lom tana lom, brochan lom sùghain.*

> *Brochan lom tana lom, brochan lom sùghain,*
> *Brochan lom tana lom, brochan lom sùghain,*
> *Brochan lom tana lom, brochan lom sùghain,*
> *Brochan lom tana lom, brochan lom sùghain.*

Thugaibh aran dha na Gillean leis a' bhrochan sùghain,
Thugaibh aran dha na Gillean leis a' bhrochan sùghain,
Thugaibh aran dha na Gillean leis a' bhrochan sùghain,
Brochan lom tana lom, brochan lom sùghain.
   Brochan lom tana lom, brochan lom sùghain,
   Brochan lom tana lom, brochan lom sùghain,
   Brochan lom tana lom, brochan lom sùghain,
   Brochan lom tana lom, brochan lom sùghain.

So an rud a gheibheamaid o Nighean Gobh' an Dùine,
So an rud a gheibheamaid o Nighean Gobh' an Dùine,
So an rud a gheibheamaid o Nighean Gobh' an Dùine,
Brochan lom tana lom, brochan lom sùghain
   Brochan lom tana lom, brochan lom sùghain,
   Brochan lom tana lom, brochan lom sùghain,
   Brochan lom tana lom, brochan lom sùghain,
   Brochan lom tana lom, brochan lom sùghain.

He changed from this to a reel, to the tune of ' Mrs. Mac-
Leod of Raasay ' as follows :

Gur e'm fear odhar biorach odhar gobhain Chillechreanain,
Gur e'm fear odhar biorach odhar gobhain Chillechreanain,
Gur e'm fear odhar biorach odhar gobhain Chillechreanain,
's dona chairich e mo chlobha gobhain Chillechreanain,
O gur biorach odhar e gobhain Chillechreanain,
O gur biorach odhar e gobhain Chillechreanain,
O gur biorach odhar e gobhain Chillechreanain,
's dona chairich e mo chlobha gobhain Chillechreanain,

I cannot say what effect these lines have on the English
reader, but if he has ever heard the music of a reel surely
something of it must jump out of the above words.

This mouth music is, I am told, of unknown antiquity.
There is an erroneous idea that it dates only from the time
after Culloden when, the pipes forbidden, dancers made mouth
music and, by inventing a word rhythm that exactly reproduced the pipes, were able to dance reels and keep the law.
But, even waiving the fact that there was no reason for
anyone to dance in the Highlands after Culloden, Puirt-a-
beul is obviously something that goes back to the very
beginnings of human expression. It is probably as old as
the pipe which it imitates.

It is said that certain apparently meaningless refrains in
English song, such as ' hey-down-derry ', go back to incredibly
remote times. The Druids are said to have had a song,
' Hai down, ir derry danno ', which summoned worshippers
to the oak groves. And likewise some of the words to the

Gaelic mouth music may have their origin in a time long before history.

I believe Gaelic mouth music would cause a sensation if it were heard in the modern concert room and I suggest that the British Broadcasting Corporation should persuade one of the Gaelic choirs in Glasgow to give a Puirt-a-beul concert one night.

While I consider mouth music to be the unique feature of the Mod, and to me the most interesting because it can be understood without a knowledge of Gaelic, it is impossible to exaggerate the beauty of the traditional Gaelic songs, each one a flawless little gem. There is a certain beauty about them, a quality of perfection, rather like that of flowers or shells, and in comparison with them the average drawing-room ballad appears tame and lifeless.

It is an extraordinary thing in these times to hear a song which has never been committed to writing. It comes from the lips of one generation to another over a great number of centuries, and the unfortunate Mod accompanist is often in grave difficulties. The singer brings no music. How can he, or she, produce a song that has lived only in the minds of remote Hebrideans? So the vocalist will often bend down and hum the tune to the accompanist and he, very gallantly, does his best.

§ 9

'The Highlander can enjoy a social glass as well as any persons; but although whisky is plentiful with them, habitual tippling is extremely rare, and there is a proverb that speaks their contempt of those who meet for the sake of drinking only. The renowned Fingal, who, by the by, delivered his maxims in Triads, said that one of the worst things which could happen to a man was to drink curmi in the morning. Measg, mixture, now pronounced meisg, signifies drunkenness, apparently from the stupefying effects of drinking mixed liquors. A gentleman assured me that, in the parish of Lairg, in Ross-shire, where he was formerly resident, there was but one person addicted to drink; and a native of Laggan, Inverness-shire, knew but one individual in that part who was accustomed to intoxication; these characters indulged their depraved tastes in solitude, for they could find no asscciates. The Highlanders seldom met for a carousal, and when they did assemble they enjoyed themselves very heartily, the "lawing", or bill, being paid by a general contribution, for which a bonnet was passed around the company. If, however, the Highlanders seldom met to drink together, it must be confessed that when they did "forgather", they were inclined to prolong their stay, and would occasionally spend days and nights over the bottle. . . . The laird of Assynt, on one occasion, having come down to Dunrobin, was accosted by the smith of the village, when just ready to mount his garron and set off. The smith, being an old acquaintance, and the laird, like the late MacNab, and others of true Highland blood, thinking it no derogation from his dignity to accept the gobh's invitation to take deoch an doras, a draught at the door, or stirrup cup, for every glass had its significant appellation, and went into the house where the smith called for the largest jar or greybeard of whisky, a pitcher that holds perhaps two gallons, meaning, without doubt, to show the laird that when they parted, it should not be for want of liquor. "Well," says Donald, "they continued to sit and drink, and converse on various matters, and the more they talked, the more subjects for conversation arose, and it was the fourth day before the smith thought of his shop, or the laird of Assynt."'

So writes James Logan in his *Scottish Gael*; and his remarks are worth the attention of any student of Scotland who attends the Mod. The Highlander carries about with him a heritage of forgatherings. The more he drinks, like the laird and the smith, the more he talks and the more subjects for conversation arise!

The Saxon, whose inn is on the village green, is a very different drinker from the Highlander, who had to cross mountains to find congenial company. There always seems to me a certain grim resoluteness, a haste, a making the most of a rare situation, about Highlanders who are drinking, whether in London, Paris, or New York. It seems that they have met together with great difficulty and will soon part, perhaps for ever, each one on some difficult journey.

Every excuse is made to keep the gathering intact. The man who suggests going away is regarded as a kind of traitor to this moment of good fellowship. The occasion achieves a rather hectic importance because of the atmosphere of mutual bereavement by which it is surrounded. Even in London, with motor-cars hooting all round, Highlanders might be drinking in some little bothy with mountains separating them from their homes ; and the reluctance they exhibit to the thought of parting is exactly the same as the reluctance of men to leave a warm fireside for the fury of a winter gale.

James Logan, whose remarks on Highland drinking are most enlightening, says that in the old days the guest, on sitting down at his host's table, found himself faced by the *bach-lamhal*, or cup-bearer, who presented him with an enormous draught of ' uisge beatha ', or whisky, in the family cup. When he had drained this he was immediately presented with a horn containing a quart of ale which it was his duty also to drain.

In this surely one can recognize the ' chaser ' of ale so dear to many Scotsmen after a dram of spirits ?

But to study Highland drinking from every angle, a man must visit the Mod and the bars of the Mod. In the course of my life I have seen men of every nationality full of drink, but never have I seen men acquit themselves with the grace and good nature of Highlanders.

Late one night, when the hotel lounge contained only myself and two elderly ladies who were sitting in remote corners, the door swung open to admit two astonishing figures. They had been celebrating their success or failure with such thoroughness that they walked very obviously on air. One, an enormous elderly Falstaff of a man, had the chubby face and the pink plump knees of a baby. His companion was slight and sandier. They came in very slowly, with their arms round each other. The large man gazed about the room with half-shut eyes, while his companion's eyes were abnormally wide. Apparently finding us invisible, the large man said with disappointment :

' Naebody here.'

They sat down in silence and I began to feel apprehensive. What was going to happen ? In England they would have been swiftly and efficiently expelled in case they offended some-one. Here, however, they were just a ' wee bit fu' ' and no one seemed to care.

One of the elderly ladies rustled the pages of a magazine, and their eyes lit up. They wanted an audience ! Very quickly they saw the three of us but, paying no attention to me, they rose unsteadily and presented themselves to the two old ladies who looked up in a mildly astonished but still kindly manner. Then the fat man made a speech something like this :

'Did ye hear me singing the day ? Ye didn't ? O woman, ye missed a grand treat. I was great. I sang this song. . . .'

He stood, an immense swaying mammoth in a green plaid, leaning on a twisted stick and, moistening his lips with great deliberation, he began to sing something in Gaelic in a surprisingly small, high voice :

'Do ye ken that song ? It means . . .'

Here he placed an enormous hand over his heart :

'Your eyes are like the little stars that shine above Sgurr an Útha, and your hair is as soft and dark as the waters of Loch Beoraid. . . . They are so. Ay, ay.'

The elderly lady smiled graciously. It was many a year since a man had said such things to her :

'I'll sing it to ye again.'

And, locking out the whole world in his terrific sincerity, he began to sing his song again to the prim little old lady until he quite ceased to be ridiculous. He ended. A tragic look came into his enormous face. He bent down towards the lady and said, just like a little boy who is on the verge of tears :

'An' I lost ! '

'I'm so sorry,' said the little old Scotswoman with a smile.

'Are ye really sorry ? ' he asked earnestly. Then, overcome by the knowledge of her sympathy, he passed a huge hand over his eyes and, bending forward as gracefully as he could, shook hands with her. At this moment he recollected his companion. He pulled himself up and looked round the lounge. Catching sight of the second man, who was singing to the other old lady, he ceased to be the pathetic failure. His half-shut eyes opened with a merry blue gleam. He was an enormous naughty boy ! He forgot all about his old lady and, turning, gambolled across the room towards his friend.

At this moment the doors opened and in swarmed a crowd from some evening session of the Mod. The two men, upset perhaps by so much rapid movement, linked arms and, with masterly disagreement in step, walked out of the room.

Throughout their escapade, which they would no doubt deny in the morning, they had behaved with a grace of manner which they would not have shown in more sober moments. The whisky had uplifted them. It had not cast them down into the gutter. It had given them wings.

While few people drink themselves into this beatific condition at the Mod, a teetotal Mod would be unthinkable. No Highland gathering would be complete without a cheerful dram or two. And one observes how under the influence of this dram the normally silent, rather dour Highlander becomes a vivid and amusing personality. It lets loose all his tremendous repressions. If he is shy, he becomes companionable, if he has the inferiority complex he becomes assured, if he is silent he becomes vocal. And the finest thing about Highland drinking is that women, while they take no part in it, do not frown on it. The attitude of the women is, I think, the reason why a Highland gathering, no matter how much drink is flying round, never degenerates into unpleasantness.

I met a man whom I took to be a laird of some sort. He wore the kilt as if he had worn it all his life. I was astonished to learn that he was a London man and very distinguished in his profession.

'I'm a dull dog for the rest of the year,' he confessed. 'But I let myself go at the Mod. I put on the kilt. I come up here. I forget London. I meet old friends, fellows who went to school with me. I've got the Gaelic in my blood and I love it. But—meet me next week in London and, man, you'll not recognize me!'

'In other words, you've gone native.'

'That's exactly what it is!' he cried. 'I've gone back to the heather. Inside every Highlander—I don't care who he is—is a fellow that he's always standing on and suppressing, a wild man who likes to feel the wind on his bare knees, who likes the reek of peat in his nose and who loves to kick over the traces and take an extra dram.'

'If I put that in a book I shall get scores of indignant denials!'

'But put it in because—it's true . . . Slainte!'

§ 10

Towards evening the Mod becomes an enormous party. The solemn daily session is over. Choirs have sung their songs. Individuals have performed the solos or recitations which they have practised for the past year. The judges have sat in grave deliberation. And now the night lies ahead and—the *ceilidh*.

This word, which you must pronounce as ' caley ', is one of the most beautiful words in Gaelic. It means a gathering, and in order to understand its significance you must imagine that you live in a small lonely bothy on the western hills. Your next-door neighbour is four miles off on the other side of a mountain. All your friends are scattered in this way. The only social occasion is the *ceilidh*, or gathering round the peat fire. Here every man tells a story or sings a song. Here the poet of the clan can give his imagination full rein, here the story-teller can produce the tale that was told to him by his father, here the singer can sing his sweetest song. We in England have no event quite like the *ceilidh*. Social life has always been too easy for our gatherings to achieve the same romance and beauty. The *ceilidh* is the sharing of a common stock of folk memories, inspired by the tradition of the clan, and sanctified by the atmosphere of the home.

The Mod splits up after business hours into any number of *ceilidhs*. The astonished traveller entering an hotel finds one in progress in the public rooms. He sees a circle of men and women round the fire, others sitting on the floor, while some one plays a piano and one by one the various members rise and sing their songs. It is the friendliest of all occasions. Good nature and generosity ooze out of it, and one looks round at the circle of faces thinking that Highland folk are the most lovable in the whole world.

Such gatherings—the legacy of a race of mountaineers— take place also in Ireland, but the Irish Gael sauces his wit with a touch of malice that is quite foreign to the Highlander. The funniest things said in Ireland are always at the expense of some one's feelings and the wittiest hits are those made against personal peculiarities. The Highland *ceilidh* is inspired by a feeling of kindness and generosity, and a desire to please and to be pleased.

And what vitality the Gael possesses! A competitor at the Mod may go on from *ceilidh* to *ceilidh*, returning to bed at 4 or 5 a.m. Yet he will in some miraculous manner be up for breakfast and on the concert platform at 9 a.m.!

At last comes the day when the Mod is over!

What a sadness spreads itself over Fort William! It is as if a light has gone out. The quick Highland spirits sink. Song is no longer heard all day and all night. Men and women discuss the formidable business of getting home. Some have to travel by steamer to the Outer Hebrides; some have long journeys by road or rail to remote villages in the mountains. So the party breaks up.

Like children whose play is over, they drift off sadly in little groups, promising to meet again next year. For three or four days they have been members of a light-hearted family and now separation, the tragedy of the Gael, faces them. There is something magnificently extreme about the farewells, about the last drink, about the last hand-clasp:

' Well, Donald, we'll meet next year.'

' Ay, lad, next year.'

They say farewell in Gaelic and part.

Fort William, looking distinctly exhausted, resumes its normal expression.

CHAPTER SEVEN

§ 1

FEW travellers bore me more than those dull fellows
who explain in great detail the mere machinery of
their progress. I must therefore ask you to believe
that when the Mod was over I went east to Laggan in order
to walk across the Corrieyarrick, and that I sent on my car to
wait for me in Fort Augustus. (It's as well to explain this,
or some one is sure to ask me how I got a car over the
Corrieyarrick !)

It was one of those mornings that arrive suddenly in the
Highlands after a week of drizzle : a day of atonement,
a day that wipes out memories of rain, as freedom from it can
obliterate even the memory of neuralgia. The rowan berries
were red as blood in Glen Spean. The river, winding its
way over moss-grown stones and foaming over rocks, lay
smooth in shallow places like melted green glass. After Roy
Bridge I saw the sun falling upon wide moorlands where the
heather was dying and the fern was russet brown.

There were improbable blues and purples on the hills
that made me thank God I am not a painter, for there are
some things you cannot ask people to believe. For miles
the road ran on the edge of Loch Laggan and on the high
part of the road, half-way along the loch, I turned and saw
one of the grandest views in the Highlands : the mighty
giants of the Ben Nevis range shouldering one another as
close as a herd of steers. In the still morning there was
hardly a wave on Loch Laggan. Its edges were ruffled by
breaths of wind that fretted the water and passed away ;
and from the high moorlands small hill burns fell through
the heather to empty themselves into the loch. At the end

of the loch is a huge dam whose waters run through a rock tunnel fifteen miles long and fifteen feet in diameter, which is driven right through the massif of Ben Nevis to provide electric power for the aluminium works at Fort William.

As I went on towards Strathspey, I began to think of the book that I carried in my haversack. I bought it one day in the Charing Cross Road for, I think, six shillings; and I regard it as a great find. It is the report published in 1749 of the court martial on Johnny Cope. The full title is: 'The Report of the Proceedings and Opinion of the Board of General Officers on their Examination into the Conduct and Behaviour, and Proceedings of Lieutenant-General Sir John Cope, Knight of the Bath, Colonel Peregrine Lascelles and Brigadier-General Thomas Fowke, From the Time of the breaking out of the Rebellion in North-Britain in the Year 1745, till the Action at Preston Pans inclusive. Taken publickly in the Great Room at the Horse-Guards in the year 1746 with a Preface containing Reasons for this Publication, London. Printed for W. Webb, near St. Pauls. MDCCXLIX.'

'Of all the books', I thought, when I saw this lying before me in a second-hand shop, 'that I would like to read lying in the heather on the Corrieyarrick, this is the one!' I bought it, but, beyond the eager cursory glance which the book collector gives to one of his latest indiscretions, I had not read it or looked at it. I knew that it dealt with John Cope's failure to meet Prince Charlie on the Corrieyarrick and I put it aside for the day when I would explore the pass.

Cope's failure to command the Corrieyarrick and his futile recruiting march to Inverness, which opened the south to Charlie's army, was a mistake so unaccountable and so farcical that no wonder it was whispered in England that Johnny Cope was a Jacobite. Poor honest, dull John Cope! It is a fact, however, that this Hanoverian general's mistake did more to give the Jacobite Rebellion a sporting chance than all the English Jacobites put together.

A narrow track ended at Garva Bridge, where a shallow hill torrent came streaming down over boulders, and ahead lay a bleak stretch of bogland and heather. The old road was at once visible. It is about six feet wide and the great blocks of stone, which the English troops put down nearly two hundred years ago, are lying in peat water with grass growing between them. My back ached to think of the labour of making the road over the Corrieyarrick, through one of the most desolate hill passes in Scotland. The road mounts and twists, loses itself, finds itself, and runs like an Alpine road round the very edge of a precipice ; then it strikes off over the heather and goes striding up towards the sky over the great shoulder of Garbh Beinn.

A dead road always fills me with melancholy. If, as some one has said, civilization is transportation, then a dead road is symbolic of the end of all things. One looks at it and wonders what in all this world is safe from the nettle and the thistle. Yet the dead road over the Corrieyarrick is not pitiful in quite the same way that the Appian Way is pitiful, or as the Peddars' Way in Norfolk is pitiful, because it was never more than a military highway and the only ghosts likely to be met with on it would be red-coats plodding wearily to the tap of a drum. This is the road whose construction the late Neil Munro described in one of his greatest novels, *The New Road*. He makes one of his characters, a Highlander, say of it :

' The hearts of all of us are sometimes in the wilds. It's not so very long since we left them. But the end of all that sort of thing's at hand. The man who's going to put an end to it—to you and Lovat and to me—yes, yes, to me ! or the like of me, half fond of plot and strife and savagery, is Wade . . . Ye saw the Road ? That Road's the end of us ! The Romans didna manage it ; Edward didna manage it ; but there it is at last, through to our vitals and it's up wi' the ell-wand and down the sword . . .'

This dead road makes one realize two things : the terrible hardship of a military campaign in the Highlands and the tremendous work accomplished by Field-Marshal George Wade when he built those now mostly grass-grown tracks which are indicated by the words ' Gen. Wade's Road ' on the Ordnance Survey maps of Scotland. Every Highlander should know something of George Wade, because it was over his roads that the Macs have advanced from their hereditary fastnesses to premierships, banks, limited liability companies, engineering works, newspaper offices, and so on, all over the world ! Wade was 53 when, in 1724, he was appointed Commander-in-Chief of Scotland. The country was just settling down after the '17 Rebellion under Prince Charlie's father. Wade's first act was to make a survey of the Highlands and to draft a report to the government, setting out what he considered necessary for the civilizing of the clan territories. His report was exactly the kind of report that a general might have made in North America before the redskins were under control, or in Afghanistan to-day. Nothing could be done, he believed, without roads. He therefore formed a road-making regiment of five hundred red-coats named by him, in a facetious moment, his 'highwaymen'. These men received an extra 6d. a day for making the Wade roads. The following eloquent but feeble couplet memorizes their exertions :

> *Had you seen these roads before they were made*
> *You would lift up your hands and bless General Wade.*

Wade's road-making activities were, of course, resented by the Highland chiefs, some of whom, says Edward Burt, who was present at the time, regarded roads and bridges as ' effeminate ' !

' Those chiefs and other gentlemen ', says Burt, ' complain that thereby an easy passage is opened into their country for strangers, who in time, by their suggestions of liberty, will destroy or weaken that attachment of their vassals which it is so necessary for them to support and preserve. That their fastnesses being laid open, they are deprived of that security from invasion which they formerly enjoyed.

' That the bridges in particular will render the ordinary people effeminate and less fit to pass the waters in other places where there are none.

' The middling order say the roads are to them an inconvenience instead of being useful, as they have turned them out of their old ways ; for their horses being never shod, the gravel would soon whet away their hoofs, so as to render them unserviceable ; whereas the rocks and moor-stones, though together they make a rough way, yet considered separately, they are generally pretty smooth on the surface where they tread, and the heath is always easy to the feet. . . .

' The lowest class, who many of them at some times cannot compass a pair of shoes for themselves, allege that the gravel is intolerable for their naked feet ; and the complaint has extended to their thin brogues. It is true they do sometimes for these reasons go without the road, and ride or walk in very incommodious ways. But why do the black cattle do the same thing? Certainly for the ease of their feet.'

It is as a road-maker and not as a soldier that Wade is remembered by posterity, although, perhaps, the chance to become a soldier arrived too late in life. He was seventy years of age when, in 1744, he was sent out to command the British troops on the Continent, where he discovered himself faced by a French army under Marshal Saxe, who had assumed command when the half-hearted French invasion of England fell through after the destruction of the transports in the gale off Dunkirk. Old Wade was so hopelessly outmatched that he asked to be recalled. The poor old man then found himself in even deeper water, for he was made Commander-in-Chief of the home forces during Prince Charlie's rising in '45! One of Wade's last acts was to sit in judgement on John Cope. He died two years after the inquiry. No man was fitter to judge Cope's conduct with regard to the Corrieyarrick, for had not he built this road?

Wade is buried in Westminster Abbey beneath a flamboyant structure which the sculptor, Roubiliac, considered to be his best work. He used to go to the Abbey and shed tears in front of it, for the memorial was placed too high for its full beauty to be appreciated.

As I plodded on over Wade's road I began to regret bringing John Cope with me. He is a slender, battered quarto of 194 pages, but, while his weight was nothing, he began to stick in my back. This, I thought, is the just reward for whimsicality—that tiresome word with which publishers so frequently embarrass a man. It suggests to my mind some one sitting in a trance in a room full of first editions of *Peter Pan*. Yet here I was on the Corrieyarrick being really whimsical in the true and awful sense of the word! So I marched on, excusing myself by the true reflection that I had been far too busy to read Wade's inquiry in any other place.

As I went on the air grew colder, and the wind, that on even the finest day never seems absent from the hill-tops, came whistling through the heather. The first six miles of the Corrieyarrick are pretty stiff, but once on the summit, which seems to withdraw tantalizingly as you approach it, the pass is conquered.

So I lay down in the damp heather, 2,510 feet above the sea, and looked back on a desolate valley strewn with rocks. Stags were belling high up on the hill-sides. Grouse, alarmed by my intrusion, crowed and exploded from the peat hags and, skimming off to a lower level, performed in the flight of a few seconds what it had taken me a weary hour to achieve, for the old road twists like a serpent as it climbs.

I took out Johnny Cope and opened the brown old leaves. When Mr. Webb ' near St Pauls ' set the type that I was reading, the footsteps of the rebel clansmen had hardly faded from the heather and heated men, who thought Johnny Cope either a coward or a Jacobite, bandied the name Corrieyarrick in the coffee-houses of London. In an address ' to the Reader ' the editor, who does not sign his name, explains that he is giving the details of the inquiry to the world because he feels that General Cope has been badly slandered. He confesses that until he attended the Board of Inquiry he fully believed Cope to be guilty of bad judgement, if not of actual cowardice, but after listening to the evidence he is convinced that the general behaved like an officer and a gentleman.

' At Dalwhinny ', he writes, ' he (General Cope) received advice of the Rebels having possessed themselves of the Fastnesses of the Corriarrick, where they proposed to wait for him ; and that thereupon, after the most serious Delibera- tion, and maturely weighing the consequences of every other Measure, it was unanimously resolved in a Council of War to march towards Inverness. And that this last step may be viewed in its true Light, it is necessary to describe the road across the Mountain, whence it will appear how great the risk would have been of attempting the Passage.'

Then follows a description of the Corrieyarrick which, I like to think, may have been either written, or corrected, by General Wade who, of course, knew this road better than any man then living :

' The South Side of the Corriarrick ', continues the report, ' is of so very sharp an Ascent that the Road traverses the whole Breadth of the Hill seventeen times before it arrives at the Top. The Road in descending on the North Side is flank'd for a considerable Space by a Wood, and is crossed by a large Hollow, which is the Bed of a Torrent, and whose Banks are so extremely steep, that it is not passable but by a Bridge, which was possessed by the Rebels, and could have been broken down in a very short time, if they had found it necessary. From this description it is plain that a very small Force, who were Masters of this Hill, were capable of stopping or even defeating a considerable Army that should attempt to dislodge them. For, each Traverse, in ascending, is commanded by that above it ; so that even an unarmed Rabble, who were posted on the higher ground, might without exposing themselves, extremely harrass the Troops on their March. Whence the attempting to force seventeen traverses, every one of them capable of being thus defended, was an Undertaking which it would have been Madness to have engaged in, with a Number inferior to the Highlanders from their Knowledge of the Country, their natural Agility, and their Attachment to Ambushes and Skirmishes, would, in this Situation, have indulged their Genius, and would, doubtless, have proved most formidable Opponents. Besides, could it be supposed that by the Bravery of the Troops, or an uncommon Share of good Fortune, all these Passes had been cleared, and the Army had arrived on the top of the Corriarrick, yet, the Descent would have been still more hazardous, and, if the aforementioned Bridge was broken down, became absolutely impossible ; for then neither a Carriage, nor a Baggage Horse could have crossed the Hollow.'

And, looking up from the pages of this book, I saw that every word was true and, knowing what a terrified handful of raw recruits Cope commanded, I began to sympathize with him.

The first question put to Cope was :

' When had you the first Notice of the intended Rebellion, and what steps did you take on receiving such notice ? '

He replied :

' The first notice I had of it was on the second of July from the Lord President of the Court of Session (President Forbes) acquainting me that he had received a letter from a gentleman of some consideration in the Highlands letting him know that there was a report current in that country that the Pretender's son was to land there this summer in order to attempt an insurrection. This report, the gentleman says, he gives no credit to, as he was convinced that the Young Man would find no gentlemen of consequence to join him.'

Cope goes on to say that he wrote on the same day to

London giving the news, and the Marquis of Tweeddale wrote back ordering him to be on the alert.

The Board then asked what happened when definite news was received in Edinburgh (about August 9) that Prince Charlie had really landed. Cope handed them a letter which had been sent to London, in which he apologized for being unable to write with his own hand because he had been blooded that day! Poor Cope! The alarm was really up by this time. It was known from a letter sent by Mr. Campbell of Aird, the Duke of Argyll's steward in Mull, that the Prince had landed in Arisaig. Cope says that he was assembling his troops and was ready to march ' with the utmost expedition '. A note of fear began to creep into his dispatches to London. Rumours came in from the Western Isles that 1,000 French had landed. Cope, who had only 1,400 recruits who had never heard an angry shot, pointed out how weak his position was in the event of anything serious happening. It took eleven days for the army to march from Stirling :

' Orders were sent at my request,' said Cope, ' to the magistrates of Stirling and Perth by the Lord Advocate to set all the bakers at those places to work night and day, Sunday not excepted, to provide bread. On the 12th of August I ordered the said Commissary to contract with the bakers of Leith—those of Edinburgh not dealing in that commodity—to provide ten thousand weight of biscuit each week and to continue baking until further orders.'

Mr. Griffith, the Commissary of Stores, was then called to give evidence about the shortage of horses. He said that although the Sheriff Deputy had a whole day's notice to find horses they were one hundred short, with the result that great quantities of rations were left behind. The transport horses accordingly came straggling in at all hours :

' It was not a day's march to Dalwhinnie,' said Mr. Griffith, ' but I was obliged to wait till eleven or twelve o'clock at noon for the horses, and that, notwithstanding the guard set upon the horses, the countrymen carried them off in the night-time.'

These difficulties, he believed, caused Sir John to shorten his marches.

Sir John Cope was called again and questioned about the horse guards ;

' Officers' guards were always put upon the bread and

baggage horses,' he stated, ' and where enclosures were to be had the horses were put into them and proper sentries placed upon them. But, there being so few enclosures to be found throughout the whole march, the horses were obliged to be grazed in the wild open country which my whole army was not sufficient to guard.'

The impression one gets from this report of the badly managed army, struggling into the Highlands on short rations, is so vivid that I am astonished the many writers on the '45 have made so little use of it :

' What were your reasons for not attempting to force the passes of the Corrieyarrick, or not continuing at Dalwhinnie to observe the motions of the rebels, or not retreating to Stirling in preference to Inverness ? ' was the next question :

' At Dalwhinnie,' replied Sir John, ' I had intelligence that the rebels were then upwards of three thousand strong, at which time the whole force I had with me did not exceed fourteen hundred effective men—and that the rebels were determined to meet the King's army at the several passes above Snugborough, a place at the north side of the Corrie-yarrick over which lay the direct road to Fort Augustus, and from which mountain there is another lying north of it, while another party of them was to march through a glen on the west side of the mountain to attack our rear after we entered the hill.'

I looked everywhere on my map for the unlikely word Snugborough, but could find no trace of it.

' A body of men with swivel guns,' continued Cope, ' which I heard the rebels had with them, by breaking down a bridge which goes over a deep hollow might render it impracticable for regular troops more numerous than we were to force their way, I had likewise intelligence of the disposition they intended to make here, which was to post bodies of men at several different places so as to be able to bring most of their fire to bear upon our troops if they attempted to pass and to rake the road with their swivel guns.'

And whom, do you think, was Johnny Cope's informant ? No other than Captain Sweetenham, the captured English officer who had seen the Raising of the Standard in Glenfinnan and had been released with Prince Charlie's defiant message to Cope.

Sir John went on to explain his Council of War. His officers

were against crossing the Corrieyarrick and, with one exception, were for pushing on to Inverness instead of going
back to Stirling. Cope's excuse for what has always been
considered a first-class military blunder is extremely interesting :

'It was evident to me from my own knowledge of the
ground where the rebels were posted,' he said, 'that it was
utterly impracticable to force a passage to Fort Augustus
over the Corrieyarrick whilst the rebels lay there to oppose
us. To attack them in this strong ground with our small
body of regular troops unassisted with Highlanders, by whom
we expected to have been joined, was to expose the troops to
certain destruction. It's true, we had two companies of Lord
John Murray's Highland Regiment and a few of Lord Loudon's, but numbers of them deserted every night with their
arms, in so much that of one of the companies which was
complete when we begun our march only fifteen remained
when we marched into Inverness. . . . If the rebels intended to march south we knew that it was not in our power
to prevent them, for they had ways to march through the
mountains to the westward of the Corrieyarrick by roads
that were practicable for Highlanders though not for regular
troops with artillery and provisions, and that by the near
route which they might take and by their being able greatly
to out-march the King's troops they would get to Stirling
before us.'

So Sir John Cope considered it wiser to go on a kind of
recruiting march to Inverness and let the Jacobite army
march past him to the Lowlands ! He thought that at Inverness he would be joined by large numbers of Highlanders, and
he also had a rather foolish plan—inspired by Whitehall—of
employing such recruits to go and drive away the cattle of
Prince Charlie's clansmen 'and so distress their families and
thereby force them to return home'.

When he got to Inverness the only recruits were two hundred
Munroes, who stipulated the same rate of pay as that received
in 1719, and enlistment for only fourteen days because the
harvest was ripe !

Cope was so hard put to it for men that he agreed. While
he was in Inverness the Jacobite army was making its all-
conquering march to the south with hardly a man to oppose it.

And at this part of the narrative I literally gasped with

astonishment, for in the dreary-looking appendix to this old book I found what I believe to be an unknown hero of the '45—the only hero, in fact, in Cope's army. Has anybody ever heard of Sergeant Molloy? It was not an age when the gallantry of sergeants was generally recognized and I am therefore hoping that I am the first to spot him. When Cope marched north he left Molloy and twelve men in charge of a small fort, or redoubt, at Ruthven, whose ruins can still be traced, I think, on the banks of the Spey near Kingussie. They were guarding an ammunition dump and a quantity of meal which, owing to the shocking transport arrangements, Cope could not take with him. As every one apparently expected the clansmen to slaughter Molloy and his twelve men, the meal was flung down the well to prevent it from falling into the enemy's hands. It was not a pleasant position for Molloy who, in spite of any fighting Irish blood he possessed, must have regarded his command with the greatest possible gloom. However, tucked away in the appendix of documents, and not even numbered, is a letter which Molloy sent on to Cope at the request of Mrs. MacPherson, the 'barrack wife', outlining his adventures. It is the only amusing document I have ever read in connection with the '45 Rebellion and I give it in full:

RUTHVEN REDOUBT
30 August 1745

HONOURABLE GENERAL,

This goes to acquaint you that Yesterday there appeared in the little Town of Ruthven above 300 Men of the Enemy and sent Proposals to me to surrender this Redoubt upon condition that I should have liberty to carry off Bag and Baggage. My answer was that I was too old a Soldier to surrender a Garrison of such Strength without bloody Noses. They threatened hanging me and my Men for Refusal. I told them I would take my Chance.

This morning they attacked me about twelve o'clock, by my information with about 150 Men: They attacked Foregate and Sally-Port and attempted to set the Sally-Port on fire with some old barrels and other combustibles which took Blaze immediately; but the attempter lost his life by it. They drew off about half an hour after Three. About two hours after they sent for me, and two of their Chiefs wanted to talk with me. I admitted and spoke to them from the Parapet. They offered Conditions; I refused. They desired Liberty to carry off their dead men; I granted.

There are two Men since dead of their Wounds in the Town and three more they took with them, wounded I am informed. They went off Westward at about eight o'Clock this Morning. They did the like March Yesterday in the afternoon, but came back at Night-fall. They took all the Provisions the poor Inhabitants had in the Town; and Mrs. M'Pherson, the Barrack-wife, and a Merchant of the Town, who spoke to me this Moment, and who advised me to write to your Honour: and told me there were above 3000 men all lodged in the Corn fields West of the Town last Night, and their grand Camp is at Dalwhinny: They have Cluny M'Pherson with them Prisoner, as I have it by the same information.

I lost one Man shot through the Head by foolishly holding his Head too high over the Parapet, contrary to Orders, I prevented the Sally-Port taking Fire by pouring Water over the Parapet. I expect another visit this Night, I am informed, with their Pateraroes, but I shall give them the warmest Reception my weak Party can afford. I shall hold out as long as possible. I conclude, Honourable General, with great respect,

Your most obedient and humble Servant,

Molloy, *Serjeant*

Sir John Cope received this letter the next day at Inverness, and sent it with his dispatch to the Marquis of Tweeddale in London with this comment, which does him great credit:

' I have just now received the enclosed from the Serjeant, whom I recommend to be made an officer for his gallant Behaviour.'

I wonder if Molloy was made an officer? If so, I wonder what happened to him. His fight with twelve men against a hundred and fifty is the only brave deed in Cope's shameful campaign and this letter to his ' honourable general ' is, in my opinion, a little treasure in the voluminous literature on the '45.

The frightful debacle of Prestonpans is described in great detail in the proceedings of the Court of Inquiry, but there is nothing new in it. I seemed to be very near Prestonpans as I turned the brown leaves and read how the whole of Cope's army turned tail and fled as the Highlanders charged at sun-rise through the stubble fields.

'Why did they run away?' Sir John was asked.

'They were seized with a sudden Pannick,' he replied simply.

The Board's verdict was 'that the Misfortune on the Day of Action was owing to the shameful Behaviour of the Private Men, and not to any Misconduct or Misbehaviour of Sir John Cope, or any of the Officers under his Command'.

The only comment one can make on this is that some one was responsible for the slowness of the army from the start, for the appalling transport arrangements, for the lack of discipline that permitted borrowed naval gunners to be con-tinually drunk upon the march, for the fact that at the battle of Prestonpans they ran away before the action began, that a Lieutenant-Colonel was forced to fire the cannon with his own hand (until three invalid soldiers ran away with the powder flasks!), and for the fact that the artillery could not be moved because the horses had gone to the rear and could not be found. One cannot help feeling that even if Cope and his officers had behaved like heroes, Prestonpans was one of the most disgraceful muddles in our military history.

Still, thank goodness, we have Sergeant Molloy of the Ruthven Redoubt!

I put down the book and looked ahead over the sweeping moorland where the dead road turned and twisted, became lost, and was found again. While I had been reading a herd of deer had moved down from the slopes of a hill and were grazing confidently on each side of the narrow track. They were far off, brown dots like ponies, but I could see without glasses the stag feeding apart, lifting his fine head now and then, listening, ready at a moment's notice to gallop like a brown streak to safety. A cock grouse crowed. Then I saw a sight which never fails to startle me in the hills. A rain cloud many square miles in area was moving slowly up the Corrie-yarrick. It was the colour of a battleship. It was moving rapidly towards me, cutting off hill after hill as it came on. I could see the shadows that it threw moving over the bright moorland beneath it. And the air grew colder and a queer ominous stillness seemed to spread over the wild landscape as if in preparation for the approaching storm. In this stillness the crowing of a grouse seemed unnaturally loud, and the wind that now sprang up had a sinister whistle as it came up from the valley and went sighing over the top of the hill.

I got up in haste and made for the summit of the pass. The cloud came behind me like an ogre. From the top of the Corrieyarrick on a clear day you can, I believe, see the Moray Firth to the east and the Coolins in Skye to the west ; but I was sadly disappointed. The weather had changed since morning and it was raining far off to the west, while a grey mist hid the east. But ahead, looking, after the brown bleakness of the mountain pass, almost like a piece of Herefordshire, was Glen Tarff, leading to the greenness of Fort Augustus.

The road down is easy. The old road twists and turns and is visible all the way. Two mountain burns are still spanned by Wade's bridges. It seemed incredible that two hundred years of Highland weather had not swept away all trace of them.

Long before I reached the ford over the Tarff a thin rain fell. The dark cloud had caught up with me and I shivered to think of the Corrieyarrick lying behind me, dark and wet, with the old road winding through that solitude and half lost among heather and peat bog.

I was glad to reach Fort Augustus, where the monastery bells were, as usual, telling the time of day.

§ 2

There is a little row of shops along the side of the Caledonian Canal at Fort Augustus. They sell the wide assortment of improbable things which surely must attract the tourists who disembark there for a time while the steamers negotiate the locks, although, strangely enough, one never sees a tourist walking about with a set of stag's antlers or a sheep's fleece. Perhaps these articles, and also the tall shepherd's crooks, are posted secretly to their homes.

I went into one shop to buy a selection of those idiotic comic post-cards about Scotland and Highlanders which are seen at their worst in Oban. I had the idea of writing something about them, but was fortunate enough to lose them in a day or two. However, when I went inside the shop to pay for these cards the shopkeeper, who was engaged in some carpentry, put down a hammer and counted the cards, while I, weary from the Corrieyarrick, leaned gratefully against the object he was making. I withdrew hastily when I saw that it was a coffin. I with my comic post-cards had disturbed him in the act of nailing black cloth over it.

Fort Augustus seems to me to possess rather a foreign air. It might be in France. This, I suppose, is due to that unusual sound in Scotland, the monastery bell, and to the sight, frequently encountered in the lanes, of a monk from the old fort sold in 1867 by the Government to Lord Lovat, who presented it to the Benedictine Order in 1876. It used to belong to this Order before the Reformation.

The old graveyard in Fort Augustus, some way out of the town, is exactly like the scene in Maeterlinck's ' Blue Bird '. It is untidy, like most Scottish graveyards. The Scots erect massive monuments above the departed and then either die themselves or forget to have the grass cut. In the country places the burial-grounds achieve an atmosphere of almost unbearable pathos. The stones lean together, or sink horribly into the earth, the grass grows high and the weeds flourish, so that if you are ever depressed in Scotland there is generally near at hand a perfect setting for your darkest moments.

In England the village church softens the harshness of death. It at least is still alive and praying—if only once a week. But in Scottish graveyards there is no church, or just a few tumbled ruins among the trees.

While I was walking round this place, wondering about these dead Highlanders and their wives, I came across a tombstone erected to the memory of John Anderson, who died at Invergarry on May 4, 1832. He was eighty-four years of age. The stone also commemorated his daughter Catherine, who died in 1852, ' relict of the late James Grearson who was lost in the *Comet* off Gourack Point, October 21, 1825.'

' John Anderson ? '

I found myself remembering the verse that has gone round the world :

John Anderson, my jo, John,
When we were first acquent,
Your locks were like the raven,
Your bonnie brow was brent,
But now your brow is beld, John,
Your locks are like the snow,
But blessings on your frosty pow,
John Anderson, my jo !

BEN LAOGHAL

WEST DOOR, ST. ANDREWS CATHEDRAL

Could this be the grave of that John Anderson?

I could not believe it because the graves of men whose only claim to fame is the fact that Burns immortalized them are so well known and so well visited, that the grass is tramped down all round them. This stone was neglected and forgotten.

I went to the Benedictine monastery. The lean father who met me was no student of Burns. Another looked thoughtful; but no, he had never heard that John Anderson was buried in Fort Augustus. So we mounted to the splendid library and ransacked the Scottish shelves for some reference to Burns and John Anderson of Invergarry. There was not a line anywhere.

I came out of the monastery feeling rather foolish. Of course, better than any library, I must ask the first man in the street or the first labourer on the road! Every step Burns took in Scotland—even if he failed to leave his autograph on the window of the local bar—is preserved in the memory of the local people. And 'John Anderson, my jo', if he ever lived at Invergarry, would be a familiar name round any fireside in Fort Augustus.

An enormous Highlander was smoking a pipe by his garden gate.

'Yes, indeed,' he said, 'that is the John Anderson. He was a friend of Burns. He came from the south, aye, from Ayrshire. He was the man who made Burns' coffin. He made it many years before Burns died—yes, indeed, and at his own request. Come inside and sit down. . . .'

In a little living-room this enormous old man, who told me that he had been a road worker, spoke of the local legends which had been handed down from father to son in Fort Augustus. I discovered that the two most vivid stories were of Bonnie Prince Charlie's adventures when he came, ragged and in flight, up Glen Moriston, and of Burns' visit to the Highlands.

The story goes that John Anderson, who was a carpenter in Ayrshire, gave up his home in the south when his wife died. He went to live with his daughter Kate, who was married to the innkeeper at Invergarry. Here Burns visited his old friend when he made his tour of the Highlands.

'Ay, it is so,' said my old friend, 'and they liked Burns so well that do ye know what they did? They turned his

8

horse loose so that he could not leave the house! They found the beast wandering in the Glen of Garry. That was a grand compliment to a guest. . . .'

After leaving this old man I called on the registrar of births and deaths in Fort Augustus. I was shown an old book in which, a century ago, his predecessor kept a private record of events. An entry in the year 1832 states, under a record of John Anderson's burial, that 'he was the maker of Burns' coffin'.

Although the burial-place of John Anderson is not generally known, I am sure it must be familiar to some at least of those earnest students of the bard who know every detail of the poet's life and the lives of every Scotsman mentioned in his verse.

But it remains for some Burns society to give a little thought and care to the grave of the man who inspired one of Scotland's sweetest songs.

I lay in bed reading a book, which I had bought from one of the monks when I visited the abbey to inquire about John Anderson. It is written by one of the brothers at Fort Augustus and is printed on the little printing press which the monks have installed in a cellar of the building. *Glen Albyn* is the title of the book, and I wish the author had not been too modest to add his name, because I would like to compliment him on a delightful account of the tragedies and comedies of the Central Highlands. The monk, whoever he is, has a nice sense of humour. He gives the following as an instance of second sight :

'In the early decades of last century a certain Protestant landed proprietor, who in his youth had led a wild life, was smitten with remorse and became a most enterprising revivalist—a brand snatched from the burning—and having settled in this district, he used to preach up and down the country to those still sitting in the shadow of sin and death. His discourses were seasoned with many astonishing, if not altogether edifying, experiences of his own early life. One evening the worthy revivalist happened to pass the little country inn, and was attracted by an unwonted glare from the kitchen window. A few minutes later he was seen returning to the window with a friend, murmuring in deep, earnest tones : " The finest vision ever you saw ; three fairies from heaven in diaphanous drapery sporting themselves by the fire. Step quietly, man, lest you disturb them and they wing their way back to the skies." His friend peeped through a chink in the blinds, and to his horror recognized his own wife and two lady friends, who had been caught in a thunderstorm, drying their "shifts" at the fire. The apparition passed, but the nymphs did not fly back to heaven. Some say that the honest revivalist knew better, and was speaking with his tongue in his cheek.'

Here is a good story about Colonel Alan Cameron, who in 1793 raised the 79th Queen's Own Cameron Highlanders in the glen. On the strength of his own name he raised one thousand men in six months. They suffered so severely on the Continent that it was proposed to draft the survivors to four other regiments. But the Hanoverian prince who was his commander-in-chief had reckoned without Colonel Cameron :

'To draft the 79th is more than you or your Royal father dare do,' cried the colonel.

'The King, my father, will certainly send the regiment to the West Indies,' said the prince.

Then Colonel Cameron lost his Highland temper :

'You may tell the King your father from me that he may send us to hell if he likes, but *he daurna draft us.*'

And the Colonel had his own way ! The regiment preserved its identity and went on foreign service as the 79th.

A certain Highland woman was asked how many husbands she had had. She replied three. On being further questioned if they had been good to her, she said the first two were honest men and very careful of their family, for they both *died for the law*, i.e. were hanged for theft. 'But what of the last ? ' 'Oh, he was a fulthy peast ; he died at home like an old dog on a puckle o' strae.'

The monk of Fort Augustus gives one of the most appreciative accounts I have ever read of the historic clan battle between the Frasers and the Macdonalds which occurred south of Fort Augustus in 1544 on the narrow neck of land between Loch Oich and Loch Lochy :

'Early in the sixteenth century the Clanranald branch of the Macdonald clan discarded their legitimate chief Ranald, at the time little more than an infant, in favour of a hardy warrior and renowned leader, John of Moidart. Ranald's mother was a sister of Lord Lovat, so according to a common custom of the Highlands the child was sent to be brought up amongst his mother's people. For the time he was lost sight of and forgotten, but when John of Moidart was carried into captivity as a hostage by James V, Ranald, now grown up to man's estate, thought fit to reassert his claim to the chieftainship.

'He arrived at Castle Tirrim, the seat of the Clanranald chief, and was favourably received. At once orders were given for a mighty feast, according to the custom of the clan, which has ever been noted even amongst the Highlanders for open-handed hospitality.

'When Ranald passed through the castle court and saw the numbers of fat sheep and oxen that had been killed and were being prepared whole over great fires in the open, he asked what all this meant. He was told in reply that it was to hold high festival in honour of his return. Turning on his heel, in an evil moment the young man said : "What need of all this fuss ? Would not a few hens be amply sufficient to celebrate the event ? " The clansmen took this as a deadly insult, and thinking him a chicken-hearted fool —which in reality he was very far from being—nicknamed him the "hen chief" and chased him back with scorn to his mother's people. This was too much for Lovat's fiery temper, and he determined to reinstate his nephew in his ancestral home.

'Having enlisted the sympathy and aid of Huntly, the Frasers swept through the Great Glen as far as Inverlochy (now Fort William), but their foes retired before them, and, deeming the expedition hopeless, the combined force resolved to beat a retreat to their respective countries.

'Following the course of the Lochy they reached Gairlochy together. Here Huntly and his men determined to make their way home by the valley of the Spean, through which the railway runs to-day, and at the same time strongly urged Lovat to do likewise. But the foolhardy chief determined to take the shorter and more direct route through the Great Glen to Beauly. This gave his enemies the very chance they looked for.

'John of Moidart, who had recently escaped from prison, made a rapid march and reached the east end of Loch Lochy, where he was joined by some of the Camerons and by the Glengarries. Here in the lap of the hill, where Ben Tigh raises its sharp-pointed mass out of the lower elevation, lies a little lake called to this day "Lochan nan Diota," or

"Lochan nan Bata", that is the tarn of the repast or of the
sticks. On the borders of this loch the little force took their
food, consisting of a small quantity of oatmeal, which each
man carried tied up in the corner of his plaid, and which
they mixed with the water of the loch. Then each one drove
his stick into the soft peat moss, a common practice in the
Highlands before a battle, and which took the place of the
modern ticket number in our army. Every survivor on his
homeward march "lifted" his stick and the remainder gave
the numbers of the fallen.

'After this John's force arrayed themselves at the little
burn which we see furrowing the brae face opposite to us,
and which is still called the "burn of the gathering," and as
the Frasers neared the end of the loch, he swept down upon
them and began the fray.

'As we have said before, Loch Lochy has been raised
several feet, and the severest fighting of the day took place
where the water now forms a large pool at the back of the
sandbank covered with grass and scrub and which at that
time was dry land. It is worth noting that an ancient song
speaks of fire-arms having been used in this battle, which,
if true, was very early for the Highlands. But it was not
by firearms nor by bows and arrows, but blade to blade and
axe to axe that this battle was to be fought and won. On
the Fraser side three hundred of the flower of the clan were
engaged ; how many John of Moidart had cannot be clearly
ascertained, but certainly his force outnumbered his opponents.

'Lovat seeing that he had been trapped determined to
fight his way through ; so having delivered a brief, inspiriting
address to his men, fell on the foe, and a furious melee ensued.
It was at noon on an intensely hot day in the middle of July
that the fight began, and the combatants not merely threw
off their plaids but their short jackets and vests as well,
and fought in their shirts and kilts, hence the battle received
its name of " Blar nan Leine ", or " Battle of the Shirts ".

'Shortly after the commencement of the battle, the Master
of Lovat, who had purposely been left at home by his father,
appeared on the scene. At this time he had not long returned
from France, where he had just completed a most distinguished
course at the University of Paris, and seemed to have a
brilliant career in front of him. The day before the battle
he had been out hunting, and on his return his stepmother,

Lady Lovat, whose conduct is not above suspicion, taunted him with idling at home whilst his father and better men were fighting for the honour of the clan. Stung by the reproach, the Master gathered a dozen stalwart followers and set out post-haste to join his father. The sight of him filled Lovat with dismay, for all was now at stake, and when a few moments later the youth was cut down in the thickest of the fray the Frasers, filled with fury, fought like tigers, not for victory but for extermination. So closely were the ranks crushed together and so stubbornly did they hold their ground without either side shrinking or giving way, that, as an ancient chronicler says, " they were felled down on each side like trees in a wood till room was made by these breaches and at last all came to fight hand to fist ".

' In the course of the battle a stalwart Macdonald made a furious slash at a burly opponent, crying out : " Take that from the blacksmith of Clanranald." The Fraser deftly parried the stroke, and taking a tremendous blow with his Lochaber axe, cried out : " And take you that from Mac-Shimie's (Lovat's) blacksmith." After the fight they were both found lying side by side dreadfully mangled.

' As the day wore on and the field gradually thinned out, the combatants, too exhausted to ply their claymores, took to their dirks, and several by mutual consent fought their way to the lake's edge to gain coolness and refreshment from the water. Here numbers were found lying in couples in the shallow water clasped in a death embrace.

' So fierce was the struggle that those who were lying almost dead upon the ground would make a desperate effort to disable a passing opponent by hacking at a leg or an arm. Lovat himself, swinging his two-handed sword like Simon de Montfort at the battle of Lewes, cut a path before him wherever he went. At length, however, he fell covered with wounds, and at once a cry went up over the field : " Thuit a cruaidh chascar " (" the lusty slasher is fallen ") and in a short while all was over. The sun went down on a dismal scene of carnage. The Fraser chronicles tell us that only one gentleman of the clan, James of Foyers, who was carried off the field on the shoulders of his foster-brother, escaped alive. If this is true the extermination must have been complete, because this James died of his wounds a few days after. Certainly not more than half a dozen escaped to

Beauly to tell the tale. The story that, like the Kilkenny cats, the Macdonalds also fought until they were exterminated is manifestly a fabrication.

'Ranald Gallda, the hen chief, who was the primary cause of all this bloodshed, fought like a hero. His swordsmanship astonished even his foes, and one after another his enemies fell beneath his blade till he came face to face with a Strontian man known as the " son of little Red Donald ". This worthy seeing himself on the point of being cut down, cried out to Ranald to beware of the man behind him. Ranald wheeled round to meet this imaginary foe and at once the Strontian man ran him through with his sword. The dying man with a supreme effort dealt a tremendous back-handed blow which struck his assailant on the head and deeply gashed his skull, but did not kill him. Some days after his return home a doctor who was dressing the wound carelessly opened the gash anew. The " son of little Red Donald ", suspecting treachery, reached out for his dirk which was hanging by the bedside and plunged it into the doctor's heart, but the violent exertion proved too much for him and in a few moments he expired. There seems good reason to believe that his intolerable boasting, together with the ruse he made use of in his combat with Ranald Gallda, had rendered him so odious to the clansmen that they were anxious to do away with him, and the action of the doctor in reopening the wound may not have been altogether unintentional. The body was buried at Eilean Fhionnan, and until recently the skull with the mark of the sword-cut upon it was to be seen under the altar in the little ruined chapel.

'There is also a tradition that Ranald Gallda's sword was preserved by a family in Strontian for a long time, and they used to show a nick in the blade proving that not without good reason were the men of that district considered hard-headed rievers.'

The monkish comment, which is perfect in its dryness, is : 'The beauty of the old clan fights was that they had as a rule little or no effect upon the general history of the country. . . . The system had its advantages and afforded a simple solution of the problem known to modern social economy as that of the surplus population.'

I cannot resist just one more quotation from the book

of a man who obviously knows every inch of the country and every word of its tradition : it concerns the attempted assassination of 'Butcher' Cumberland. It appears that after Culloden, when the Duke of Cumberland's savage treatment of the defeated clans roused the horror and indignation of the Highlands, a noted sheep stealer named Corrie was persuaded to murder the Duke near a bridge on the outskirts of Fort Augustus.

'The road at that time took a slightly different course, and a person placed near the corner of the bridge commanded a long straight stretch before him. Here a little trench was dug and Corrie took up his position. A mighty charge of powder was poured into the blunderbuss, and then "she" was crammed almost to the muzzle with pieces of lead, rusty nails and pieces of scrap-iron, such as the heart of a poacher loves. Then the weapon was adjusted in the fork of a tree. Unfortunately for the success of his enterprise, Corrie, in his predatory expeditions, had never fallen in with regular troops. The steady tramp of the soldiers, the rattle of their accoutrements and the prancing steeds, took him by surprise, and when the Duke came clattering past on his charger the unwonted sight completely destroyed the poacher's nerve. He missed his aim and fled, hotly pursued by the soldiers.'

He went to a cave which is still pointed out near Fort Augustus, where, strange to say, he managed to escape discovery.

After Culloden the wild joy with which England greeted the downfall of the Jacobites was expressed with touching sincerity in the appearance, all over the country, of the Duke of Cumberland's head as a tavern sign. And how many people realize that gory Cumberland is perpetuated by the name of one of the prettiest garden flowers. A verse that became popular after Culloden went as follows :

> The pride of France is lilly white,
> The rose in June is Jacobite ;
> The prickly thistle of the Scot
> Is northern knighthood's badge and lot ;
> But since the Duke's victorious blows,
> The lilly, thistle and the rose
> All droop and fade, all die away,
> Sweet-William only rules the day—
> No plant with brighter lustre grows
> Except the laurel on his brows.

There is something exquisitely inappropriate in the sweetness of Duke William! The flower, originally named after William of Orange, was re-dedicated, and became a sign of Whiggery during the rejoicings which marked Cumberland's return from Culloden.

§ 3

If you wish to penetrate a country as wild and desolate as anything in the British Isles, take the road from Fort Augustus that branches right at Invergarry and leads you, in the course of forty miles or so, through Glen Garry into Glen Shiel.

Glen Garry is exquisite. Beyond the still, blue loch the river flows with Highland grace through a valley green with birch trees. Even an unobservant eye will notice the dark clumps of nettles that mark the ruins of old crofts in this sweet glen. They dot the flat lands near the river and they lie like old sores on the hills. These are the remains of houses burnt down or left to rot during that barbaric and disgraceful episode in the history of Scotland known as the ' Clearances '.

I doubt whether the agrarian history of any country in Europe can match the heartlessness of that time, when Highland families were burned out of their homes and shipped abroad to make way for sheep runs and deer forests. The Clearances were, of course, a result of the '45 Rebellion. As an old Highland chief said in the year 1788 : ' I have lived in woeful times. When I was young the only question asked concerning a man of rank was, How many men lived on his estate ? Then it was, How many black cattle it could keep ? but now it is, How many sheep will it carry ? '

The disarming of the clans after the defeat of Prince Charlie, the abolition of feudal power, the sweeping away of hereditary jurisdiction, spelt the death of the old Highland social system. In the old days, when every Highland chief was a little king with his own army, his wealth and pride were naturally in the number of men who would follow him to the cattle-lifting or the clan battle. When Lowland law came into the Highlands and such things were made illegal, the clansman, if not an actual burden on his chief, became a tenant, and the chief himself became a laird.

The old feudal splendour vanished and the Highlands joined in the modern rush for money. Clear out the men, women and the children and make way for sheep! That was the terrible cry which depopulated the Highlands. And the grandsons of those beloved chieftains who had led their clans to battle, and whose great names still haunt the Highlands, turned on the men of their own clans like tigers and saw them driven, broken and homeless, overseas. If you want to read the full horror of that time, get Alexander MacKenzie's *History of the Highland Clearances*. It makes bitter reading.

I can never pass through a glen such as Glen Garry without wondering what these clan territories were like before the system was broken up. Were they very squalid and poverty-stricken? Or did the piper really play by moonlight in shieling time? It seems terrible that whole counties which once supported a great population should now be desolate. From this lonely glen in 1745 no fewer than six hundred men followed their chief to Culloden. In 1777 Major John MacDonell of Lochgarry raised a fine regiment, the 76th, or MacDonald Highlanders, mainly from this glen, and in 1794 another regiment was mainly recruited from the men of Glen Garry. The ingratitude and harshness which met them on demobilization drove them from home. The Glen Garry men emigrated in a body to Canada, taking two Gaelic-speaking ministers with them, and there, far away from the land of their birth, they showed their love of that land by naming their settlement in Ontario, Glengarry.

To-day there is hardly a MacDonald to be encountered in this district which, less than a century and a half ago, held thousands of them. It is a wilderness given over to sheep and deer. But sometimes in the summer you will encounter a Canadian walking through the glen, standing for a moment as if puzzled, then going on as if he were following some carefully memorized direction. He will stop at one of the many clumps of dark nettles and stand among the moss-grown foundations of an old bothy. He has come home, called back by the strange pull of Highland blood. He should hate and loathe that glen, perhaps, but he does not do so. Although he may burn with indignation at the thought of the injustice and cruelty that drove his ancestors across the seas, he finds in Glen Garry something more powerful than sorrow or hate. He finds love. It is the land of his own folk.

§ 4

The road climbed towards Tomdoun. It grew bitterly cold. Down below the clouds moved sluggishly over the hillsides; sometimes they thinned, or the wind blew rifts in them, and I saw a gleam of water where the River Garry ran like a silver thread through the dark valley.

I might have been the last man left on earth. Whichever way I looked was a majestic wilderness with never a hint of life to soften it, never a sound but the belling of stags high on the misty slopes, no movement but the fall of hill burns, the slow procession of clouds, the heavy flight of an eagle.

I remembered the story of the last Glengarry, Colonel Alastair Ranaldson MacDonell, who died in 1828. It seems impossible that such a character could have existed in modern times. He was the last Highland chief to travel the country with a band of retainers, known as Glengarry's ' tail '. He seemed quite unconscious of a changed age and lived, dressed, and behaved as if he existed in the Highlands of the sixteenth century. Walter Scott knew him well; it was, in fact, Colonel MacDonell who gave Scott his famous deerhound, Maida.

' He seemed to have lived a century too late,' wrote Scott, ' and to exist in a state of complete law and order like a Glengarry of old, whose will was law to his sept.' Scott is supposed to have painted this unique character as ' Fergus MacIvor ' in *Waverley*.

The colonel always wore Highland dress and behaved like a great potentate. When George IV made his famous visit to Scotland, Glengarry marched south with great pomp and ceremony, accompanied by his ' tail '. George may have been slightly alarmed by the ' tail ' for we learn that each member of it was sworn in as a member of the King's bodyguard! During a ball at Fort William, Glengarry quarrelled fiercely with a grandson of Flora Macdonald, a young subaltern called Norman MacLeod. The outcome was a duel in which MacLeod was slain. Glengarry was charged with murder at Inverness, but was lucky enough to be acquitted.

There is a reference to him which has, I think, escaped all his commentators. I discovered it in a small, dry little book called *Two Excursions to the Ports of England, Scotland and*

Ireland, translated from the French of Charles Dupin, Captain in the Corps of Naval Engineers, London, 1819. M. Dupin, who seems to have regarded the Highlands in 1818 as savage territory, was at Fort Augustus when the Caledonian Canal was under construction, and on his way there he says :

'I crossed the vale, or glen, of Garry. I passed first in front of an indifferent house built near the ruins of an old castle, a remnant of the power of the MacDonells over the surrounding country. Over the door of the new mansion I saw suspended, as emblems of triumph, heads of deer and carcasses of wild birds : these were the trophies of the chieftain in the annual hunting matches in which he assembled the Highlanders of his clan, together with the visitors from the neighbouring clans, all clad in kilts and their thighs bare. These hunting matches last three days. At night they sleep in the forests, and at length they return to the castle to eat the produce of the chase and quaff their favourite whisky to an excess that not unfrequently terminates in savage broils.'

The Frenchman does not attempt to disguise the horror with which the survival of Colonel MacDonell in the modern world inspired him ! But he suffered a worse shock at Loch Oich, when he saw the Well of the Seven Heads with the inscription written by Glengarry. 'May my feeble voice make known this infamous monument from one end of Europe to the other ' wrote Charles Dupin !

Glengarry died in 1826 when attempting to escape from the wreck of a steamer on the coast near Fort William.

His funeral must have been the last of its kind in the Highlands. A howl of fury went up from his clansmen when it became known that a hearse was to be sent to take the old chief to his grave. They threatened to smash it if it should attempt to enter the glen. 'It is by the hands of his people and shoulder high ', they said, ' that he should be borne to the grave. Never would we see Mac-mhic-Alastair carried to Kilfinnan in a cart.'

And so it was. At sunrise on the funeral day parties of the clan came down from the hills, each section headed by the pipes. They lined up on the lawn of the castle. In front of the open door was planted a yellow standard, the clan banner, surmounted by a holly bush, the badge of Clan Donald. Four clansmen carried the coffin. Four others stood at the corners bearing flaming torches. Wax tapers

had been fixed to the stags' antlers which decorated the outside of the castle. The ' ceann-tigh ', the heads of the cadet
families, then took up the coffin, and, as they began to march
off Glengarry's piper, who had taken his post beside the
clan banner, blew up the march ' Cille-Chriost '. It was a
frightful day in the middle of January. A thunderstorm
was moving over the glen. As the coffin passed through the
gates a flash of lightning and a peal of thunder caused Glengarry's old blind bard, Allan Dall, to break out into a funeral
dirge, waving his bonnet in the air and crying, ' Ochon,
ochon, ochon,' in the storm.

When the funeral party reached the graveyard the stream
was swollen to the size of a mad torrent—there was no bridge
over it as there is to-day—and the Highlanders plunged in
with the coffin. It seemed for a moment, when they reached
the middle of the stream, that they would be swept away,
for the coffin lurched and remained stationary as the bearers
strove for a foothold. Then a loud voice was heard crying
on the opposite bank. It was the chief's eldest son, Angus,
giving the clan war cry—' Lamh dhearg bhuadhach Chlann
Dhomhuill ! ' And at the sound of it the bearers pressed
forward into the torrent and safely gained the bank.

So the last Glengarry was placed to rest near his famous
ancestor, ' Black John ' of Killiecrankie. The son who
succeeded to the title was only ten years of age. It was
soon discovered that Glengarry's attempt to carry the splendour of the sixteenth century into the bleak realities of the
nineteenth had left him with debts of £80,000. There was
nothing for it but to sell the estates. They were sold again
in 1840, and for a third time in 1860.

And to-day the traditions of this great clan are to be found
in Canada, where there are said to be something like 20,000
Macdonalds in Glengarry, Ontario. If I know anything of
Highland blood, these Canadian Macdonalds are weaned on
stories of the old glen, and I suppose many a child in
Ontario could give an historian points on legends of Glen
Garry.

I went on over the roof of the Highlands, mounting steadily,
until, at the crest, the road dipped down and I ran out of
the clouds and passed into the next valley—Glen Clunie.

Leaves were blood-red and plum-yellow in the woods.
Bracken was rusty-brown on the smooth hill slopes. In the
air was the bite of a cold autumn day, with its hint of winter.
So I went down, down, down into one of the loveliest glens
in Scotland—Glen Shiel.

This is the 'road to the isles'. This is the way Johnson
and Boswell came riding on a September day in 1773, and
it was here that the Highlanders clustered round them like
Red Indians as Boswell handed out bits of bread and twists
of tobacco, while the large doctor lined up the children and
gave them pennies. Boswell observed to Johnson that it
was much the same as being with a tribe of Indians :

'Yes, sir, but not so terrifying,' said the doctor.

I suppose these poor Macraes were the ancestors of the
men who became millionaires in Canada.

This road is haunted by a Spanish colonel. Spanish troops
landed in 1719, but were captured here by the bridge. The
skirmish made no mark on Jacobite history ; in fact, the
colonel's ghost is the only thing remembered about it, and he
is sometimes, I am told, met on the road. They believe in
ghosts, second sight, and corpse lights in these hills.

Every step through Glen Shiel is more lovely than the
first. It is one of those glens which unfold gradually. The
mountains on either side, seen from the winding road which
is at sea-level, appear tremendous, and you are continually
stopping to gaze back, wondering whether the view that lies
behind is grander than that in front. On my right the Shiel
River tumbled over its rocky bed. Half-way up the hill-slope
is a large black boulder under which, it is said, Prince Charlie,
cold, starving and ragged, spent a night when he was hiding
from the royal troops with a £30,000 reward on his head.

So I went on to the climax: the sudden view, at the head
of the glen, of Loch Duich. This is a salt-water loch that
thrusts itself inland between the mountains. Its shores are
gold with salt weed. I saw it with the sun on it. The sky
was blue. The loch was blue. The mountains were a
darker blue. Backward through the glen I saw a wild cluster
of mountains with the sun shadows over their deep corries,
desolate slanting uplands, deer forests, dark little valleys
which the sun never touches, steep precipices streaked with
thin white lines of falling water.

I was as far from civilization as it is possible to be in Great

Britain. The nearest market town was Inverness, and it was over fifty miles away.

Just before the sun set I mounted the great hill above Loch Duich, the road that runs up over the summit of Mam Rattachan to the little coast town of Glenelg.

I reached the summit. It is 1,116 feet above the sea, and of all the great views I know in Scotland this is the one I place for its grandeur, its magic beauty, its terrifying splendour, beside that of the Coolins in Skye. . . .

The sun was setting. Far below me the loch, edged with its rim of bright gold, reflected clouds that were edged with yellow and soft pink. I was so high that I looked out over the heads of the smaller mountains to the great brown monsters that lie round Ben Attow onward to Glenaffric. And southward I looked over Sgurr Mhic Bharraich to the mighty Saddle which lifts itself above the dark valleys and the lesser peaks.

Imagine something like the frontier of another world, something like the mountains of the Moon ; range after range fretting the sky with their varied lines, mountain piled on mountain like frozen thunder, peaks shooting up above smooth moorlands, broad monsters shouldering the sky. And you look over the heads of mountains across valleys where rivers rush and tumble, across terrible gorges where the trees hide from the wrath of the wind, across miles of bleak moorland until you come to some giant greater than the rest.

This view is finer than anything except the view from the top of Ben Nevis ; infinitely more Scottish than Skye ; a strange mixture of sweetness and strength. The view from Mam Rattachan is a scene a man could watch with the same reverence and love every day of his life.

As the light was drawn from the sky the mountains became grape-blue. Grey mists crept through the valleys ; dark mists were hung from gorge to gorge high up in the wildness of the hills. Above, the first star burned ; and the mountains settled into silence and the dark.

§ 5

I had not seen a human being for hours. Suddenly I saw one. He was lying on his back on a bank of wet heather beside the road. He was a big man with a reddish beard. He

wore a shaggy suit of plus fours and a deer-stalker cap with
a brown waterproof cover on it.   As he lay back he held up
his left arm, which grasped a stick, and he used the handle as
a rest for the telescope which he directed with his right hand
on the opposite mountain.

The enormous Highlander grunted, and, heaving himself out
of the heather, turned upon me a pair of exceedingly blue,
frank eyes and said, with something like a smile :

'Have ye ever seen a stag shot ? '

I said, 'Yes ; in Arran.'

'Well, ye'll see a stag shot in about half an hour,' said the
Highlander.   'They're just working round the corner of
yon hill. . . .'

And he handed the telescope to me.

It is difficult for a person unaccustomed to deer-stalking to
pick out with a telescope a brown stag on a brown hill.   I
wriggled and squirmed about in the heather, seeing almost
everything but the stag in a series of misty magnifications
about the size of a half-crown.

'He's lying down,' my large friend insisted.   'And he's
got his head up !   He's been lying down all morning !   Look
now under that dark patch by the corrie ! '

It was stupid and exasperating, but no stag could I see !
So my new friend, instead of stamping me to death beneath
his tremendous brogues or calling me a fool, as men would
have done in many parts of the Lowlands and practically all
over England, expended divine patience on me.

He tore up a great fistful of moss from the side of the
stream and, walking up to the bridge, he patted the moss
into a kind of tee ; then, resting the telescope on this, he
focused on the stag, warning me not to move the instrument by a hairsbreadth.   I looked through and—I saw the
stag !

He was lying in the heather high up on the mountain,
about three miles away.   He was a light brown stag. . . .

"Nineteen stone if he's a pound," put in my friend.

The stag was still as a rock, and his head was lifted high as he
looked down to the valley.   I could see the darker shape of
his antlers.   He was beautiful.   There was no way of warning
him !

Suddenly, in excitement and anxiety for him, I placed my
eye too near the telescope.   It moved upward an inch, and

showed me something else. Three men were creeping round the side of the mountain! They were heather colour; only their white faces and their slow movements gave them away. They were above the stag. They could not see him, but I could tell by their slow, sinister approach that they knew exactly where he was.

'I hope he gets away,' I said.

'Ye'd not say that,' he replied, 'if ye'd been stalking him since breakfast!'

I saw the stag, still as a rock with lifted head. The men were crawling on their stomachs. In a few moments they would creep up over a projecting ledge, and then . . .

Oh, the awful ignorance of that stag! I felt sure that his eyes were half shut, dozing. He had no idea that three men had been plotting his end since breakfast. He did not know that, while he sat at peace, death was creeping behind him through the heather. I stared at him fascinated. Had he a chance? Could he still cheat them?

'Do they see him yet?' asked the stalker calmly.

'Not yet!' I told him. 'No, not yet . . . wait a bit! I believe they do! One stalker is lying down! The man with the gun is behind a bit! Now they've stopped! The stag . . .'

'He's quite still . . . he doesn't know!'

The beautiful brown creature sat with his head lifted. Could there be a greater contrast than his absolute unconsciousness of approaching death and the expert, grim, determined approach of the stalkers?

How difficult to believe that his nerves were set on a hair trigger, that the faintest whiff of man blown back on him by a wind cast from a remote corrie would send him off like a brown streak of light! Slowly, painfully, the stalkers crawled forward—so slowly, wriggling like worms through the heather. But the stag did not know!

Suddenly—he moved! He disappeared, backward, it seemed, in the heather! There was a thin cloud of brown dust in his place! He was rolling like a horse! I smiled. How strange that he should have chosen that critical moment to roll!

Crack!

I heard the crisp sound of a rifle from the distant hill. Then I knew that I had seen him die two seconds before the sound of the shot that killed him came down from the mountain.

I found myself surprisingly angry. I believe at that moment I could have shot the man who had killed the stag. A sitting stag! It was not sentimentalism. I would have felt the same rage had I seen a man with a knife slashing a picture in the National Gallery. I hated like fury to see such a lovely thing turned into dead meat. I did not, perhaps, mind the death of the stag: I did mind the end of his beauty.

Then through the glass I saw a rush of three men to the scene of the assassination. They lifted his head by the antlers, and the poor thing flopped down into the heather; and only a second ago it had been so lovely and so proud! Then they brought out knives and set about the corpse.

As I went on my way a tall, bleak Englishman climbed out of the heather to the road. I knew him.

'Did you kill him instantly?'

'I did,' he said with a gentle smile. 'I would hate to wound a stag.'

Then came a pony and across its back was laid the lovely brown fellow from the hills, his antlers trailing, vermilion blood on his muzzle, and his Sheraton-thin legs stuck straight out. I felt his iron-hard muscles; he was still warm, just freezing into death.

'Nineteen stone . . . a grand stag!' said some one.

I wish I could have seen him as only a beast. Perhaps, had I stalked him all day, I could have killed him. I think not, but I don't know. I looked back at the mountain with the sickening feeling that something lovely had quite needlessly left the earth.

§ 6

Sir John is an old friend of mine, but at times I dislike him almost as much as he, at times, dislikes me. He is tall, thin, bleakly blue of eye, and has a complexion which is a network of tiny blood vessels. His face always looks chilblained, due, I think, to the frosty nature of his prejudices. He wears shrill tweed clothes reinforced at the shoulders with strips of leather.

He believes first of all in the divine right of kings, then in Eton and Oxford, then in the Carlton Club, then in the superiority of London under the Empire (promenade), and lastly in the Church of England. He is about sixty, but the fact that he has not given birth to an original thought since he was twenty has helped to make him appear younger. He is, therefore, happy and enviable. I like him because I think he is funny ; he dislikes me because he thinks I am funny.

' Look here,' said Sir John, ' I can't for the life of me make out why you should be one of these confounded sentimentalists who are ruining the country. Come out and have a shot at a stag ! '

' I won't have a shot at a stag because I used to be a marksman and I might hit him, but to prove that I'm not ruining the country I'll come out stalking with you and I'll swear not to shout, sing, wave my arms, throw stones, or in any way interfere with the assassination.'

' There you go—assassination ! Can't you see, my dear fellow. . . .'

' Perfectly. You think these stags belong to you, and— what is really in your favour—you like venison, therefore you shoot stags ; and I understand. I detest venison, and I like the look of stags when alive, so that for me to shoot a stag would be both untidy and criminal.'

Sir John then made that sound which writers interpret as ' Tcha ! '

If fox hunting holds all the thrills of cavalry warfare, deerstalking is the infantry equivalent.

It was while we were at breakfast that a scout arrived to say that the enemy had been sighted ' on the hill '. It is usual in the Highlands to employ this vague phrase ' on the hill ' to indicate square miles of mountains. (A stranger unaware of the map might think that there was only one hill north of the Caledonian Canal !)

Breakfast, therefore, broke up in some disorder and in a few minutes the room looked like a G.H.Q. surprised by a sudden enemy offensive.

The troops had paraded near the stables. We told off the advance guard—two earnest young ghillies armed with telescopes. Sir John and I then fell in to lead the main body, composed of an odd stalker or two carrying guns and leading two shaggy Highland ponies saddled ready for the dead bodies.

So we plodded on through a wood beside a stream, over a moor and up to ' the hill '. We reached an undulating heathery space and we saw before us brown hill after brown hill, a fretted skyline of peaks, and a valley with a foaming torrent dashing through it over rocks.

We flung ourselves in the heather, opened telescopes and, lying on our backs, examined the face of a hill which was perhaps four miles off.

' Bad day,' said Sir John, ' the wind's all wrong.'

' They may get away ? '

' They may ! I suppose you'd enjoy that ? '

' I shall smile ! '

' Well, we'll see if we can't do some shooting.'

' You bloodthirsty old brute ! '

Sir John turned to me a face purpled with passion, for this is the one remark you must never make to a deer-stalker. No deer-stalker regards himself as bloodthirsty so long as he rations himself to one death a day.

I saw a number of brown creatures grazing on the distant hill. They looked to me like ponies until I saw their hind-quarters. There were about thirty hinds. Some distance from them in lordly isolation was the stag, a fine fellow with an arched neck and a magnificent head.

It is now the time of year, explained one of the ghillies, when the stags roam the hills and round up the hinds. They wander about like sultans with their harems. Sometimes they meet another male, who at once challenges them. They fight. If the newcomer wins, the old sultan gallops off and leaves the victor in possession of the hinds, but sometimes their antlers become locked, and when the winter snows have melted you find on the hills the skeletons of two stags.

' What happens to the hinds when both stags are killed ? '

' They just go off and get rounded up by other stags.'

While I watched the distant hill I saw our stag rise up and exert his authority. A few hinds had strayed from the herd. He pranced up, lowered his head, and said very plainly : ' Now come along, you girls must stick together,' and having brought them back he retired to his place.

' He'll do. A big chap,' said Sir John.

We then set out, leaving the ponies and the ghillies behind.

There followed two hours of enjoyable but exhausting physical hardship. If you think deer-stalking is just spotting a stag and walking cautiously for a mile or two, and then shooting him, try it. In the first place, the deer-stalker has, like the fox hunter, to be able to anticipate the actions of his quarry. He must know with tolerable certainty what the stag will do in about three hundred unforeseen circumstances. Every set of antlers is the wireless aerial which communicates to a stag in some mysterious way the latest news bulletins from the surrounding hills.

It is not necessary for the deer-stalker to be seen to be believed. The stag is an acute bundle of nerves and instincts. He smells trouble more than a mile off. The clumsy stalker has no chance. Although the wind may be blowing from him, a small gust blown back to the stag from a ledge of rock and up he springs and off he goes. . . .

I felt the excitement of this stalk. There were moments when it was necessary to lie in brown streams of peaty water ; there were moments when it was necessary to remain prone in the heather with one's face pressed affectionately against the hob-nailed boots of the stalker in front ; there were moments when one hardly dared to breathe in case a loose stone became dislodged in a gully and, bounding down, started an avalanche which would ruin Sir John's day.

Then, weary, wet, starving, covered in mud and bleeding in places from scratches, we came after two hours' crawling, peeping, whispering, and lying about in streams, to the crest of a hill which would give us a shot at the stag. It was a steep climb through a miniature valley ; just a cleft in the hill which had become filled with stunted trees and brushwood.

Sir John was interesting. His blue eyes gleamed frostily. He had in some way retained his dignity while he lay in river-beds. In an incredibly wild flight of the imagination he reminded me of some high staff-officer engaged in a desperate enterprise in no-man's-land. Not a word was said. He and the stalkers understood one another perfectly by nods and looks and liftings of the eyebrows.

The moment came when he took his loaded rifle. It was an exciting moment. I must admit that he had earned his stag. I nearly wrote on an envelope, ' Over the top and the best of luck,' but his expression forbade any such flippancy. It was deathly quiet. The wind remained on our side. Sir John began to crawl onward and upward. We lay below watching him. Every movement was important.

He was but a short distance from the crest of the hill when it happened ! We saw with astonishment that something had come over the crest and was looking down at him. It was a sheep! For one awful instant the sheep and Sir John gazed into each other's eyes. Both seemed to say:

'You idiot, what are you doing there?'

Then the sheep's head disappeared, and Sir John topped the hill. He turned and waved to us. We scrambled up to him. The hillside was bare!

Not a hind! Not a stag! And no need to ask the reason why! That sheep, starting back suddenly, had given the alarm! The stag had bounded up crying:

'Come on, girls, here's Sir John!'

In one second they had streamed round the mountain-side. I admired Sir John; he had made no mistakes. I admired the stag; neither had he; and he had won.

'Well, well,' said Sir John as a stalker produced sandwiches, 'you see how it is.'

'You're a sportsman,' I said. 'I expected you to have a fit or shoot the sheep.'

'Don't be an ass,' he said. 'It's the stalking that matters. He got away. He deserved to get away. Better luck next time.'

§ 7

Fifteen miles of beauty lie between hills. They are called Glen Moriston. There is dark Loch Clunie, there are scraggy deer forests, then the glen seems suddenly to peal with laughter as the road dives into thick birch woods alive with rabbits. This glen is the scene of one of the most romantic adventures in the wanderings of Prince Charlie. It is the story of the Eight Men of Glen Moriston. . . .

It was July, 1746. Charles had been hiding since April 16 —the day the clans died for him in a sleet storm on Culloden Moor. He had put on petticoats in Skye and had passed rather clumsily as Flora Macdonald's Irish maid, he had concealed himself in woods and caves, he had been starving and wet through, and at last he had gained the mainland.

He was out of the frying-pan into the fire. The western Highlands were alive with wandering bands of Hanoverian troops. They sat round their camp fires at night and decided how they would spend the £30,000 reward when they caught Prince Charlie. All the time he was near them, hiding in caves and grottoes, so near, in fact, that one morning he awakened to discover that he had come in the dark to sleep within gunshot of a camp.

He came creeping through the heather of Glen Shiel with one companion. He bore no resemblance to the fine young prince who, a few months before, had gone in state to Holyrood with the Star and Cross of St. Andrew on his breast. He had a bonnet on his head and a wretched yellow wig. There was a knotted handkerchief round his neck. His coat was of dark, coarse cloth, he wore a frayed Stirling tartan waist-coat, a fairly good belted plaid, tartan hose, and brogues tied with thongs so worn that they hardly remained on his feet. His shirt, which had once been white, was, it is reported, the colour of saffron.

He had been forty-eight hours without meat when he came into Glen Moriston on July 24. He saw at a distance a little hut with smoke rising from the roof. He decided to go there and beg food. His companion, Glenaladale, pleaded with him not to enter the hut. Although the poorest of High-landers could not be bribed with £30,000 to give him up, who knew that the people in this hut might not be Govern-ment men?

'I had better be killed like a man than starved like a fool,' said Charles as he made for the hut.

He entered. Eight tough-looking men were at dinner upon a large piece of boiled meat. They were all noted thieves who had sought refuge in the hills. They were surprised when they saw the strange figure of Prince Charlie. One of them, who had served in the army, recognized him, but thinking it unsafe to tell his companions, said with great presence of mind:

'Ho, Dougal M'Cullony, I am glad to see you!'

The Prince knew then that he had been recognized. He thanked the man and cheerfully sat down to the boiled beef.

After dinner the Prince and the man who knew him held a council of war. The other seven men would have to be told! Although they were poor, and probably had not a shilling between them, they swore to protect him. It will stand to the eternal glory of the Gael that while Charles was in the heather and £30,000 was to be had for the asking, there was no Judas in all the Highlands.

The scene is now a cave called Corriedoe, which you can see about two and a half miles up the River Doe. Here the

Eight Men of Glen Moriston brought the Prince for greater safety. They made him a bed of ferns and heather-tops. They mounted guard at the head and the foot of the glen. They went out on cautious foraging parties and brought back food. On one occasion, anxious to procure some delicacy worthy of a prince, they ventured at great peril into Fort Augustus, where they bought for Prince Charlie a penny-worth of gingerbread.

About this time patrols were moving through the glens. Within a few miles of the Prince's cave an Edinburgh merchant called Roderick MacKenzie, who resembled the Prince in build, was challenged by troops and shot. Here again magnificent loyalty flamed up, for as he died he shouted :
' You have killed your Prince ! '

The soldiers cut off his head and took it to Fort Augustus to claim the £30,000. The Duke of Cumberland, believing that MacKenzie's head was that of Prince Charles, left for London with the conviction that his work was over and the rebellion crushed. The news that Prince Charlie had been shot spread over the Highlands, and the troops relaxed their watch ; which was useful to Charles and the eight men of Glen Moriston.

There is, to my mind, no finer picture of Charles than that of his stay with the Moriston men. It is a picture infinitely finer than that seen all over Scotland, which shows the Prince dressed heroically in fancy Highland dress covered with orders. When these loyal fellows heard that the Prince was considering the possibility of linking up with some neighbouring Highland gentlemen, they went to him and swore that he was safer with them. If they betrayed him, they said, they would have to leave the country because no one would speak to them, except to curse them, whereas, they pointed out, a sum of £30,000 would be a great temptation to a small country gentleman who could disappear Londonwards and spend it.

And the end of the story ? The men befriended Charles for weeks and led him stealthily to his friends. The Prince became more ragged. When he embraced Lochiel he was barefoot, he had grown a beard, he wore an old black coat, a kilt and a plaid. He held a gun in his hand and had a pistol and dirk in his belt. He said good-bye to the Eight Men of Glen Moriston and—here again what a subject for a painter !

In September a French privateer, armed with thirty-two carriage and twelve swivel guns, crept in under cover of the hills to a loch in Moidart. A boat put out to her and Prince Charles' adventures ended where they began.

And what of the Men of Glen Moriston? Many years later a man named Hugh Chisholm caused great interest in Edinburgh. He was one of the men. There was curiosity to hear his own story of the cave. He was a poor man and people treated him kindly and gave him money. But he would always shake hands with his left hand. He explained that when Prince Charlie said farewell he had shaken hands with him, and he had sworn never again to give to any man the hand he had given to his prince.

It may be interesting to give the names of the Eight Men of Glen Moriston : there were two Macdonalds, three Chisholms, a Macgregor, a Grant and a Macmillan.

Their names shine for ever in the history of Jacobite loyalty.

§ 8

I went in bright sunlight through the deepening beauty of Glen Moriston. What a perfect glen it is ! If you wish to see a sudden switch over from wild Highland to soft Highland scenery go through this glen. The deer forests end suddenly. You are in dark fir and birch woods, and the River Moriston tumbles over falls which put Killicrankie in the shade.

I have never seen so many rabbits elsewhere in Scotland. The woods are full of them. They dash across the road in suicidal clubs. Enormous families sit up and watch your approach and then go tumbling to cover with a bob of white tails.

Glen Moriston ends on the banks of Loch Ness. I took the Inverness road along the north bank of the loch and, as it was rather late, decided to stay the night in one of those small hotels designed for English trout-fishers.

The hotel stands beside a brown river which its guests are not allowed to fish. If I had a rod I could cast a fly from my bedroom window.

There is a big, bloated trout in a glass case in the hall. It was caught by Colonel Somebody in Eighteen Something, and looks like the origin of all fishing lies. In the smoke-room is a gigantic salmon lying like an airship above imitation green weed. Retired generals, and ex-governors before whose rage whole provinces have trembled, turn their backs on a picture of Queen Victoria and sigh at this massive and improbable fish with something like calf-love in their eyes.

There is always a chocolate coloured spaniel lying at the foot of the stairs. Stags protrude indignant heads from the walls and watch you with their round black eyes, as if accusing you of having shot them. In the hall is a big silver platter, the catafalque on which spotted trout lie in state every evening, for it is the custom in the fisherman's hotel to make public the best basket of the day.

It is the right thing to do, when you descend for dinner to review the trout and to mutter impetuously, as if carried away, ' By Jove, what a jolly nice . . .' for it is highly probable that the man who caught them is lurking about, as artists are supposed to hang round their pictures in the Royal Academy, drinking in public comment.

You must never make a disparaging remark when you pass the bier. You must never on any account say :

' Heavens, I got twice that number with a bent pin in Ireland ! '

For in days when the water is too high or not high enough, and the only thing that remains consistently high are the fishing rights, fishermen in Scotland work hard for their trout.

Now, all round this hotel are the Highlands of Scotland. The nearest shop is fifteen miles away. You look out of a front window and you see the river and hills, and you look out at the back and see more hills.

It is really a remarkable organization. It was established, thanks to the Waverley novels, when Queen Victoria took the Highlands to her heart, and it has been run on the same lines ever since. Its first guests were women with bustles and men with Dundreary whiskers, who suddenly discovered, thanks to Scott and Balmoral, that scenery hitherto considered barbarous was entrancing.

And this hotel, linked spiritually with Bloomsbury and certain homes in Streatham, is one of the last strongholds of the Victorian age. Where else would you find a painted drain-pipe for the storage of walking-sticks? Where else would you discover a spray of bullrushes painted in the left-hand corner of a mirror? Here, although I suppose a man might try a thousand shops for macassar hair oil, the anti-macassar is still in position. Here you may come suddenly, with a strange twinge of emotion, on a bamboo table and a box of stereoscopic views of Switzerland!

There is red plush, Spanish mahogany, a bookcase with Burke's *Peerage* side by side with a novel by Zola, and, of course, a complete set of Scott. From many a wall ' The Queen ' herself presides over these survivals of her day.

If you sit alone for any length of time in the drawing-room, it would not surprise you should a hansom cab arrive with a noise like a clap of thunder and drive straight through the hotel!

You go down to dinner. Can it be true? You are indeed back in the days of Victoria! You are surrounded by Victorians. Here is gathered together an assembly such as only the country towns and the country houses of England could produce. Those old men with drooping white moustaches and eyes like bloodhounds were evidently the young subalterns whom Kipling wrote about—Wee Willie Winkie and the rest of them.

Those ancient brittle women, who are distinguished by an enormous disapproval, belong, too, to a distant day. There is nothing pathetic about them. They know how to take care of themselves. They appear unaware of the death of the ruling classes.

There is a baronet with an exceedingly red nose and a bottle of port beside his plate ; there is every kind of retired Army officer, there is a prosperous clergyman with a thin, badly dressed daughter, whose spurious youthfulness and bright speculative eyes are positively thrilling in such an assembly.

So the stranger sits among them, knowing that he is on probation until it has been discovered whether he was at Eton or Sandhurst. He sits on the outside edge of the social ice slightly amused and hating them all heartily, wishing the baronet would get drunk and sing, as he probably would, ' Ta-ra-ra-boom-de-ay,' or hoping that, in some way impossible to imagine, humanity might come into the room.

Each table has its own social attitude. The baronet is on cordial speaking terms with a man at the next table :

'Any luck?'

'No.'

'Filthy weather.'

'Yes.'

The most exclusive table is one occupied by an ancient man in a check suit so loud that his coat seems to be trying to play a tune with his trousers. With him are three majestic women. He was probably once a Colonial Governor.

'George!' says one of the women in a piercing voice, 'go up and get my indigestion mixture! It's on the table by the bed. Not the pills. . . .'

And His Excellency rises and marches obediently from the room like the massed bands of the Brigade of Guards.

After dinner the stranger finds himself wandering about the drawing-room, but he is apparently invisible. It all helps the fantastic idea that he is a ghost lost among ghosts. No wonder other nations hate us, he thinks, as he watches little groups humming and hawing over their bridge cards.

In the manager's room, which is marked 'Private,' is the real holy of holies. Here certain privileged old men have fled from their wives. They sit and drink real whisky and tell extravagant stories about fish and stags. You can see them through a glass window. They form the most exclusive club in the Highlands. A man would have to visit the hotel for ten years, or catch a salmon bigger and even less likely than the mammoth in the smoke-room, before he would be given the freedom of the hotel.

So in despair the stranger drifts into the public bar, where a crowd of ghillies are discussing the deficiencies of the sportsmen: how the colonel hooked a fine 'fush' and behaved like an 'auld fule'; how the baronet lost a stag; and so on.

This is also bleak and unfriendly. The stranger is still a stranger. So up he goes to bed, where the rush of the river comes through the open windows. There is a picture by Marcus Stone on the wall. A pretty man in knee breeches is just going to propose to a girl who sits, with a 'do I hear angels?' expression, on a complicated and uncomfortable rustic garden seat.

There is a stamping down the passage. A door opens and shuts. There is an enormous bang as the baronet flings out his vast brogues. Then—just the rush of the river flowing by under the moon like liquid ebony.

It is difficult to know how it happens.

In the morning the stranger, having bathed in a bath of brown peat water, finds himself walking up and down before breakfast wondering if it will rain. He is joined by the baronet.

' Well, what about it ? Clouds a bit low, eh ? '

He is joined by the parson :

' The wind's high and it's blowing from the right quarter.'

He is joined, to his astonishment, by one of the Trojan women, immense in tweed and carrying a stick :

' Are you fishing to-day ? ' she smiles, sweetly.

There is a gusty blare as of trumpets, and the ancient viceroy comes out to look at the sky :

' Let's hope those clouds will blow over ! '

So the stranger says to himself : ' How delightful and unaffected these people are : how simple and charming and how sincere. What a pity I have to go away ! How could I have misjudged them as they brooded over their bridge ? How delightful of the baronet to ask me to shoot in Shropshire. . . . How delightful are the English when they decide that you are visible. . . .'

This tender regret lasts for a few miles and then the stranger remembers the stags' heads popping out from the walls, the incredible salmon swelling in the smoke-room, the red plush, the bullrushes on the mirror, and the massive silence of the English soviet when some unknown quantity comes in from the storm.

At least this is what I thought as I followed the Caledonian Canal into Inverness.

CHAPTER EIGHT

§ 1

I CAME to a mighty resolution in Inverness. I decided
to go north and see what John o' Groats is like. This
place has always exerted a fascination over me. It
suggests a wind-swept shore with perhaps one house standing
bleakly on the brink of waves. Unlike other territorial
extremities, it does not own an impersonal name : it carries
down to fame in a most provoking manner the name of John.

Early one morning I took the road that runs along the
south shore of Beauly Firth, so close to it that you can hear
the small waves lapping on the weed-covered stones. Never
has Beauly Firth looked more wonderful : blue water, white
gulls, yellow sea-weed, and in the distance hills the colour of
blue smoke.

At Lentran the road dived inland into flat green country
where the last sheaves of the year were being carted in a still,
mellow sunlight. Just before I crossed Beauly River I saw
the towers of Beaufort Castle rising above trees on the left.
The name of this castle is associated with one of the most
remarkable men in the history of Scotland—Simon, Lord
Lovat. It is extraordinary that, in the course of the present
craze for biography, no writer has tackled this perverse but
attractive old villain. I wish Mr. Compton MacKenzie, from
whom this district has no secrets, would lend his graceful and
vivid pen to this exciting theme. And old Lovat is exciting.
His life during the '45 was surrounded by all the essential
qualities of a modern thriller : plot, counter-plot, spies,
double-dealing and the rest of it.

The power of the caricaturist is sometimes terrible. When-

254

ever one thinks of Simon Fraser one recalls Hogarth's hideous portrait of him in old age, bloated, villainous, with satanic eyebrows and the mouth of a satyr, a portrait painted just before that time when, wracked with rheumatism and gout, the old man had to be helped up the steps of the scaffold.

I would like to see a portrait of him in his youth. He must have been a remarkably handsome adventurer. His ability put him in a class apart. He was, in his way, a genius. Certainly his ability for extricating himself from what, to other men, would have been hopeless situations, amounted to genius. He was thrice imprisoned for Jacobitism before he was sixteen. He saw the inside of prison in France. He was outlawed with a price on his head, and he was once condemned for treason in a court of law. Yet with the agility of an eel he slipped out of these situations. His personal charm must have been quite out of the ordinary and I cannot help feeling that, had he been capable of honesty and single-mindedness, he might have been the greatest man in Scotland since Montrose.

He was born about the year 1667. He took a degree at Aberdeen University in 1683. His study of the classics was such that he always had an apt Latin tag on the end of his tongue—even during his last moments on the scaffold. His intention on leaving Aberdeen was to study law, but an easier path to wealth and success presented itself. I should have explained that he was a landless young man, the cousin of Lord Lovat, and when he was invited to accompany his kinsman to London he saw a chance to ingratiate himself and persuade Lord Lovat to make a will in his favour ! On Simon's authority Lord Lovat was ' of contracted understanding ', so possibly the task was not so difficult as it might seem ! Young Simon returned to Scotland rubbing his wily hands, having secured a universal bequest that, should Lord Lovat die without a male heir, Thomas Fraser of Beaufort, Simon's father, should inherit the estates. The devil who looks after the affairs of people as clever and as charming as Simon Fraser decreed that Lord Lovat should die soon after making this ridiculous bequest.

Simon's father became Lord Lovat and Simon styled himself Master of Lovat. But it was not so easy as it sounds. The dead Lord Lovat had left an heir by a marriage contract in the person of his daughter, who, backed by powerful relatives, assumed the title of Baroness Lovat. Young Simon thought that the quickest way to settle the dispute would be to marry the lady. This he was unable to do, even at the point of the sword. Finding himself opposed, he lost the smile that never deserted him while things were going his way, and flew into an unbridled passion. He plotted a frightful outrage; if he could not get the girl he would marry her mother by force. He therefore seized Castle Dounie, in which the Dowager Lady Lovat was living, and in the middle of the night carried through an act which, without the record of the evidence in *State Trials*, it would be frankly difficult to credit:

' He and his said accomplices make the lady close prisoner in her chamber under his armed guard, and there come upon her with Mr. Robert Munro, minister of Abertarff, and three or four ruffians, in the night time, about two or three in the morning, and having dragged out her maids, Agnes M'Bryar and — Fraser, he proposes to the lady that she should marry him, and when she fell lamenting and crying, the great pipe was blown up to drown her cries, and the wicked villains ordered the minister to proceed. And though she protested with tears and cries, and also afforded all promises of anything else, and declared she would sacrifice her life sooner than consent to their proposal, nevertheless the said minister proceeds and declares them married persons, and Hugh Fraser of Kilmonavic and Hutcheon Oig, both of them thieves and murderers, are appointed for their waiting maids. And though she often swarved (fainted) and again cried most piteously, yet no relenting. But the bagpipe is blown up as formerly, and the aforesaid ruffians rent off her clothes, cutting her stays with their dirks, and so thrust her into her bed.'

I do not think the history of Scotland, which contains many a grim and dreadful episode, has a more frightful scene than the rape of Lady Lovat while the bagpipe screamed to drown her voice. But, unbelievable as this was, the sequel was still more extraordinary. Lady Lovat was removed to an island where she remained for a long time in a state of complete mental and physical prostration; but when she recovered she appears to have fallen in love with Simon! I absolutely refuse to fall into the temptation of any comment except this: that Lovat, as his subsequent career proves, must have possessed a personality that verged on wizardry.

He was outlawed for this deed, and he took to the hills with a

band of faithful ruffians. Every time they captured a member
of the enemy forces they administered this oath on their dirks :

'I renounce my claim in Jesus Christ and my hope of
heaven and devote myself to the devil and the torments of
hell, if ever I venture into the territories of Lord Lovat or
occasion him directly or indirectly the smallest mischief.'

The country became too hot for them. Simon's old father
was forced to fly. He went to the Isle of Skye, where he died
in Dunvegan Castle. Simon now became Lord Lovat. This
was in 1699. His cause looked hopeless. There was a death
sentence on his head and he was wandering the hills, living
on his wits. But what magnificent wits ! He understood the
subtle art of setting men against each other, of sowing trouble,
of saying the poisoned word with an innocent smile. He set
the rival dukes of Argyle and Atholl against each other to
such effect that Argyll interceded for him with William III.
William was abroad. Simon crossed the Channel. He took
his famous smile first to the exiled James at St. Germains,
where he professed loyalty ; he then fawned on William III
at the Loo and said exactly the same thing ! From James
he got the promise that, if ever he gained the throne, the per-
fidious and traitorous house of Atholl should be exterminated :
from William he got remission of all his many sins ! So
having won something from both sides, he returned home !
Such is personality !

He was one of those convincing men who have no convictions. His star was self-interest. Rarely has history presented a more perfect example of the shameless opportunist.
In 1703 he was again in France, spying on the Jacobites.
They detected his treachery and flung him into prison. He
made an exciting escape and returned to England on the
eve of the 1715 Rebellion. It is said that his was the idea of
assembling the clans on the Braes of Mar under the pretext of
a hunting-party. In true Lovat style he also got the credit
from the other side of playing a leading part in putting down
the Rebellion ! He certainly broke its back in the north by
his capture of Inverness. However, his action in double-
crossing his Jacobite friends and acting for the Hanoverians
founded his fortunes, as he intended they should. He received
his estates and also many honours. From that moment he
became a great man in Inverness-shire. At Castle Dounie,
the scene of his violent marriage, he kept a kind of rude court :

9

'His table', says Sir Walter Scott, 'was filled with Frasers, whom he called his cousins, and he took care that the fare with which they were regaled was adapted not to their supposed quality but to the actual importance of his guests.'

At the head table were claret and French cooking, lower down were beef and mutton, lower down still sheeps'-heads and ale. Provisions for an enormous crowd were brought in each day and were devoured before nightfall, so that any one arriving late could never get a thing to eat. He exercised the rule of a feudal lord, and often hung up his followers by the heels from trees on the estate.

Although he was surrounded by a certain barbaric splendour, he was an extremely cultivated man of the world. The most polished and affectionate letters were perpetually passing from Dounie Castle to the great ones of the earth. Lord Lovat became the greatest exporter of 'soft soap' in his day. He even wrote to Sir John Cope as 'My dearest general'! A brain that was capable of outwitting governments played with men and causes from the library of Dounie Castle.

As soon as Lovat found himself securely established, it pleased him to regard his forced marriage with the Dowager Lady Lovat as a youthful jest. He got rid of her and without the slightest difficulty married Margaret, daughter of Ludovic Grant of Grant. This occurred in 1717, when Lovat was fifty years of age. King George I was godfather to a son by this marriage!

But Lovat had not done with matrimony. His third marriage took place when he was an old man. It was a characteristic piece of work. He wanted an alliance with Argyll. He anticipated the modern broadcasting announcer by sending to Miss Primrose Campbell, daughter of John Campbell of Mamore, an S O S stating that she was to go at once to an address in Edinburgh where her mother lay dangerously ill. The girl went with all speed, to be confronted by Lovat, who informed her that she was in a notorious house of ill-fame and that he would blast her character unless she married him. She consented, stayed with him long enough to present him with a son, and then separated from him.

Prince Charlie's Rebellion of 1745 found this extraordinary character an old man of seventy-eight, gouty, rheumaticky, the most important potentate in the north of Scotland, and with a brain as keen as a knife and as cunning as a fox. Although his skill in intrigue had not weakened with age, his luck turned against him. He backed the wrong horse. Since 1737 he had been secretly the head of a Jacobite association of Highland chiefs which was plotting a restoration, while outwardly he professed to be a Hanoverian pillar in the north. The Government became in time suspicious and deprived him of his sheriffship. This roused his fury. He began openly to entertain spies and agents. The Battle of Prestonpans decided him. He believed that Prince Charles was winning. He made the fatal step of throwing off his mask.

Old, helpless, and unable to move without support, he waited the result of Culloden in the house of one of his clansmen at Gortuleg. Suddenly the vale was filled with flying horsemen. A lady who was present in this house as a small child has left an account of the scene. The confused multitude, she says, the sudden sight of so many flying men, seemed to her to be a vision of the fairies, and as she looked she superstitiously tried not to blink her eyes in case the vision faded. But, alas for Charles Edward, it was no vision! And Simon Lovat, the old fox, knew that it was one of the grimmest realities he had ever witnessed. But he did not despair. He was carried on a couch over hill and through glen for nearly seventy miles to the head of Loch Arkaig where, alone of all the Jacobite lords, he put forward a plan that, if carried through with resolution, might have saved the clans from complete destruction. He suggested the old and invincible expedient of taking to the hills with a standing army of 3,000 men, each clan supplying its quota and changing the force in rotation. Murray liked the idea and suggested that all should sign a pact; but the old fox would put nothing in writing!

Things were now desperate with Lovat. He had burned his boats and Cumberland was burning his castle. The crafty old man had some time before prepared for himself a secret hiding-place which he boasted 'would make a hundred good men defend it against all the soldiers that King George can have in Scotland'. This was on an island in Loch Morar. He accordingly placed his fat and gouty body in a litter and was carried by his devoted clansmen from Loch Arkaig to Loch Morar. The final hiding-place on the isle was a large hollow tree, and to this Lovat retreated one day when alarmed by some sailors from a man-o'-war, who had launched a boat on the loch. But he was discovered by a sailor who, peeping through a hole in the tree trunk, saw with astonishment a pair of elderly legs muffled in flannel. Lovat was dragged forth with his hoard of 6,000 guineas.

The old man was hoisted on a litter and taken to Fort William. The desire for life burned still in his ancient gout-ridden frame, and the cunning old schemer decided to have one last throw of the dice.

'I often carried your Royal Highness in my arms in the parks of Kensington and Hampton Court, to hold you up to your royal grandfather that he might embrace you, for he was very fond of you and the young princesses,' he wrote in typical Lovat vein to Cumberland. But even Lovat was mistaken in the belief that memories of childhood's days could move Duke William !

'Now, sir,' he continued, 'all that I have to say in my present circumstances is that your Royal Highness will extend your goodness towards me in a generous and compassionate manner in my present deplorable situation ; and if I have the honour to kiss your Royal Highness's hand I would easily demonstrate to you that I can do more service to the King and the Government than the destroying an hundred such old and very infirm men like me, passed seventy, without the least use of my hands, legs or knees, can be of advantage in any shape to the Government.'

What a revolting old ruffian he was ! Here, at the very end, and caught in the one definite act of his life, he offers to turn traitor to the lost cause. One can have no pity for him although one must respect the dignity, almost the contempt, with which he eventually met death.

He was sent to Fort Augustus in a horse litter ; from there he was sent to Edinburgh. He entered Newcastle in a coach and six. He moved by slow stages to London, the astonished country people watching his bloated body heaved out of the coach at his lodgings each night ; and as he tottered in on the arms of two dragoons, his sharp, malicious eyes moved over the crowd, still, even in his extremity, fixing themselves on any fresh young girl. In the White Hart at St. Albans he met an old acquaintance, who drew out paper and charcoal and made a sketch of him. Thus Hogarth got the portrait that sold in such numbers, so that the printers were forced to work night and day.

The old man conducted his trial with ironic dignity. He

made jokes at the expense of the judges who tried him. As his coach trundled off to the scaffold an old harridan pushed her face into it crying :

' You will have your head chopped off, you ugly old Scotch dog ! '

To which Lord Lovat, sinking back in his seat, replied :

' I verily believe I shall, you ugly old English bitch.'

A sea of curious faces surrounded the scaffold :

' Why,' he said, ' should there be such a bustle about taking off an old grey head that cannot get up three steps without two men to support it ? '

So great was the crush that the scaffold collapsed, and a gleam of the old malice lit Lovat's eye as he commented :

' The more mischief the better sport ! '

He felt the edge of the axe, examined his coffin, tipped the executioner, and then, with a line of Horace on his lips— *Dulce et decorum est pro patria mori*—he placed his head on the block, and the executioner struck one blow. So perished the last man to be beheaded in England.

In 1815 his descendants died out and the estates devolved on the Frasers of Strichen, from whom the present Lord Lovat is descended.

I lost sight of Beaufort Castle among its trees and, crossing Lovat Bridge, came to the pretty village of Beauly. The first man I met was the proverbial stranger, and the second told me that when old Lord Lovat was being carried away in his litter after the Battle of Culloden he saw the flames rising from Beaufort Castle, which had been fired by Cumberland's men. If this is not possible—and I cannot say—it must be a legend. And what stories, I wonder, of that remarkable character linger on in the Fraser country and will probably never see print.

§ 2

From Inverness to John o' Groats is about 153 miles. The road, nearly all the way, lies along the coast. Geographically, the coast-line is a replica of the Scottish coast from Dunbar up to Peterhead. You must replace the deep indentations of the Firths of Forth and Tay by the Firths of Moray and

Dornoch, and the long straight coast-line from Dundee to Peterhead is reproduced in a similar coast-line from Bonar Bridge to John o' Groats.

There, however, the resemblance ends. In the north, instead of the fertile lowland seaboard of Fife, Angus, Kincardine and Aberdeenshire, you have the brown moorlands and the mighty hills of Ross and Sutherland rising almost from the very brink of the sea. There is nothing inland except mile after mile of desolate deer forest, cut to the seaward by beautiful little glens and by several exquisite rivers, such as the Fleet, the Brora, and the Ullie, which come tumbling from the remote, high moorlands to empty themselves into the sea.

These three most northerly counties—Ross and Cromarty, Caithness, and Sutherland—are the least known in all Scotland. If you look at a railway map you will see that, with the exception of one line running along the east coast from Inverness to Wick and Thurso, these enormous counties are without the railway. The total area of Ross and Cromarty is 3,260 square miles, the total area of Caithness is 701 square miles, and that of Sutherland, 2,028 square miles. So here in the extreme north of Scotland is an area of nearly 6,000 miles which is right off the main line of communication. If any part of Scotland can in these days be called 'unknown', when one of the most efficient systems of motor coaches explores the Highlands, I think these three northern counties deserve the name.

A straight road through low, green country runs from Beauly to the Muir of Ord and a mile or two farther on, standing some distance off to the left, is Brahan Castle, the last seat of the MacKenzies of Seaforth. Every one in the Highlands knows the story of the Doom of the House of Seaforth and the Curse of the Brahan Seer ; and I looked towards this house with more than usual interest.

Second sight, which puzzled Dr. Johnson and has puzzled nearly every one who has seriously inquired into it, is, as I found in Glen Shiel, still respected in the Highlands. The Brahan Seer was the most famous magician of his day and his prophesies are still talked of round every fireside in the Highlands and the Outer Isles. Kenneth MacKenzie, or

Coinneach Odhar, to give him his Gaelic name, was born in the early seventeenth century in the Island of Lewis. He seems to have been a crystal gazer, and in the course of time his visions were feared and respected throughout Gaeldom. His most famous prophesy, and the one that brought him to his death, concerned the Seaforth family.

The story goes that during the reign of Charles II the third Earl of Seaforth had occasion to go to Paris. He rather unkindly left Lady Seaforth at home in Brahan Castle. When he had been absent for several months without sending word to her she became anxious and, calling in the Brahan Seer, asked him for some information about her absent lord. On this occasion the tact of the famous prophet seems entirely to have abandoned him for, on gazing intently into his divination stone, or crystal, he gave a loud laugh and told her that Lord Seaforth was not only well but merry. The word ' merry ' used in conjunction with Paris should have told Lady Seaforth quite a lot but, with feminine persistence, she badgered the wretched Coinneach to tell her more. He, no matter how much he knew of the future, seems to have known absolutely nothing about women, because he replied : ' Ask no questions. Be assured that your lord is well and merry.' This, of course, was asking for trouble on a large and undignified scale.

Lady Seaforth questioned the seer so persistently that he, with lamentable honesty, described the absent Seaforth in words which left nothing to the imagination. He saw his lord seated richly dressed in a gilded room, and upon his knee sat a lady of remarkable beauty.

It might have been thought that no knowledge of second sight would have been necessary to forecast the immediate future. Lady Seaforth turned with fury on the Brahan Seer and called him a liar and a traducer. She told him that he had defamed a mighty lord in the midst of his vassals and sullied his name in the hall of his ancestors. He must pay for his lie with his life.

The poor prophet was led out to execution, but before he died he uttered the famous Doom on the House of Seaforth. He pronounced these prophecies : that the Seaforth family would die out in sorrow. The last chief would be deaf and dumb. He would be the father of four sons, all of whom would predecease him, and that after his death no MacKenzie would rule in Brahan. After the death of this chief the estates would be inherited by a ' white-hooded lassie from the East '. He gave as a sign that men might recognize the time of his prophesy that four great neighbouring Highland lords would suffer from the following infirmities : one would be buck-toothed, another hare-lipped, a third half-witted and a fourth a stammerer.

Now we come to modern times. The Baron Seaforth and MacKenzie, who inherited the estates in 1783, was a distinguished soldier. He had one suspicious peculiarity. He was stone deaf.

There is a strange story about this deafness. When a child his hearing was normal until he suffered from measles at school. About fifteen boys suffering from this complaint were placed together in one dormitory. The nurse in attendance was alarmed one evening by hearing one of the boys cry out. It was Lord Seaforth. He told her that he had seen a hideous old woman enter the dormitory with a bag round her neck. She had paused at the bed near the door and, after gazing closely at the boy in it, had passed to the next bed. She looked at this boy and then, creeping stealthily to the head of his bed, had taken from the bag round her neck a peg and a mallet. She had placed the peg on the boy's forehead and driven it into his head. Seaforth said that he heard the crunch of the bones although the boy never moved. The old woman moved on down the line of beds, passing over some boys and driving pegs into the heads of others. When she came to Seaforth's bed he said that he tried to cry out but could not utter a sound and, to his immense relief, the old woman passed him by. She gave a last look round the dormitory and slunk out without a sound. As soon as she had gone Seaforth found himself able to scream.

The nurse told the doctor of the child's delirium, and he made Seaforth repeat it and wrote down the dream word for word. The doctor discovered to his horror and astonishment that every boy named by Seaforth as having the peg driven into his head died from fever. Seaforth himself recovered, but remained stone deaf for the rest of his life.

His deafness was not seriously alarming to his clansmen, however, because the prophesy of the Brahan Seer concerned a deaf and dumb Seaforth. By his marriage Lord Seaforth had four sons. Each one of them died before their father. On the death of the fourth son Lord Seaforth became dumb with grief and is said never to have spoken again.

It was at this time that the various physical peculiarities cited by the Brahan Seer were noted in the persons of four neighbouring chiefs. These men were Gairloch, Chisholm, Grant, and Raasay. Lord Seaforth died at Brahan Castle on 11 January, 1815, the last of his race. And the prophesy of the ' hooded lassie from the East ' was rapidly fulfilled. The estates went by act of entail to Seaforth's eldest daughter, who had lived abroad and had recently become the widow of Admiral Sir Samuel Hood. So she came from the East Indies to Brahan Castle to enjoy her melancholy inheritance hooded in two senses ; by name and in the coif of a widow.

That is the story of the Doom of Seaforth and you can, if you like, try to convince the Highlands that it was all coincidence.

§ 3

I was now in the county of Ross and Cromarty—the only double-barrelled county in the British Isles. The boundary-line is somewhere just north of Beauly. The double name of this county is due to the amalgamation of two sheriffdoms. In the old days Cromarty included a small hereditary sheriff-dom near the town of the name and also eight or ten detached portions of north Ross-shire. In 1891 the Boundary Commissioners straightened out this inconvenient legacy from the past and formed one county, including in it—which strikes one as rather strange—the distant Isle of Lewis in the Outer Hebrides. It seems rather odd that the county town of Lewis should be Dingwall, several hours' journey by boat and rail from its dependent island !

In the ancient town of Dingwall I saw a strange war memorial, the most interesting I have come across in all my travels. It stands in the station square and is in the form of an intricate rustic cross. It was originally erected in the village of Fontaine Notre Dame in France by the pioneers of the 4th Battalion Seaforth Highlanders, in honour of comrades who fell in the Battle of Cambrai.

For six years this cross stood on French soil, bearing an

inscription in French which the villagers placed on it. This reads as follows :

Mort Pour La Patrie
4 eme Bataillon
Les Seaforth Highlanders
Honneur aux Hommes
Mobilisés dans cet village
Pour La
Bataille de Cambrai
1917.

In the year 1924 the Reunion Club of the battalion decided to bring home the cross and set it up on Scottish soil. So it stands in Dingwall to-day, the very cross, with the exception of a few minor restorations, which the men themselves made in France and erected ' in memory of their beloved dead.'

England, Scotland and Wales are scattered thickly with war memorials, most of them the uninspired work of committees and many the loving labour of individuals, but not one of them is half so touching as this : the only war memorial in Great Britain made by soldiers in the sharpness of their own grief, a rough cross set up in a foreign land for none to see but the peasants who would pass by and perhaps tell their children how the Highlanders marched out to die at Cambrai.

It is good to see this cross in the heart of the Seaforth country, and I am sure that Dingwall, whose pride for it no man need emphasize, has taken every care to preserve its fragility in the years to come.

The road ran beside Cromarty Firth, where a few slate-grey destroyers lay at anchor. It ran on to Alness and to Tain, whose name is a corruption of the Norse word Thing—a place of assembly. Dingwall, by the way, is also a Norse word —Thingvalla, the field of the assembly. This part of Scotland bears many a trace of the Norse settlement and, as one goes north, the Gaelic place-names become less frequent and such places as Dibidale, Amat, Langwell, Cadboll, and Culbo, preserve in them a memory of the Viking pirates who ages ago drove their long boats into the creeks and river-mouths of these counties. But I notice that the Gael has managed to retain the hill-tops. In Ross, at any rate, there are more Bens than Sgurrs.

At Bonar Bridge I said good-bye to Ross and Cromarty and

entered Sutherland. The road runs for some time on the very edge of Dornoch Firth, then it goes inland and comes out along the coast again. If you ever take this road look out for a little place with a ruined mill called Spinningdale, and about half a mile from it lie in the bracken beside the road and look south over Dornoch Firth. I have seen many a view in Scotland of blue sea water and hills, and this one I place among the very finest. You look back over the road you have travelled—for the northern road performs a hairpin bend and runs along the north side of the firth—and to the south lies the panorama of the Ross-shire hills. It may have been some trick of the light, but I thought that never had I seen such blue water in Scotland as the water of Dornoch Firth. Hills covered with fern sloped down to the firth and behind rose thick woods of birch and fir. Across the water the opposite hills were spread with all the browns and deep blues of autumn, and behind them lay wilder, more fearful hills, the trackless wilderness round Ben Wyvis : a barren desolation given over to deer, where a man might wander for a week and never meet a living soul.

I looked over the deep blue water, where the darker blue currents were like sunk purple, and I thought how surely various parts of Scotland evoke the spirits of her people : Scott on the Borders, Burns on the south-west coast, Claverhouse in Galloway, Prince Charles in the west, and Mary in Edinburgh. Each one has a part of Scotland which is singularly his own, and their names pin down the map as surely as those little flags with which tacticians once marked the progress of battles. Here, in this bleak land of deer forest and lonely river, of long twilight and dark sea water, I remembered a man, the most perfect knight in the long and splendid history of Scotland, a man who has no district of his own because he was always here, there and everywhere—the Great Montrose. This was the wild country that sealed his fate and brought him to the earth ; and that is why I remembered him as I looked at Dornoch Firth as it runs up to the Kyle of Sutherland and the moorland round Corbisdale.

If one could put back the clock and stay the hand of Fate, preserving for a few years one life in the history of Scotland, which life would you preserve ? I would have saved Montrose. I would have come to his rescue when he wandered lost in this awful wilderness of moors, and I would have spared him from the clutches of the Highland Judas—the Laird of Assynt—the only Gael in history who betrayed a hero for gold ; and so Montrose in a few years would have seen all that he fought for and believed in come true when a Stuart came into his own. But Charles II as a king might have been Montrose's disillusion. If so, it would have been very interesting. In the harmless game, which any one can play, of trying to imagine what *might* have happened, the Great Montrose at the court of the Merry Monarch is a provoking problem.

No matter whether it seems at times that the war of principle, in which Montrose staked and lost everything, was a fight between the Covenanters led by Argyll on the one hand and the countless hereditary enemies of Clan Campbell on the other, the fact remains that Montrose saw his duty clearly and in his manner of fighting for it stands head and shoulders above every man of action in the history of his country.

'It is a figure that must always haunt those who travel the rough roads of Scottish history,' writes Colonel John Buchan in his magnificent biography, *Montrose*. 'We see him in the brave clothes which still dazzle us in his portraits, the long, north-country face, the broad brow, the inscrutable grey eyes. He is thinking, wondering, brooding on the needs of his land, while others are preying on them. Then he reaches his conclusions, and, with something between the certainty of the thinker and the enthusiasm of the boy, he sets out on his desperate errand. We see him in battle, a flush on his cheek, a youthful ardour in his eye, but his mouth set like iron. We see him among his friends, conquering all hearts with his wit and grace. We see him in triumph and in failure, careless of self, his course set unfalteringly towards his dreams, carrying, in Keats' words, "an awful warmth about his heart like a load of immortality". He is always very human, very much the man, for Alasdair and his kerns would never have followed the ordinary dreamer. And then, when the last blow has been struck, he has neither fears nor reproaches. Clearly and reasonably he states his defence, and when it is flouted and he is condemned to a shameful death, he takes it meekly, knowing something of the fallibility of mankind. The Edinburgh mob is awed into a hush by his appearance ; his enemies declared that it was his fine clothes and noble looks ; more truly we may read it as that inward vision which is the beatitude of the pure in heart.'

Montrose must always be the darling hero of every young man and every young woman, for in his life the purity and the idealism of youth are exalted and for ever glorified.

When this young man—he was only thirty-eight when he died—who had been up to the neck in the Covenanting fight, believed that the security of the State and everything in which he believed were threatened by the Kirk's war against the King, he turned against his former associates and became their most ferocious enemy. He became the most splendid champion the Stuarts have ever known ; and their cause has enlisted many brave and gallant men. The ' Year of Montrose ', 1644–5, that amazing twelve months when he galloped from victory to victory, was one of the most extraordinary years in Scottish history. For twelve months this young man performed an act that seems impossible : he united the clans of the Central Highlands and he exhibited, in the words of Sir John Fortescue, ' perhaps the most brilliant natural military genius disclosed by the Civil War '.

The execution of Charles I filled Montrose with a sense of an almost divine mission. If he had been an idealist before, he became now a crusader. ' I never had a passion upon earth so strong as to do the king, your father, service,' he wrote to Prince Charles two days before the execution. On the day of the King's death he swore to write his epitaph with blood and wounds.

In April, 1650, we see him arriving from the Continent as Viceroy in Scotland of the exiled Charles II. He lands in the Orkneys with a few foreign troops. He plans one of his whirlwind campaigns. He invades the mainland at Thurso and marches south, expecting to be joined by the local clans. No recruits come to him. He finds the northern castles held by the Covenanters. His plight is desperate and he takes to these wild Sutherland hills. Near the head of Dornoch Firth he is met by a superior Covenanting force, and his little army of Danes and Germans and Orkney fisher lads is hacked to shreds.

Montrose is forced to fly. Flinging his sword-belt and his Order of the Garter in the heather, he gallops off on a friend's horse, for his own has been shot under him. He swims the Oykell River, borrows Highland clothes, and wanders lost on the moors. Neither of the two men with him knows the country. They miss their way in the dark. Instead of travelling north, as they hope, they wander west. They sleep under the cold April sky for two nights. They are faint from hunger. They separate on the trackless hills in the hope of finding help. One of them, Sir Edward Sinclair, is never heard of again. The mystery of his end is known only to the hills. Montrose wanders on, lost and famished, and falls at length into the hands of a man who has been watching for him—MacLeod of Assynt. This man sees that Montrose's head is worth enough gold to give him security for life, and he hands Montrose to his enemies.

'The name of the Laird of Assynt', writes Colonel Buchan, 'lives in Scottish history with that of Sir John Menteith, who sold Wallace. It is remembered as a solitary case of a Gael who betrayed a suppliant for gold. . . . He was awarded 25,000 pounds Scots for his services, of which 20,000 were to be paid in coin and the rest in oatmeal. It does not appear that he ever got the money, but the receipts for the meal were long extant, and Highland tradition is positive that two-thirds of it were sour.'

And what of Montrose ? Crofters on the road south saw a strange and fearful procession. A man with the face and bearing of a prince, mounted on a little shelty horse, is beaten along the roads, a quilt of rags and straw for saddle, a rope for stirrups, his feet fastened under the horse's belly. This is the proud Montrose. He is in a high fever. Every town turns out to see him pass, and here and there people curse him ; but his expression never changes. He comes at length to Edinburgh.

Here a murder almost as swift as Rizzio's is carried through under the name of justice. The Covenanters are in touch with Charles II. It is only a question of days before he will land at their invitation. Montrose—the Viceroy—must be executed before every one becomes a royalist ! They meet, mount him on a cart horse and escort him into the city where a gallows stands ready to receive him. His eyes burn with fever. There is the look of a saint about him. He looks like a man who is beyond vengeance and who cannot be hurt. At the sight of him the common women, who have lost husbands in his wars and have been hired to stone him, drop their missiles and follow his pale face, the tears running down their rough cheeks.

They take him in a few days' time to the Mercat Cross, where a thirty-foot scaffold is erected. He wears, by the kindness of friends, a suit of black cloth with a fine scarlet cloak, a black beaver hat with a silver band, and stockings of carnation silk. There are ribbons in his shoes and white gloves on his hands. A minister, who in his cell has ventured to reprove him for dressing his hair, receives this rebuke : ' My head is still my own.'

A great crowd fills the market-place. They listen in awe to his last words : ' I shall pray for you all. I leave my soul to God, my service to my prince, my goodwill to my friends, my love and charity to you all. And thus briefly I have exonerated my conscience.'

His arms are tied. He mounts the ladder. He cries : ' God have mercy on this afflicted land ! ' The tears run down the hangman's face as he performs his office ; and, when the hushed crowd see him swinging, a great sob comes from them and they break up, terrified, and scatter to their houses.

After three hours and a half they cut down the body of Montrose and fulfil their barbaric sentence. The head is hewn off and placed on a spike over the Canongate. The four limbs are hacked off and sent, one to each of the four towns : Perth, Glasgow, Stirling and Aberdeen. And in the darkness of night, the poor headless and limbless trunk of the Great Montrose is buried beneath a gibbet on the Boroughmuir. . . .

In three weeks' time Charles II landed in Scotland. He must have seen the ghastly relic of Montrose in Aberdeen. And nine years afterwards—the year of Charles II's Restoration—a little Londoner, writing in his diary on January 30, began : ' This morning, before I was up, I fell a-singing of my song " Great, Good and Just ", etc., and put myself thereby in mind that this was the fatal day, now ten years since, his Majesty died.' The song that Samuel Pepys had set to music went like this :

> Great, good and just, could I but rate
> My grief and thy too rigid fate,
> I'd weep the world to such a strain
> That it should deluge once again.
> But since thy loud-tongued blood demands supplies
> More from Briareus' hands than Argus' eyes,
> I'll sing thy obsequies with trumpet sounds,
> And write thy epitaph with blood and wounds.

These words, which the comfortable Samuel Pepys hummed to himself, were those with which Montrose dedicated his life anew to the cause of the Stuarts when the news came to him that Charles I had walked through a thin shower of sleet to a scaffold in Whitehall.   There is, to my mind, something so strange in the thought of these two men, so incredibly different, meeting together in this lovely verse : the one who died in the high Roman manner for Charles and the other, the lovable, vulgar little gossip, who was to see and record so much of Charles in the act of enjoying those rights for which Montrose suffered and died.

The road swings round the Dornoch headland, running inland a bit and giving a view of the towers of Skibo Castle, where the late Mr. Andrew Carnegie used to plan his bene-factions.   I was in two minds about Dornoch, which lies two miles off the main road towards the sea.   It is no longer the see of a bishop, but, if it were, it would be the smallest cathedral city in the British Isles, with a population of 725 ; this distinction is now claimed by St. Asaph in Wales. The last woman in Scotland to be burnt to death as a witch died at Dornoch in 1722.   The poor old thing was believed to have turned her daughter into a pony and procured the devil to shoe her.   With some strength of mind, for I would like to have seen Dornoch, I held straight on.   John o' Groats still seemed incredibly far away. . . .

I could not get the memory of Montrose out of my mind. And as I went on thinking of him, and of the verse he wrote, the only political verse I know that is lit by real beauty, I remembered the strange story of his heart.   I wondered what became of it and if it will ever turn up again.   Not every Scotsman knows this story, and I am sure few Englishmen have heard it.

Two days after the execution a few daring friends of the dead leader went by night to the grave on the Boroughmuir. They had come for the heart of Montrose.   It was the custom in ancient times—and a popular custom in Scotland—to bury the body of kings and heroes in several places, the heart in one spot, the head in another, and so on, in order that the departed might derive benefit from the prayers of several congregations.   Bruce wished his heart to lie in the

Holy Sepulchre of Jerusalem, and Devorgilla, wife of John Balliol, founded, as I noted in Galloway, an abbey to receive the heart of her husband. But the heart of Montrose was wanted for another reason. The sudden tragedy of his end caused a friend who loved him to desire this relic.

The grave diggers had to work swiftly. There was no time to prise open the coffin. They bashed in the wood over the chest and took the heart from the body. Then they filled in the grave. The heart was taken to a skilled chirurgeon and apothecary, who embalmed it.

This unpleasant but pious act had been performed by the orders of young Lady Napier, whose husband, the second Lord Napier, one of Montrose's most ardent friends and supporters, was in exile on the Continent with the son of Montrose. Lady Napier, grief-stricken by the frightful death of their hero, decided to send the heart to the son, the young Marquis. She therefore had a steel box made from the blade of Montrose's sword. It was a small oval box about the size and shape of an egg. It opened when a small knob was pressed down, and inside she placed the embalmed heart of Montrose, wrapped in a piece of coarse cloth painted with a preservative resembling glue. This steel box was enclosed in a gold filigree box of Italian workmanship, which had been given to John Napier, the inventor of Logarithms, during his Italian travels by a doge of Venice. So the heart of the Great Montrose crossed the Channel and came into the possession of his son ; and so began its astonishing wanderings.

The young Marquis was in Holland when he received the heart of his father. This must have been in the year 1650, or, at the latest, 1651. But from the moment the heart left Scotland it disappears for a long time. There is no record of it. The young Montrose flung himself into the violent politics of Scotland. Returning from exile, he took part in the Highland rising under the Earl of Glencairn, and in the course of his stormy fortunes the relic was, no doubt, forgotten.

But, many years after his death, the heart appeared in the most surprising manner. The fifth Lord Napier—great-grandson of the Lady Napier who had caused the heart to be embalmed—happened to be travelling in Holland with an intimate friend of his, a Dutchman. Lord Napier told his friend the old story of the egg-shaped box containing the heart of Montrose and, to his astonishment, the Dutchman mentioned that a collector of antiquities possessed the very box. Napier saw it and there was no mistake about it. The collector was persuaded to give up the box and so, by a miracle of chance, the heart of Montrose came back into the Napier family. The gold filigree box was intact, and inside it was the small steel case with the spring knob that opened to reveal the brown, cloth-covered heart.

Lord Napier took the treasure back to Scotland with him. It was fairly obvious that when young Montrose left Holland the relic was either lost or stolen, and had come by chance into the hands of a collector. That part of the story was indeed not half so strange as the fact that it should have been discovered by a Napier. But the story of the heart had hardly begun.

Two days before Lord Napier died, he called his favourite daughter to him and entrusted to her the heart of Montrose. She was then sixteen years of age. In time this daughter, Hester, married Samuel Johnston. This was about the year 1776. After a few years of married life Hester and her husband sailed for India, where he had received a civil appointment at Madras. Among her treasured possessions on this voyage was the heart of Montrose in its gold filigree case.

The East Indiaman in which Mr. and Mrs. Johnston were travelling fell foul of a French squadron off the Cape Verde Islands. The French ship opened fire and the British ship replied. Mr. Johnston took charge of four of the quarter-deck guns and Mrs. Johnston stood on deck, unwilling to leave her husband in the moment of danger, and grasping a large, thick, velvet reticule, into which, during the excitement of the moment, she had crammed jewels and other valuables, including the heart of Montrose.

A shot from a French frigate struck one of the East Indiaman's guns, killed two gunners, and sent up a shower of splinters that wounded Mrs. Johnston and blew away her precious velvet bag. When the gallant lady recovered she rushed to her bag and examined it. The splinters had damaged it. The delicate gold filigree box was shattered to pieces, but the small steel box containing the heart was uninjured. The French ships were beaten off, and, in due course, Mr. and Mrs. Samuel Johnston, accompanied by the heart of Montrose, reached India.

One of the first things which the devoted guardian of the heart did, when she had set up house in Madras, was to seek out a skilful native goldsmith and submit to him the broken fragments of the gold filigree box. From these, and from Mrs. Johnston's description of the original, he managed to make a box as beautiful as the one that had been shattered. He made also to her order a silver urn, engraved on the outside in native dialects with a history of the heart and of the outstanding events in the life of the great Montrose. In this urn, which was placed on an ebony table in the drawing-room, Mrs. Johnston kept the heart of Montrose. One day it vanished. So great was Mrs. Johnston's distress that the rumour spread through the district that the silver urn contained a talisman of so powerful a character that he who owned it would never die in battle or be taken prisoner. So for a second time the heart of Montrose disappeared ; and it remained hidden for nearly twenty years ! There were rumours that a certain rajah had bought it, but an inquiry, or a search for it, was impossible.

The son born to the Johnstons was the distinguished colonial administrator who became Sir Alexander Johnston, the reorganizer of the government of Ceylon and the founder of the Royal Asiatic Society. He it was who found the heart again and restored it to his family :

' My father was in the habit of sending me every year during the hunting and shooting season to stay with some of the native chiefs,' wrote Sir Alexander Johnston in 1826. ' One day, while I was hunting with the chief who was said to have purchased the urn, my horse was attacked by a wild hog, which we were pursuing, but I succeeded in wounding him so severely with my hunting pike, that the chief soon overtook and killed it. He was pleased with my conduct on this occasion, and asked, before all his attendants, in what manner I would wish him to show his respect and regard for me. I said, if the report was really true, that he had bought the silver urn that had belonged to my mother, he would do me a great favour by restoring it ; and to induce him to do so, I explained to him all the circumstances connected with it. He replied that it was quite true that he had purchased it for a large sum, without knowing that it had been stolen from my mother, and he immediately added that one brave man should always attend to the wishes of another brave man, whatever his religion or his nation might be ; that he therefore considered it his duty to fulfil the wishes of the brave man whose heart was in the urn, and whose wish it was that his heart should be kept by his descendants ; and, for that reason, he would willingly restore it to my mother. Next day, after presenting to me six of his finest dogs and two of his best matchlocks, he dismissed me with the urn in my possession, and with a present from himself to my mother of a gold dress, and some shawls, accompanied by a letter, expressing his great regret that he had innocently been the cause of her great distress by purchasing the urn, which he assured her he would not have done had he known that it had been stolen from her.'

Once more the heart of Montrose had been lost and found again ! But still more adventures were in store for it. The Johnstons left India in 1792 to return home to Scotland. They reached Boulogne in safety, and were just about to cross the Channel when the French Revolutionary Government issued an order that no gold or silver must leave the country. The silver urn containing the heart of Montrose came under this ban. In the confusion of the moment Mrs. Johnston confided the urn to the keeping of an English lady in Boulogne, a Mrs. Knowles, who promised to hide it securely, pending the time when the political situation would make it possible to smuggle it over into England. But the political situation did not improve. From 1792, until Napoleon's downfall at Waterloo in 1815, England and France were at war. The Johnstons made every effort to recover the heart of Montrose but, alas, it had vanished. Mrs. Knowles had died and all trace of the hiding-place was lost. Sir Alexander Johnston took the search upon himself and ransacked Boulogne for the heart ; but never a trace of it could he discover. He died in 1849.

Every word of this incredible story is authentic. It crops up in letters of the period and is mentioned in Mark Napier's *Memorials of Montrose*. The best summary is that by J. G. Lockhart in a book, published recently, called *Here are Mysteries*. Mr. Lockhart winds up his account with this tantalizing vision :

' As more than one hundred and thirty years have passed since the heart of Montrose was lost, we may doubt whether it will ever reappear. Yet stranger things have happened.

One day, perhaps, some one exploring the dusty contents of an old shop in the back streets of Boulogne, may chance upon a little gold box of Indian craftsmanship. Opening it, he may even find that it contains a steel case " the size and shape of an egg ". Let him then be careful of his discovery, for in his hands may be resting no less a treasure than the heart of the Great Montrose.'

§ 4

I found myself at Brora, which, like all these little sea-coast places in the extreme north, seems to specialize in golfers, fishermen, and devoted parents who enjoy an un-sophisticated holiday. And the north road, looking more than ever like the Aberdeen-Montrose road in the south, went over cliffs by the sea, crossed burns, and passed glens where rivers came pouring down under a tunnel of clustered green.

A few miles from a little place called Loth a stream falls through a glen, and nearby on the roadside is a memorial which states that the last wolf killed in Scotland was slain at this spot by Hunter Polson about the year 1700.

I wonder if this is accurate. It has been said somewhere that the distinction of killing Scotland's last wolf belongs to that great fighter Sir Ewan Cameron of Lochiel, who killed one in 1680, but there can be no doubt that wolves existed in remote corners of the Highlands long after this. Lochiel's wolf may have been the last one on his territory in western Inverness-shire, but not the last wolf in the country.

There is a story that the last wolf in Scotland was killed as late as 1743 by a mighty hunter named Macqueen of Pall-a-chrocain in the Tarnaway Forest of Morayland. The story is given in *Lays of the Deer Forest* by the Messrs. Stuart :

'One winter's day Macqueen received a message from the Laird of Mackintosh that a large " black beast " supposed to be a wolf had appeared in the glens, and the day before killed two children who with their mother were crossing the hills from Calder ; in consequence of which a " Tainchel ", or gathering to drive the country, was called to meet at a tryst above Fi-Giuthas, where Macqueen was invited to attend with his dogs. Pall-a-chrocain informed himself of the place where the children had been killed, the last tracks of the wolf, and the conjectures of his haunts, and promised his assistance.

'In the morning the "Tainchel" had long assembled, and Mackintosh waited with impatience, but Macqueen did not arrive ; his dogs and himself were, however, auxiliaries too important to be left behind, and they continued to wait until the best of a hunter's morning was gone, when at last he appeared and Mackintosh received him with an irritable expression of disappointment.

' " Ciod e a' chabhag ? "—" What was the hurry ? " said Pall-a-chrocain.

'Mackintosh gave an indignant retort, and all present made some impatient reply.

'Macqueen lifted his plaid and drew back the bloody head of the wolf from under his arm—" Sin e dhùibh "—" There it is for you ! " said he, and tossed it on the grass in the midst of the surprised circle.

'Mackintosh expressed great joy and admiration and gave him the land called Sean-achan for meat to his dogs.'

I wish I knew more of Hunter Polson and the Sutherland wolf. This county must have been one of the last fastnesses of the Scottish wolf, and to-day there is a ford at Coulin called Pait nam Madadh—the Wolves' Ford.

I thought, as I went along, that an appreciation of Sutherland scenery must be for ever marred by the memory of the Sutherland clearances in the nineteenth century. A dispossessed Gael in Canada once said that in eight years a land that had waved with corn, whose mountains were studded with sheep and cattle, whose hills resounded with the note of the bagpipe, and whose people were always ready to take up arms for their chieftains, was converted into a solitary wilderness. Looking at the Sutherland Straths to-day, a man might think that they had never nourished human beings but had been lost in their primeval harshness since the cooling of the earth. Yet it has been recorded that a ship once lost her way at sea in the smoke of the burning crofts of Sutherland. She had to lie to until night, when the glare of the blazing houses guided her to shore. Starving men and women, who had taken to the Sutherland hills, used to flock in hundreds down to the shore to grub for cockles.

They used to bleed cattle and, mixing the blood with oatmeal, cut the paste into slices and fry it. Although no social change as great as the demobilization of a nation of warlike tribes, and the substitution of a normal land-tenure system, can be made without hardship and the creation of a surplus population, the fury of fiends seems to have been let loose upon the Highlanders of Sutherland.

I have often wondered why this proud and warlike race did not turn and rend its oppressors. I wonder whether the ministers of those days were on the side of the evicting tyrants ?

Beyond Helmsdale the road became serious. It left low, green country and shot up into the hills. It twisted and turned into a brown solitude of smooth moors and windy heights, running on and upward over the bleak face of hills. There was mile after mile of it. I felt that I was on the boundary. This was the Ord of Caithness : a pass between Sutherland and her northern neighbour. It is supposed to be unlucky for a Sinclair to pass this road on a Monday. It has been so since the distant Monday when the Sinclairs passed that way to Flodden, whence only one returned. In winter-time the Ord of Caithness must be one of the most terrifying roads in Scotland. The posts along it serve to mark the way when snow hides the road. From the top, what a magnificent drop down into the greenness of Berriedale ; and into a new country too : a queer bare, treeless country bound by iron cliffs, where the wind sweeps in straight from the Orkneys and the Shetlands, and every shrub and every thatch has the appearance of crouching head-down before it, even on a sunny autumn afternoon.

Caithness is a strange, fascinating county. It is a strong, definite county. The mysterious Picts have left their fang-like towers in the fields, and the Vikings have named the creeks and the bays and the hills. Wick, to which I was travelling, is Vik—a bay, and Thurso is Thor's-a—the river of the god Thor. If the Isle of Skye could marry a county of Scotland, he should marry Caithness, a placid fit mate for his storminess. The Norse influence has made of Skye a vast, bearded warrior armed to the teeth, and of Caithness a strong, blonde Viking maiden at her spinning-wheel.

§ 5

I came into Wick as a protracted twilight was beginning
to darken into night. A long, crooked high street was full
of young men and girls. The men were big fellows, mostly
fishermen in blue jerseys, and the girls conformed to a pattern
that, thanks to the mass production of hats, skirts, shoes,
and almost-silk stockings, is becoming the same all over
the world. There were a few old women whose yellow,
incredibly lined faces were framed by black knitted shawls
and from whose barrel-like waists hung long black skirts and
aprons ; but they were like the ghosts of another day.

I went across a bridge and saw the roof-line of Wick, a
church tower or so and rows of chimneys, printed in jet-
blackness against a queer, quivering sky. It was not a
dead twilight : it had an unearthly vitality about it ; and
the water that rushed under the bridge lay in pools of startling
livid brightness, cut across by shadows in which it swirled
darkly like boiling pitch. I asked myself whether Wick
was not like any other small seaport in Scotland, and whether
my feeling that it was rather weird was not, perhaps, the
result of fatigue and preconceived opinion. But no ; I looked
at those sinister black buildings against a sky that should
have been that of night, and I knew that the northern sun
puts a spell on all this country. I have never seen a quayside that looked more ripe for treasons, stratagems, and spoils.
Some dark treasonable plotter among my ancestors awakened
in me as I looked at Wick and wanted to fling his cloak over
his mouth, pull his black hat down over his ears, and go
slinking over the cobbles beside that silver and black water
to tap thrice on a dark door.

I came to a splendid harbour with an immense breakwater :
it had that look of an empty stable which the absence of
the usual trawlers, which are out at sea, lends to such places.
Along the quaysides were the stacked boxes and the scaly
machinery of the herring industry. One or two fishing boats
were tied up, their riding lights swinging with the tide ; and
over them was the hearty smell of powerful tobacco and the
pungency of recently vanished bacon. . . .

It was with a great effort I tore myself from Wick, for
I was dreadfully weary ; but had I not promised myself to
sleep at John o' Groats ? Another seventeen miles . . .

seventeen long, awful miles at that time of night, and after such a day, when each mile seems like ten. Every shadow on the road became a grotesque flying demon, and the blanched walls seemed to beckon me to destruction.

I could feel a sea wind blowing. I could see the minute light of Duncansby Head sweeping a yellow sword over the Pentland Firth. There were other lights too, as the jagged headlands of Scotland gave their warning to the night.

A long straight road runs to John o' Groats. There is nothing there but the John o' Groat's House hotel and a cottage or two. I have seldom felt a greater sense of adventure than the rushing forward to this little hotel on the very edge of Scotland.

I entered a porch hung with postcards, and went into a room in which an English clergyman was playing some kind of card game with another elderly man and two women. They all looked as though they had enjoyed a good meal, and the parson was smoking a curved meerschaum. Even then, tired and hungry, I remained in the room for a moment, charmed by the sight of this unlikely group at John o' Groats. The place sounds so remote, so beyond the normal trafficking of man, yet this little group seemed to link it firmly with the unswerving normality of South Kensington.

You can always tell whether a small hotel is good or bad by the expression it assumes when you arrive at ten o'clock at night and ask timidly for something to eat. The bad hotel frowns and implies sinfulness on your part, growling unwillingly of slumbering maids and waiters, and locked larders. But the good hotel smiles and says that you must have had a frightful journey and—would you like an egg on a haddock, or would you like grilled ham, or perhaps some soup which it will not take one second to warm. Such a hotel is this on the tip of Scotland's craggy nose. And, when I had eaten, I went up to a small room where a fire of peats was burning in the grate, filling the room with the smell of Gaeldom, reminding me of Connemara and Arisaig and of all the fine men and the good-looking, black-eyed women I have met in those places, so that, tired as I was, I poked the peat and sat down and wrote a lot about the Gael which I tore up in the morning.

Over the mantelpiece was a picture I have not seen for many a year. A woman is on her knees crying, sitting at the

feet of a clean-cut man with a firm jaw-line, who gazes vacantly
into the distance. The name of the picture is 'A Fallen
Idol'. I believe it puzzled the Royal Academy in Victorian times, when 'problem' pictures were the fashion, but
it puzzled me far more as a child when it hung in my nursery.
I used to wonder and wonder about it. Why was the woman
crying? Why did the man look so stern? And in the
little room with the turf fire I looked at the picture again,
but not with the same bewilderment.

§ 6

I was up and out soon after six on a bright, windy morning. The hotel stood on grass-covered sandhills, with the
waves of the Pentland Firth breaking a few yards from its
windows. Straight ahead to the north, dwarfed by distance,
the Orkney Islands rode the blue water like anchored ships :
Hoy to the left and South Ronaldsay to the right. I could
see the green on them, and the shape and colour of their
cliffs as the sun caught them. Much nearer, a mile or two
from the shore, was the lovely green island of Stroma.

John o' Groats itself is wind-swept but comfortable-looking
country, well kept and trim, straight little tracks running
through the fields, cone-shaped haystacks held down by
ropes and stones, and so flat, and with such enormous clouds
rolling over it, that I am sure old John de Groot must have
been more than once reminded of his native Holland.

It is an extraordinary thing that the name of a man of
whom practically nothing is known should have gone right
round the world. John de Groot, from whom this place
takes its name, is said to have been a Dutchman who settled
on the extremity of Caithness in the reign of James IV. He
is supposed to have worked a ferry from this point to the
Orkneys, and some say that he got the nickname of John
o' Groats because he charged a 'groat' for the passage.
The deed, however, which brought him fame was the construction of an octagonal building, pierced by eight doors
and containing an octagonal table. This, says legend, was
made to settle a dispute on precedence among his eight sons.
The eight men could each enter the building at the same
moment and sit at a table which possessed no head to it.
An ingenious explanation of this story, in which one can trace

the skilful brain of the modern antiquary, is that possibly John de Groot built near the ferry an octagonal wind-shelter for his passengers.

Whether it was wind-shelter or house, not one stone of it stands to-day or has been visible for many a year. The hotel is built, I believe, on the supposed site of it.

Not far from John o' Groats is a whitewashed church whose walls stand within sound of the Pentland breakers. Here John o' Groats is said to have been buried. I found a tombstone said to be his, which has been taken up and let into a wall of the church, but I could not decipher one word on it. I did find one stone, however, which suggests that his family was flourishing in the seventeenth century. It stated: ' Heir Lies Findlay Grot. Duncansby. Departed 18th of Mai. 1601. Spes altera Vita.'

But John o' Groats has not the finality of Land's End or the Mull of Galloway. It is not, in fact, really the most northerly point in Scotland. Dunnet Head, not far off, thrusts itself a mile or so farther into the Pentland Firth; and so wild are the seas that beat around it that stones flung by the waves have been known to smash the windows of the lighthouse three hundred and forty-six feet above.

I walked to the lighthouse on Duncansby Head, to which a track leads through the fields from John o' Groats, and there I had a view of the Orkneys and the Pentland Skerries which I shall never forget. The deep blue firth was whipped into white here and there by the wind, the cloud shadows were passing over the water, and the air was so clear that I could see a thin line of white where the waves dashed themselves against the Orkneys. The famous Stacks of Duncansby are three pillars of sandstone, like the Needles, isolated by the water from the mainland.

§ 7

I was talking to an Edinburgh lady, a visitor to Caithness, who has known the district from John o' Groats to Cape Wrath since she was a child. We were sitting on a stone wall not far from Duncansby Head :

' Old superstitions that have died out all over Scotland are still flourishing here,' she said. ' Although the railway is only seventeen miles off at Wick, there are literally hundreds of people who have never sat in a railway train and have no desire to do so. I remember, not so long ago, two men from this part of Caithness came to Edinburgh and my husband agreed to show them round. Neither had ever been in a train before, nor had they seen a big city. What do you think impressed them about Edinburgh ? An elephant in the Zoo. They would look at nothing else. They were fascinated. The train seemed nothing to them ; the crowds and the trams, and all that sort of thing, left them unmoved ; but they watched the elephant all day.'

While we were talking a fisherman came through the fields, and, seeing us on the wall, let forth a great shout. The lady laughed :

'There you are ! ' she said. 'That's superstition ! It is frightfully unlucky to meet a woman when you are going off in a fishing boat ; and it is still more unlucky if she speaks first to you. That fellow is going across the fields—a long way round—in order to avoid meeting a woman. He sees me on this wall, and shouts something to me so that he spoke first ! '

'You'll make me believe in witches ! ' I said.

'Witches ! ' she cried. 'There are dozens of them ! I could introduce you to a woman, not far from this very wall, who is supposed to have a most baneful effect on the fishermen. If any fisherman in this part of the world met her on his way to launch a boat, he would turn back and refuse to go out that day.'

She looked across to the little island of Stroma :

'Over there,' she said, 'they still believe in the evil eye. There is an old woman—apparently an ordinary harmless old thing—but the crofters drive their cows away into byres or anywhere out of her sight. You ought to go over to Stroma. In the stormy winter nights they take turns to watch for wrecks. Nothing will ever persuade the people of Stroma that wrecks are not sent by providence to help them through the winter. They adore them ! No one could prevent them boarding a wreck immediately it touches the rocks and removing everything, including, as they did recently, the engineer's false teeth.'

I remembered the story of Alan Stevenson, engineer to the Lighthouse Commissioners, who, in the middle of the nineteenth century, toured Scotland, seeking ideal situations for lighthouses :

'Why are your sails so ragged?' he asked an old sailor on a rocky strip of coast.

'If it had been God's wull that ye had not built sae mony lichthooses, I wad hae had new sails last wunter,' was the indignant reply.

And I suppose the inhabitants of Stroma, who now see lights flashing all round them, regarded these in the beginning as a frightful infringement of their immemorial rights.

§ 8

The dialect at John o' Groats is peculiar, and is very different from speech in either the Highlands or the Lowlands. My first discovery was that, when men meet each other, they frequently cry: 'Oh boy!', which I, in my ignorance, put down to the regrettable Americanization of current British speech. But it is not so. It is an ancient greeting in this part of the world.

I collected a number of phrases and exclamations which struck me as very peculiar, but I readily abandon them in favour of a genuine piece of Caithness dialect which I found in the *John o' Groat Journal and Weekly Advertiser*. This was headed 'Cracks on Current Topics', and is a conversation between an English-speaking character, named Mr. Lear, and two Caithness worthies called Sandy and Tam. Here is a bit of their talk:

Mr. Lear: Are you aware that at the World's Fair at Chicago tea-drinking has been revolutionized?

Sandy: Ochanee, stop til A get ma auld dictionary doon fae 'been 'e amery.

Mr. Lear: For five thousand years, since the discovery of the tea plant, people have been drinking hot tea, but at the World's Fair a tea is brewed in cold water and served with ices.

Tam: Ding'd, man, hid's a peety 'at A didna ken 'at a month ago, A wid heden aff word til Robbie or J.M. for a puckle.

Sandy: Ochanee, we hev plenty o' tea an' mair at Heather Inn if fat we hev rins deen; fat mair could ye seek?

Tam: Man, yir doited; dae ye no' see 'at wi' cauld water tea A widna need til teem mine in 'e saucer an' blaw on'd 'at hid widna burn ma mooth fan 'e simmer veesitors is here.

Sandy : A did hear 'at Johnnie Jack looked at ye wi' 'e tail o' his e'e fan he saw ye blawin' on yir tea.

Tam : Och, yes, yes, an' Proodfeet straiked his liv' ower his face 'at A widna see he wis lek till lauch, an' Kirsty pat doon her broos, but feint's ma cares, A wisna gaun til burn ma mooth wi' heyt tea.

Mr. Lear : The new tea plant has been found in Shizuoka.

Sandy : Oh, boy, 'at will be some beig toon in 'e sooth 'at we ken naething 'boot.

Tam : Ochanee, ye can be lek Johnnie Jack fan he is sippin' thick milk an' meyl, he aye says til me : Eh iman hid's graun', hid's graun', we noor see 'e lek o' this in Gleski.

Mr. Lear : It will be unfortunate if the grand display which is anticipated at our annual show will be spoiled by a wet day.

Sandy : Ochanee, yes, yes, a weet day will pit 'e shine aff o' man an' beyst.

Tam : Faigs, A houp there'll be nae rain for last Setterday nicht A wis in Casselton A treated masel' til a pair o' spleet new plus-fowers, an' Donnie h'arkened in ma loog 'at they wir a good bit better than Roggey's, so mind ye 'at's good waun an' fan A'll go in at 'e show gate wi' 'at fufflin' 'boot ma knees an' Hornag at ma heel wi' her new branks an' helter shank, A'm tellin' ye A'll hev ma heid in 'e air an' nod till 'e president an' 'e secretary an' every simmer veesitor, an' mind ye, cup or no' cup, A'll be thinkin' masel' as beig as twa-three.

Mr. Lear : Special trains and crowded omnibuses will be a feature of our show day.

Sandy : Ochanee, there'll be fouk 'ere fae far an' near for a Caithness boyag fae wa' doon on 'e ither side o' London wrote me 'e ither day sayin' he wid meet me at 'e show an' he span up a bit o' poetry in his letter. A hev 'id on ma tongue an' A'll just tell ye fat hid wis :

> *A try ma 'prentice han' at times*
> *'At wee bit simple, hamely rhymes,*
> *An' if they've gi'en ye any pleasure*
> *A'm higher paid than if by treasure.*
> *The time for goin' home is near,*
> *Why, lo ! it scarcely looks a year*
> *Since A tried til buy ma cousin's coo,*
> *An' chuckens fae a wifey kent by you.*

She attery-lek til me did say :
A've nothin' for ye, sir, 'e day,
Some o' ye fae Wick comes here
An' offers little for wur gear.
Ochanee, woman, A've always thocht
A've peyed ye weel for all A've bocht,
An' aye A've gi'en ye highest prices
For butter, eggs, an' even grices.

I am afraid that I find this very difficult to understand.
Here, however, are a few translations : ' Hid's a peety '
(It's a pity) ; ' A wid heden ' (I would have had) ; ' We
noor see 'e lek o' this ' (We never see the like of this). The
popular word ' boy ' comes out in the above as ' boyag '.

It is a fascinating dialect, but a difficult one for a stranger
to pick up. Its store of local words must be enormously
rich.

§ 9

The north coast of Caithness is flat, green, rich country,
with the sea roaring at its iron cliffs. For the first time since
Inverness I was out of sight of hills. I had the strange feeling
that I was in East Anglia. It was utterly unlike Scotland,
and many of the people I met as I went towards Thurso were
those tall, blue-eyed, blonde people who, like many a family
in East Anglia, owe their fair hair to the Vikings.

Two things one notes at once about Caithness : the flag-
stones that are up-ended in the fields and serve the purpose of
hedges, and the number of mounds called ' Picts' Houses '.
Caithness stone is grey and hard, and I have read somewhere
—but I cannot remember where—that Paris was once paved
with it. The ' Picts' Houses ' must not be confused with the
stone forts, or duns, which are always attributed to the
mysterious Pict. Apparently any green mound in a Caithness field is a Pict's ' house '. The legend survives here, as
it does in every part of Great Britain which was once occupied
by the Picts, that they were very little people who lived in
the earth. It is probably quite common for conquering races
to regard their predecessors as small people, and in Ireland,
of course, the Picts have in the course of time become the
fairies or ' little people '.

But it is not of the Pict that one thinks in Caithness : it
is of the Viking. The Norse pirates have left names all over

the map of this county.   They called the neighbouring county, the most northerly in Great Britain, Sutherland, or Southern land, as indeed it was to them.   Their influence stopped at the hills.   They did not want hills : they had enough of their own in Norway !   But Caithness was a lovely slice of flat, arable land, for which any man would go a-Viking.   What an extraordinary thing was that wave of sea thieves in the eighth and ninth centuries, a wave that covered the Shetlands and the Orkneys and, spreading right down the west coast of Scotland, covered the Isle of Man—which became a kind of naval base to this queer coast-wise Empire—and, founding the Irish towns of Dublin, Cork, Limerick, Wicklow and Waterford, turned east to make a mark on England and to create Normandy. Nowhere in Great Britain is the Norse influence more interesting than in Caithness.   It existed there as a living force until well into the eleventh century.   All the pleasant agricultural districts have Norse names, only the hills and the useless moors far inland, where the Scot was driven by the pirates, preserve the Gaelic names.

Thurso is a grey town with a long main street and a harbour that fronts the magnificent sweep of Thurso Bay.   In front of the church I saw a statue of Sir George Sinclair, the distinguished laird of Thurso Castle, who died in 1868. Scotland owes him gratitude for his editorship of the *Statistical Account of Scotland*, that amazing mass of information compiled by the ministers of every parish in Scotland.   It was called ' the most valuable repertory of statistics at the command of any country in Europe ' and, in spite of the League of Nations, I imagine that it must still be the most informative compilation of the kind since Domesday Book. But Sir George was more interesting than any mere surveyor of statistics.   He was at school with Byron and Robert Peel. Byron described him as ' the prodigy of our schooldays '. When he was sixteen he left Harrow and went to Gottingen where, arrested as a suspicious character, he was brought before Napoleon.   He was dismissed and wrote a narrative of the interview, published privately in 1826, which I would dearly like to possess.   And I am afraid I looked at his statue with an admiration sharpened by the rapacity of a book collector.   He had a long and distinguished parliamentary career and caused a great stir when William IV was king by refusing to lunch with his Majesty on the Sabbath !

In the main street of Thurso I saw a sight I have not noticed before in Scotland : good-looking young fisher lassies, wearing rough skirts and aprons, and carrying on their heads big, flat, oval-shaped wicker trays of fish. In Edinburgh and Leith I have seen only incredibly old fish wives, or women who have lost the first bloom of youth. There was something beautiful about these young women as they passed, laughing and chatting, with silver loads upon their heads.

And now, as I went on, the road climbed Scrabster Hill and ran ahead through fields, giving constant views to the right of steep rocks falling to the sea. In no part of Britain that I know is the cliff scenery so consistently fine. Something more than ordinary rock is necessary to bind Scotland in the north, and to withstand the terrific seas that foam and thunder at her. After thirteen miles I crossed a slight ridge and entered Sutherland again ; after forty miles I came to a lovely village called Tongue, that lies on the shores of the Kyle of Tongue, and here I was in another world : the world of loch and yellow weed, of high, impregnable hill and dark gorge, of brown moor and wild forest.

There is a little ferry at Tongue that takes the foot passenger across in a few minutes, but the motorist must make a twelve-mile circuit of the long inland loch. And it is worth it !

Far ahead I saw a range of hills which seemed to me one of the grandest in the whole of Scotland : Ben Loyal to the left and, flanking him, Ben Hope. What a magnificent contrast these two giants make as they stand side by side : Ben Loyal, the Coolin of Sutherland, rising in a series of precipices to a height of 2,505 feet, to end in a series of shattered crags like the spires of a cathedral ; and Ben Hope, a great dome, higher by 500 feet, but smooth and tame, one spur rounded like Glamaig, the other fanged like Sgurr nan Gillean. Ben Loyal is a hill on which Norse gods might have sharpened their swords. Thor must have come from Thurso to use it as his whet-stone.

Ben Loyal rose up into a blue sky, his highest pinnacle clear of cloud, and I thought that he was one of the most fearsome mountains I have ever seen. His sides are scored by fearful ravines and dark gullies, and the eye moves over his grim and

10

awful bulk, noting secret blue recesses, high up, where the splintered rock has fallen apart, making caverns and ledges, a fit playground for devils or a cradle for the Valkyrie.

What a wilderness it is, this northern coast of Sutherland! I felt, as I invaded it, more remote from civilization than when I crossed the Sierra Nevada from Granada to Almeria. Every mile plunged me more deeply into the wilds. It is the very workshop of God. The hills lie piled in aloof majesty above the sea, lonely salt-water lochs wind their way like spies into the land, sometimes desolate and bare of life upon their shores, sometimes with two or three small houses ; and nothing else except yellow weed, the fern, the wind, the lapping wave, and the blue reflection of the brooding hills. So few travellers come this way that it is not worth any one's time to run ferries larger than a rowing boat. So for twelve long, mountain miles I ran down the east side of Loch Eriboll and along the opposite road up the west side, performing a journey that could have been made by water in less than five minutes.

I dived into lanes as green and lush as any in Warwickshire, I came out to glimpses of loch and moor and hill, of pine-covered slopes and slopes as bare as iron, of small rivers rushing over broad stony beds, of thin burns singing through leaves, and of slender white waterfalls leaping into the air from rock ledges. And always, sooner or later, at the mouths of the lochs, I heard the thunder of waves dashing against the cliffs and saw the broad splendour of the open sea.

Loch Eriboll lies nestled in the hills. Its narrow waters are darkened by the mountains that rise to the west of it. Two, or perhaps three, small crofts stand along the twenty miles of its shattering, but superb, indifference : poor little places, with low roofs cowering from the wind, and in front of them a few yards of raked earth on which some meagre crop has been sown. I saw the evening mists gather in the hills. There was no sign of life save the slow flight of some large bird and the bolt of a rabbit into the fern. And as it grew dark, and the long northern twilight fell over Loch Eriboll, all sense of adventure deserted me. I wanted to hear some one speak. I wanted to see a fire. I wanted to get away from the threat of the hills and their implication that I, and all men, were intruders on the surface of the earth.

I ran into a straggling little village called Durness, but

could find nowhere to stay. It was now almost dark. I was directed to an hotel some miles off, on the side of the Kyle of Durness. I mounted a hill and came in sight of a fearful panorama of hills, black now against a faint pulsation in the sky, drawing the cold mists about them and preparing for the dark.

I found a fisherman's hotel almost on the water's edge. It was quite accustomed to battered-looking travellers. It offered food and a great fire in a brick hearth. The only other guest was one of those lonely Englishmen with a crimson face, a white moustache, a genius for silence, and a tweed coat reinforced at the elbows with leather. He resented me as if I had got into a first-class carriage which he had been hoping to keep all to himself. He had been so happy, sitting in his plus fours and his carpet slippers, with a glass of whisky and soda on the arm of his chair ; and I had interrupted his dreams of trout.

He looked at me as I wolfed bacon and eggs, and perhaps he thought that we might have gone to the same school, for he actually spoke to me. Like all these taciturn old Englishmen, who are apparently either lost or in hiding in Scotland, he was a charming fellow when brought to the point of self-expression :

'Lonely spot,' I said.

'Yes,' he replied. 'Only licensed house for eighty miles.'

'Sixty from a railway station.'

'Yes. Are you a fisherman ? '

To have said 'no' would have earned his contempt, and to have said 'yes' would have earned his rancour, for he would have hated my intrusion.

'I am,' I said, 'but I am not fishing at the moment.'

'Motoring about, eh ? ' he said.

'Yes.'

And a look of blank incomprehension settled over his face. He looked at me as if I were slightly mad, as no doubt he thought I was. I was a fisherman and I was—motoring ! Something queer. Our friendship never ripened. It expired in his vague uncertainty about me.

So I went upstairs to bed, passing on the way his waders and his oilskins, his rods and his creels and his basket, and a pair of giant's boots studded with nails. In my room burned a glowing pile of peat.

§ 10

In the morning I ate an enormous breakfast as I chatted to the fisherman, who sat there ready for the fray.

Caged in a case of frail-looking glass on the mantelpiece was a wild cat wearing a ferocious expression. He was a huge beast, fully as large as a big fox terrier, with a small lynx-like head and enormously powerful hindquarters. The fisherman told me that this wild cat had been shot on the hill at the back in 1931.

'Are there many of them about ? ' I asked.

'Oh, lots, I expect,' he replied. 'The shepherds say that they take the lambs, and in the winter they'll attack you almost at sight.'

He apparently knew quite a lot about wild cats and had shot one many years since in the Highlands :

'When it was skinned,' he said, 'the body was a mass of muscle—all sinew.'

He said that many cats supposed to be wild in the Highlands are domestic cats that have taken to the hills or the woods. But there is, however, no mistaking the real wild cat, as this specimen in the case proved.

'Once a tame cat goes hunting,' said the fisherman, 'she'll never give it up. I knew a shepherd once who had a cat that used to bring him home game every morning. He wouldn't have parted with her for anything. Some mornings she'd come back with a grouse or a pheasant, and sometimes even a hare. The trouble with this sort of cat is that she becomes very destructive. There's only one way—bar shooting her—that will stop a cat once she's gone native. Clip her ears close to her head. Cats don't like the water dropping in their ears. That'll keep her at home. . . .'

An enormous ghillie with a deer-stalker hat on his head, a suit of hairy tweeds and black boots with the tabs sticking out at the back over his heels, stood outside holding rods and a landing-net. The fisherman wiped his white moustache carefully and stamped with the noise of a shod shire stallion from the breakfast-room.

Sunlight shone on the Kyle of Durness. The hills lifted their wild heads in a clear sky. I wondered, as I ran beside the loch and struck westward through a bleak valley, how I could have been so cast down by them the night before.

The valley was another Glencoe, and with Glencoe's air of dark brooding. The road went between two lines of enormous hills ; on one side rising to the height of 1,700 feet and on the other to giants like Beinn Spionnaidh, which is 2,537, and Grann Stacach, which is 2,630. Dark little glens opened up on each side and, looking down them, I saw mile after mile of desolate grandeur. The ten miles or so of this valley from Durness to Rhiconich are among the wildest and the finest in the Highlands of Scotland. Half-way along this road I came upon an engraved stone which in itself speaks for the solitude and the bleakness of the district. It read :

1883

As a mark of gratitude and respect to the inhabitants of Durness and Eddrachillis for their hospitality while projecting this road this inscription is placed over this well by their humble servant

PETER LAWSON
Surveyor.

It is not often nowadays that a surveyor discovers himself in such bleak and untamed country ; and Mr. Lawson paid a graceful and eloquent tribute which must delight every one who passes along the road.

To go through this valley is like playing hide and seek with giants ! At the end of the glen near Rhiconich I caught my breath at the sight of a monster called Arkle, or Arcuil, who stands by himself to the left, towering all alone, to the height of 2,580 feet, a finely curved isolated mass rising like a Gibraltar.

Then the country changed. From Rhiconich, where the long arm of the western Loch Inchard comes swinging in from the Atlantic, to Laxford Bridge is six miles of enchanted gnome-like country. The road is at sea-level and there is a lacework of small lochs. They lie by the hundred : all shapes and all sizes. I looked out to the Atlantic and along the slender curving sea lochs, but always I came back to the water-logged land over which the road, it seems, picks its way so timidly.

Some of the wildest parts of the Western Highlands—Morar

and Arisaig and the country round Glenelg—are, by comparison with this stretch of unspoilt and unexplored beauty, on the main line. And, as you come through this Uist-like tangle of lakes, you are faced by another tremendous glen, formed this time by the stupendous bulk of Arkle to the left and the perfect outline, a cone-shaped volcano, of Ben Stack to the right. If I could show a stranger just one glimpse of Highland scenery, this is the one I would choose for him. . . .

The road runs along the foot of Ben Stack, beside Loch Stack, with the mighty bulk of Arkle changing shape all the time on the other side of the water. You will meet nothing on this road except, perhaps, a man with a gun, or a deer cart making for some remote rendezvous.

This strange district, washed by the magic of the Atlantic seaboard, has no written history. Its story is a record of clan wars and of deeds that have been handed down round the peat fire from one generation to another. It is an unforgettable solitude that must always haunt the memory of any one who has seen it.

I came through the terrific glen by the edge of Loch More and, with the waters of Loch Shin alongside me for sixteen miles, arrived at last in Lairg, almost worn out by a succession of Glencoes.

And that night, very late, I slept in Inverness.

CHAPTER NINE

IN WHICH 1 DECIDE TO WALK THE LARIG GHRU, SET OUT FROM
AVIEMORE WITH MRS. MURRAY OF KENSINGTON, SPEND A NIGHT
ON THE FLOOR OF A STALKER'S HUT, WALK THROUGH GLEN TILT,
HAVE SOMETHING TO SAY ABOUT THE ORIGIN OF ATHOLL BROSE
AND ARRIVE, WITH FORTY MILES BEHIND ME, AT BLAIR ATHOLL

§ I

BACK in Inverness, which I now regarded as a southern
metropolis, I mooned about for some days in a perfect
fog of indecision. I had promised to go to Aberdeen
to have a night's salmon poaching with a man on the River
Hush-hush. I also wanted to walk the Larig Ghru, but I
was not too sure of being able to walk forty miles. This is
a frightful admission in these days, but it is a true one.
While in this unpleasant state of suspended animation I met
the Honourable Mrs. Murray of Kensington.

What a woman !

I met her among the second-hand books in an Inverness
shop, and I took her back with me, in two volumes, to the
hotel. Her real name was Mrs. Sarah Aust, but apparently
she preferred to use the more aristocratic one of her first
husband, the Honourable William Murray, brother of the
Earl of Dunmore. Murray died in 1786, and his widow, then
forty-two years of age, married a Mr. George Aust. Thirteen
years after this marriage, when Mrs. Aust was fifty-five,
she descended on Scotland in a specially reinforced coach
as 'the Hon. Mrs. Murray of Kensington'. With the eye
of a hawk and the campaigning spirit of Hannibal plus
Cæsar plus Napoleon, she drove her coach right into and
over the Highlands ; and nothing could frighten or deter
her or blunt her stupendous curiosity. Her book was published in 1799 and was so well reviewed that she printed the
reviews in a second edition. Again, what a woman !

The title of her book is : *A Guide to the Beauties of Scotland,
Etc., to which is added a more Particular Description of Scotland, especially that part of it called the Highlands.*

This is how she begins :

' Provide yourself with a strong roomy carriage, and have the springs well corded ; have also a stop-pole and strong chain to the chaise. Take with you linch-pins and four shackles which hold up the braces of the body of the carriage ; a turnscrew fit for fastening the nuts belonging to the shackles ; a hammer and some straps. For the inside of the carriage get a light flat box, the corners must be taken off, next the doors for the more conveniently getting in and out. This box should hang on the front of the chaise, instead of the pocket, and be as large as the whole front, and as deep as the size of the carriage will admit : the side next the travellers should fall down by hinges at the height of their knees to form a table on their laps ; the part of the box below the hinges should be divided into holes for wine bottles to stand upright in. The part above the bottles to hold tea, sugar, bread and meat ; a tumbler glass, knife, fork and salt cellar, with two or three napkins : the box to have a very good lock. I would also advise to be taken, bed-linen, and half a dozen towels at least, a blanket, thin quilt, and two pillows.'

Having frightened off all but the most intrepid of her readers, Mrs. Murray of Kensington then goes on to advise visitors to Scotland to dispense with a servant on horseback and make the unfortunate man sit behind the coach on a specially made seat :

' In a journey of near two thousand miles, my carriage was only *once* near being down ', she says, ' and would certainly have been so had my servant been anywhere but on the seat behind. He felt and saw the shackle belonging to one of the hind springs break, and instantly called to the postilion. Had the carriage not stopped immediately, I do not know what might have happened. This accident happened on the road near Loch Awe, far from assistance of any kind, and in torrents of rain.'

She set off—from Kensington, of course—on May 28, 1796, with her maid by her side and the manservant on the seat behind, and she was, although unconscious of the fact, the most extraordinary traveller Scotland had ever seen, with the possible exception of Dr. Johnson. She was the first woman to write about the Highlands and she was probably the first English person, man or woman, to explore many of the more remote Highland hills and glens. We can gain some idea of the sensation she must have caused, in her relentless search for death or pneumonia, in the following light-hearted pen-picture of herself :

'Mrs. Murray appears,' she writes, 'accompanied by gentlemen and ladies, dressed in a red leather cap trimmed with brown fur and a habit of Tartan such as is worn by the 42nd regiment of Highlanders. She mounts a white horse with a Fingalian stick in her hand, cut out of the woods in Morven.'

But this was not her usual appearance. She was normally in her coach, commanding the wretched driver to take her over the Corrieyarrick or over the roads which men trembled to contemplate, or else, jumping out, and disappearing before the puzzled eyes of the Highlanders, to lean over some ghastly chasm or drench herself in the spray of a waterfall. How the maid and the manservant must have loathed this tour ! How they must have tossed restlessly in some foul bothy dreaming of the Royal Borough, and wishing that their mistress would come to her senses.

Mrs. Murray of Kensington helped me to swing myself out of my laziness. Something of her terrific energy and her enthusiasm for peril and exploration soaked into me and shamed me. I decided to walk the Larig Ghru. And I would take her with me and read her on the way.

But forty miles without a shelter. Could I . . .

'Nonsense, man,' I seemed to hear the Hon. Mrs. Murray of Kensington say. 'Of course you can do it ! Listen to me. . . . When I quitted the narrow road under the rocks by the side of Loch-a-chravy it became amazingly jumbling and winding amongst various-shaped rocks and crags covered with wood ; and rended chasms deep and dark on every side, no trace of man or living thing to be seen, every sound reverberated from rock to rock, flying through the gloomy labyrinth to announce the approach of unhallowed steps. My heart was raised in awe to heaven's solemnity, whilst that of my poor man was depressed to the dread of hell. He was walking before the horses, who were step by step thumping the carriage over rocks, when he suddenly stopt the chaise and, coming to me with a long face, said : " Madam, I believe the devil is in this place ! Do you hear that noise ? " All was echo : the whistle of a bird, the sound of the foot of an animal, the rustling of the wind amongst the trees, the gush of a torrent or the fall of a pebble resounded through the solemn pass as through a ruined cloister. I listened—it was a sonorous deep noise—dying away ; and again regularly resuming the same key. I had no fears, and bid the men advance. But the road, getting worse and the pass narrowing, I got out of the carriage, thinking it more advisable to explore it on my own legs than shut up in the chaise : I thus became the vanguard of my servants as the fittest person to encounter the devils. . . .'

What a woman !

Who, after reading the Honourable Mrs. Murray of Kensington, could fear even the Larig Ghru ?

§ 2

Leaving Inverness one evening, I took the road to Aviemore. It leads up into a deserted region of hill and moor. I saw the sun set from the treeless glen of the Findhorn and I mounted in a chill wind to the gloomy pass of Slochd Mhuic —the wild boar's den.

I thought that Mrs. Murray of Kensington might have raised her heart in awe could she have seen the miles of lonely road : mountains rising in the dusk, grouse getting up before me, whirring off and then skimming low down over the moor on motionless wings, miles of heather, dead and brown on the hill-sides, and dusk creeping through the glens. At Aviemore I came to an hotel in a park.

I was told that half-way through the Larig Ghru, at the end of the first twenty miles, was a stalker's hut in which I could stay the night if the man was not on the hill. This pleased me because, encouraged perhaps by the intrepidity of the Honourable Mrs. Murray of Kensington, I had been quite prepared to bivouac in the heather.

That night I unpacked the provisions I had bought for my walk. Then I went to bed and studied maps and read about the Larig Ghru :

'There is no pass to compare with it in all Scotland,' says Mr. Seton Gordon.

'One of the wildest and grandest passes of the lofty Cairngorm Range,' says Mr. Muirhead, who adds, 'There is no inn or house of shelter on the route.'

'This is about the longest day's march in the Highlands,' says Mr. Baddeley.

Forty miles! It was a rash and impetuous adventure for one who had done no walking since the War. But the vision of that indomitable figure in a red leather hat trimmed with fur and a habit of Tartan 'as worn by the 42nd regiment of Highlanders' came to uplift my drooping spirits; and so I fell asleep.

I was awakened in the morning by the sound of a bagpipe. I jumped from bed and went to the window. The smartest Highlander I have seen for many a day was striding slowly up and down the hotel lawn, playing 'Up in the Morning Early'. His brogues printed a black track in the dew. He wore a blue bonnet, a snuff-brown jacket, and a kilt of Murray tartan.

In the foreground lay green Rothiemurchus Forest, with the mists of night still stealing like old witches through the pine trees; beyond rose the brown uplands round Glen More; to the right was a vast barrier of dim mountains lost in cloud, the Cairngorms. I could pick out the rivers and streams by the grey banks of fog that lay above them, twisting here and there like serpents. Clouds had crept down the flanks of the mountains in the night and lay there in the windless morning like the smoke of old battles. The icy air came over miles of mountain, with the sweetness of autumn in it and smell of wet earth.

The sound of the reveille ended suddenly in the squeal and groan of a dying pig. Who, I wondered, was this piper? Was he some eccentric Highland chief who amused himself by awakening the guests? Was he the hotel proprietor?

I thought there was something vaguely familiar about him. He saw me at my window and gave me a salute. He was the hotel porter! My mind went ahead to the moment when I would be forced by custom to offer this splendid creature a paltry piece of silver. It was an embarrassing prospect. I felt that it would be more in keeping with his appearance if I tipped him with a dagger.

After breakfast I strapped on my pack, grasped an ash stick, and strode self-consciously through the assembled fishers, golfers and motorists, feeling rather like Christian in the *Pilgrim's Progress*. So the Honourable Mrs. Murray of Kensington and I went down the road towards the Larig Ghru.

In certain lights the Larig Ghru, seen from Aviemore, looks like an early Italian painter's idea of hell. It is seven and a half miles away : a great cleft in the Cairngorms : steep, dark, cruel, with something about it that suggests to you that there, if anywhere, a man might find the last dragon.

It is the longest high hill pass in Great Britain. Eight miles of it are at the 2,000-feet level, and parts of it are as high as 2,800 feet. Some say that the name means ' The Gloomy Pass ' ; others, the more modern Gaelic scholars, say it means something else ; but what they think it means I do not know, and neither, I believe, do they.

I went through a brilliant, insincere morning to Coylumbridge. The sun was shining, and in England the day would have remained fine. But in the Highlands of Scotland a promising morning too often fades into rain.

I saw a house, the last one I should see for twenty miles, and bidding it farewell struck off over a grassy track to the right, which led onward and considerably upward through trees beside a stream.

I think it was after the sixth mile that my breath came fast and the pack, which seemed so easy at the start, felt like a piece of granite.

I was among the bare hills and climbing steadily. The sun had gone and I could see the texture of the clouds which steamed over the heads of the mountains. Looking back, I saw, remote and framed in blown mist, fair, green Strathspey, a hint of sunlight, and a few white dots which were houses.

I flung myself down in heather, rested, and ate sparingly. I was at the entrance to the Larig Ghru.

The clouds grew darker and nearer. Rain fell, thin, wetting rain, as I climbed up into the gaunt mouth of the pass. Before me was a narrow, stony track twisting between boulders on the edge of the mountain-side. The clouds cut off sight of the skyline. Avalanches of stones had shot down from the heights during storms and lay in clefts at the base of the hills. In this rain and mist there could be no more melancholy sight than the Larig. Its gloom seemed to engulf me. I might have been a lost soul plodding on in some heartless region of Purgatory.

In the middle of the pass I rested my pack on a great boulder and listened to the sound of the Larig. There was the sound of the mountain torrent in the valley. Then, quite near in the mist, came a hoarse croaking, rather like a corncrake: a queer, uncanny, appropriate sound. It came many times from the shelter of boulders. It was the sound of ptarmigan.

Once I saw the birds in flight, dark birds with a flash of white in, or under, their wings. They were remarkably tame and must be the easiest birds in the world to shoot. But what the ptarmigan can find to eat, in the middle of a rocky ravine surrounded by mountains as bare of nourishment as the side of a battleship, is a mystery.

I was unspeakably tired. The rain stopped for a moment and, selecting a dry place beneath a vast overhanging boulder, I ate my bread and cheese and consoled myself with a few pages by Mrs. Murray. I noted with a certain satisfaction that the Larig Ghru was one of the few places which had resisted the invasion of this resolute female. She had penetrated, however, to the shores of Loch Einich in the Cairngorms, from which position she says : ' I got a near view of the rugged pass called Lairg Cruaidh, signifying a hard rocky narrow pass between two hills. The rocky mountains on each side of this pass are wonderfully fine from every point of view where they can be seen ; and I longed very much to go through this pass to Mar Lodge, the Earl of Fife's.'

I learnt with some concern that it was while admiring the rugged grandeur of the Larig that she suffered a rather undignified accident. She was riding a pony on this occasion :

' The shepherd who held the bridle was explaining the name of the hill, and the eyes of the pony, I suppose, were deceived by appearances, so down sunk the legs of the animal who, finding himself in a trap, began to struggle and in an instant threw me over his tail. I fell fortunately on soft peat moss and had the presence of mind to roll myself out of the way of the heels of the struggling pony and got up without any kind of hurt.'

She tells an excellent story of the '45 which is new, at least to me :

' In the last Rebellion,' she says, ' Robertson of Strowan,

the poet, was a man at that time near eighty years of age, his body hale and strong, and his mind in vigour. He was at the battle of Preston Pans and for his share of booty was allotted the carriage of Sir John Cope, there defeated. Strowan drove it in triumph as far as he could towards his district, and when the roads became impassable he summoned his vassals to carry it into Rannoch. Amongst the other contents in Sir John's chaise were a number of rolls of brownish stuff which were concluded to be very valuable specifics for wounds, particularly as they were safely packed in a soldier's carriage to be ready, as it was thought, in case of accidents. The precious rolls were cried in the streets of Perth. "Wha'll buy Johnny Cope's salve?" They were rolls of chocolate.'

As the rain began to fall again I put Mrs. Murray of Kensington away and prepared to go on. The mists were steaming down the hills. I heard a hoarse roaring and knew that somewhere in the mist a stag was seeking a hind.

The first day's walk was divided into two portions: the time when I tried to keep dry and the time when I tried to get as wet as possible. There is a great pleasure in getting wet. When you realize that it is no longer possible to keep dry a kind of recklessness takes possession of you. It came to me when I felt the first cold trickle of water inside my shoes. When little squirts of water shot between the eyelet holes I took off my limp hat and let the rain soak down through my hair into my eyes. And with this wetness came a desire for more wetness.

No longer did I leap nimbly from boulder to boulder when crossing streams; I just walked through them! And after three hours of this I think every unused muscle in my body was aching and—I have seldom been happier in my life. . . .

The stiffest part of the Larig is a crazy wilderness of red granite boulders. Here the track ends and you have to climb and slide over the rocks. They lead down to a reward: the lovely Pools of Dee. Here are three tarns of icy water. Streams run underground to these tarns beneath mossy hummocks, and in some are holes through which you can see the water flowing. It makes a sound like the glass Japanese harps which people hang up before open windows.

A few miles farther on I rested by the Dee. I had done twelve or thirteen miles, and I was exceedingly tired. Another eight miles lay between me and the stalker's house. I was now through the pass and before me was spread the splendour of Glen Dee. Opposite was Cairn Toul and the Devil's Point, immense, boulder-strewn, and magnificent. I lay in wet heather soaked to the skin watching the mists roll up from the mighty desolation of Glen Guisachan. It was here, flying high out of mist and going into mist, that I saw an eagle, and, lying on my back, I held him for a little with field-glasses, just long enough to enjoy his slow, leisurely flight and the cruel curve of his wing-tips.

Men who have walked the Larig in a storm will know that I longed to take off my brogues at the Dee, but feared to do so in case I could not fit my feet into them again ; they will also know the grand agony of getting up and making for the distant, almost friendly, pine trees of Glen Lui Beg.

I tramped on, striking good firm grassland, and, looking back at the savage Larig Ghru, wondered what on earth could induce me to turn about and retrace my steps through it. On these grasslands are little hills of sphagnum moss. I dug my hands into the red cold stuff and pulled it up by the roots : it smelt earthy and clean. I came down to the Dee, which is here a swift stream about twenty feet wide. I walked straight into it—the water rose to my knees—and I walked out on the other bank.

Every step was now agony. I had nearly completed twenty miles and was not only anxious to know whether the stalker, whose hut should be somewhere near, was in, but was slightly panic-stricken by the thought that he might be, as the hotel at Aviemore put it, ' on the hill '. If he were ' on the hill ' I considered it ten to one that I would get pneumonia if I had to sleep in the heather, because nothing would have induced me to go on over the next twenty miles to Blair Atholl.

Far off to the right I saw a small white building—great joy !—and from its roof curled a spire of smoke ! There was no sign of life as I came near. On the walls of the hut were nailed six fox-brushes. I knew that these foxes had been shot and, having once lived in Warwickshire, I concealed a shudder and banged on the door. A dog barked. A large calm man came to the door, listened to me and, understanding me completely, made way for me to go in as if he were quite accustomed to half-drowned visitors. I went in to the joyful warmth of a peat fire.

§ 3

The stalker's house stood in the shelter of hills, some little distance from the Dee. A small stream ran past it towards the river. It was the first inhabited dwelling I had seen since I left Coylumbridge, nearly twenty miles off over the mountains.

I was wet to the skin. No fire had ever seemed to me more gracious or more lovely. It burned in a room which, obviously the living-room of my host, was like a biography of its owner. It was the room of a man who lives from one year's end to another alone in the solitude of the hills. There are rooms just like this in the back blocks of Canada and on the edge of the Australian bush. Several guns were slung from hooks on the wall. A waterproof gun-case hung from the roof. Clothes were drying before the fire, for my host, as I learned, had been twice drenched on the hills that day. A string was stretched before the fire on which steamed two pair of hand-knitted stockings. A pair of iron-shod boots lay sole upwards before the blaze, their insides stuffed with paper, which is the only right way to dry boots.

On a side table near a window was that marvellous link with the world : a wireless set.

You can go all over the world and find nothing more dignified, or more charming in its ease and good breeding, than the hospitality offered to you in the humblest hut in a Gaelic-speaking country. In Ireland I have accepted food and shelter from poor people who would have been shocked and insulted had I offered them money : and here in the Highlands of Scotland I met again that aristocratic generosity which belongs to a younger world.

My host might have been fifty or sixty. He was bitten brick colour by wind and rain. We shook hands and he smiled at me, for I must have looked like a man fished out of a river ! He waved his hand to the fire :

' Now take off your clothes and dry yourself, and I'll get you something to eat.'

He went to a cupboard and set a table as only a lone bachelor can ; but in London, Paris, or New York, there was no dinner that night which looked better than the loaf of bread, the plate of butter, the tin of condensed milk, and the big, brown tea-pot which he got ready for me.

I found a tin of bully beef. This we opened.

Then for half an hour there was no sound from me. My host smoked his pipe in a dark corner, and twinkled his blue eyes now and then, saying, 'Ay, it was a bad day,' and that the stags were going over from Mar to meet the hinds above Aviemore.

Dusk filled the room. He lit a paraffin lamp and put more fuel on the fire. The storm had blown itself out and the sky above the hills was innocent and pale : a wan, repentant yellow.

I knew, for I have an eye for these things, that I was in a Catholic house. Much of the Catholicism of the Highlands is pre-Reformation. The violent revolution which has marked the character of Scotland so clearly never roused many a mountain glen or western isle. The faith planted in the Highlands when St. Columba came flying to Iona, in search of some place from which he could not see his native shores, has continued to this day. Little Catholic communities exist in the hills like unmelted snow, for the fires of Calvinism never reached so far.

Drenched in peace I lay like an old dog in the blaze. I tried out the wireless, but put down the earphones because the woman who was singing in Stockholm seemed wildly improbable in this place. . . .

The Larig Ghru !

Always I came back to the Larig. Now that I was beside a fire, it seemed tougher than it really was ! I told the stalker, as he sat quietly and massively smoking his pipe, of the stag I had heard belling in the mist, and of the eagle that passed over Glen Dee.

He told me of things he had seen on the hills ; and he told them as well as only a man who does not read too many books can tell a story. As he waved his pipe stem to the darkening hills I felt myself in the mist again, and drew nearer to the fire. He told me how the stags bell in October mists, and how the fighting of stags in a mist sounds like the rattling of sticks in a hat-stand.

Once or twice he had seen an eagle attack a herd of deer. The eagle hovered low over them and panicked them ; then it worked to break one beast away from the herd. The deer, bunched together, were terrified by the awful thing over them, until one, more startled than the rest, a young hind, flung up her head and broke away, with the eagle after her.

I had passed through the Larig, and this sort of thing was more interesting to me than anything that was happening in the world. At that moment I would have almost—almost —hobbled another five miles to see this sight. And did the eagle kill the hind ? No ; the bird chased her for a mile and left her half-dead with fear. . . .

I went to the door. The moon was rising. It was an enormous autumn moon. A thin, honey-coloured rim was just showing above the round back of Carn Mhor, and so bright was it that a gold haze crowned the mountain-top. All the beauty, all the melancholy, of night seemed gathered in this place as bit by bit the moon got up over the crest, and every little stone had a shadow. . . . . .

' And now I'll show ye to your bed,' said the stalker.

I took off the earphones. I had been listening to an hotel dance band in London. I could hear the dancers go back to their little gold chairs ! London never seemed so unreal to me as it did that night in the Highlands.

I followed my host upstairs, where I discovered that he had given up his room to me. No ; he would much rather sleep downstairs and see that my shoes did not burn ! He was so gracious and so undeniable, standing there with a lit candle and the smile of a grand seigneur.

There was a knock at the door. The stalker flung me a couple of deerskins and a fawn coachman's coat with the Duke of Fife's arms on the buttons :

' If ye're not warm enough,' he said, ' ye'll maybe be glad of these.'

I placed a mattress on the floor, pulled deerskins over me, blew out the candle, and the moon came shooting in through the skylight. A silence unutterably deep enclosed the world. The moonlight was on my face and, although I was dog-weary, I could not sleep. I heard the stalker moving below. Once there was a sharp scream in the night, abruptly and terribly stilled. Some small creature had met death in the moonlight.

It was morning.

The light was pale and grey and cold. I found myself lying in a corner of the floor, half in and half out of the deerskins. I wondered, as I lay looking at the light through the sloping glass of the skylight, which part of me was hurt more than other parts. I knew that some day I would boast and brag about walking forty miles without any preliminary training, and when that time came I would forget all about this weary ache from head to foot.

But I was sorry for myself as I lay there in the stalker's hut, wrapped in the pinkish-brown coat of the late Duke of Fife's coachman, the deerskins smelling faintly, rather like a hot horse. What a terrific constitution Charles Edward must have had ! I wondered if he had any idea of putting himself into training for the '45 when he went out hunting in France and Italy before he set sail for Scotland.

I roused myself and went downstairs. The stalker greeted me with a slow smile, asking me, with the innate good manners of the Highlander, if I had slept well. A pale sun was struggling over the hills and the morning wind was cold. I had put my shaving things on a little window-ledge in the porch of the hut. It gave me a queer twinge of amusement to see my shaving-brush standing next to the windpipe of a stag.

A little burn of ice-cold water came tumbling down behind the hut. I went there and washed and shaved :

' Another twenty miles to-day ! ' I said to the stalker, trying to throw a little heartiness into my voice.

' Ay ay ', he said as he submerged a teaspoon covered in condensed milk into a cup of black tea. Twenty miles ! It was nothing to him.

The turf fire, which would go out only when he left his hut for ever, was glowing brightly. The dog lay in front of it and the light wavered over gun-barrels and hanging clothes. I would like to have talked to him about women, for I have never seen a place which needed a woman more. Women can be most irritating in their perpetual passion for niggling tidiness, but inanimate objects have a way of obeying women while they resolutely defy man. Men alone in solitary places are always rather pitiful. They have a rough and ready expertness about them, but their surroundings lack the air of efficiency which the touch of a woman gives to every room in which men live and die. It is not until one sees a place utterly devoid of female influence and interference that one realizes how much we owe to women for a thousand unnoticed touches of graciousness and ease.

We had a monosyllabic breakfast. We talked of stags and hinds and grouse and salmon. At last I got up unwillingly and prepared to go.

We shook hands and I went off over the soft wet grass.

§ 4

The day was as fine as the previous day in the Larig had been foul. The sun, although it was barely nine o'clock, was almost warm.

Something had happened to my right knee which made the act of going downhill sheer agony. On the level, however, I appeared uncrippled.

I crossed the Dee near the spot where Byron, as a boy, was nearly drowned, and, mounting a track which led up to wide, smooth-backed moorlands, all brown with dead heather, I left behind level green grass and trees.

If you would in two days see an unforgettable glimpse of the Highlands, do this forty-mile walk from Aviemore, through the Larig and Glen Tilt, to Blair Atholl ; for here is concentrated a succession of what I consider to be among the grandest mountain views probably in Europe. I have years ago climbed mountains in Switzerland, and it is incredible to me that thousands of British people should make that long and wretched journey when, within a few hours of London, there are the Coolins of Skye and the giants of the Grampian Range. If I were fond of climbing mountains I would rather belong to the Scottish Mountaineering Club than to any Continental climbing organization. . . .

Somewhere near the Bynack Shieling I flung myself down in a sweet bed of heather and looked back. I was about 1,600 feet up, and before me stretched an astounding panorama of hills, great and greater, colossal things shouldering the sky, heather-brown or stark naked as they came from the earth's womb. I looked back at the whole Ben Macdhui range, with the great and spectacular mass of the Devil's Point in the foreground, its graceful flanks grey with fallen boulders. Beyond rose the vast masses of Cairn Toul and that mountain, Braeriach, in whose corries there is a fall of snow that never melts.

As I turned from this, the bulk of Beinn A'Ghlo almost took my breath away. It lay before me in the centre of the glen

—the Mountain of Mist. But there was no mist about it that morning as I looked up at its great precipices. This mountain has three distinct summits, and they say that in this terrible wilderness of rock are nineteen corries, in each one of which you can fire a rifle that cannot be heard in the next.

I came to the Falls of Tarf, cascading in showers of foam under a bridge which commemorates the death of an Englishman, a man named Bedford, who was drowned in 1886 while attempting to ford the river at this spot. The planks shook and moved under my feet. In a few more years the bridge may be as dangerous as the river.

I was coming slowly—very slowly—into civilization again. The name Falar Lodge on the map, some mile or two over the hills, reminded me of a good story. It stands 1,750 feet above the sea, probably one of the highest and loneliest places of its kind in the whole of Scotland.

In the August of 1822 Lord Kennedy, who had the shooting, made a bet of 2,000 guineas that he would shoot forty brace of grouse in twenty-four hours and afterwards ride his horse 140 miles to Dunnottar and back. And he won the bet! He began his shoot at a quarter past four in the morning, bagged his forty brace by nine a.m., mounted his horse and reached Dunnottar at two p.m. Seventy miles in a little over four hours! He then rested for an hour and rode the seventy miles back to Falar, where he arrived at about eight p.m. I think he earned his 2,000 guineas.

I was now at the entrance to Glen Tilt. Before me stretched a deep, straight gorge with a track running through it high on the mountain-side. At the bottom the Tilt ran over a rock bed. The steep sides of the gorge carried up to me the sound of the river as it rushed and tumbled on its course. The strange thing about Glen Tilt and its river is that it looks as much like a canal as the Caledonian Canal is unlike one. The rocks through which the Tilt goes might have been cut by man to give this river a straight route to the Garry at Blair.

Seldom have I seen a greater contrast to the Larig in rain than Glen Tilt in sunlight. I had for a day plodded through twenty miles of mist that parted only to reveal dim and awful shapes of monster hills, cruel gorges with the rain shining over them, precipices leaning out over chasms where the mist steamed and boiled ; and when the air became darker I knew that somewhere above in the clouds was a monster greater than the rest, more terrifying in its unconsciousness of man and in its inability—even, so it seemed, its unwillingness —to offer him anything but death. Such is the Larig Ghru on a bad day : an inferno, a Valhalla, if you like, where the old gods might moan for blood from hill to hill.

Now in the glorious sunlight of Glen Tilt the Highlands were smiling. The river laughed and chuckled its way over rocks, pausing reflectively here and there at deep black pools flecked with foam, then, taking to its heels again with a laugh, it cascaded onward merry as a colt in a meadow.

On the great sloping mountains a few sheep grazed, and once, looking upward, I saw against the sky a stag standing as if cut in bronze.

The road high up on the mountain was sheer joy. Trees had crept down into the shelter of the glen and had hung their branches over the river ; there were groves of alders, and birches gnarled and twisted as old men. The Tilt is surely one of the most beautiful of Highland streams.

I remembered a famous lawsuit of the 'forties, in which the then Duke of Atholl tried to close Glen Tilt to the public. Money was unsuccessfully poured out like water. The fight was the subject of an amusing poem written by Sir Douglas Maclagan. It concerns a party of botanists, led by Professor Bayley Balfour, who were on their way to Ben Macdhui when they encountered the furious Duke in the glen :

> *The Duke at this put up his birse,*
> *He vowed in English and in Erse,*
> *That Saxon fit*
> *Su'd never get*
> *A'e single bit*
> *Throughout his yet,*
> *Among the Heilan' hills, man.*

> *Balfour he had a mind as weel*
> *As only Duke could hae, man,*
> *Quo' he, ' There's ne'er a kilted chiel*
> *Shall drive us back this day, man.*
> *It's justice and it's public richt,*
> *We'll pass Glen Tilt afore the nicht.*
> *For Dukes shall we*
> *Care a'e bawbee ?*
> *The road's as free*
> *To you and me*
> *As to his Grace himself, man.'*

And so it proved. I remembered in this glen something I had read about a drink which is, I believe, famous in the Duke of Atholl's country—Atholl Brose. It is a mixture of whisky, honey, and raw eggs.

The Honourable Mrs. Murray, of Kensington, has something to say about it.

'To a lover of whisky,' writes Mrs. Murray, 'it is a delicious treat, and much prized by the people of Atholl, having good reason, I suppose, for so doing. One instance of its efficacy I will mention : the daughter of an inhabitant of Atholl, having been placed at one of the finest boarding schools in Edinburgh, was seized with a violent fever ; her father was sent for, as she was thought in great danger ; and upon his arrival, being told that his child was on the point of death, and that everything the physicians could do for her had been done without effect, he earnestly exclaimed : " But has she had any Atholl Brose ? " " No." He then had a good dose of it instantly prepared, and making her swallow it, she soon recovered.'

I was once told a curious and amusing story about the origin of Atholl Brose. It appears that in the dim past an heiress of the Tullibardine family adopted an exhausting habit of wandering about the glens from the banks of the Tay at Dunkeld to the banks of the Garry at Blair Atholl. Her wanderings were, however, seriously endangered by a gigantic wild man, who would suddenly pounce upon strangers and rob them, not of gold, but, being an unusually unsophisticated savage, of food, and particularly of fruit. The heiress of Tullibardine announced that she would marry the man who could either kill or capture the savage.

This appealed to a gallant young Highlander in the Atholl country. He studied the habits of the wild man and noticed that he came to drink regularly at a certain spot in the forest, where a hollow stone received water from a burn. The young Highlander turned aside the burn, emptied the stone of its water and filled it instead with honey and whisky. When the wild man came to the burn, he fell flat on his stomach and began to drink. He enjoyed the whisky and the honey so much that he drank it to the last drop and then began to feel rather sleepy. As soon as he fell asleep, the young Atholl Highlander leapt upon him and securely bound him.

The heiress of Tullibardine gladly fulfilled her compact,

for, the story goes, all the time she had been secretly in love with the young man. These two, when they founded their family, took as their crest a wild man in shackles. Now the Murrays of Tullibardine were in time created Marquises of Tullibardine and Dukes of Atholl and, in support of this legend, it is pointed out that to-day the Duke of Atholl bears on his coat-of-arms a savage shackled with the significant motto : ' Furth fortune and fill the fetters.'

The drink which proved too strong for a wild man was, it is said, called ever afterwards Atholl Brose. That, of course, may be the whole point of the legend ; for many such stories are not complete without a moral.

Unfortunately, alas, for legend, I am afraid that the savage in the Atholl coat-of-arms cannot be the wild man of the woods. Anyone who has been interested in Scottish heraldry must have noticed how frequently naked savages or wild men holding clubs appear, generally as supporters. I believe I am right when I say that this fashion for savages can be traced to a tournament which James IV gave during his marriage festivities in 1503. The King himself assumed the disguise of a savage knight and many of the lords who tilted on his side dressed up Highlanders as hairy savages and stood them as guards over their arms. This is a dangerous subject ; and some one is sure to remember that John, Earl of Carrick, used savages as supporters as early as 1369 ; to which I have no answer !

I tramped on to Forest Lodge, where the Tilt flows over an incredible rock bed of rosy granite. If I had to give a beauty prize to Highland rivers, I would give it to the Tilt at this point by the arched bridge.

Onward, onward, with the miles heavy on my feet.

Onward to a road . . . a hill . . . a dreadful hill . . . an endless hill . . . an aching hill. Every mile now seemed like ten. I was dog weary. Then over the shoulder of the hill I saw the distant Vale of Atholl, where there would be an inn, beer, a bathroom, hot water, food. I saw a motor-car. I wanted to stop it and tell the people that I had walked forty miles.

There was an agonizing downhill walk to Blair Atholl. Then—how can words describe the beauty of the inn ?

A stern woman looked at me.

'Sign the book !' she said—and I realized that it was Sunday.

So I limped over to the book and declared, according to the comic law of Scotland's Sabbath, that I, who had walked all the way from Aviemore—every yard of forty miles—was a *bona fide* traveller. That I thought was one of the funniest things that had ever happened to me.

On the following day I limped about Blair Atholl until I found someone who could give me the recipe for Atholl Brose. Here it is :

Take a pound of liquid honey, put it in a basin, add half a pint of water and stir until they are mixed. The spoon must be a silver one. Then add, very slowly, a pint and a half of whisky. Stir until a froth rises. Bottle the mixture securely and let it keep.

This potion, I am assured, is, like John Peel's 'View holloa ', calculated to awaken the dead.

'You can use oatmeal instead of honey ', I was told, ' and some like to beat up the yolk of an egg with the brose.'

Late that afternoon I took the train to Aviemore, where I regained my car. And so, by a wide half-circle through Grantown, Keith and Huntley, I arrived at last in Aberdeen.

The Highlander, bless him, who had promised me the salmon poaching, had evidently forgotten all about it. When I called at his house I was told he was 'away '. He was not merely out, or from home, or on his holiday : he was ' away '. This is an extraordinarily vivid Scotticism. I imagined him striding through the forests of Central America or paddling a canoe up the Amazon. (He was really in a fishing inn within fifty miles of Aberdeen.) But when his landlady said the word ' away '—she said ' awa' '—I seemed to see an empty road stretching to the uttermost ends of the earth.

CHAPTER TEN

I GO TO SEA IN AN ABERDEEN TRAWLER, JOIN A STRANGE COM-
MUNITY, HELP TO STEER THE SHIP TO THE FISHING GROUNDS,
ENCOUNTER 'OLD GEORGE', SEE THE NETS COME UP, SLEEP IN
A BADGER'S DEN, LEARN THE TRAGEDY OF TRAWLING AND SET
FOOT ON LAND WITH A DEEP RESPECT FOR THE MEN WHO SWEEP
THE NORTH SEA

§ I

I MET 'the Skipper' in the Aberdeen fish market. It
was that grey moment before sunrise. He was smoking
his pipe and shouting advice to deck-hands who were un-
loading the catch.

The market rang with the early-morning noises of thousands
of fish being slapped on a stone floor, with the crying of
hungry gulls, with the creak of derricks, the stammer of
steam winches, and the hoarse sirens of trawlers trying to
get out from the stem-to-stern and port-to-starboard crush
at the quay-side.

The Skipper was a short, grey-haired Yorkshireman with
the shoulders of a bull. He wore a blue jersey and a cap
that years ago had been new. As we talked about fish and
fishermen I thought to myself how strange a life is theirs,
how mysterious to the landsmen, how unconsidered by the
millions of women who go to a fish-shop every day.

There are in Aberdeen alone nearly 3,000 fishermen in 300
trawlers, who sweep the North Sea by day and night, in
summer and winter, in order that you—who never think
about them—may have fish for breakfast.

'When do you go out again?'

'Morning at eight,' said the Skipper.

'Will you take me with you?'

The Skipper turned to me a couple of bleak blue eyes.

'Many a visitor has spoilt good fishing,' he said. 'They
get so sick we have to turn back to port with the nets hardly
down!'

'I swear to die quietly—but I'm a good sailor!'

'If you can stick a trawler you can stick anything,' he said.

After a long and persistent conversation I found myself very reluctantly invited to go with him.

'But mind,' he said, 'you've got to muck in with us. It's no blooming Savoy. We don't wear pyjamas and we don't shave, and as I'll lend you oilskins you need no luggage. . . . Eight sharp, and if you don't turn up I'll know you've been sensible and changed your mind!'

Sharp at eight I pulled on a fisherman's jersey and went down to the dock. There she was with steam up. She looked terrifying, but attractive. She was built for wild seas ; her stem was up in the air, and her stern settled firmly in the water, like a hen on its nest. The bridge, or wheel-house, rose up amidships in front of a jet-black smoke-stack. The decks were littered with every kind of gear. An unconvincing lifeboat was parked astern.

'So you've come,' said the Skipper with a grin.

I jumped aboard.

A man in shirt sleeves and a cap was peeling a potato. Other men were mending nets, which were slung up on the starboard side. The trawler smelt of hot oil, onions, fish and boiling soup.

'This is the cabin,' said the Skipper.

I went backwards down a perpendicular ladder, hit my head a fearful crack on an iron girder, and found myself in a queer little oblong dug-out lit by jets of acetylene gas. My first impression of a trawler's cabin was overpowering. It smelt of men, fish, tobacco, acetylene and Scotch broth.

The entire cabin was occupied by a V-shaped table with a bench running round it. At the back, let into the side of the cabin, were four dark cupboards. One appeared to be occupied by a dead man. A bare arm with an anchor tattooed on it moved slightly and I saw a large face looking at me with a slightly resentful expression. Then the figure heaved round with a grunt and turned its back on me.

In this little badger's den the crew of a trawler eat and sleep. The discomfort was almost priggish. It was a sight to make a woman faint. It was just a retreat from wind and rain and sea which men, inured to a harsh life, had carved out for themselves in the bowels of a ship otherwise occupied with 'gear'. No attempt had been made to make the place even faintly attractive. One glance at it told me that in a trawler there is no leisure.

'Park your gear in my bunk,' said the Skipper.

In a little box in which I could just stand upright, I deposited a small bag containing a towel, a razor, and a tooth-brush.

'You'll be comfortable here,' said the Skipper.

'Rather,' I replied, with just a little too much heartiness.

A faint shudder ran through the trawler and we moved. The Skipper up in his wheel-house took her within a yard of other craft without smelling their paint. He did things with the ship that no man could do with a motor-car. In a few minutes we reached the open sea. Up went the trawler's nose and down went her tail. She seemed determined not to miss one wave !

I sat on a pile of nets astern, and thought that this would be the first time since the War that I had slept for three nights in my clothes. In half an hour I knew that I was not going to be ill ! I was delighted !

Immense men in thigh boots clumped about the deck, but I could get nothing but monosyllables out of them. I wondered whether they would ever become human. An elderly man, with the most depressing expression I have ever seen, was swearing quietly and continually at a steam winch. This was my first meeting with Old George, one of the hardest workers on the North Sea. I did not then know that he seldom speaks to anyone.

'Good morning,' I shouted. 'A grand day.'

A glance of incredible hatred was my answer.

'What the hell has that to do with you ? ' said George's eyes.

He turned and went on swearing at the winch with a kind of savage joy :

'This,' I thought, ' is not going to be a sociable party.'

'Skipper wants you on the bridge,' shouted some one ; and I staggered forward, with the sea hissing by and the trawler's nose now high in air and now down deep in the trough of the swell.

The wheel-house rose high above the deck and its windows rattled like the windows of an elderly taxi-cab. The Skipper stood with one arm flung in a friendly way over the wheel. A compass swung from the roof, but there were no maps or charts.

'Don't need 'em,' said the Skipper. 'Been on the North Sea for fifty year.'

I learnt that he was the first man to take a minesweeper out of Aberdeen during the War. He explained to me the routine of life in a trawler.

Ten men compose the crew—skipper, first mate, two engineers, fireman, cook, and four fishermen or 'deckies'. Every one except the engineers takes a hand with the nets and the gutting of the fish. The ordinary members of the crew receive 9s. 6d. a day, and a bonus of 5s., 7s. 6d. and 10s., if the catch at the end of the fishing has averaged £30, £40 or £50 a day, which does not always happen ! The trawl is put down and pulled up every three hours by day and night. The crew sleep in snatches of one hour, or one hour and a half, between putting out and pulling in the nets. No one is ever off duty. 'It's the hardest life a man can live,' said the Skipper . . .'

I took the wheel and steered the plunging thing through the sea.

'Keep her sou'-west,' I was told.

It was not easy. I would turn the wheel until two marks came together on the compass, and then the mark would waver and I would have to swing her back. I could feel the wind and the sea pulling her. I could see the waves curling and breaking over the bows. Now and then she seemed to lift right out of the water and shudder. There was a thrill in guiding her, in seeing her nose almost imperceptibly turn at the bidding of my hands on the wheel.

So we went on for two hours or so, the skipper's blue eyes roving over the sea, which he knows as well as a policeman knows his beat. In another half-hour, he explained, we would steam at slow speed and drop the trawl.

The first mate climbed up into the wheel-house.

'Dinner,' said the Skipper ; and we lurched aft to the cabin.

Here were gathered four members of the crew. The cook —still wearing his cap—climbed down the ladder with a saucepan full of something that would have made anyone liable to sea-sickness die on the spot. It was unskimmed Scotch broth ! There were peas and leeks and carrots and beans and turnips ' intilt,' and the surface was a golden pattern of grease bubbles, some large and some small. After this he again returned, bearing a tin full of meat roasted in fat. This was followed by a gigantic batter pudding served with custard.

While this witches' Sabbath was proceeding in the cabin, the trawler seemed to be taking hurdles. A mug of tea would suddenly slide six inches to the left or right, or I would find that a spoonful of soup designed for my mouth swerved suddenly towards my left ear. It was a difficult meal; but for the second time I knew that I was not going to be ill. . . .

The meal was taken in dead silence. I have a vivid memory of large, black hands digging knives into a pound of butter, and I understood what the Skipper meant when he said that many a visitor had spoilt good fishing! But I liked it. It was exciting! It was worth doing.

Here we were tossing about the North Sea, trying to earn a living by an effort that would kill nine men out of ten. There was something heroic about it; something new, and something no one could possibly imagine. I knew—even when I met the baleful eye of George—that here was a crew of first-class fellows. I could feel that soon we would conquer a mutual suspicion, and be telling stories. First one and then another left the table to get on with the job.

' It's time to fish,' said the Skipper.

Almost as he said it the engine changed its tune and we were steaming at half speed. I went up on deck to see how an Aberdeen trawler catches fish.

§ 2

The trawler rode a wild sea. The crew were busy with a complicated net that ran practically the length of the starboard side.

This net is so designed that it moves along the bed of the sea. There is a wide opening that drives the fish into ' the bag '—a net big enough to hold a horse—from which there is no escape. On every trawler, slung up fore and aft, you will see two wooden boards as large as a front door. After the net has been flung, these boards are lowered on steel ropes and, running far apart at parallel distances, they serve to keep the mouth of the net distended.

The skipper directed operations from his wheel-house.

' Let her go! '

There was a great splash as the net went overboard with its floats and runners. The steam winch began to chug on the fo'c'sle, and in splashed the trawl boards. Then many fathoms of steel line were let out, and we began to steam at about four miles an hour over the wide and enigmatic North Sea. What would come up in the trawl in three hours' time ?

The three hours which elapse between the first time of flinging in nets and pulling up are the only three hours in which a trawler's crew can—to use a rather absurd word—rest. The men clamped off over the wet and swaying deck. Four of them went to the little dark cupboards in the cabin and curled themselves in sleep.

Trawler fishermen have Napoleon's genius for sleep. They can come in from a bitterly cold wind, after prolonged physical effort, to snatch an hour's sleep, and awaken immediately the bell sounds for the next haul. I was astonished by their stamina until it occurred to me that much of their work was automatic. They had been doing it for years. They could not conceive of any other kind of work. For years they had been awakened from a sudden sleep at intervals of three hours, day and night, to go up on deck and haul away, to knock out the pin and pull up the trawl boards.

In the bridge-house the Skipper, a pipe between his teeth, steered a deserted ship over a swelling sea. Far off to the right was a dim line of land :

' Montrose ! ' said the Skipper.

I looked down on the dead ship. Every one save the engineer and the firemen was snatching sleep. Even ' Old George ' was asleep somewhere, wearing, I have no doubt, the same resentful expression that he wears in his moments of baleful consciousness. Possibly even Alec, the cook, was asleep, still wearing his cap.

' How do you know where to trawl ? ' I asked the Skipper.

' Oh : it's just knowing,' he replied, helpfully.

And the wheel turned, taking us in the track of fish ; for the Skipper's china-blue eyes are said not only to be able to see astern, but to see right down to the bottom of the sea !

' Prices are bad and there's no money in fishing to-day,' said the Skipper. ' Numbers of boats are in debt.'

Each boat in a fleet is like an individual company that

shows a loss or a profit. Although they may belong to the same firm they set out as individuals, going where they think the fish are to be found. The money which an ordinary eighty-ton trawler must make in a year, before it can show a profit, is incredible.

'This boat cannot begin to pay,' said the Skipper, 'until we have sold £6,000 worth of fish in twelve months; and that takes a bit of doing in these times. . . .'

We talked of the fisherman and his life, for the men who comb the North Sea are a type as distinct as the miner. The sea and fishing run in their blood. They cannot settle down ashore. I was surprised to learn that every member of the crew except one was married. In fables and folk tales it is always a man who marries a mermaid, but in real life, it seems, it is the woman who links her lonely life to that of a merman! It was odd to think that the crew of this trawler, who seemed married only to their perpetual labour, had any link with the shore.

'Ay, we're queer folk,' said the Skipper. 'I remember the days of the old sailing ships. Men used to go out fishing with charms about them. And good luck or bad luck always had something magic about it. In the old times many a ship's crew would refuse to sail on a Friday because they thought it was unlucky. And if you mentioned a parson, a salmon, a rabbit or a pig when you were at sea—well; they were cruel days too! And if you mentioned any of these words ashore, you used to see the fisherman lift his foot until he could touch the iron of the boot heel, which broke the spell.'

He gave a turn to the wheel, and we talked of the War and the art of mine-sweeping.

'There were some great boys in the mine-sweepers,' he said, 'and some queer ones. Funny things happened, too! I remember there was a fellow we could do nothing with. He was no use. And we tried every way to get shot of him! And one day the commandant of the shore depot comes along in his launch and says: "Have you got anyone you can recommend for a job?" So we see our chance. "Yes," we says, "we've got a very good man!" and we give his name—glad to get rid of him at last. The next day comes an order to fall in in full uniform, if you please! So we fall in. Up comes the launch, and what do you think they do? They pin a blessed medal on the mug's chest! They were dishing out decorations, not looking for a spare man ! Can you beat that ? Time to haul-in. . . .'

He rang a bell. One by one the sleepers awakened and grouped themselves along the starboard side. The net was coming up !

The sky, which had been as deserted as the sea, became suddenly full of wings. First twenty, then thirty, then a hundred gulls of all kinds appeared, it seemed, by magic. Soon there were thousands wheeling over us, or riding the sea with smug, expectant expressions : gulls, saddle-backs, pretty, dove-like kittiwakes, with beaks the colour of pistachio nuts, great herring gulls, and, loveliest of all, solan geese, long of neck, hawk-eyed, and cruising high up ready to dive.

As these birds heard the winch, and saw the movement of the trawl lines, they became frantic with excitement. Slowly the net was pulled up. Out came the trawl boards. Men placed their hands on the net and began to pull. First one gannet dropped like a stone into the water and then another. They rose from their dive, each holding a small wriggling fish.

As the bag of the net came up the sea grew sandy. Twenty solan geese dived together. Their white bodies cut a green line deep in the water. I could see a white blur of feathers where they fought to take fish from the net. They were the shock troops of this enormous winged and hungry army.

The dripping mesh was gradually pulled up and the bag was swung on the derrick high above the fo'c'sle. It hung there dripping sea water. It shook with struggling fish. It was an enormous bag of life dredged from the sea bed. I could see between the coarse mesh the flapping tails of flat fish, the gasping head of a cod or a haddock, and coral pink sea urchins by the thousand. Some one pulled a rope, and with a great wet splash thousands of fish fell struggling on the deck.

It was an astonishing jumble. It looked like the end of some famous aquarium. Soles, plaice, cod, haddock, cat-fish, monk fish, eels, mackerel, hake, and dozens of fish unknown to me lay in a great pile two feet deep.

They lay forgotten. The crew was putting out the net for another three-hour trawl. Only the Skipper stood gazing at the fish, picking up a cod by the tail, examining a sole, or flinging some worthless object overboard where the gannets dived and the gulls screamed.

II

' Is it a good catch ? '

' Not bad. It's lemon soles I want.'

' And, by heaven, you've got them ! '

' Might have been better. . . .'

No sooner was the net out than the work began. The Skipper took the wheel. Every member of the crew—save the two protected by the engineers' union !—sat side by side on the wooden edge of the ' fish pond ' with penknives in their hands. Even the fireman came up from his hot iron cave into the cold spray. Even the cook left his galley and lent a hand. Then began a rather horrible slaughter. The living fish were taken up, one by one, and gutted. The bodies were flung into baskets : flat fish in one, cod in another, haddock in a third, and so on. In this first bag was an octopus. George gloomily discovered it and flung it back into the sea. It was the only fish whose death I really desired, because I felt that it might some day turn up at Bournemouth.

The strangest fish was the Angler Fish, which is merely a huge mouth attached to an edible tail. This horrible thing lies on the sea-bed with an antenna supended over its cavern-ous mouth. At the end of the antenna, or fishing-rod, is a spot of phosphorus. Small fish, approaching to investigate this light, find themselves inside the mouth !

The fiercest fish was the cat-fish. It opened jaws of steel and, making the face a cat makes when it sees a dog, dug its fangs into the nearest solid matter. This fish is known in shops as ' rock salmon '.

' It's the cleanest fish that swims the seas,' I was told. ' It lives on nothing but shell fish.'

In an hour and a half every fish was gutted and packed away in ice. The Skipper smoked his pipe, and calmly swung us here and there above the fishing ground. The crew trooped back automatically to the dark little cabin, where they flung themselves down and were asleep in ten minutes.

An hour passed. A bell rang :

' Haul in ! '

They trooped out on deck to gain another bulging bag of varied life from the North Sea. It was now almost sun-down. I was already wondering what night would be like on this strange ship.

§ 3

The trawler rises and falls in the darkness. In all other trades and occupations the day's work is over. In factories and in mines the new shift is replacing the old. But here day and night are alike ; and the same shift carries on through the twenty-four hours.

The last daylight ' bag ' has been gutted and the fish stowed below in ice. The crew are taking one of their two-hour ' rests '. The mate is on the bridge. The cook is washing up. The jolly young Scots engineer is sitting below in heat and oil listening to the rhythm of his engine. And the North Sea hisses past us, sometimes leaping over the side in a shower of spray.

I climb below into the fug of the cabin. It smells of strong tobacco and the ghost of the last meal. The wall cupboards contain sleeping men. Old George sits gloomily at the table, holding a mug of tea. He never appears to sleep : he has massive reveries instead. He gazes right through the vibrating cabin walls, right across the North Sea, across Scotland, across Ireland, perhaps across America, to some grim Valhalla known only to himself. If he wore a spiked helmet instead of a cap he would look a bit like Bismarck. Suddenly a loud and refined voice shouts from behind Old George ; and this is what it says :

' The poetrah of dot-dot-dot-dash-dash is—bzzzzwheeeee dot-dot inevitablah divided into three main divisions dash-dash-dash his lyrics for example are things of sheer and flaw-less beautah dash-dot-dot for instance his—wheeeeeeee dot-dot employment of words, so right, so lovelah, so, as one might say, picked like a flowah from a hedge-row dot-dot-dot-dot . . .''

It is the Voice of the World speaking to us as we toss about trying to catch the world's breakfast. The skipper turns over in a bunk :

' Yarmouth herring prices come through yet, George ? '

George makes a noise which means ' No,' and the skipper turns and is instantly asleep. There is no sound but the puff-chug-chug of the engine—regular as heart-beats—the creak of wood, the hiss and bang of the sea against our hull and the incredible Voice of the World saying :

' Take this gift of expression so perfectlah shown in his lines on immortalitah. . . .'

Old George sits there with the face of a ruined emperor, cursing, cursing, cursing, with a ' gift of expression ' undreamt of by the Voice of the World, that white-bellied, green-eyed, leprous, misbegotten monk-fish that bit through his new thirty-shilling rubber boots.

I go up on deck and look at the stars. The moon is rising over the sea. It looks like a segment of an orange. It glows dully like the glow from a furnace, then clouds cover it and the sea is the colour of steel. I sit on a pile of nets astern, enjoying the kick of the boat as she buckets along, thinking how uncomplicated life can be. All the finer, more exquisite, pains of life are absent in this constant physical wrestle with elemental things. I could never retire to a monastery to expiate my sins, but I could retreat to a trawler ; or I think I could.

I speculate on the possibility of sleeping on these nets and so avoiding the heat and fug in the badger's den below. If I put on the great coat with the hood which the skipper lent me, perhaps it would not be too cold. It is a long time since I have slept under stars.

A bell rings . . .

Slowly the crew lumber up into the starlight. Their ' rest ' is over ; and once more they must pull in whatever the generous sea has given. Acetylene lamps are lit on deck. They illuminate the starboard side and the fo'c'sle. As the net comes up the sea is faintly luminous. Fish flash and vanish. They dart madly on the surface like streaks of quicksilver. Their eyes are green, like the eyes of cats at night—thousands of green pin-pricks in the sea—and, gradually the huge phosphorescent bag bulging with its living harvest is hauled high in the air and emptied with a cold splash on deck.

It is a tremendous ' bag '. It is better than the day catches. A voice from the bridge sings :

> ' Daisy, Daisy, give me your answer do.
> I'm half crazy all for the love of you.
> It won't be a stylish marriage ;
> We can't afford a carriage. . . .

ease off that main derrick there or you'll have the damned board in the sea !

> But you'd look sweet, upon the seat
> Of a bicycle made for two.'

This song indicates that the catch is good:

'Aye,' says a Scots voice in the dark, 'but when the bag comes up bulging like a tam o' shanter fu' wi' lemon sole ye'll hear the auld man sing his masterpiece.'

'And what's that?'

'It's called: "I'm dancin' wi' tears in my eyes." '

Rain falls. It slews across us, icily cold. I huddle myself in the hooded cloak. The crew clump aft, their hands red with blood from the gutting.

'Man, come awa'; ye'll surely freeze oot there,' says a great voice.

I stick it a while longer, but am driven down. The cabin looks cosy. There are tea, jam, and a tin of hot minced meat. This is the fourth, and last, meal of the day. It is eleven o'clock.

The Voice of the World says:

'This is Jack Brown and his band playing to you from the Dorchester Hotel, London.'

The cabin rings with a fox-trot. When it ends I can hear the murmur and rustle of people leaving the floor. I wonder who has the little table near the gold screen to-night and if Hugo has taken them into the kitchens to see the live trout.

'Do they dance in yon place till midnight?' asks some one, gazing solemnly over a mug of tea.

'Sometimes later.'

'They must get awfu' tired. . . .'

This is not irony! The great fellow who has been hauling nets for twenty-four hours really means it! I want to go up on deck and howl my laughter to the stars. By heaven, how funny!

Gradually, the men knock out their pipes and climb into their cupboards. The band in London plays an energetic tune. An enormous boot protrudes from one bunk, a hairy arm from another, a pair of blue trousers, much worn, from a third.

I find myself falling asleep, so I climb into the bunk which the skipper kindly evacuated and, taking off my shoes, lie down on a hard hill with my head on a leaden pillow. I can hear the sea moving past in long swelling waves that rise up along the hull and dip astern into watery hollows. The engine sounds exactly like a train puffing slowly . . . just like a train. Oh! the trains I have known in my life, sad trains and happy ones. . . .

Hell is suddenly let loose over my head! Something like a shell seems to have got us amidships! I sit up, hit my head on the ceiling, curse, look at my watch! It is 5 a.m. Then I have been asleep! They are up on deck pulling at that eternal net. The bang was the trawl board coming up. I can hear men stamping and shouting. I pull on sea boots. The cabin is empty.

Up on deck I see them braced against a dawn wind, their hands wet, their fingers crooked in the brown meshes, pulling in together—'aaaay—up!'—as the net comes aboard to the scraping sound of crushed shells and stone from the bottom of the sea.

What an epic of labour it is—and they don't know it!

Towards the east is a troubled line in the sky like a little ache. It breaks the blueness of night. Soon it will be day.

§ 4

It is 7.30 in the morning, with a fresh wind blowing, the gulls screaming, and the latest haul of fish lying gasping on the deck.

I wonder why the sight of so much suffering life rouses no compassion in me. If they squealed, or made any sounds of pain, it would be unbearable, but these creatures, possibly because they live in a different element, have no kinship with us. Perhaps that is why a fish-shop is always interesting and a butcher's revolting.

A trawler's crew is not given to the softer emotions. They stamp about in the pool of squirming life in their great sea boots. I hate to watch this, yet if I were a fish I would prefer to be crushed quickly by the boot of a fifteen-stone man than gutted alive with a penknife.

The waste that goes on every day and all day in a trawler is appalling. The skipper tells me that fish are less plentiful than they used to be because of the amount of trawling that goes on, but no one dreams of sorting out the little ones and throwing them back.

During my first day at sea I caused loud laughter by gathering up all the small, rejected soles and plaice, and carefully carrying them to the port side (away from the unappeasable gulls), where I flung them back to marry and have families. But it was disappointing! Fish caught in a trawl get 'drowned'. They are brought up in a breathless condition, after having been dragged for miles over the sea bottom. Nine out of every ten flat fish—codling and haddock have greater vitality—just turn a white belly to the sky when returned to the sea and drift slowly and depressingly downward.

A figure in shirt sleeves and a cap comes along the deck holding a tin pan. He gazes critically at the catch, pulls out one or two lemon soles, a hake, a haddock and a few plaice and flings them into the pan. This is our breakfast. In half an hour we shall be eating these fish.

How can I describe the experience of eating fish straight from the sea?

We troop down into the little cabin. We are hungry. We have been out for hours in the salt winds. The cook climbs down the ladder with the fish, which he has fried in the same pan into which he gathered them half an hour before. It is a kind of fishy mixed grill. We dive into it with our forks and—there is dead silence for a time! A lemon sole straight from the sea and fried in the most primitive manner in Alec's inadequate galley tastes finer than any *sole bonne femme* or *sole Colbert* that you will find in the great hotels and restaurants of the world. It is white and firm. It has the tang of the sea in it. When you cut it, the flesh parts and reveals a clean, polished skeleton.

As we light our pipes after breakfast and finish the good old army tea, the skipper tells us stories which begin:

'Have ye heard about the Yorkshire man who . . .'

Just as he is launched there is a great clatter down the stair, and a man comes into the cabin. One look at him tells the skipper and his men what is the matter. Their action takes place simultaneously with his words:

'*She's fast!*' he cries.

There is a rush for the door. The skipper jumps up on the seat that runs round the cabin and leaps down to save time. The others lumber up after him. The awakened engineer pokes a head out of his bunk:

'What has happened?' I ask.

'Och; she's fast. . . .'

'Who is *she,* and why is she fast?'

'The net,' he explains. 'She's caught up on a wreck or something. If ye'd learn some new words ye should go up on deck now. . . .'

Up on deck is the only scene of excitement that ever occurs on a trawler. Every one is gathered on the starboard side gazing down into the water. The first mate on the bridge has stopped the engines. The little ship rolls from side to side in the swell. Old George is swearing to himself in his quiet, deliberate way as he pulls a rope. The skipper directs operations; and on every face is anxiety.

The trawl net has become entangled in something at the sea bottom. The first sign was the ship's refusal to steer. Then the enormous weight of the net with its attendant boards had brought the trawler to a standstill. This is the frequent tragedy of trawling: sometimes the damage is slight; sometimes it runs into more money than the day's fish are worth, and sometimes net, boards and everything have to be cut away.

The skipper puts an inch of grease on a lead weight and drops it into fifty fathoms of water. He pulls it up, looks at it critically, and says:

'Aye, I thought so—it's a wreck.'

He then takes the wheel. He can do anything with his trawler. He is the taxicab driver of the sea. He can turn her almost in her own length; he can make her advance, or retreat or passage like a charger in a musical ride. And on this occasion he does all his tricks. The ship jazzes round the captive trawl. The steam winch stammers away for a while, but—no—the net is fast! At last, after half an hour's coaxing, we go half steam ahead and, far below at the bottom of the sea, our net is torn over the wreck—and up she comes!

The net is woefully torn. There is nothing left of the ' bag '. There are great rents and gaps in the meshes. And this is the tragedy of trawling! No fisherman can tell as he casts the trawl overboard whether it will sink to a clean sea-bed or drag itself over a rock.

Fishermen, like agriculturists, and all those who occupy themselves with the eternal verities, have great philosophy. No use crying over torn nets! Unship the port trawl! The crew leave the ruined net on the starboard side and rush over to the port side, where they sink the other net ; and the trawler goes on her journey.

You might think that in an occupation which allows men casual snatches of sleep during a working day of twenty-four hours a sudden accident of this kind—which means more work and less sleep—would cause a deal of grousing and bad temper. But not a bit of it ! The crew hang up the tattered net and begin to mend it, almost good-humouredly, almost as if they were sorry for it. And as the new net sinks with a great splash into the green swell a tousled red head looks down at it and a Scotsman cries :

'Gang doon to hell and—come back fu' o' fush . . .'

That is the sailor's farewell to the new trawl !

§ 5

Much of the hatred and mistrust in this world of ours is caused by the inability, or the lack of opportunity, to study our fellow human beings.

When I joined the trawler she appalled me. I called her a floating slum. I thought of her as a compromise on a large scale between a clog and a coal bucket. Her elaborate discomfort seemed to me almost a kind of snobbishness. I disliked the basket of onions and potatoes which lay on what I priggishly nicknamed the 'quarter-deck'. The absence of lavatories, and the habit of washing hands in a bucket of water brown with blood and sea slime (and the knowledge that this 'fresh' water was filtered and used again and again), revolted me.

In the first few hours I had redesigned the ship in my mind, repainted her, cleaned her up and had discovered the potentialities of a disused cabin under the wheel-house. You see, I was looking at her with my own eyes.

After a few days at sea I find myself getting fond of her. I am looking at her with the eyes of a fisherman. I like the basket of vegetables in the stern because I know that even if there were room for it in the cook's galley it would not be as fresh as it is out in the rain and the wind.

The overcrowding is inevitable in an eighty-ton ship in which ten men are trying to win, in the most economical manner, a living from the sea. She is a floating workshop. There is nothing about her, no matter how clumsy it may seem to ignorant eyes, which is not there as the result of experiment and experience. She is as grim and specialized and as efficient as a woman. She is made for only one job : to go out in wild seas and catch fish.

The hold forward, where the fish lie in the dignity of death (and crushed ice), is more spacious than our cabin ; and that is all part of her efficiency. She is firstly a machine for trawling the sea ; secondly a storehouse for the catch ; and thirdly —but a long way after—a place in which we eat and try to sleep.

It is strange, too, how quickly one becomes fond of a ship and how quickly a ship becomes a personality. The smaller the ship, I think, the more endearing she seems. No one, for instance, could love the *Majestic*, just as no one could love a town hall. Some things are too big and impersonal for affection. But this funny little trawler, as she kicks and buckets about the North Sea, is in some way gallant and pitiful.

I am sure she is the best trawler on the North Sea. I am sure she is more efficient at her job than any other. I am beginning to share the unexpressed, and perhaps inexpressible, pride of the crew in her, for no team of men can work so hard and so continuously unless they are united by a quality of mind which perhaps they would not recognize as pride or loyalty. And it is a fine, clean thing to meet. Trawling is, judged by ordinary standards, a terrible life. But it has a certain hard dignity, whereas the labour of a person who automatically pushes sheet after sheet of cardboard into a fearful machine that can never err is, to my mind, lacking in dignity.

This floating stage on which the drama of the North Sea fisherman is played has a mystical and a spiritual significance. I go up on her deck at night, and, in a solitude of stars and sea and a fierceness of rain and wind, know that there is nothing trivial or second-rate about her. It is dangerous to be alone with the sea too long, because you might begin to think too much. And our pride in this ordinary, rather dirty little steam trawler takes this form :

' She cost six thousand pounds before the War,' says the skipper, ' but could you get a ship as good as she is—full of pre-War stuff—for twelve thousand pounds to-day ? Not blooming likely . . .'

And I glow with reflected pride and agree. The engineer rubs an oily rag over some portion of his engine, and says: 'I can screw eleven knots out of her. . . .'

And I say 'Damned good'; and mean it.

The last catch is on deck. The ship tosses along at four knots. Suddenly the voice of the Skipper is heard from the bridge. It sings:

> *Dainty Dolly-Daydreams,*
> *Pride of Idaho; so now you know . . .*
> *La-di-da-di-da-di-da,*
> *Pom-pom-pom-pom . . .*
> *For no one's got to kiss that girl but me.*

The men smile as they slit open the bellies of fish. The 'old man' is pleased! We have had good fishing. We have filled one hundred eight-stone boxes of fish on what is known as a three day 'scratch'. Our first day was poor. No quality. The skipper said to me:

'I wonder if you're a Jonah!'

Then the lemon soles came in! Then the 'bag' came up, bulging and round, not cone-shaped with poor stuff, and the sound of songs that still drift round the corners of elderly hearts came from the wheel-house at night. Once in the middle of the night we paused in the darkness and waited:

> *'I'm dancing with . . .'*

Would the Skipper sing his masterpiece? Would he dance with tears in his eyes? Would he sing that song reserved for a superlative bag? With Yorkshire caution he peered down into the thin pool of acetylene light where the fish flapped and gasped, and —never finished the line! It was not quite good enough . . . nearly; but not quite! But it was a 'You are the Honeysuckle, I am the Bee' catch!

So the daily gamble went on. Fifty, sixty, seventy boxes filled. Now, with a hundred boxes of good fish in ice, the Skipper bursts into song, flings over the engine-room signal to 'Full steam ahead', and the tough little ship shudders and quickens, lifts her nose, drops her stern, and a cloud of salt spray lifts itself over her to fall foaming on the deck.

Old George, caught without his oilskins, retains his inscrutable expression and addresses a few terrible words to his inveterate enemy, the steam-winch.

Clothed from head to foot like an armadillo in stiff oilskins,

I go right to the stem and hold tight to ropes as I enjoy the wild lifting of the ship and the sudden exciting drenching as the wave breaks over us. I wonder why the old wooden figure-heads generally wore such gloomy and dignified expressions. They should have been carved shouting or singing. There is nothing more maddening to the blood than to stand right in the stem of a ship, and to feel her rising and falling to the sound of hissing water and the sharp lash of spray.

When I look back over the steep fo'c'sle I see the stern low down in the water, settled firmly like a rider in his saddle, and all round is a lovely wash of angry sea, with a white, swift pattern of gulls screaming in our wake, the solan geese, flying high, dropping like darts into the green water. The skipper removes his pipe and shouts something which I cannot hear. But the next moment I know, as she goes down, down, down, into the very depths of the swell, lifts till I am swung up into the sky and then—crack, and I am drenched from head to foot !

Far off to the left the roofs of Aberdeen rise from the sea. Although I am dying for a hot bath, I begin to feel sorry to leave this ship. If I could have spent another month aboard her perhaps Old George and I might have been on speaking terms. But I must not get vain.

What a good crowd they are ! I shall never pass a fish-shop again without remembering them and their companions in the little ships that sweep the North Sea day and night. For they are as uncomplicated as we in cities are complicated. They are, in the true sense of the word, sea men.

The Voice of the World, that gives them a children's hour downstairs in the cabin, and something they cannot understand from Spain or Germany or Rome, is significant only when it speaks to them of storm or tempest or the price of fish :

'Ah, that fellow who does the weather must be a clever chap,' they say. 'He's often right . . .'

And in the middle of the Prime Minister's impassioned speech one night, when the destiny of our unhappy country seemed to vibrate in his voice, some one switched off and remarked :

'Fifteen bob a cran for herring's no blinking good, Alec.'

So I stand on the quay at Aberdeen in a blue jersey, shaking enormous hands :

' Come back some day.'

' I will—some day.'

I tell the Skipper I would like to take the crew for a drink :

' No liquor on this ship,' he says.

' What are you all going to do to-night ? '

' Oh, we'll go to the pictures ! '

I try to visualize them, enormous in the gloom, watching something wicked and improbable happening in a world that is strange to them. It is an astonishing thought—as strange as if one came suddenly on a band of Vikings eating chocolate cream !

' Good-bye ! '

I turn away with regret ; and as I walk I feel the sea rising and falling in my head.

CHAPTER ELEVEN

TELLS HOW THE HONOURS OF SCOTLAND WERE SAVED, HOW THE
CAPTAIN OF THE 'ROYAL AND ANCIENT' PLAYS HIMSELF INTO
OFFICE, WITH SOMETHING ABOUT ST. ANDREWS, STIRLING, INCH-
MAHOLME AND THE SIGNIFICANCE OF 'THE CURSE OF SCOTLAND'

§ I

I LEFT Aberdeen with the knowledge that winter was on
the way. The storm that had rocked me so thoroughly
on the North Sea had swept with fury over the land.
In these few days the roads were choked with leaves and
the wind held a bite in it that spoke of approaching snow.
'It's snell,' said a man in Aberdeen. What marvellous words
slip out of Scotsmen now and then! Snell! That is exactly
what the wind was—snell: a word that sends a shiver of
cold up the spine, a word straight from an ice-box, a word
that must have been coined at the North Pole.

As I went south along the coast, autumn still lingered in
the quiet fields, combed now of the harvest but dotted with
cone-shaped ricks; and in the woodlands of the Dee trees
were expiring in a last blaze of red and gold.

When I was about four miles from Aberdeen, I had a desire
to see a village on the coast which has given its name to a
fish known all over the world—Findon. This is the birthplace of the 'Finnan' Haddock.

I turned down a side road and came at length to a few
houses standing on hilly ground beside an ashy-grey stretch
of the North Sea. The only sign of life was a man in blue
overalls mixing concrete beside a gate-post. I asked him
where I could see a Findon Haddock, and he looked surprised.
No haddocks are Findoned there these days! Years ago
every little house in Findon used to smoke the fish, but
nowadays this is done in Aberdeen.

I went on south. Dunnottar Castle rose on a mighty rock
beside the sea. It was in this castle that, during the wars
of the Commonwealth, the 'Honours of Scotland'—the
Regalia—were hidden. There are dozens of stories about

them. One says that they were smuggled out of the castle in the creel of a fishwife. Another says that Mrs. Grainger, wife of the minister of Kinneff Church, bore them through the ranks of the besiegers, carrying the Crown of Scotland in her lap and the Sceptre disguised as a distaff.

That is the popular story, but any one who has seen the Honours of Scotland in the Jewel Room of Edinburgh Castle will find it rather difficult to credit. Even if, as the story goes, Mrs. Grainger received permission from General Monk to take certain bundles of flax out of the castle, it is hardly possible that such bulky bundles as those wrapped round Scotland's crown, sceptre and sword, could pass through the least-vigilant sentries without difficulty. And as we know that General Monk was chiefly interested in gaining possession of the Regalia, even inserting a clause about it in the subsequent treaty of surrender, it is surely not possible that Mrs. Grainger could have performed this act. The story says that General Monk himself assisted the lady to mount her horse!

It would seem far more likely that the simpler plan would work, that of letting down the 'Honours' on a rope from the steep rock, while some one gathering sea-weed came along and casually pitched them in a cart.

It is, however, an historic fact that the 'Honours of Scotland' were gallantly smuggled out of Dunnottar Castle and taken to the Rev. James Grainger, minister of the neighbouring parish of Kinneff. He hid them for a time at the foot of a bed in the manse, until he found a more secure hiding-place, which he described in the following document, signed June 4, 1642, drawn up in case he should die before Scotland's Regalia was claimed :

" I, Mr. James Grainger, Minister of Kinneff, grant me to have in my custody the Honours of the Kingdom viz. the croun, sceptre and sword. For the croun and sceptre I raised the pavement-stone just before the pulpit, in the night tyme, and digged under it ane hole, and put them in there, and filled up the hole, and layed doun the stone just as it was before, and removed the mould that remained, that none would have discerned the stone to have been raised at all. The sword again, at the west end of the church, amongst some common saits that stand there, I digged down in the ground betwixt the twa foremost of these saits, and laid it doun with the case of it, and covered it up, as that removing the superfluous mould it could not be discerned by anybody ; and if it shall please God to call me by death before they be called for, your ladyship will find them in that place.'

The 'ladyship' to whom this letter was addressed was the Dowager Countess Marischall, widow of the hereditary guardians of the Scottish Crown Jewels and feudal proprietor of Dunnottar Castle. As soon as Charles II was restored to the Throne this lady at once hastened to Whitehall to tell the secret of the hiding-place, and to claim for herself and her son the full glory and honour of having rescued and preserved the Regalia. This was a monstrous injustice, because the people who saved the Regalia were Sir George Ogilvie of Barras, Governor of the Castle, his wife, Elizabeth Douglas, and their kinswoman, Anne Lindsay. The Dowager Countess Marischall may have been in the plot, but Ogilvie and the two gallant ladies carried it out.

The result of this dispute was a bitter family quarrel between the Keiths and the Ogilvies, and King Charles rewarded them most unjustly : young Sir John Keith (who had been in France at the time the Regalia was saved) was made Earl of Kintore and Knight Marischall with an annual salary of £400, while Ogilvie was made only a baronet and given a slightly more favourable tenure of his estate at Barras.

The late Lord Cowdray, who owned Dunnottar Castle, spent a small fortune in restoring it, and the castle to-day has been brought back to life. It is one of the most loving and intelligent reconstructions of an ancient fortress that I have seen. There is a room which is kept locked. Its windows look down from the steep cliff to the sea. Lord Cowdray reconstructed this room as a luncheon place for guests of the family who visited the ruins. Over the fireplace is the following inscription :

In commemoration of the Defence of the Honours of Scotland from Sept. 1651 to May 1652 by George Ogilvy of Barras, Governor of Dunnottar, and of the help given to him by his wife, Elizabeth Douglas, and by her kinswoman, Anne Lindsay.

It is slightly consoling to know that the walls of Dunnottar give credit to those who strove so bravely to preserve the symbols of Scotland's independence.

Montrose, whose fine steeple shows up far off along the

coast road, is a quiet, good-looking country town with a distinguished, wide main street. All sorts of things have happened to Montrose in the course of its existence. Balliol surrendered the Scottish throne there, and Sir James Douglas, carrying the embalmed heart of Robert Bruce, embarked at Montrose for the Holy Land. And it was from Montrose that James Francis Edward, the Old Chevalier, stole through the snow of a winter's night to the harbour and a ship, and so the '15 ended.

I was looking in a shop window in Montrose and noticed a pie called a Forfar Bridie. I went inside and ate one. They are extremely good and should be eaten hot. They are made of minced steak cut into inch-long lengths and seasoned with salt, pepper, and sometimes with a little minced onion. This pie was the speciality of a Mr. Jolly, a baker, who made them in the county town of Forfar about half a century ago. . . .

Thirteen miles from Montrose is Arbroath.

What a delightful town. The guide book says : ' Noted for its fine Abbey Church and as the " Fairport " of Scott's " Antiquary," but otherwise uninteresting.'

On the contrary, I found Arbroath one of the most interesting towns on the east coast of Scotland ! Its cleanness delighted me ! It looks as though every street has a valet to brush it and press it into neatness and smartness. Baskets of flowers hang from every lamp-post. This may be a habit caught from Dundee, which is the only other place I know with garlanded lamps. Dundee's lamps, if I remember them, go in for nasturtiums and geraniums ; Arbroath's lamps hold out baskets of pink geraniums and marguerites.

These flowers give a pretty, festive appearance to Arbroath. You feel happy and pleased as soon as you see them. I wish all towns in England and Scotland would take a tip from Arbroath and deck their streets with flowers.

The red-sandstone abbey is one of the grandest ruins in Scotland. It is in charge of one of the best guides in the land. Mr. Wilson, who stood in the face of a flaming red sunset and rebuilt the abbey for me, filled it with incense and monks, waved his hand and reconstructed the Old Regality Hall where—how many Scotsmen know ?—the Scottish Act of Independence was planned in 1320.

He showed me the famous ' O ' of Arbroath, a fine round

window in the south transept, which in the old days was lighted with a beacon for the use of sailors. Then he took me into the Chapter House, where I saw the gigantic leg bone of William the Lion.

A Scots Parliament, that assembled in this place in 1320, made a pronouncement that is not only a landmark in Scotland's struggle for independence but is also one of the finest things ever uttered in Europe on Nationalism. The statement grew out of the Pope's unwillingness to recognize Bruce as King of Scotland. This was the answer sent from Arbroath to Rome :

' If this prince ', it ran, ' should leave the principles he has so nobly pursued, and consent that we, or our Kingdom, be subjected to the King or people of England, we shall immediately endeavour to expel him as our enemy, and as the subverter both of his own and our rights, and will make us a king who will defend our liberties ; but as long as there shall but one hundred of us remain alive, we will never subject us to the dominion of the English. It is not glory, it is not riches, neither is it honour, but it is liberty alone that we fight and contend for, which no honest man will lose but with his life.'

Near the harbour a street of whitewashed cottages fronts the North Sea. This is where women prepare that most delicious of all smoked fish, the ' Arbroath Smokie '. The kipper is coarse, and the Finnan haddock uninteresting, compared with the ' Arbroath Smokie '. It is a haddock caught with hook and line, salted for a short time and then smoked.

I visited these cottages and was told all about the art. The men catch the fish and the women smoke them. Behind every house is a big, black barrel half-sunk in the earth. A fire of non-resinous wood is lit in the depths of the barrels, and after a time damped down with wood chips until a thick dense smoke is created. The haddocks, which are never split open like the familiar smoked haddock, are merely decapitated and cleaned and after immersion in a solution of salt are tied tail to tail in pairs and slung over a pole in the smoke. Layers of sacking are hung over the mouth of the barrel to keep in the smoke, and in half an hour or so the ' Arbroath Smokie ' emerges done to a turn and coloured a beautiful bronze-brown.

I was told that there is at least one place in London—a large cooperative store—in which 'smokies' can be bought, but, generally speaking, the beauty of this fish is appreciated only in Scotland. This is a pity. No one who, after spending a day in the open air, encounters an egg riding an 'Arbroath smokie', is ever likely to forget it.

There is, I am told, some peculiar virtue about a 'smokie' smoked in Arbroath. Aberdeen makes them, but the Arbroath fisher-wives—as an old lady with a clay pipe told me —do it much better.

This fishing community with plenty of work to do, and nappy in its work, is a delightful thing to find in any modern town.

There was a time, said a policeman, when the fisher folk rarely mixed much with the townspeople, but now many a pretty fisher girl who bears a creel on her back during the day appears in the evening in silk stockings and a smart costume.

'But,' he said, lowering his voice, 'ye can aye tell her because of her walk. She bends forward, ye ken, from bearin' the creel.'

§ 2

In Dundee I met a man who had some business with a marmalade factory. He persuaded me to go with him. While he was engaged I was allowed to wander about and watch the making of marmalade, cakes and sweets. I came to a room in which something quite out of the ordinary was happening : girls were making sweets that were at least two centuries old, sweets which none of us has seen for many a long day. They are known to the trade as 'Love Hearts', but I remember village children calling them 'Mottoes' when I was a boy. I thought they had quite departed from this earth, and to see them again reminded me of the village grocer's congested window with its post-cards and boots, fly papers and flannel shirts and bottles of ink and sweets. The 'Love Heart' is generally round and about the size of a penny. Some are pink, some blue, some white. Each sweet has a pleasing message written across it in either blue or red sugar :

'There has always been a big sale for these in Scottish country towns,' I was told. 'It is probably the oldest sweet made by us—and we have been making sweets since the year 1793.'

The mottoes have remained more or less constant for a century. As the sweets came cascading through a machine I read:

> *You like to Tease.*
> *Time will Unite Us.*
> *Certainly, Darling.*
> *Guid folk are scarce.*

And the perfectly good Scottish remark: 'Hands off till you are better acquaint.'

'But who buys these?' I asked.

'Oh, they go into village shops all over Scotland.'

These 'Love Hearts' are unsophisticated. Their message is one of provoking simplicity. But in the next room I discovered another kind of sweet—precisely the same in essentials—but absolutely different in its attitude towards life. These, like the 'Love Hearts', were pink and white and blue; some were triangular, some square, some round and some crescent-shape. They said:

> *Say, kid, I like your style.*
> *Gee, but you're some baby.*
> *You're some jazz hound.*
> *You're a regular fellow.*

'These sweets,' I was told, 'we call "Cupid's Whispers".'

'But why does Cupid whisper with such an American accent?'

'Ah, you see, the blocks from which the mottoes are printed come from America.'

'But do these sweets circulate in, say, Mull or Skye, or north of the Caledonian Canal?'

'No; they are only popular in towns which have cinemas.'

'In other words, towns which can translate them?'

'Yes.'

What a strange contrast! In one room thousands of sweets were being made which would have conveyed a tender message to our great-grandmothers, while next door the machines rattle out Americanized triteness for an entirely new generation.

It is a strange and unexplained fact that now and then a motto becomes unpopular. It is instantly changed. But most of them have been in existence since the heyday of Gretna Green.

' Which are the most popular ? ' I asked.

' The simple old ones like : " Time will Unite Us " and, of course, a very popular one is, " I Love You ".'

I crossed the ferry and was soon in St. Andrews.

§ 3

When the sun shines on St. Andrews you see a coast town as lovely as any in Europe. It has the attraction of character and the charm of quality. Although I cannot play golf and have now too many interests ever to be able to include it among the things I do badly, I could never be bored in St. Andrews, except probably on a very wet day in the Club House of the ' Royal and Ancient '. This ordeal would, I imagine, be a supreme test of self-control for a non-golfer.

St. Andrews gave to Scotland her patron saint, and since the Reformation she seems to have cast her genius for canonization on the game of golf. For golf in St. Andrews is quite different from golf in even the most ecstatic centres of the game. Just as in the old days the shrine of St. Andrew drew pilgrims to this spot, so to-day golfers arrive in the town with a pilgrim's ardour in their faces, some of them hardened perhaps by much prostration at the shrine, but many timid and exalted by the knowledge that they tread on holy ground.

I had always calmly accepted the fact that St. Andrew should be the patron saint of Scotland until, after a recent holiday in Capri, happening to go over to the mainland, I motored from Salerno to Amalfi, where I stopped for lunch. I was taken by a young Italian guide, who, incidentally, had never heard of Scotland, to the tomb of St. Andrew in Amalfi Cathedral. The saint is buried in a dim crypt where he lies in a gold coffin surrounded by a forest of lit tapers. It seemed to me rather appropriate that the patron saint of a country whose rainfall has always been adequate should lie in burnt-out Amalfi, where every now and then the faithful prostrate themselves before him and pray for water. The young Italian crossed himself and told me that if he had any trouble he always prayed to St. Andrew, who was, according to his estimate, the most rapid worker in heaven. He told me of the miracle of the 'manna di Sant' Andrea' which exudes from the saint's bones once a year in November, when the Archbishop descends into the crypt with a glass phial which miraculously becomes wet with the fluid. This phenomenon is, by the way, repeated at other shrines in Italy where the blood of saints is believed to liquefy on stated days.

But why, I asked myself, did St. Andrew, whose body is in Italy, become associated with Scotland. This is the story.

Andrew was, of course, the brother of Simon Peter and he was the first disciple called by Our Lord. He was 'the most gentle of the Apostles'. After the Ascension he travelled in Scythia and Russia as the first missionary to the Muscovites. He then returned to Jerusalem and afterwards set out on a mission to Greece. Among his converts was the wife of the Roman governor of Patrae. The husband was made so angry by his wife's conversion that he ordered Andrew to be crucified. The legend is that the saint himself chose the X-shaped cross on which he died because he professed himself unworthy to die on the same kind of cross as that on which Christ suffered. His hands and feet were not nailed but bound with cords in order that his agony might be repeated ; and in this manner St. Andrew died.

The body was buried by the governor's wife, but the bones afterwards taken up and translated to Constantinople where they were placed with those of St. Luke in the Church of the Apostles. There they remained until the year 1208 when Cardinal Pietro Capuano, a native of Amalfi, brought the relics as a gift to his native town.

But, if the Aberdeen Breviary is to be believed, he brought only a portion of the skeleton. The Scottish monks stated that before the first translation of the relics a certain St. Rule, or St. Regulus, the custodian of the relics at Patrae, was visited by an angel who ordered him to take three finger-bones, an arm-bone and the knee-cap of St. Andrew and journey to the western limits of the world and establish there a city in honour of the Apostle. The monks then describe, with supreme inaccuracy, the voyage of St. Rule to Scotland and the foundation of St. Andrews.

It is believed that in the remote times, of which no clear

record exists, a church, built where St. Andrews now stands, was enriched by certain relics which were said to be the bones of St. Andrew, and from that time it grew famous as a shrine and became the ecclesiastical capital of Scotland.

By the time of the Norman Conquest of England the shrine of St. Andrew had a European reputation. A votive tablet, which is said to have hung in a chapel in the town, reads rather like a modern guide-book :

' The bay and the shore of the sea,' it stated, ' though rough and boisterous, contains a most fertile country ; this region once poor, foul and desolate is now rich, beautiful and flourishing. Hither come to pray a crowd of men from the most distant regions—the loquacious Frenchman, the war-like Roman, the Flemish weaver, the uncivilized German, the Englishman, the Saxon, the Hollander, the naked Pict, the savage Angerian ; and strangers from the Rhone and the Tiber come to seek the prayers of St. Andrew.'

Indeed so many pilgrims came from different countries that a special ferry boat was maintained on the Forth to take them on the last lap of their arduous journeys.

So St. Andrew became the patron saint of Scotland. It was a vulgar jeer in England that the Scots acknowledged no other saint, and the suggestion was made by the ' auld enemie ' that St. Andrew became a saint because he gave Our Lord an oat cake after the forty days' fast ; in which blasphemous jibe we can read a dig at the frugal Scot !

§ 4

Had St. Andrews Cathedral not been destroyed, the town might well have been called the Oxford and Canterbury of Scotland. It is the only town in Scotland which is soft and mellow as Oxford is mellow ; and the ruined cathedral, although no larger than Chester Cathedral, must have been the finest example of pointed Gothic in Scotland.

Knox, who is usually blamed for inciting the populace to tear down the Popish churches, did, as a matter of fact, on several occasions, attempt to restrain the frenzy let loose by his eloquence. When in 1559 he came to St. Andrews to denounce ' the hellish priests, belly-gods and shavelings ', his sermons did, it is true, cause the multitude to tear down the images from the cathedral, but there was no wholesale sabotage. The building is a ruin to-day because it was allowed to fall into ruin, and once the roof of a large building like a Gothic cathedral is allowed to collapse the end is not far off. Also, the size of the parish church of St. Andrews contributed more to the ruin of the cathedral than even the anger of Knox's followers because, as soon as the priests fled, Protestantism transferred itself to the Town Church and permitted the cathedral to fall slowly into decay.

I walked round the ruins, admiring the view of the west window seen through the arch of a fine Romanesque gateway, and then I climbed to the top of the tall stone tower of St. Rule's. This strange-looking slender tower is 108 feet high and in a remarkable state of preservation. In its shadow lie contrasting personalities : Samuel Rutherford, the Covenanting divine, and Tom Morris the golfer. Not far away is a grave which no writer on Scotland can pass by : the grave of Andrew Lang. It has always been a mystery to me why Scotland, which is capable of an almost exaggerated admiration for Scottish men of letters, has extended to Lang only a lukewarm admiration. He was a genius who—with the possible exception of his book on St. Andrews, the town he adored—illuminated every subject that attracted his fertile and questing mind. He was journalist, poet, anthropologist and historian ; but possibly the word ' loyalist ' describes him best of all. He had a passion for lost causes. He was a sincere Jacobite and I think that, although he admired the Old Chevalier more than his son, it will be agreed that his best book is *Prince Charles Edward*. Lang had a genius for transforming himself into a literary detective. His most famous ' case '—the result of being asked for some information about the Jacobites by Robert Louis Stevenson—was *Pickle the Spy*, in which, to the fury of many Highlanders, he pinned the badge of treachery upon Alastair Ruadh MacDonell— Young Glengarry. A life of Andrew Lang is a book that ought to be written, but I believe there is, or was, some difficulty. He was opposed to the publication of his biography and also to that of his letters. . . .

The tower of St. Rule is mounted by way of a chilly, damp spiral stair and as you go up you can hear the coo-ing of the pigeons which now inhabit the tower. But, once on the lead roof, what a view lies round you ! On a clear day you can see two green humps to the south-west. They are the Lomond

Hills of Fife that rise near Loch Leven, and to the north are the Sidlaw Hills beyond Dundee. It is not a great view in a country of tremendous panoramas, but it is a beautiful blend of sea and land and at your feet are the graves in the Cathedral kirkyard and all round you the clustered roofs of St. Andrews and a castle, like a broken sword, lying on a rock.

It is a dizzy tower because of the sheer and terrifying drop. If you are affected by heights and feel the forces of gravity tickling the soles of your feet, you will be glad to go down to the earth and, standing before the ruined altar of the cathedral, remember that Bruce stood there at the consecration of the building, a ceremony which he regarded as a memorial of Bannockburn. And, before you turn away, remember also that at this altar James V and Mary of Guise were ' spousit with great glory ', and the child of their marriage was Mary Queen of Scots.

I went to the Castle of St. Andrews which stands on a jutting cliff above the sea. There is little left of it save a gate-house, a dungeon and a secret passage that must delight the heart of every boy who visits this town because, unlike most secret passages, you are given a lamp and permitted to explore it.

The guide took me to the ' Bottle Dungeon '—a ghastly *oubliette* shaped rather like a bottle, its only entrance the neck, the body being shaped out of the solid rock. The imagination of St. Andrews has consigned every distinguished unfortunate in the town's history to this dungeon, and the guide told me how victims were lowered by a rope into a darkness deeper than that of the blackest night.

He took me to the gate-house and told me how in March 1545 George Wishart, the Protestant reformer and friend of John Knox, was burned to death at a stake in front of the castle, and how Cardinal Beaton, lying at ease on velvet cushions, watched him die. He said that when Wishart had forgiven the executioner he saw Beaton at the window of the tower and prophesied his early death by violence.

And then the guide went on to describe the murder of Cardinal Beaton ; but how improbable it all sounded in the air of a fine autumn afternoon in St. Andrews, with three elderly Englishmen in plus fours standing round with expressions which proclaimed that, while they had heard of the immortal Mrs. Beeton, the Cardinal was a total stranger to them. . . .

This murder was perhaps the most terrible in Scottish history. Rizzio's murder twenty-one years later was admittedly a political assassination of the first magnitude, but Rizzio was only an Italian minstrel and Beaton was the Pope's representative in Scotland.

The Cardinal was a worldly man of the type of Wolsey and Richelieu. His immorality was notorious. He was the father of several children by Marion Ogilvy and his opponents in their zeal credited him with a perfect seraglio of mistresses. When James V died the Cardinal seized the supreme authority and became Regent, some said by forging the royal will. He was fighting to stamp out Protestantism and to resist the scheme of Henry VIII for the marriage of the infant Mary Stuart with young Edward, Prince of Wales.

Two months after Wishart had been burned, men who had sworn to be revenged on Beaton gathered at St. Andrews. There were sixteen of them. The leaders were John and Norman Leslie, William Kirkcaldy and James Carmichael. They gathered in knots of twos and threes round the castle rock and the cathedral churchyard. Beaton, who had heard of an English plot on his life, was strengthening St. Andrews castle, heightening the walls and generally stiffening it for a possible assault. The men, who were bent on a sacrilegious murder more terrible than any since the murder of Thomas à Becket, waited until the drawbridge was lowered to admit the night shift of workmen, and then they edged up to the gate. It was a matter of moments to rush it, slay the warder, fling his body in the fosse and run for the Cardinal's apartments.

Here they were faced by a locked door :

' What meaneth this noise ? ' cried Cardinal Beaton.

' The Master of Rothes hath taken your castle,' came the wild shout from outside.

The Cardinal tried to escape by a private stair. He saw Kirkcaldy of Grange standing there with a drawn sword. He ran back to his bed-chamber and, with the help of his page, or chamber-chiel, piled heavy furniture against the door, hoping that time would bring rescue. But St. Andrews was not yet awake. The town lay silent in the flush of a May morning :

'Open!' cried the murderers, hammering on the door.

'Who calleth?' asked Beaton, standing behind the door grasping a double-handed sword.

'My name is Leslie!' came the answer.

'Leslie?' echoed Beaton. 'Which of the Leslies—is it Norman?'

'Nay, my name is John,' answered Leslie.

'I must have Norman,' cried the Cardinal. 'I must have Norman—he is my friend.'

'Content yourself with those that are here, for you shall have none other,' was the sinister reply.

Then began a battle with the door. They ran with their shoulders at it, but could not burst it in. The Cardinal sank down in a chair and begged for terms. All he could hear were voices outside crying for fire. Then he smelt burning wood. They were piling coals and faggots outside the door. The Cardinal sprang up and shouted:

'Sirs, will you spare my life?'

'It may be that we will!' said a voice.

'Swear, then, unto me by the Wounds of God, and I will admit ye!'

Some promise was given and he opened the door. He faced his murderers in all the authority of his holy office and with all the power of his personality. They looked at him and realized that they had come to kill the most powerful man in the country, Cardinal of St. Stephen, Legate of Paul III and Lord High Chancellor of Scotland. He stood before them holding a huge old sword:

'I am a priest,' he pleaded. 'Surely ye will not slay me?'

Then his air of authority left him and he turned pale, gazing from face to face. For one second the murderers hesitated and then they rushed him. John Leslie drove an arm-pit dagger into him. Peter Carmichael followed with his sword. James Melville of Carnbee struck up their weapons with a long, thrusting stag-sword:

'This sacrifice is the work of God,' he said quietly, 'and, as such, ought to be conducted with becoming deliberation.'

The wounded man cowered before them:

'Repent thee, thou wicked cardinal, for all thy sins,' said Melville, 'but especially the murder of the pious Wishart, that instrument of God for the conversion of these lands. His death now cries for vengeance and we are sent by God to inflict the deserved punishment. Remember that the stroke I am about to deal thee is not the mercenary blow of a hired assassin but that of a most just retribution . . .'

He then ran the stag-sword into Beaton's breast. The Cardinal fell back :

'I am a priest,' he cried. 'Fie, fie . . . all is gone.'

By this time the bells of St. Andrews were ringing, the provost and the town guard were assembling and the citizens had leapt from bed. They came to the castle and demanded to see the Cardinal. There was a lapse of time. Then, horrified, they saw something being pushed out over the wall of the fore-tower. It was the murdered body of Beaton suspended by a foot and an arm. The shudder that went over the crowd in St. Andrews spread over Europe. To the Catholics it was an act of unspeakable horror and sacrilege ; to the Protestants of England and Scotland it was a sign of hope and triumph . . .

The murderers managed to consolidate their position. Supporters flocked to their standard—among them John Knox. The castle was besieged by the Regent Arran. The defenders got in touch with Henry VIII, who financed their defence and promised an English fleet.

The Regent planted the royal Standard of Scotland before the castle and opened fire with brass cannon. Fire was kept up from seven in the morning until four in the afternoon. But the castle held out. It held out for more than a year ! Then one day a fleet of sixteen warships with the *fleur-de-lys* on their sails dropped anchor in St. Andrews Bay. They were the belated contribution of the King of France towards the avenging of a cardinal's sacred blood. The fleet was in charge of Leon Stronzius, a famous Italian soldier. He unshipped his cannon, drew them through the streets of St. Andrews and, mounting them on the old tower of San Salvador's College, on the walls of the cathedral and on all high vantage points, opened a murderous fire into the very heart of the castle.

John Knox, inside the castle, made the situation much worse by dinning into the ears of the garrison that this last misfortune was a just reward for their licentious lives !

There could be only one end—surrender. The gallant outlaws gave in and were bundled into the galleys by the French troops and taken to France. Among them was John

Knox. For nineteen months the man whose voice was to shake Scotland to her foundations was a slave chained to the bench of a French galley.

On one occasion a ship in which he was slaving came within sight of St. Andrews. A fellow slave asked him if he knew the place. Yes, he replied, it was at St. Andrews that he had preached his first sermon and he did not doubt but that God would preserve him to preach there again.

As soon as St. Andrews castle was captured, the victorious army discovered a gruesome relic in the ' Bottle Dungeon '. The body of His Eminence, Cardinal Beaton, was found preserved in a solution of salt.

§ 5

Mary, Queen of Scots, considered St. Andrews the most attractive town in her kingdom. She visited it several times, notably during her first eighteen days' tour of Scotland shortly after her arrival from France. She was only nineteen years of age at the time and may still have remembered her early years. At any rate she was very interested in the scenes of her childhood. She set out on horseback—the first lady in° Scotland to use a side-saddle with a pommel—and she visited Linlithgow where she was born, Stirling, where, as an infant, she was crowned, Perth, Dundee, St. Andrews, and Falkland where her father, James V, had died.

A charming old house in St. Andrews is pointed out as Mary's lodgings during her visits to the town. It is now the library of St. Leonard's School for girls. I was shown a beautiful little room that has been lovingly restored to its former condition. There is a window recess cut off from the rest of the room by a panelled partition and inside is Queen Mary's bed. She could lie in her little shut-away box of a bed and look down on a quiet garden and trees.

This is the house, or a portion of it, which Mary hired in 1573 when she retired with her ladies to spend a bourgeois holiday. The only man admitted to their councils, apparently, was Randolph, the English Ambassador, who was head over ears in love with Mary Beaton. In those odd moments when he remembered that he was an ambassador he tried to

find out whether the Queen intended to wed Darnley or
Leicester ; but Mary rebuked him prettily, telling him that
he must remember she was on holiday and that politics were
barred.

In the little panelled bed box in the room overlooking a
garden Mary may have dreamed of marrying Darnley, who in
time, she may have thought, would become the Catholic
Henry IX of England. What a dream for a devout daughter
of the Church !

The Queen was never merrier than at St. Andrews, but now
and then she would fall into sudden passions of weeping,
crying that she wanted assured friends ; but these storms soon
cleared and the Queen was as happy at St. Andrews as ever she
was in Scotland. In the morning she worked in the little
garden behind the house and in the afternoon she often
studied Livy under the tutorship of George Buchanan, the
principal of St. Leonard's College. On one occasion Randolph
was invited to go into the garden and watch her practise at the
butts.

Nearly every town in Scotland is associated with the storm
and stress of Mary's life. Only in St. Andrews can we imagine
her in more or less calm waters ; and it is the prettiest picture
in the tempestuous history of this old grey town.

§ 6

Why should the Nine of Diamonds be called the ' Curse of
Scotland ' ?

I have for some time collected legends current in Scotland
on this subject, and in St. Andrews I heard a new explanation.
It may be interesting to tabulate the various stories.

I have heard the suggestion that the Nine of Diamonds
refers to the arms of John Dalrymple, 2nd Viscount and
1st Earl of Stair—' Or on a saltire azure nine lozenges of the
field ', or, in non-heraldic terms, nine diamonds. His acquies-
cence in the Massacre of Glencoe caused his name to be
execrated throughout Scotland, so that card-players when
they came to the Nine of Diamonds called it ' The Curse of
Scotland '.

. An earlier and rather unconvincing legend is to the effect
that during the reign of Mary Queen of Scots a thief named
George Campbell—a kind of Colonel Blood—attempted to

steal the 'Honours of Scotland'. He succeeded in forcing nine stones from the crown. (In an inventory of 1539 there are twenty diamonds mentioned among the jewels in the Crown.) In order to replace the stolen gems, it is said, a crushing tax was laid upon the country so that the buying of the nine diamonds was considered to be a national curse.

Grosse has another explanation. He says that diamonds imply royalty and that every ninth king of Scotland was a tyrant and a curse to the country.

Dr. Houstoun in his memoirs, published in 1747, says that in his time the Nine of Diamonds was called by card players 'the Justice Clerk', a reference to Lord Justice Clerk Ormistone who helped to put down the '15 Rebellion with the utmost severity.

A fifth explanation is that Mary of Lorraine introduced the game of *comète* into Scotland in which the winning card was the Nine of Diamonds, and so many noblemen were ruined at the card tables that the game became known as the 'Curse of Scotland'.

There is a sixth, and rather similar, explanation which traces the phrase to a game called 'Pope Julio' or 'Pope Joan' in which the winning card represented the Pope.

The story I heard in St. Andrews was that the Duke of Cumberland issued his 'no quarter' order after Culloden on the back of a card which he picked up from the floor. The card is said to have been the Nine of Diamonds.

Still another explanation is that the phrase should be not the 'Curse' but the 'Cross of Scotland', and that the shape of the Nine of Diamonds suggested a St. Andrew's Cross. This, I venture to suggest, is rather a far-fetched theory.

It is, I think, surprising that in all these stories not one suggestion is made that the 'Curse of Scotland' may be a far older term than any of these stories would lead one to suppose. Edward I was known as 'The Hammer of the Scots' and on his tomb in Westminster Abbey is inscribed: 'Edwardus Longus, Scotorum Malleus, hic est'. If only one could establish some link between Edward and the Nine of Diamonds one would have, I feel, a much better explanation than is to be found in any of the current legends.

§ 7

A feeling of excitement spreads through St. Andrews when the time arrives for the new captain of the Royal and Ancient Golf Club to play himself into a year of office.

Golf is really a royal and ancient game. The enemies of Mary Queen of Scots charged her with heartlessness because she played ' goif ' soon after Darnley was murdered. She was seen at Seton one day ' richt oppinlie in the feildis with the palmall and goif '. Charles I was playing golf at Leith when the news of the Irish Rebellion was brought to him. James, Duke of York—afterwards James II and VII—was a great golfer and played what was probably the first Scots-English international at Leith Links. The title of the ' Royal and Ancient ' was approved by King William IV in 1834 and this monarch, although not a golfer, presented a gold medal to the club on which the word golf is spelt ' golph ', probably the error of some London goldsmith.

The royal connection with golf was continued by King Edward VII who, when Prince of Wales, became Captain of the ' Royal and Ancient ', allowing himself to be played in by proxy. The present Prince of Wales and his brother, the Duke of York, have both played themselves into office, the Prince in 1922 and the Duke in 1930.

I rose at 7 a.m. to watch the Captain take office. It was a magnificent morning. The North Sea was breaking against the sandhills and the Old Course looked as if it had been pressed by its valet during the night. An old man was sweeping the first green with a long switch of hickory, obliterating the evidence of any worm which had had the impertinence to intrude. An official of the Royal and Ancient was dragging out a little old-fashioned cannon of the kind seen sometimes in the gardens of retired sea captains. And so, with the dew still on the grass, the stage was set for the most solemn ceremony of the golfer's year.

I am, as I have already admitted, not a golfer, and in St. Andrews I feel much as a Christian must feel in Mecca or as an infidel ought to feel in Jerusalem. I am an outsider, one who does not know what Tom Morris did long ago or what Harry Vardon or Bobby Jones have done in our own time.

ST. ANDREWS GOLF COURSE

FISHERMEN OF EYEMOUTH

I can only look with reverence at the Royal and Ancient Club, which stands beside the sea like a strip of Pall Mall on holiday, and marvel at the atmosphere of solemnity which precedes the new captain's ceremonial whack.

The citizens of St. Andrews appear on the course and surround the clubhouse. It is the greatest day of the year in a town dedicated to golf. Few would be absent from the ceremony. No one in St. Andrews would care to say that he, or she, had not seen the new captain drive off from the first tee. The caddies, who are as distinct from other men as stable boys or fisher lads, gather in great numbers. When the new captain plays himself in every year, they scramble for the ball and the caddy who retrieves it receives a golden sovereign. They stand about in the cold morning air, terribly alert and cynical, as if they already know all the caustic jokes about golfers that will eventually appear in the pages of *Punch*.

The terrace fills with people. Men and women stand about gazing out lovingly over the greens and the bunkers. At last the new captain appears. He is an elderly man in a noisy suit of plus fours. The retiring captain walks with him to the green. Some one looks to the priming of the cannon.

Old Andrew Kirkcaldy, the professional of the ' Royal and Ancient ', whose name is known all over the world, bends down and tees up the ball. Crowned heads call him ' Andrew ', and he has at one time or another told the House of Lords exactly what he thinks of it—and Andrew never minces his words. When the Prince of Wales played himself in as captain some years ago old Andrew sniffed contemptuously, and told the Prince that his golf clubs were nothing but a set of old shinty sticks. It is Andrew's proud boast that he has teed up the ball for the captains of St. Andrews for the last twenty-two years and, as soon as he does this, the caddies spread out over the course and wait ready to race for it. The crowd gazes at the new captain as worshippers in ancient times might have watched a high priest in the act of performing a sacrifice.

The new captain takes a practice swing. Then he takes another one and looks out over the course.

I think how dreadful it would be if he missed the ball altogether ! I have a vision of baronets dying by the score, of old county families losing their heirs and of the grey stones of the Royal and Ancient crashing down as if an earthquake had struck St. Andrews.

'Has a captain ever missed a ball?' I whisper to a friend in the crowd:

'No,' I am told sternly, 'but many a one has foozled or sliced his drive.'

This sounds terrible, and I stand inwardly praying that the new captain will neither slice nor foozle.

Up go his arms, bang goes the sea captain's little cannon, and a white pill soars swiftly over the links in the direction of the waiting caddies. As its arc declines, the caddies begin to run. The ceremony, which began like a game of golf, now develops into a Rugby scrum. The caddies fight for the ball as gulls fight for fish. I see a mass of waving arms and kicking legs. Men retire from the battle nursing their fingers. At last a rather startled young man comes running towards us holding a golf ball. Reporters dash at him:

'How did you get it?' they ask him.

'I was underneath,' he says with stark simplicity, 'and some one kicked it my way so I just lay on it.'

They lead him to the captain who shakes hands with him and gives him a golden sovereign. So the ceremony ends. St. Andrews has a new captain. The Parliament that draws up the laws of golf has welcomed its annual Prime Minister. All over the world golfers may drive and foozle secure in the knowledge that somewhere in the sacred city of golf is enthroned that authority which extends itself to every green and bunker throughout the world.

And the captain, well pleased with his drive, after receiving the congratulations of his fellow golfers, goes off to—slice his morning egg.

§ 8

I went to Stirling by way of Cupar and Kinross, and on the way I wondered what is the correct pronunciation of the word golf. In St. Andrews I had heard it pronounced in three different ways: as goff, gowff and go-l-f.

The educated Scotsman almost eliminated the 'l' sound, the uneducated Scotsman stressed the 'ow' (as in how) and the Englishman pronounced the 'l'.

I believe the English pronunciation is all wrong. The

word, like 'Calf' and 'Half', is one in which the '1' sound should be omitted. It should be 'goff' and golfers should be pronounced 'goffers'.

In the reign of Mary Queen of Scots the word was spelt 'goif'—with no '1'. In Shadwell's *Royal Shepherdess*, which was published in 1669, there is a song which goes:

> *Thus all our life long we are frolick and gay*
> *And, instead of Court Revels, we merrily play*
> *At Trap, and at Keels and at Barlibreakrun,*
> *At Goff and at Stool-ball and when we have done*

Chorus: *These innocent sports, we laugh, and lie down,*
> *And to each pretty lass we give a green gown.*

Baily, in 1728, mentioned the game in his dictionary as 'goff—a sort of play at ball'.

Perhaps the '1' sound came into favour during our intimate relations with the Low Countries, because as early as 1658 Hexham's Dutch Dictionary mentioned 'Een Kolve—a banding staff to strike a ball', while in 1754 Sewel's Dutch Dictionary gives the word as 'Kolf—a club to strike little bouls or balls with '.

Still, I shall call the word 'goff' until some 'goffer' can convince me that I am wrong.

§ 9

Stirling is the best centre from which to explore one of the most fascinating parts of Scotland. Bruce, Wallace and Mary Queen of Scots have left their names to the countryside: Bannockburn is near-by; Stirling Bridge is only a few yards out of the town, and the Lake of Menteith is not far off. The ancient capital of Dunfermline is a few miles to the east and the Trossachs about the same distance to the west. But, in addition to this, you have Stirling Castle, which, with Edinburgh, is the finest and most romantic castle in Scotland. . . .

Early in the morning I decided to climb the Wallace Memorial. It was the right day for it: a clear, windy day with plenty of high cloud. This great tower, which reminds me of a castle on the Rhine, rises on the height of Abbey Craig and stands sentinel above the 'Links of Forth'. It was built about sixty years ago as a national memorial to William Wallace.

An old man took threepence, and I plunged into a stone corkscrew. I climbed up and up; and the wind grew bitterly cold as it whistled through the Victorian arrow-slits.

A half-way house is called the 'Hall of Heroes'. You are faced by the marble stares of sixteen notable Scotsmen. It is dangerous to quarrel with heroes, but the temptation is sometimes too great to be avoided. Walter Scott is, naturally, first on the list; then comes James Watt, Allan Ramsay, Robert Tannahill, Adam Smith, Sir David Brewster, Hugh Miller, Carlyle, William Murdoch, John Knox, David Livingstone, Robert Burns, Thomas Chalmers, George Buchanan, Bruce and—William Gladstone!

I respectfully suggest that the list should be revised. Heroes, like all things, are subject to periodic reassessment. The above selection of sixteen of Scotland's greatest sons, while it may have suited the nineteenth century, is hopelessly out of tune with to-day. Some one told me that Stirling was about to advertise itself. I can think of nothing more calculated to draw attention to it than the decision to put the reorganization of this 'Hall of Heroes' to a national vote.

The little guide-book says, after naming the heroes: 'The object which will claim the most devoted attention of the visitor will undoubtedly be the shrine containing the Wallace Sword.'

I have no idea how many swords Wallace possessed, but if only a percentage of those said to be his are genuine he must have had some difficulty in deciding which one to choose when he wanted to kill an Englishman. This sword is, of course, the genuine one from Dumbarton. It was lying by his side when he was betrayed as he lay asleep in a barn at Robroyston in 1305.

Up I went again through the stone corkscrew. The top of the tower is a windy place that offers you one of the most wonderful sights in the world. It was a clear and perfect day.

Stirling, in a blue haze, lay below with the 'Links of Forth' twisting round her like a serpent. But what a barrier is that stupendous mass of the Grampians lying to the north-west! I saw Ben Lomond, Ben Venue, Ben Ledi, Ben More, and, far to the east, Ben Vorlich, without a cloud on their old heads, standing up blue in the sun, magnificent, far off, and in some way ominous.

I saw five battlefields ; Bannockburn and, just beyond it, Sauchieburn ; Falkirk below the ridge of the Pentlands ; Sheriffmuir on the high land by the Black Hill and, right below me on the fringe of Stirling, that place where Wallace swept down from the site of his memorial and smote the stupid Surrey and the fat and foolish Cressingham.

There is probably no other view in Great Britain which tells so much of a country's history.

When I had climbed down again, past the ' Hall of Heroes ', and downward through the uncomfortable stone tube, I came to the old man who sells the tickets.

' And do you believe that the sword upstairs is really the sword of William Wallace ? ' I asked.

' A man would be a fool if he didna',' he replied, and turned away.

There was nothing more to be said. These devastating replies are not uncommon in Scotland.

When we became friends again, I found that he was a man of Fife, was seventy-three years of age, and had served fifty years ago in the London police force. He was on duty at the Tower during the ' dynamite ' outrages.

But he had not been in London for half a century, and had, I gathered, no desire to see it again.

' They tell me there's a bridge over the Thames by the Tower,' he said. ' There was aye a bridge there—London Bridge—but this one lets ships in.'

' They call it Tower Bridge.'

' Ay, ay.'

We talked about hansom cabs, horse omnibuses, barmaids, ' Piccadilly Johnnies ', silk hats, and Queen Victoria ; and so, leaving him to his memories and his illusions, I went down to that windy plain where the crag of Stirling crouches like a lion.

§ 10

The hot, damp smell of autumn was in the air, and a robin was singing of death. When he paused and waited, as he always does, in the middle of his grief, the silence deepened so that the fall of a red leaf was somehow important and arresting.

Beyond the brown woods and the withered bracken lay a

sheet of water grey as the breast of a dove. There was about it something like smoke and something like glass. It was hushed and lonely, as if it had withdrawn itself from the world. A water fowl, rising suddenly on loud wings, cut two lines of silver in the lake as it lifted itself into the air. This was the Lake of Menteith.

Far off in the middle of the lake was a low greyness that rose and fell in queer shadows, as though the once holy isle of Inchmahome was built up out of lake-water like a mirage.

This little island is one of Scotland's shrines; it was here that we can think of Mary Queen of Scots living, for once, a happy hour in ' that first garden of her simpleness '.

On Inchmahome she was hidden when the English were hammering at the gates of Stirling, and from Inchmahome she passed out into the world, a little child with a crown upon her head, a child of storm and destiny. And in these autumn days, when the lake is like a sheet of grey smoke, there is no sound in the dying woods but a robin recalling something pitiful that has been happening since the beginning of the world.

I took a boat and rowed over the grey water to Inchmahome. There come moments—you may have felt them, too, if you have ever been alone—when it seems that there is no such thing as Past, Present or Future, but as though Time were a maze in which we, suddenly turning a corner, might find ourselves in the Past or the Future. At such moments the Present is the least probable convention. And Inchmahome spreads this queer enchantment over the Lake of Menteith; and the soft woods whisper it. Even the high hills echo it.

Scotland is a land of lochs, but Menteith is her only ' lake '. There is a gentleness and a softness and a kindness about it that is absent from every other sheet of water. In the woods that fringe the lochs of Scotland you might expect to meet a man with a sword; but among the little birch trees that run down to the Lake of Menteith you would meet a man with a harp.

On the island is all that is left of an ancient monastery. The Office of Works—the only lovable Government Department we possess—has placed reverent hands upon it so that the old stones rise up with dignity.

It is of Mary Stuart only that a man thinks as he explores

this little island. Legend has labelled every yard of Inch-mahome. There are the ' Queen's Bower ', the ' Queen's Garden ', the ' Queen's Tree ' and the ' Queen's Chamber '.

The story goes that the young Queen held a mimic court on the island, attended by the Four Maries. She is also said to have begun to study languages there and to have employed herself with needlework.

There is a strange circle of boxwood, perhaps fourteen feet high, planted, so the story goes, by Mary. In the centre of this dark circle is a memorial, placed there last year by the Holyrood Club of Glasgow.

How cruel it is to question any legend about Mary ! But is it likely that this little girl—she was only five—would have planted a box hedge or learnt languages or made tapestry on Inchmahome ? If any one can prove to me that she did these things I will be only too glad to abase myself ; for the story is very beautiful. But the truth should be told. . . .

The storms were already breaking over her. Henry VIII, who had worked so hard to unite the two kingdoms by the marriage of Mary to his frail boy, Edward, died, leaving orders that the union was to be arranged. The Protector Somerset invaded Scotland with a great army of mercenaries.

Scotland struggled to resist him. The Fiery Cross—the S O S of the Highlands—was, for the first time, sent round the Lowlands on the point of a lance. It was a cross of hazel that had been thrust into a fire and dipped burning into the blood of a newly-slain goat. Scotland rallied ; and an army of 36,000 men faced the English on the eastern border.

Then followed ' Black Saturday ' at Pinkie-cleugh when the Scots after a terrific fight were scattered with the red earth rising in clouds from the field. In the panic that followed, the little Queen was hurried to the lonely island of Inchmahome.

England was wooing her with an army and France with promises. It was, perhaps, on this island, while she played in the monastery gardens or watched the autumn trees turn-ing brown, that the arrangements for her marriage to the Dauphin of France were completed.

So, if we cannot quite believe that she planted a boxwood hedge, we can at least imagine her playing with fallen leaves on Inchmahome, unconscious that over her small auburn head were gathering the first storm-clouds of her tragedy.

Mary was taken from Inchmahome after a stay which is said to have been only a matter of weeks. Somerset had not pressed his victories.

The child was taken to Stirling, and, at length, to Dumbarton, where she waited five months for the French Fleet. In the autumn of that year a little girl of six embarked on a French man-of-war. There were with her four other little girls named Mary and a retinue of 200 gentlemen and servants.

Twelve years later a girl of eighteen watched the French coast fade into the night.

'The darkness that is now brooding over France,' she said, 'is like the darkness of my own heart.'

Her galleon dropped anchor off Leith in a blinding sea mist, and Mary Queen of Scots came—home. . . .

Inchmahome, on a still autumn day, with a robin piping his heart-breaking little song, will always be sacred to the memory of the most tragic of the Stuarts.

CHAPTER TWELVE

IN WHICH I TELL YOU SOMETHING ABOUT FOOD, GO TO HAD-
DINGTON, SLEEP IN CARLYLE'S BED, GO ON TO DUNBAR AND
EYEMOUTH, WHERE I HEAR ABOUT A 'DISASTER', AND TO
BERWICK, WHERE I HELP TO RING THE CURFEW AND SEE SALMON
NETTED AT TWEEDMOUTH. I VISIT FLODDEN, EXPLORE THE
ETTRICK FOREST, SIT AT SCOTT'S DESK IN ABBOTSFORD AND—
ALAS—SAY FAREWELL TO SCOTLAND

§ 1

DUSK falls over a rock that wears a castle like a crown.
This rock, which carries something of Glencoe into
the very heart of Edinburgh, slopes gently towards
Holyrood, bearing on its ridge black spires and pinnacles
which in certain lights resemble the spears and banners of an
army.

Down on the level plain is modern Edinburgh, planned in
straight lines. Tramcars run through the town and crowds
fill the north side of Princes Street. But beyond the empti-
ness of a deep valley the wall of rock rises, dark and brooding, lifted against the sky in a passionate concentration
like sleep.

Once, when I lived in a room overlooking a harbour, a great
liner was tied up to the dockside. I would find myself going
to the window to assure myself that it was still there. It was
something improbable and, in a way, fantastic that belonged,
yet did not belong, to the land. And, like many a stranger
in this aristocratic city, I am always going to the window to
make sure that the Castle and its embattled ridge have not
sailed away into the region of those 'old unhappy far-off
things' to which they so clearly belong.

I find myself looking with the eyes of an artist at the rock
on which old Edinburgh crouches. I would like to paint it
in all its disconcerting moods : in the chill freshness of an
autumn morning, in the calm sunlight of an afternoon, but
most of all in that time which is not day and not night when

the shadows gathering on the rock steal down like a band of cloaked men.

I climbed the Rock to visit again the Scottish National War Shrine. I have put into words elsewhere the emotion which this shrine creates in the mind of one who sees it for the first time ; and a second visit deepens the conviction that it is the most beautiful memorial in the world.

Genius, it would seem, haunts this rock. It might have been thought that nothing more could have been done to add to its over-whelming significance. But not far from the shrine I found the recently opened Scottish Naval and Military Museum, another labour of love that tells the story of ' an old and haughty nation proud in arms '.

Scotland is rightly grateful to the three men who are mainly responsible for this stirring record of a nation's chivalry, the Duke of Atholl, Major Mackay Scobie and Mr. Wilson Paterson.

In a little over three years they have assembled a wonderful and colourful collection of naval and military relics, a harvest from the countless fields on which the Highlands and the Lowlands have drawn the sword. Most museums of this kind are pathetic and dusty. They speak not of the glory of causes and the splendour of conviction but of death and decay. It must be very difficult to keep the chill atmosphere of the tomb from a museum of this character. But the organisers have succeeded brilliantly and unforgettably. They have brought together mementoes of old wars and they have shown them in the heroic manner, so that one is conscious, not only of the gallantry of Scotland's long war record, but also of the ideals for which Scotsmen have so often given up their lives. It is not the funeral march that one seems to hear wailing through this museum, but the blood-stirring tap of a drum and a jingle and creak of cavalry on the march.

I cannot find words to praise the oak statuettes made by Mr. Pilkington Jackson. They show men of the Scottish regiments at various periods in history. He has given to each figure, whether it wears the long wig of the Marlborough period, the cropped hair of Covenanting times, or the bag-wig of the Georgians, a good Scottish face. If ever I meet Mr. Jackson I shall ask him how many of these splendid little figures are portraits. If the Naval and Military Museum contained only this series of statuettes it would have justified itself. It is a gallery in which Scotsmen may see their forefathers to the very life, dressed in the varied splendour of old uniforms, grasping pike, musket and sword.

There are relics in plenty ; bonnets and helmets and tunics, also the fine Colville collections of ancient weapons which, but for the patriotism of the Marquis of Bute, might now be in America.

I suppose the most interesting of all the relics is the uniform which Prince Charlie wore at Culloden. He must have presented a variegated sight, for tunic, trews and jacket are all of different tartan. Even with the knowledge that such garments would be treasured and handed down with veneration from father to son, one marvels at the freshness of the colours.

What a magnificent war record Scotland possesses ! As I went round this museum it occurred to me how much history can be hidden in a button, and how much courage may be summed up in a plume.

The Scots Greys, or 2nd Dragoons, is the only cavalry regiment that wears an infantry bearskin. This right was won by the regiment at Ramillies in 1706, when they surrounded and disarmed the French Regiment du Roi. They captured no fewer than seventeen standards. The bearskins worn by the Scots Greys are the bearskins of the Royal Bodyguard of the King of France !

The Royal Scots are the oldest regiment in British service and perhaps in the world. If you go to the Royal Scots Club in Edinburgh you are certain to hear someone use the regimental nickname—'Pontius Pilate's Bodyguard.' Their uniform has gone through a number of remarkable changes, and, like many a Scottish regiment, they have served overseas against England, playing the part of soldiers of fortune. It was Charles II who recalled them to Scotland, an act which is commemorated on their colour in the royal cipher within the collar and badge of the Order of the Thistle. Charles also gave the colonelcy of the Royal Scots to the Earl of Dumbarton ; and that is why the regimental march is ' Dumbarton's Drums.'

But when the Royal Scots are inspected by royalty they do not play ' Dumbarton's Drums '. They play : ' The

Daughter of the Regiment.'   The reason is that Queen Victoria was born in the Regiment. Her father, the Duke of Kent, was colonel in 1819.

The King's Own Scottish Borderers have an involved archæology of their own. They are the old 25th. It is said that the whole regiment was recruited within four hours by the Earl of Leven in 1689. They are the only Scottish regiment allowed to wear a rose in their caps on August 1— a distinction won at the Battle of Minden in 1759.

The Cameronians, or Scottish Rifles, take their name from that stubborn old Covenanter, Richard Cameron, who fell fighting against the King at Ayrsmoss. They went into action for the first time in 1689, when they defended the kirkyard of Dunkeld against Viscount Dundee. Like certain other godly Scottish regiments, the Cameronians, on taking service under William III, stipulated that every company should have an elder of the Kirk who, with the assistance of the regimental chaplain, should deal with all ' crime ', including bad language !

It was also, I think I am right in saying, the only battalion in the army whose kit contained a compulsory Bible ! Among the regimental peculiarities cherished by this regiment is that buglers wear two bugles on their arms and that officers wear their swords at the trail like the cavalry. I do not know why.

The Black Watch—the ' Gallant Forty-Twa '—is the oldest Highland Regiment in the service. Its companies were raised independently in 1729 and as its members belonged to a number of different clans a new tartan, the now famous Black Watch, was designed to overcome an obvious difficulty.

There is an interesting piece of history to be read in the colour of the hackle in the bonnets of the Black Watch. This red hackle once belonged to the 11th Light Dragoons. At the Battle of Gueldermalsen, in 1795, the Black Watch retrieved a situation lost by the cavalry, and Sir George Dundas decided to humiliate the dragoons by taking the red hackle and giving it to the Highlanders.

The ' bugle ' worn on the collar and cap badges of the Highland Light Infantry—a regiment that has more battle honours on its colours than any other in the British Army—is different from the ordinary bugle badges. The ' bugle ' is really a French horn and it was won by the old 71st for bravery during the Peninsular War.

The only Scottish regiment which wears two collar badges is the Seaforth Highlanders. One bears the letter ' F ', the initial of the Duke of Albany and York, and the second is an elephant, a badge won at Assaye. It was the skirl of the Seaforth's pipes that warned the defenders of Lucknow that the relief force was near at hand.

The Queen's Own Cameron Highlanders have the distinction of being the last British regiment to carry a flag into battle. This happened at the Battle of Atbara in 1898 when the Camerons charged the Zareba with a Union Flag carried by Staff Sergeant Wyatt. He fell shot in the knee but another sergeant took up the flag and rushed forward with it.

The famous ' thin red line ' that withstood the charge of the Russian cavalry at Balaclava was a Scottish regiment, the Argyll and Sutherland Highlanders, and when the Birkenhead troopship went down in 1852 the men who put the women and children in the life-boats, and then stood to attention on deck as the ship sank, were men of the Argyll and Sutherland Highlanders and the Highland Light Infantry. . . .

These are only a few of the memories awakened by a walk round the Scottish Naval and Military Museum. In this purely Scottish museum of war it is possible as nowhere else to gain a true conception of the tremendous part that Scotland has played in the military history of these islands.

And a few yards away rises the Shrine of Scotland, which commemorates, with a dignity, simplicity, and beauty which have few equals in the world, the part played by Scotland in the greatest of all wars.

§ 2

I went to the National Gallery in Edinburgh—one of the choicest and best-lit galleries in Great Britain—to see ' the Honourable Mrs. Graham '.

She stands against a Georgian pillar in the full fashion of her day, a rich dress looped back over an underskirt, pearls about her lovely neck, one ostrich feather in her right hand, a feathered hat tilted on her head, mounting like a ship the high wave of her hair, and on her exquisite face an expression, slightly stern but already melting, as if she were waiting for some one who has had the bad manners to be three minutes late.

When Gainsborough was told that much of the beauty of this picture was due to the richness of Mary Graham's clothes he violently disagreed and accordingly painted her—as she is to be seen in the National Gallery, London—on a doorstep holding a broom.   And Gainsborough was right : she is just as lovely.

I have always admired this picture.   When I was a boy Mrs. Graham was my ideal of a great lady.   It took me years to realize that she was merely a girl of eighteen assuming the manners of a grand duchess.

Mary Graham and Annie Laurie are two Scotswomen whose names have been rescued from oblivion, one by a song, the other by a picture.   Behind the song ' Annie Laurie ', as I pointed out somewhere near the beginning of this book, is a commonplace love story, but behind Gainsborough's portrait of Mrs. Graham is a sad one.

She was the daughter of Lord Cathcart.   She was married in 1774, when she was seventeen years of age, to Thomas Graham of Balgowan.   They were a devoted couple.   After seventeen years of married life they still wrote to one another like lovers.   In the eighteenth year, however, Mary Graham fell ill and died suddenly during a health cruise in the south of France.   Her husband was in Scotland, distracted with grief.   Friends brought the body home, running the gauntlet of French revolutionary troops who on one dreadful occasion broke open the coffin.

Thomas Graham, in order to forget his grief, travelled abroad and eventually became a soldier.   He was forty-four years of age and he believed that life held nothing more for him.   But his sorrow had launched him on a remarkable career.   In 1809 he became a Major-General.   He was one of the few persons present at the burial of Sir John Moore.   He became second in command to Wellington in Spain.   He commanded forty thousand troops at the Battle of Vittoria.   He refused a Spanish dukedom and returned home, covered in glory, to accept a peerage and the title of Lord Lynedoch of Balgowan.

' What is it to me ? ' he wrote to a friend.   ' I stand alone in the world.'

He was thinking of the woman who had been dead for twenty-two years.   He never forgot her and his grief remained so sharp that he could not bear to face her portrait. As soon as she was dead the picture vanished.   It was whispered that the lovely thing had been bricked up in the wall of one of his houses. This was not true. After his death it was discovered black with age in a London storeroom where it had been neglected and forgotten for nearly half a century.

So Lord Lynedoch lived out his long life, accumulating honours and leaving behind him, when he died at the age of ninety-five, many memorials of a distinguished career. Among them is the United Service Club in Pall Mall, which he instituted with the object of ' affording officers a respectable place of meeting in London without resort to taverns '.

After his death his lovely young wife came to life again. Robert Graham, a cousin, who inherited the property in 1843, heard of the picture that was stored in London. Could it be the exquisite Gainsborough that had been lost for nearly fifty years ? He was so excited that when the picture was on its way to Lynedoch he galloped out along the road to Perth and met the carter on Dalcrue bridge. He insisted on opening the packing-case there and then. On Dalcrue bridge he saw through half a century's grime the proud young beauty whom Gainsborough had painted exactly seventy years before.

So Mary Graham came back to Scotland, and she will never leave it again. This Gainsborough was Robert Graham's gift to the people of Scotland on the proviso that it should never leave the country.

§ 3

And now—food.

When I described, with an exactitude which I flatter myself is infallible, how to make Scotch Broth in my book *In Search of Scotland*, I had no idea how much happiness I was spreading over the earth. Since that time I have received many letters from distant places—notably from Canada and Australia—to say how superlative is this soup, and how well I have described the process of its composition. Among such letters were others, from Scots at home, generously offering to teach me how to make all kinds of Scottish dishes, including even a haggis. These startled me. I detected in them the quite erroneous assumption that I am an expert chef, the kind of man who shows off to his guests with a chafing-dish, tossing brilliant omelettes into the air, conjuring delicious sauces in full view of the audience out of rum bottles and sugar. The truth is that no man has ever known less about the mysteries of the kitchen than I, and no man could be more futile and helpless with the raw materials of any meal, with the single and notable exception of the peas, barley, leeks, carrots, etc., which, when blended together with mystic art, make Scotch Broth.

There was, however, among my correspondence one letter from a resident in Edinburgh offering to teach me how to make the favourite dish of a Scottish king. It is called ' Friar's Chicken '. At first I rejected the proposal as one quite beyond my powers. I said that I felt flattered that any one should think me capable of making ' Friar's Chicken ', but, if the truth must out, the manufacture of Scotch Broth had really tested my capacity for detail and organization to the uttermost and had made any kitchen in which I had performed this miracle of skill and judgement a perfect hell until the act was completed and the grated carrot sprinkled, in final benediction, on the brew.

The answer to this, by return of post, was a thick bottle. Inside was a ghastly sight. I will refrain from description except the slight indication that, at first sight, it seemed that a frog had died and been bottled in a jelly of sphagnum moss. A covering letter fulfilled my worst anticipations—this was ' Friar's Chicken ' ! I was ordered to bring it to the boil and eat it. Strangely enough, I did so. And at the first mouthful I said : ' This is great and romantic food—a dish to banish melancholy ! ' It was haunted by a strange spice. Was it musk, or saffron or ambergris ? I did not know. But I decided to find out. In a few days' time I began to desire it again, until, as the weeks lengthened, I decided to try and make it myself. I discovered that ' Friar's Chicken ' was regarded in the eighteenth century as a Scottish dish of great antiquity. Scott in *The Fortunes of Nigel* mentions it as the favourite dish of James VI and I, a man who, although a coarse feeder, was probably a good judge.

So I went to a house in Edinburgh which had been duly warned, and in a few hours I had added the accomplishment of ' Friar's Chicken ' to that of Scotch Broth. I will now tell you how to make it without the ambiguity which pervades all known cookery books. I will tell you this mystery so that it will be impossible for you to go wrong :

First. Take two pounds of knuckle of veal. Place this in a good average saucepan. (Ah, you say, what is a good average saucepan ? The one used by me held six pints of water when full to the brim.) Place the veal in the pan and cover well with water—that is to say, when the veal is lying in the pan the water should cover it to the depth of an inch. Now put on the lid and let it boil for two hours. When the water starts to bubble so that steam comes hissing through the lid, rush to the stove and turn down the gas until the water just turns over pleasantly and without anger. At the end of an hour and a half take a look into the saucepan. You will see two or three unpleasant green scum-like deposits floating about on top. Take a spoon and sharply fish these out. While all this is happening you must :

Take a nice young chicken ; dismember it. This means that you disjoint it : two legs, two wings, two sides of the breast, and so on. (This part is perfectly revolting, but it is worth it in the long run.) You should now have on the plate about six or seven pieces of chicken. You then remove the skin. You will have great difficulty in removing it from the lower parts of the legs and the more secret places of the wings, but it will peel off from the larger portions as bark peels from a tree. Now——

Take parsley. Chop it up until you have enough of it to fill a tablespoon. Have ready beside you a tin of cinnamon. This is a fine brown powder like snuff. Have also salt and white pepper. At the end of two hours the critical moment in the making of ' Friar's Chicken ' arrives, and you proceed to :

Take the boiling veal from the fire, remove the meat, and strain the stock, or soup. Now put the pan back and add to the soup the various portions of dismembered chicken. Let the brew boil gently. Then season with salt and pepper and add the chopped parsley. Every one must season to his own taste. The best way is to try with small quantities of salt and pepper and keep tasting until the mixture is right. Now add the cinnamon. Do so in very small quantities and go on tasting. Then stir the pan and allow the brew to boil until the chicken is tender. This period varies with different chickens. (The only way I could tell was by sticking a fork into the chicken.) While the chicken is boiling :

Take two eggs. Whisk them up in a basin. See that the

chicken is done, then slowly pour in the whisked eggs and stir them in one direction only. This process will alarm you slightly. The eggs will curdle. Never mind. Then take the pan off the fire and—'Friar's Chicken' is ready!

If you do not like it, I shall be surprised. It is a most unusual dish. It has a distinction that is absent from modern cookery, and in the old days when every farmer and crofter in Scotland paid part of his rent in 'kain' hens, it must have been eaten from one end of the country to the other. It is useless to ask me who invented this, because I do not know. It may possibly be an old French dish that came over in the train of Mary Queen of Scots. It may be much older. The monks of Melrose may have invented it. But whoever did so understood the art of composing an unforgettable dish.

Now, in conclusion, I must add a few additional comments on 'Friar's Chicken'. I have made this three times. The first and third times I used cinnamon to flavour it. On the second occasion I used mace, which is a brown powder from the outer covering of the nutmeg. I find it very difficult to say which is nicer. Both flavourings are authorized by antiquity. Sometimes I think the cinnamon is the better, and sometimes I like the mace. The opinion of those who have been privileged to eat 'Friar's Chicken' as cooked by me is worth little, because these unfortunate people have been so bewildered, and rendered so apprehensive, by my accounts of the romantic and historic associations of this dish, that they approach it in an unbalanced condition, thankful only that they could honestly praise it.

There is one more point about 'Friar's Chicken'. An intelligent woman who tasted it said that it would be the ideal way to cook a rabbit; and this I am inclined to believe. If this is so, I have, I consider, rendered a great service to mankind because, of all foods, stewed rabbit is surely the most dreary, the most depressing and the most mean-spirited.

§ 4

I got into Haddington in the dark and went straight to bed. The bed was a great catafalque with a claret-coloured awning above it. In the morning the girl brought in tea and said:

'And did ye sleep sound?'

' I did. Why ? '

' Yon's Thomas Carlyle's bed,' she said. ' The Americans come from far and near to sleep in it.'

What astounding things Americans do ! I had an absurd vision of a man in horn glasses reading *Heroes and Hero Worship* and trying to keep awake. Yet it is an interesting bed, for to it the ' Sage of Chelsea ' took a love-stricken brain : he slept in it when he was courting pretty Jane Welsh who lived in the main street.

It was seven a.m. I looked with some curiosity out of the window. Haddington is one of the best tonics I can pre-scribe in a world that seems none too sure of itself. Nothing could look more permanent than Haddington. Its wide, long main street with its worsted-grey houses is built for eternity. We hear a lot about the solidity of English country towns, but they are sweet and soft compared with those of Scotland, where the grim stone houses take on the massive permanence of mountains.

Outside each house or shop a dustbin stood on the pave-ment's edge. A black and white collie with an old man in remote attendance took a flock of sheep up the street. The morning sun fell over the house-tops. The stern stone houses stood with shuttered windows as if closing their eyes to the regrettable sight of dustbins.

It was just the sort of place in which Carlyle would make love.

All round Haddington lie the fat farmlands of East Lothian. There is no finer land in the kingdom and no finer farmers. Haddington spreads over this rich region an air of prestige and experience.

No farmers have, of course, made money within the memory of living man, but you feel that if farmers could make money they would do so in East Lothian and bank it at Haddington in a grey stone building which solidly suggests that the pound is still the pound, and will continue to be so—in Haddington ! When France made long and passionate love to Scotland in the old days, Scotland acknowledged her advances with a stern compliment in the form of town squares. These old love tokens are to be seen all over the country. There is one in Kelso, another in Stirling, a third in Jedburgh. Had-dington's contribution is a main street that, with a few minor alterations, would not look out of place in Normandy.

In Hardgate Street is Bothwell's house, where Mary Stuart's wild man performed one of his lesser known exploits.

Bothwell had waylaid a convoy of money and was hard pressed by his pursuers. He stole into this house—which belonged to Cockburn of Sandybed—and confronted a terrified serving-maid, who was turning meat on a spit, with a demand for her clothes. He changed into them and—so the story goes —did the turnspit's work for three days until he could escape.

There can be no other town in Scotland of this size—the population is about 4,000—which can claim a longer or a more varied roll of fame. John Knox was born here. So was Jane Welsh, the wife of Thomas Carlyle. So was Samuel Smiles, the author of *Self Help*; and John Brown, ' of Haddington ', the famous divine, although not a native of Haddington, spent all his life here.

Another famous son of Haddington who has never received recognition is George Miller, the founder of the *Cheap Magazine*. Had he lived to-day—or preferably as a schoolfellow of the late Lord Northcliffe—Miller could not possibly have avoided becoming a millionaire. He erected the first printing-press in East Lothian at Dunbar in 1795. He removed it to Haddington in 1804, where nine years afterwards the *Cheap Magazine* was published—the first attempt ever made to provide good popular literature. Its success was astonishing. It penetrated into cottages all over Scotland, and reached a circulation—and in days before railway transport—of twenty thousand a month. Copies of this magazine should be treasured as a landmark in the history of popular literature.

Although Miller must have had sympathy for his public, he designed an almost unforgivably sententious title page :

THE CHEAP MAGAZINE
A work of humble import,
yet
Claiming the attention of all ranks
As having for its object
PREVENTION OF CRIMES,
And being calculated to ensure the
PEACE, COMFORT, AND SECURITY
OF SOCIETY
by alluring the young and thoughtless
To a taste for reading subjects of real
utility,
Having a tendency to counteract the

BANEFUL INFLUENCE OF DEPRAVED
HABITS ;
Promote the interests of Religion,
Virtue and Humanity ;
Encourage a Spirit of industry, economy
and frugality
AND
Dispel the shades of Ignorance, Prejudice,
and Error, particularly from among
the lower orders of mankind.

It says much for the quality of Miller's periodical that the
' lower orders of mankind ' forgave this terrible title-page
and bought the magazine ! But it died for want of a distri-
buting agent, and poor Miller died also, a sad and disillusioned
man. But he deserves a statue for making Haddington the
birthplace of popular literature. . . .

There is a fine old bridge spanning the often flooded waters
of the Tyne. On one of its arches the rough Border justice
was administered. Thieves and malefactors were hung from
an iron hook and allowed to kick themselves to death above
the smooth slow river.

' The last time the hook was used,' a local antiquary told
me, ' was after Bonnie Prince Charlie's rising in 1745, when
the hand of one of his supporters was hung there. It remained
hanging, black and shrivelled, for ten years. . . .'

The Tyne flows under the bridge past the lovely old Abbey
Church which has inherited from a still more ancient church
the title of ' Lamp of the Lothians '. This was an openwork
spire like that of St. Giles in Edinburgh or that spire in Newcastle still known as ' the Eye of the North '.

Here I met a grave-digger who, like all his kind, and in the
good Shakespearean tradition, was a cheerful, smiling man.

' And was John Knox born here or in Morham ? ' I asked.

He pointed over the river in the direction of the tree which
was planted at Carlyle's request on the legendary site of
Knox's birthplace.

' Well,' he replied, ' Thomas Carlyle wouldna have gone
to the expense of planting yon tree, or of putting a rail
around it, if he hadna been certain. . . . Jane Welsh was
a direct descendant of John Knox, ye mind.'

After a conversation about mortality—conducted in the
most cheerful manner—I left him to find that tombstone
which moves the heart more than anything in Haddington.

In the ruined nave of St. Mary's lies that once lovely and brilliant woman, Jane Welsh Carlyle. Forty years of marriage with a mountain of philosophy were not easy, even if a woman married, as she once said in her impetuous way, for ambition ; and she also had temperament.

But at the end Carlyle came to her, to stand, an old man with a melting heart, gazing up at the window as if she might pull aside the blind, as she did when she was young. In the dusk he went like an old grey ghost to the ruined nave to kiss her tombstone and to write perhaps the most pathetic tribute a husband has ever written to a wife :

'In her bright existence', he wrote, 'she had more sorrows than are common, but also a soft invincibility, a capacity for discernment, and a noble loyalty of heart which are rare. For forty years she was the true and loving helpmate of her husband, and by act and word unweariedly forwarded him as none else could in all of worthy that he did or attempted. She died in London April 21, 1866, suddenly snatched from him, and the light of his life as if gone out.'

So upon her tombstone he placed a little of that warmth and tenderness which in life might have made the 'Mocking Bird' a happier woman.

§ 5

I think that some places, like some men, should never be met. A preconceived opinion is often more satisfactory than reality. My preconceived opinion of Dunbar was clear and distinct. It was, I thought, a romantic crag—a kind of Scottish Tintagel—thrusting itself out into the North Sea. There was always a mist over it, wind round it, waves against it and the sound of gulls crying in the sea fog. On the top of the crag was a castle in ruins, great walls ending and beginning nowhere, stairways rising to the stars, high windows at which, on dark nights, ghost lights would shine. Such was my idea of the castle that might have saved the life of Mary Queen of Scots. . . .

When I saw Dunbar for the first time I asked at once for the castle ; and someone said, in the beautiful, blunt Scottish way : 'Man, ye're looking at it.'

But I was not ! I was looking at three girls in green bathing dresses who dived one after the other into a circular swimming-pool beside the sea. The temperature, said a notice board rather callously, was fifty-eight degrees Fahrenheit. In addition it was raining. A wireless gramophone connected with a loud speaker tried to cheer up the bathers.

Then, looking beyond the swimming-pool and its pavilion, I saw sitting on a rust-red crag a pitiful little wall like the wall of a shelled house in a devastated area. Even the most timid of boys would not have troubled to climb it. It was all that time and cannon have left of that stronghold from whose gates Mary Stuart went to play out the last act of her tragedy. . . .

And the wireless gramophone suddenly shrieked the latest dance croon to the corpse of Dunbar Castle.

Of course, when an historic town decides to become a holiday resort this sort of thing is bound to happen. And why not ? How Mary Stuart would have loved the laughter that in these days rises from a swimming-pool to those stumps and caverns which were once the proud ramparts of Dunbar !

The part of Dunbar I like best is the old tumble-down fishing quarter, which has seen better days. It looks like some seaside relative of the Canongate in Edinburgh. Here the survivors of a once prosperous community put up a pretence at fishing. The harbour which Cromwell built is dead. The newer harbour is dead. And the old men and the old women, who sit baiting the hooks with mussels and neatly coiling the long lines in baskets under layers of hay, seem to be working in a dream.

There is something terribly tragic about these bits of disappearing Scotland. In a few years they will have vanished. One has the impression that youth, which makes vivid all things, has withdrawn the promise of continuity, so that when the last old man has taken his last look at the still harbour there will be nothing but silence.

I walked to the red ruins above the harbour. In its day Dunbar Castle was one of the strongholds of the eastern seaboard. The rich stream of Scottish history flowed through its gates for centuries. Oriel College, Oxford, was born there one day in June 1314, when Edward II and his bodyguard rode up in flight from Bannockburn.

The King had narrowly escaped death on the field. Four

dismounted Scottish knights had seized the trappings of his horse. Edward felled them with his battle-axe. His horse was slain. On a fresh horse he spurred south, vowing that if he reached England in safety he would dedicate a house for poor Carmelites to the Mother of God. From Dunbar he escaped to Berwick. So Oriel College has its roots in the red ruins of Dunbar as surely as Balliol springs from the green hills of Galloway.

But as a man stands among these tumbled stones there is one question only which he would wish to wring from them. What is the truth about the love story of Mary Queen of Scots and Bothwell? Did Mary love her wild man or did he take her by force? We shall never know, and pens will fight about it until the end of the world.

In centuries of alarms and excursions Dunbar can have known no stranger night than that in April, two months after Darnley's murder, when the Queen of Scots was led to this castle by the man who had slain her husband.

She had been riding with twelve attendants when Bothwell, with eight hundred armed men behind him, rode up and, taking her by the bridle, led her away. The twelve days she spent in this castle are a mystery. Within three weeks she had married Bothwell in Holyrood; and she still wore her widow's weeds.

Whether she loved Bothwell or not, her fate was sealed, and these old stones were soon to witness the beginning of the end. The Associate Lords interrupted the honeymoon at Borthwick Castle. Bothwell was forced to flee. At midnight, Mary, booted and spurred, in man's clothes, let herself down from a window twenty-eight feet from the ground and galloped off into a June night alone. Is there a less probable picture in history? Or a more pitiful one?

If she had hoped to escape from Bothwell the dawn must have brought despair; if she were trying to flee after him it must have brought happiness. He found her—only a few miles from her starting place—and once again these stones of Dunbar saw the Queen of Scots, a weary figure in the clothes of a man, enter its mysterious walls.

They found for her the gown and kirtle of a countrywoman, and in these the Queen of Scotland rode out with the man who was her lover, or her captor, to Carberry Hill and—defeat.

So a man stands above the North Sea at Dunbar wondering what was in her heart ; and there is no sound but the waves on the red rocks and the cries of the gulls, and a whisper, which may be the wind in the old stones, saying : ' Perhaps, strange as it may seem, she loved him.'

If you want an anti-climax—and I enjoy them at times— go down from the ruins along the sea wall and beneath the castle you will come to a trim, small stone building with the date 1913 on it. The door, which is often open, reveals a clever-looking piece of machinery which might be astronomical, typographical or even medical. A man bends over charts. A needle in the machine traces wavering lines on a cylinder.

This is one of the only two tidal observatories in the British Isles. The other is near Penzance. Dunbar and Penzance establish what one might have considered a simple problem —sea levels.

It appears that the water at the entrance to Dunbar Harbour is a place where tidal levels remain constant. Every hour a plummet descends into the water, and every week the tidal charts go up to the Ordnance Survey in London. (That is all I could understand about it !)

Immediately above this mystery of the tides is the rock that holds the even deeper mystery of Mary's heart.

§ 6

A few miles from Berwick the road runs sharply to the sea and to a small, mysterious-looking fishing town called Eyemouth. This place is as Scottish as any place could be ; a dour, grey, restrained little town whose queer old houses nod together as if caught in the act of remembering smuggled brandy.

Eyemouth is unknown to fame. No tourists prowl about it. No guide-books extol its charm. No artists ever camp out on its ' Marine Parade ' and attempt to capture the rather tragic, defensive attitude which Eyemouth adopts towards the wild North Sea rollers that year by year eat into the land. In other words, no one has ever heard about Eyemouth. It stands facing the sea like someone warding off a blow.

It is interesting to go into such places because you soon learn, if you just sit down and listen, that the Eyemouths of this world have lived as vividly as more famous places. Their memories are as long and as strong. Eyemouth is the town of ' The Disaster '.

Since the year 1881 disasters have shocked the world; towns have been wrecked by earthquakes; ships have gone down to the bottom of the sea; millions of good men have died in battle; thrones have tottered; plagues have stalked across the world; but to Eyemouth there has been only one real disaster in the last half-century.

The War was an unhappy affair to Eyemouth, but the disaster was—'The Disaster'.

I first heard about ' The Disaster ' when I was sitting on a herring-box on the quayside, learning that in these days it does not pay a man to own a drifter. Even if your two sons man the ship it does not pay, with prices as they are.

On a neighbouring barrel an old man was baiting fish hooks with mussels. He wore a fisherman's peaked cap, a blue jersey and blue trousers. He joined in the conversation. His remarks were treated with great respect. I asked who he was.

' He's one of the few men,' I was told in a loud whisper, ' who escaped from the Disaster.'

' What Disaster ? ' I asked.

I received a glance which told me that I had forfeited whatever respect my previous conduct had gained for me:

' Man, have ye never heard of the Disaster ? '

' Which one ? '

' The Disaster of 1881.'

Then I was told a story which, after all these years, is alive in Eyemouth; a story that is still a thing of terror to every woman whose man goes out fishing in the North Sea.

In 1881 Eyemouth was a prosperous fishing town. It was the first community to adopt the modern deep-sea fishing-boat with closed deck. Its fleet was regarded from Peterhead to Yarmouth as one of the finest and most seaworthy on the East Coast of Britain.

On Unlucky Friday, October 14, 1881, the fleet sailed in a queer calm.

(Old Thomas Burgon, the survivor, stopped ' sheelin' ' the mussels and said :

' There was not a breath o' wind and the glass was never sae low.')

There were two hundred and seventy-nine men in the forty-five boats, and one hundred and twenty-nine of them belonged to Eyemouth. They had shot their lines about eight miles from the shore when an even deeper calm came over land and sea. Dark clouds appeared. A wind rose.

(Old Thomas Burgon suddenly made a loud clap with his hands : ' It happened like that ! ' he said.)

And with the suddenness of a clap of thunder one of the most fearful storms within memory swept the country from the Orkneys to the English Channel. The Eyemouth fleet had a terrible experience. Some of the vessels were driven ashore and lifted by the force of the waves high over the rocks ; but most of them were never seen again.

In a few hours Eyemouth learned that half her men had perished at sea. One hundred and twenty-nine of the hundred and eighty-nine fishermen who were drowned belonged to this small town. That is Eyemouth's memory. In an hour of storm a prosperous fishing community was, so it seemed, ruined.

' There was not a house without a hearse at the door,' said the man who told me the story. ' Things will never be what they were before the Disaster.'

While we were talking, the only excitement which now invades Eyemouth drove up in the shape of two motor lorries loaded with barrels of herring.

The women of Eyemouth, aproned and booted and with fingers protected by bandages of rag, lined up on each side of long wooden troughs in a curing yard. The herring were poured barrel by barrel into the troughs. The girls were not allowed to start until the whole convoy had been unloaded. At a signal there was a flash of a hundred knives and the work began.

Herring gutting is expert, hard, and badly paid work. The girls work in gangs of three. Their skill and speed are uncanny.

But here again the blight that seems to have settled over the fishing industry has resulted in a glut of salt herring for export markets. A drifter's catch is rushed to the yard. The girls gut and pack them in brine. Then—the rush over —the fish are stacked in barrels to wait, either in Scotland or on the quayside of Hamburg, sometimes for months.

Eyemouth should have produced a Barrie. It is full of

character, and somewhere beneath the surface there may be humour, but I must admit that first impressions are either grim or tragic.

There is a graveyard which must surely be unique in Great Britain. Years ago, when a dispute arose about a new burial-ground, a solution was reached by piling six feet of earth on the old one ! This meant that all upright stones had to be removed. These were used to erect the most grisly building possible to imagine. Its walls were tombstones, many of them the old eighteenth-century Scottish stones covered with skulls and cross-bones.

This ghastly place was a watch-house in the days of those ' Dandy Doctors ', or body-snatchers, who provided Robert Louis Stevenson with a theme for one of the most blood-curdling short stories ever written.

But one memory of Eyemouth is at least happy. Here it was on a May day in 1787 that a good-looking young man called Robert Burns came riding on a stout mare. He had come to Eyemouth to be made a Royal Arch Mason. The local lodge had decided that ' on account of R. Burns's remark-able poetical genius ' he was to be admitted without payment of the usual guinea admission fee.

We can imagine the careful fathers of Eyemouth having a solemn meeting about this ! And they were repaid ! Burns was in his usual cheerful mood for he wrote in his diary that his host was a ' warm-hearted, jolly fellow—takes a hearty glass and sings a good song '.

So on this happy and illustrious memory it seems well to say good-bye to Eyemouth and its sad little harbour.

§ 7

The Liberties of Berwick end at Lamberton Toll. There is nothing in the landscape to indicate a frontier. You would, in fact, pass into England without realizing it, were it not for a rather drunken-looking standard by the wayside. ' Scotland ' it proclaims.

The dignity of the announcement is slightly interrupted by the attitude of the standard, which leans heavily to the right, like a patriotic Scot on Burns Night. I attempted to straighten it ; but it requires a spade.

I stood with one foot in Scotland and the other on English

soil. The Border line runs through a pigsty that is actually in both countries, and so arranged that the animal sleeps in Scotland and eats in England. Mr. Logan Mack says in *The Border Line* that the farmer once bought a pig half a mile off on the English side and was fined £5 for introducing the animal to Scotland without a licence ! Presumably, if he had changed the pig's bedroom he would have avoided the fine.

One of the little white cottages on the side of the road used to be Lamberton Toll House. In the old days the toll-keeper was often awakened by the drumming of hoofs along the road from Berwick. He would look out of his window and see below the steam rising from the post horses and hear a man and a maid yammering like a couple of lunatics for marriage.

Lamberton's toll-keeper was, as recently as 1856—when Lord Brougham's Marriage Act put an end to Over-the-Border romances—as notorious as the ' blacksmith ' of Gretna Green for his ready assistance in these matters. I believe the man, with sublime lack of humour, but with perhaps a perfect grasp of irony, had a notice in his window :

' Ginger beer sold here and marriages performed on the most reasonable terms.'

Along the lane to the left, and through a farmyard, is one of Scotland's forgotten memorials. It is the ruin, difficult to discover now, of Lamberton Kirk. On this spot an event took place which, through a long century of tragedy and romance, led to King James VI of Scotland riding south in a very good humour to become James I of England.

It was in 1503 that a cavalcade crossed the Border and turned up the hill to Lamberton. After years of war England and Scotland had decided to make a premature peace by the marriage of Margaret Tudor, daughter of Henry VII, with James IV, King of Scotland. At Lamberton she was received by the Scots Commissioners.

In Edinburgh the little bride—she was only fourteen years of age—was given a Scottish welcome. The bells rang. A fountain flowed with wine. The wicked old stone houses in the Canongate were hung with tapestries ; and the poet, William Dunbar, wrote ' The Thistle and the Rose '.

So among the nettles of Lamberton was sown that seed, the tragic stem of which bore in time Mary Queen of Scots and her son—James VI and I—and all the exiled Stuarts.

§ 8

I could, I suppose, have found my way to Selkirk by other roads, but the temptation to invade England was too strong. I found myself determined to spend the night in Berwick. I was technically in England, but that was all. In every outward way Berwick is as Scottish as Kelso or Jedburgh.

I walked round the walls. Berwick, Chester, York and Londonderry are the only completely walled towns in the British Isles. Berwick's ramparts are grass-grown. Strange, green hummocks seem to cover the debris of old battles. Now and then I came across an old gun lying in the long grass. I leaned over the Scots Gate and looked down into the quiet wide High Street that still, so it seems, is waiting and listening for a sound from the North. On the seaward side, the wind comes cold from the North Sea, and the long rollers break on Fenham Flats. Lindisfarne—one of the loveliest names on the map—lies like a gold ship at sea.

But more interesting even than the walls of Berwick is a climb to the steeple of the town hall. I went there in the evening when the chimneys of Berwick were smoking. The town hall was empty. I wandered into the queer old court-house, with its panelled bench, dock and gallery. I met a young man who turned out to be William Ormston, master bellringer.

'Ay, I'll let ye up,' he said in good Lowland Scots, as he unlocked the door of the tower.

'Are you Scots or English ? '

'Half and half, like all Berwick,' he replied.

We went up a winding stair and then up a perpendicular ladder into a dusty place, where the bells of Berwick hang. There were more ladders, darkness, and we came to a clock that has been ticking off time since 1756. We stepped out at last into the open air ; and below us lay the clustered red roofs of Berwick-on-Tweed, and the three bridges across the river ; to the north the green hills of Scotland ; to the south the Cheviots.

What a view ! How eloquent are the red roofs of Berwick ! You could wander round this town for weeks and never know much of that strange, hidden area called ' back-yards '. From a height you look right down into them. You see how the houses of old Berwick were all huddled together within the walls like sheep in a pen. These ' back-yards', which are entered by a narrow passage, must have seen some fearful sights when the Scots were over the Border ! One man with a sword or a bow could hold them against a crowd.

Another thing you notice from the tower is that all the old houses have eaves like those A-shaped eaves of Norwich, which still remind us of the dead Flemish cloth industry. In Berwick the attics once held the rich grain of East Lothian.

' Ay, in the old days,' said William Ormston, ' all the grain in East Lothian was stored in Berwick, and was shipped south ; but the attics are empty now. . . .'

The clock struck a quarter to eight.

' I'll be going now,' said William Ormston.

' What's the hurry ? '

' I must ring the curfew ! '

So together we clambered down the ladders to tell Berwick-on-Tweed that William the Conqueror would like all the fires put out.

We stood in a wooden loft where the bell-ropes hang from the roof. William Ormston (who, when not ringing the bells, is sweeping the chimneys of Berwick) stood by the rope of the curfew bell waiting for the striking of eight o'clock. In the old days the curfew bell was rung also at five a.m. as a signal for the opening of the town gates.

' And until the War ', said Mr. Ormston, ' there was a " Dead Bell " that was rung when a buddy died. It was verra profitable for the bellringer, for the cost went in wi' the undertaker's bill, and the bellringer went round to collect his money. It was verra profitable, too, for the undertaker, but verra depressing for Berwick. . . .'

At this moment something became alive in the darkness overhead. There was a whirr of wheels like the flight of some enormous bat, and slowly the belfry gave out the strokes of eight.

William Ormston grasped the rope of the curfew bell. He pulled it down until its tail writhed on the wooden floor, then up it shot to the end of its length and from high above us sounded the curfew.

' Ay, it's been rung since the old days,' said William Ormston, as his arms moved to the rope, ' and although you'd think nobody cared now, there's many a body listening for it to set a clock or to put a bairn to bed . . . ay ; ay. . . .'

And as the bell rang out over Berwick I knew it to be the voice of the Border.

I went down. Dusk filled the grey streets. Carts creaked homewards. Lights shone in windows. English Berwick said good night in the accents of Scotland. The last notes of the curfew died on the wind, and the first stars burned above the old grey town of battles.

§ 9

The salmon has a bad time in Scotland. Every one is on the look-out for him. His only hope of survival is to gain the freedom of some expensive river in the Highlands where there is nothing more dangerous than a colonel or two with a rod bought in St. James's Street. Here, with luck and common prudence, the salmon may live to undertake those mysterious migrations which no one, I believe, understands.

But woe betide the salmon at the river mouths of Scotland! I have sat up on a platform above the Solway Dee on the west coast watching men trap salmon in what is called a Yair net. I have, as you know, been out at night in Kirkcudbright with a shoulder net ; but the most dangerous place for any salmon is surely the mouth of the Tweed at Berwick.

I was walking up a hill towards Berwick in the evening. A horse was pulling a heavy cart up the road in front of me. The driver paused to rest his steed. The cart was loaded to the brim with the kind of salmon that men tell lies about in every public-house in the Highlands! They were enormous. The life was hardly out of them.

' Where do they come from ? '

' The Tweed Fishery.'

' Netted ? '

' Ay.'

I said that I would like to watch this organized murder.

' Ye'll have to be quick,' said the man, ' for it's the last day o' the salmon fushin'. We stop at midnight. . . .'

I went down to a strip of shore at Tweedmouth. Here the great river that for twenty miles is the boundary between England and Scotland pours itself into the North Sea. Half the idle population of Berwick was gathered on the shore. I learnt that the salmon season had not been

NEWARK TOWER, YARROW

SUNSET OVER THE ETTRICK WATER

good, but that phenomenal catches on the last day of the netting had thrilled Berwick.

The crowd stood watching operations with the eyes of fishermen, and even the dogs of Berwick were excited about it.

Nothing could be simpler than the methods of the Berwick Fishery. This is the time of year when the salmon make for the fresh water to spawn. Anyone who has looked over Galway Bridge, in Ireland, when the salmon are moving up, will know that they come in a great instinctive army, sometimes shoulder to shoulder, so that you could not drop a twig in the water without hitting a fish.

The netters of Berwick merely interrupt this procession with a huge net. They are by law allowed to keep the net in the water for only twenty minutes; but they economize their time (and get more fish) by using two nets; the instant one is pulled in the second one is cast out. This fishing is a continuous drama in twenty-minute stretches.

The fishers prepared to pull in the net. The twenty minutes were up!

As soon as the men on shore put their hands to the ropes a rowing-boat shaped like a clog—its prow sharp as the beak of a Viking galley—was pushed off with the second net. The boat skimmed over the long rollers that break on this part of the coast and from the stern fell the net, making a great circle outside the net that was being hauled in, so that any fish escaping the first trap would fall victims of the second.

But no one looked at the second net. Every eye was fixed on the wide semicircle of sea faintly indicated by cork floats. At first we saw nothing. Then as the men pulled, narrowing the circle every minute, we saw an odd commotion out at sea as if the water were boiling:

'Yon's a big fush!' shouted a boy.

'Ay; he's a twenty-pounder!' cried a spectator, gripping me by the arm.

An old man in plus fours with a salmon fly in his hat looked faintly sick.

The crowd began to shout excitedly. The dogs began to bark. As the great net came into shallower water we could see that the bag, or bosom, at the end of it, was full of salmon, lashing out, leaping, fighting for life. The desperate struggle of the silver-flashing life was terrible. They fought like sharks.

13

When half the net had been gathered in we saw our first fish. They had been caught in the body of the net, and had at once become aware of their peril. They were spent with a fight of twenty minutes. They lay exhausted. Men pulled them out and placed them on the beach. They lashed the stones with their tails once or twice and lay still.

But in the end, or bosom, of the net an awful fight of great salmon was taking place. They leapt into the air. They lashed out powerfully. One four-foot fellow leaped a yard from the water, and we saw that he had thrust his head through the mesh.

When the net was pulled in thirty-two salmon lay on the shore. They ranged from fifteen to thirty pounds in weight.

The fly fisherman began to look positively ill. . . .

Many of the fish, I noticed, bore bruises underneath, which I thought were gained in their struggle :

' Nothing of the kind,' I was told. ' Those are seal bites. Every salmon you see with these red marks on him has at some time had a narrow escape from a seal. . . .'

When it became dark I was weary of watching salmon drawn in from the sea. Sometimes the net would hold ten ; sometimes twenty or more.

' We shall fish right on till midnight,' said one of the men.

In the dusk the netters of Berwick form one of the most picturesque sights in Scotland. They are silhouetted against the pearl-grey sea. Half a dozen men strain against the weight of the boat and push it out over a line of white rollers. So they stand braced in effort, eternal and unchanging, for the fisherman and the ploughman are the only two permanent figures in the world.

§ 10

On a grey day with rain falling I motored from Berwick to the royal burgh of Selkirk.

This is a distinguished place with the ripe flavour of age over it. The triangular market-place with its queer, spired town hall is, I think, rather French. I would not have been surprised if Athos, Porthos and Aramis, suddenly clatter-ing round a corner, had flung themselves from their horses and stamped thirstily into the Fleece.

I plodded round in the wet, learning quite a lot. Andrew

Lang was born in Selkirk. There is a statue to Mungo Park, the explorer. Burns, so a tablet says, once lodged in the old, now vanished, Forest Inn, and Walter Scott stands in front of the town hall. It was to this statue that poor old John of Skye, who had been piper of Abbotsford, came with his pipes beneath his arm. He gazed for a long time at his old master, then, tuning the pipes, marched round the statue playing Scott's favourite airs. But he was an old man and his strength and skill had vanished. His pipes gave out during the 'Land of the Leal' and poor old John sat down at his master's feet sobbing his heart out.

The most arresting of all Selkirk's monuments is a sentence of three words on the memorial to the Battle of Flodden :

'*O Flodden Field.*'

That is all.

If there is a more eloquent or more poignant inscription on any war memorial, I have yet to read it. These words conclude each verse of J. B. Selkirk's lovely poem, *Selkirk after Flodden*. And the mad idea came to me to visit Flodden. I had never been there. It was a mad idea, because the rain was falling, as it can in Scotland, with a grim enthusiasm.

I came to a narrow lane. The cart-tracks were full of water. I opened a gate and began to climb a green hill. On top of this was a stone cross. Far off to the left the Eildon Hills lifted themselves from the flat lands of Tweedside like a ship left high and dry by the tide. Beyond them the long, smooth outline of the Lammermuirs shouldered the sky with grey clouds touching them. So this was Flodden.

I am surprised at times that certain places can be found on any map. I feel this when the train slides into Rome. I feel it at Bethlehem. I feel it at Tintagel. That Flodden, lifted high above common things by centuries of song and story, should be a green hill with wet sheep mournfully cropping grass seems somehow strange.

I would say that the only two battles fought on British soil that still awaken sorrow are Flodden and Culloden. England's battles have been many and magnificent, but one feels that there must have been an element of fox-hunting about them. They are not really tragic. Even the Wars of the Roses seem like the amusement of a privileged class, and one feels that the ploughman pulled up his horses and watched them, as he would watch hounds.

Scotland's battles have been desperate. They have been national. Flodden turned Scotland into a graveyard.

One of the most interesting recent books on Flodden is a small volume called *The Secret of Flodden*, by W. Mackay Mackenzie. No one can deny that this writer is a good Scotsman, but he has had the detachment to take a new and impartial view of Flodden. He thinks that the Scots should have won. They were superior in numbers and in artillery.

Most writers on medieval warfare call Flodden the last victory of the arrow. Mr. Mackenzie denies this. He says that the English archers were out of action as soon as the armies became locked in conflict. He traces Scotland's defeat to the failure of the Scots to employ the German pike —a cumbersome eighteen-foot weapon—and the superiority of the English brown-bill, or halberd.

It is good to find some one with the courage to defend the gallant King of Scotland, James IV, one of the finest of the Stuarts.

Like all Stuarts, he resented advice. But some of the greatest battles in history have been won by generals who rejected advice. Nelson, one remembers, once put a telescope to a blind eye. Had Scotland won the Battle of Flodden, James would have gone down in history as perhaps the greatest general his country had ever produced. When a man succeeds in the face of advice he is called a genius ; let him risk and lose and he is ' impetuous ' or ' ill-balanced '.

As you stand on the green hill of Flodden it is not difficult to imagine that September day in 1513, with the rain falling and the English Army begging James to descend and fight on the plain. You look at lovely Twizel Bridge—the most beautiful Border bridge—and you can, in imagination, see the English forces crossing that bridge to take the Scots in the rear. That bridge is one of Scotland's saddest relics.

Evening falls over this green hill and the battle is over. King James lies dead and round him lie the bodies of ten earls and three bishops, eleven barons, the archbishop of St. Andrews, three other church dignitaries, the Treasurer and sixty-eight knights and gentlemen.

It was Lord Dacre who found the body of the King of

Scots. It was carried to Berwick, where it was identified. It was then embalmed and taken first to Newcastle and then to London, where it was placed in the Carthusian monastery at Sheen. Although James had been excommunicated, the Pope gave permission for Henry VIII to bury him in St. Paul's Cathedral. There is no evidence that this was ever done.

Stow, on the other hand, says that when the monasteries were sacked the body of the King of Scots was found lying wrapped in lead in an attic among waste timber and rubbish. He tells how some workmen ' for their foolish pleasure ' cut off the King's head and how Queen Elizabeth's master glazier, a man called Young, took possession of it and kept it in his house for some time until, scared, perhaps, by his ghastly relic, he had it buried in the church of St. Michael's in Cheapside.

I walked down the green hill in the rain. . . .

The story went through Scotland, as it goes whenever a hero falls, that the King was not dead. Had not ten men worn the royal armour at Flodden to mislead the English ? A servant swore that he saw the King ride across the Tweed on the day after the battle. Over the hearthstone it was whispered, and believed throughout Scotland, that the King was in Palestine on a pilgrimage.

I looked back at the green hill.

The wind that blew over it on that September night so long ago has been blowing through the heart of Scotland ever since. They call it ' The Flowers of the Forest '.

The sorrow of a nation found its voice in that lament. There is nothing else like it. And when the pipes play it a man knows that in the sound of it is all the sorrow that has bruised the heart of mankind since the beginning of the world.

§ II

For two days I lay in bed with a cold reading Hogg's poems, but on the third day I realized that there is no point in being ill unless there is some one to sympathize with you, so I got up and, with the energy of ten thousand men, went out into this magnificent country. The rain was over. The sun was out. The Yarrow was full of water from the hills ; and I thought that rarely had Scotland looked more beautiful.

I gathered from Hogg that Selkirkshire is more full of ghosts, fairies, goblins, witches, wizards, spells and incantations than any other part of Scotland. And for proof of this you have Oakwood Tower overlooking Ettrick Water near Selkirk, where Michael Scott once lived. He was the famous wizard who split the Eildon Hills in three and rode Satan as the Souters o' Selkirk spur their annual nags to a Common Riding on a June morning.

The two streams that above the many others lend an enchantment to this county, the Yarrow and the Ettrick, join together on the plain of Philiphaugh where the Covenanters defeated Montrose. And the road to St. Mary's Loch says good-bye to Ettrick Water and follows the Yarrow, mounting into an enchanted country where there is nothing but hill folded against hill, the slide and murmur of water, the flight of birds and the slow movements of grazing sheep. It is a countryside that must instantly awaken the interest of anyone who is sensitive to landscape. It appeals to the eye in a thousand ways, in the sweetness of its sudden little glens and belts of trees, in the singing of the river over its shallow bed of pebbles, in the majestic sweep of moorlands, in the magnificent clouds that mass themselves to sail over hill-tops where the curlews cry, and the brown slopes where sheep crop grass. But there is also in Yarrow a feeling of homeliness and cosiness because on the sky-line lie wilder, higher moors whose harsh remoteness fling into relief the softer beauties of the ' Dowie Dens '.

Yarrow Water appeals also to the mind as a land supreme in legend. Every child born in this part of Scotland inherits a whole library of ballads. There is no stone that is without its fairy and no ruin without its ghost. From belts of trees or stark from the moor rise up all that is left of Border peel towers. They are tall stone keeps with twelve-foot thick walls and turrets from which, in the old days, men always looked for trouble. The marks of the iron cresset which held the bale, or need, fire can be seen still on the stones. Sometimes there was a special beacon turret for the fire-pan whose flame by night and smoke by day sent the men of the Border to boot, saddle and spear.

I came to one in a loop of the Yarrow, standing quite near the road among trees. This was Newark Castle, one of the most famous of the Border keeps. It is the tower in which Scott set the scene of *The Lay of the Last Minstrel*. It was originally a hunting-seat of James II of Scotland and later it became the property of the ' bold Buccleuch ', a family that is said to take its name from a buck that was slain in this district. But Newark, standing calmly above the Yarrow, has looked down on scenes of murder and violence. It was in the courtyard of this castle that the Covenanters massacred their royalist prisoners in cold blood after Philiphaugh, while one of their ministers watching the ghastly sight commented : ' This wark goes bonnilie on ! ' The field in which the bodies were buried is still called ' The Slain Men's Lea ' and Scott somewhere speaks of the skulls and bones that in his time were dug up in it.

Every yard along this road led me into a deeper enchant-ment. I crossed and re-crossed the river and passing Yarrow, in whose ancient kirkyard lies the maternal grandfather of Walter Scott, went on into a land that became harsher. The woods ended and the moors became wilder and higher, and only the gleam of lovely Yarrow Water to the left softened a country-side that had an almost Highland bleakness. Then suddenly the scene changed and I came to an exquisite sheet of water, woodlands fringing it, brown moorlands rising from its banks in long, gentle lines. This was St. Mary's Loch. It is, with the exception of Loch Lomond, the most famous loch in the south of Scotland. There is no song about it as famous as the Jacobite *Bonnie Banks of Loch Lomond*, but the poets who have been inspired by ' lone St. Mary's ' are many. It is a pity that none of them has written a really great poem about it. There is plenty of pretty music in the minor key, like Alexander Anderson's :

> *What boon to lie, as I lie now I lie,*
> *And see in silver at my feet*
> *St. Mary's Lake, as if the sky*
> *Had fallen 'tween those hills so sweet.*

But even Hogg, who responded now and then with un-erring skill to the sights and sounds by which he was sur-rounded, failed to do justice to St. Mary's Loch. I think Wordsworth hit the right note when he spoke of Yarrow's ' pastoral melancholy '. There is an odd melancholy about it even on a sunny day, and the many little hill streams and moorland burns that find their way into it seem like the tears of all the women of Yarrow who, if balladry can be believed, normally spent their lives weeping for lovers or husbands slain by the light of the moon.

On the hill-side above the loch I discovered all that remains of the little church of St. Mary: a few gravestones leaning from rough grass and bushes. Somewhere among this green tangle lie the two unhappy lovers of that magnificent ballad, *The Douglas Tragedy*, one of the few Border ballads, by the way, whose progress you can actually trace on the map. It was from Blackhouse Tower on the Douglas Burn that 'Lady Margaret' and her lover eloped one moonlit night and took the bridle-path over the moors. But the father awakened and discovered the absence of his daughter and:

> ' Rise up, rise up, my seven bold sons,
> And put on your armour so bright,
> And take better care of your youngest sister,
> For your eldest's awa the last night.'
>
> He's mounted her on a milk white steed,
> And himself on a dapple grey,
> And with a bugelet horn hung by his side,
> And lightly they rode away.

So the seven brothers and the father run to horse and gallop off into the night. They overtake the lovers. A frightful battle takes place on a bleak moor-top and the girl sees her father and her brothers fall.

> O she's ta'en out her handkerchief,
> It was o' the holland sae fine,
> And aye she dighted her father's bloody wounds,
> They were redder than the wine.
>
> ' O chuse, o chuse, lady Marg'ret,' he said,
> O whether will ye gang or bide ? '
> ' I'll gang, I'll gang, lord William ' she said
> ' For ye have left me no other guide.'

So he lifts her again on the milk-white steed and they ride slowly away. They stop to drink at a burn and suddenly a mortal wound, that the lover has suffered in the fight, breaks out, and the stream is stained with his blood. They ride swiftly to his mother's house:

> ' Get up, get up, lady mother,' he says,
> ' Get up and let me in !—
> Get up, get up, lady mother,' he says,
> ' For this night my fair lady I've win.

'*O mak my bed, lady mother,' he says,*
'*O mak it braid and deep !*
And lay Lady Marg'ret close at my back,
And the sounder I will sleep.'

But in the morning both lovers lie dead. They are buried close together in St. Mary's kirk, and from the lady's grave grows a bonny red rose and from his a briar. Their branches twine together until, as the last verse tells, the Black Douglas in a fury tears up the briar and tosses it into St. Mary's Loch.

These Scottish ballads cannot anywhere be equalled for simplicity, intensity, a stark sincerity and a beauty of expression that shines in them like a flower growing in the cleft of a rock. In all Scotland there is probably no spot richer in great ballads than the vales of Yarrow and Ettrick waters. The three that I think the finest are the Douglas Tragedy, the *Dowie Dens of Yarrow* and the superb *Lament of the Border Widow*. Is there anything more vivid and more pitiful than the poor widow's description of her husband's death ?

He slew my knight to me sae dear,
He slew my knight and poin'd his gear
My servants a' for life did flee,
And left me in extremitie.

I sew'd his sheet, making my mane ;
I watch'd the corpse, myself alane,
I watch'd his body, night and day ;
No living creature came that way.

I bore his body on my back,
And whiles I gae'd and whiles I sat ;
I digg'd a grave, and laid him in,
And happ'd him wi' the sod sae green.

But think na ye my heart was sair,
When I laid the mould on his yellow hair ;
O think na ye my heart was wae,
When I turned aboot away to gae ?

Nae living man I'll love again,
Since that my comely knight is slain ;
Wi' ae lock o' his yellow hair,
I'll chain my heart for evermair.

It is perhaps something of all this tragedy, the centuries of the salt ache of widowhood, the bitterness of thwarted love, the horror of sudden raid and counter-raid, that finds

13*

its way into the atmosphere of St. Mary's Loch, making it
on the fairest day overcast and thoughtful or, as Wordsworth
said, pervaded by a ' pastoral melancholy '.

§ 12

Near the head of St. Mary's Loch I came upon a bronze
man on a slight hill among trees. He sits thoughtfully with
a plaid on his shoulder and his sheep dog beside him, gazing
out towards the loch and the distant waterfall which he
knew so well—the Grey Mare's Tail. So James Hogg the
Ettrick Shepherd, one of Scotland's greatest singers, and, with
Burns, a classic example of natural genius, surveys the lovely
stage on which his life was played.

Hogg was one of the most remarkable characters of his
time. His ' opportunities ' were far less than those of Burns.
He was a shepherd boy who taught himself to read and write.
He admitted that his total schooling amounted to less than
a year. When he was seven he was herding ewes, and when
he was twenty he was a shepherd to Mr. Laidlaw of Blackhouse,
near the site of the castle mentioned in *The Douglas Tragedy*.
He taught himself to write and to rhyme. His life, like that
of Burns, was a constant struggle against his environment,
yet it was this environment—from which I suppose he would
have given his right hand to escape—that inspired every out-
standing poem that he wrote. He was an unequal poet. He
could write the most banal nonsense and follow it in a few
pages with something of flawless beauty. Unlike Burns, he
could not criticize himself and, unlike Burns, he remained
all his life essentially a peasant, and not entirely in the Scottish
sense of the word. Scott was a great friend to him and I
think Scott's handling of Hogg—by no means an easy person
to handle—is a fascinating sidelight on the greatness and the
sweetness of Scott's character. Hogg, consciously or un-
consciously, copied Scott and assumed Scott's obligation to
help him, not only with money, until at times his demands
must have tried Scott's temper to the utmost. There was,
an uncouthness about Hogg that is not natural to the Scottish
peasant and I have the idea that there was a twisted strain
of envy in him. It has become the fashion to criticize Hogg's
vanity. Vain he undoubtedly was, but then the vanity of
a shepherd who can write immortal verse cannot be judged

by the normal standard. Had he been mean as well as vain there would have been nothing to defend about him ; but he was generous and open hearted and his humble little home was, in its way, as great a social centre as Abbotsford.

Burns was the poet of humanity ; Hogg the poet of nature. No poet has had a keener sense of the unearthly than Hogg. He had wizard blood in him and, during the long years that he herded sheep on the melancholy moors and beside haunted burns, he knew by sight every elf in Border legend. Just now and then Hogg could write with the exquisite humanity of Burns. I think his poem to his old sheep-dog should have a place in every anthology. No lovelier poem has ever been written to a dog :

> Come, my auld, towzy, trusty friend,
> What gars ye look sae dung wi' wae ?
> D'ye think my favour's at an end,
> Because thy head is turnin' grey ?
>
> Although thy strength begins to fail,
> Its best was spent in serving me ;
> An' can I grudge thy wee bit meal·
> Some comfort in thy age to gie ?
>
> . . . .
>
> O'er past imprudence, oft alane,
> I've shed the saut and silent tear ;
> Then, sharin' a' my grief and pain,
> My puir auld friend came snoovin' near.
>
> For a' the days we've sojourned here,
> And they've been neither fine nor few,
> That thought possesst thee year to year
> That a' my griefs arose frae you.
>
> Wi' waesome face and hingin' head,
> Thou wadst hae pressed thee to my knee
> While I thy looks as well could read,
> As thou hadst said in words to me :
>
> 'Oh, my dear master, dinna greet ;
> What hae I ever done to vex thee ?
> See, here I'm cowerin' at thy feet,
> Just take my life, if I perplex thee,
>
> 'Whatever wayward course ye steer ;
> Whatever sad mischance oe'rtake ye ;
> Man, here is ane will hold ye dear !
> Man, here is ane will ne'er forsake ye !'

> *When my last bannocks on the hearth,*
> *Of that thou sanna want thy share;*
> *While I hae house or hauld on earth,*
> *My Hector shall hae shelter there.*

> *And should grim death thy noddle save,*
> *Till he has made an end o' me;*
> *Ye'll lie a wee while on the grave*
> *O ane wha aye was kind to thee.*

For this one touching and beautiful poem about his dog I can forgive James Hogg for his occasional roughness to men. And the shepherd who wrote this wept because at the age of twenty-five he did not know enough to enable him to commit his poems to paper! He taught himself the alphabet as he watched his sheep, making letters an inch high and using for his book the slate stones of the hill-side. Poor, ambitious Hogg! And we see him later in life crouched beside some boulder on Yarrow Water, a pen in his hand and an ink-horn stuck in the buttonhole of his waistcoat, as he transmits to paper the things seen and unseen which lie around him. Recognition came to him when he was about forty-five, but bad luck attended everything he did. If he made any money he lost it; and a book by Hogg seemed the natural preliminary to any publisher's bankruptcy. His life was made easier by the gift at a nominal rent of the farm of Altrive, left to him in the will of his patroness, the Duchess of Buccleuch. Here, in later life, Allan Cunningham described Hogg as the possessor of ' the best trout in Yarrow, the finest lambs on its braes, the finest grouse on its hills, and as good as a *sma' still* besides '. One reads this with a sense of relief. Well did he need his trout, his grouse, his mutton and his ' sma' still ', for the visitors who flocked to his door demanded entertainment out of all proportion to his means.

He fits in to that pleasant Abbotsford landscape, taking his place among the characters who basked in the sunlight of Scott; and now that the sunlight is over he stands alone in the chilly gaze of posterity a much greater man than he seemed to Scott—as great almost as he seemed to his fellow shepherds and farmers—the next vernacular poet to Burns. If you would read Hogg at his best read *Kilmeny*, *The Witch of Fife* and *The Queen's Wake*. They are, in their class, supreme.

He was also an excellent prose writer. What could be

more vivid and revealing than this pin-sharp picture, printed after Scott's death, and describing their first meeting :

' The first time I ever saw Sir Walter was one fine day in the summer of 1801. I was busily engaged working in the field at Ettrick House when old Wat Shiel came posting over the water to me and told me that I boud to gang away down to the Ramsey Cleuch as fast as my feet could carry me, for there were some gentlemen there who wanted to see me directly.

' " Wha can be at the Ramsey Cleuch that want to see me, Wat ? "

' " I couldna say, for it wasna me they spake to i' the bygangin', but I'm thinking it's the Shirra an' some o' his gang.'

' I was rejoiced to hear this, for I had seen the first volumes of the *Minstrelsy of the Border*, and had copied a number of ballads from my mother's recital, or chaunt rather, and sent them to the editor preparatory to the publication of the second volume. I accordingly flung down my hoe and hasted away home to put on my Sunday clothes, but before reaching I met the Shirra and Mr. William Laidlaw coming to visit me. They alighted and remained in our cottage perhaps nearly two hours, and we were friends on the very first exchange of sentiments. It could not be otherwise, for Scott had no duplicity about him. He always said as he thought. My mother chanted the ballad of " Old Maitlan " to him, with which he was highly delighted, and asked her if she thought it ever had been in print ? And her answer was, " O, na, na, sir, it never was printed in the world, for my brothers and me learned it and many frae auld Andrew Moor, and he learned it frae auld Baby Mettlin wha was housekeeper to the first laird o' Tushielaw. She was said to have been another nor a gude ane, an' there are many queer stories about hersel', but O ! she had been a grand singer o' auld songs and ballads."

' " The first laird o' Tushielaw, Margaret," said he, " then that must be a very old story indeed."

' " Aye, it is that, sir.—It is an auld story. But mair nor that, excepting George Warton and James Stuart, there war never ane o' my songs prentit till ye prentit them yoursel' and ye hae spoilt them awthegither. They were made for singin' and no for reading ; but ye hae broken the charm now, an' they'll never be sung mair. An' the worst thing of a', they're nouther richt spelled nor richt setten down.'

'"Tak ye that, Mr. Scott," said Laidlaw.

'Scott answered with a hearty laugh, on which my mother gave him a hearty rap on the knee with her open hand, and said, "Ye'll find, however, that it is a' true that I'm tellin' ye." My mother has been too true a prophetess, for from that day to this these songs which won the amusement of every winter evening have never been sung more.

'We were all to dine at Ramsey Cleuch with the Messrs. Bryden, but Scott and Laidlaw went away to look at some monuments in Ettrick Churchyard, and I was to follow. On going into the stack-yard at Ramsey Cleuch I met with Mr. Scott's groom, a greater original than his master, at whom I asked if the Shirra was come.

'"Ow ay, lad, the Shirra's come," said he. "Are ye the chap that mak's the auld ballads and sings them sae weel?"

'I said I fancied I was he that he meant.

'"Ay then, lad, gang your ways into the house and speir for the Shirra. They'll let ye see where he is, and he'll be very glad to see ye, that I'll assure ye o'."'

I walked round the end of the loch and over a bridge to the little inn of 'Tibbie Shiel's' where Hogg and his friends used to gather. 'Tibbie's' to-day has become slightly sophisticated, but it has not lost the look of an 'auld clay biggin'. The old box beds are still in position in the kitchen walls.

Tibbie Shiel was an Ettrick woman who married a Westmorland mole-catcher named Richardson. When he died she, encumbered by six children, began to let her spare room to lodgers, the first being Robert Chambers. So the inn developed that became famous throughout the Scottish Lowlands. Tibbie was a woman of character and managed her difficult literary guests with great skill. Her trout fried in oatmeal, her luscious slices of ham, and her fresh fried eggs brought many a genius, who had been wandering the lochside all day, rushing to her like a starving schoolboy. She was acquainted with all the vagaries of the literary mind.

And she had many a good laugh too! One night when a group, which included Hogg, had talked themselves dry and the bottles were empty, Hogg begged her 'to bring in the loch'.

On the way back I stopped a moment at the Gordon Arms Inn that stands where the road runs north to Traquair. There is a plate outside which announces: 'At this inn in the autumn of 1830 Sir Walter Scott and the Ettrick Shepherd met and parted for the last time.'

This was when Scott, worn out after four years' incessant literary knight errantry, already faced the end. He had suffered a slight stroke in the February of that year and he walked slowly for a mile down the road leaning heavily on Hogg's shoulder:

'There was something in his manner that distressed me,' wrote Hogg. 'He often changed the subject very abruptly and never laughed. . . .'

Poor Scott. This was the time when, reading 'Otterburn', he had broken down in tears at the lines:

> My wound is deep—I fain would sleep—
> Take thou the vanguard of the three,
> And hide me beneath the bracken bush,
> That grows on yonder lily lea.

Opposite Yarrow a road winds southward into the valley cut by Ettrick Water. It is a smaller, lonelier version of the neighbouring vale. I soon approached a place where the Ettrick flows through a miniature river gorge, and a few miles farther on beside the winding river I came to the most perfect little kirk in the Lowlands of Scotland.

If you wish to see the ideal Scottish kirk you must see Ettrick. The old building stands in its shady kirkyard, covered in dark ivy. Inside, it presents to the eye an intricate arrangement of pews, the clear glass windows admit the light of pure reason and there is over the place an atmosphere compounded of centuries of Presbyterianism, centuries of god-fearing Sabbaths, and of admonition and rebuke. And I seemed to detect the smell of peppermint hiding wistfully and timidly behind the more powerful staleness of a building that is used only on the seventh day.

In the peaceful shadow of the ivied kirk lie James Hogg,

and Tibbie Shiel, and also Hogg's maternal grandfather whose epitaph is as follows :

> Here lyeth William Laidlaw, the far-famed Will o' Phaup, who, for feats of frolic, agility and strength had no equal in his day.

In the same place is buried Hogg's mother, the woman who coloured her son's mind with the beauty and the fantasy of the ballad country.

§ 13

I have spent a long time in Sir Walter Scott's study at Abbotsford House. It remains just as he left it when, on a hushed September afternoon a century ago, his great soul retired from the most terrible struggle into which any man of letters has ever flung himself.

How Sir Walter Scott at the age of fifty-five shouldered his publisher's debt of £117,000, how he solemnly dedicated his brains to the creditors, how he worked like a slave for honour's sake, and how in six terrible years he earned a great fortune every penny of which went to others, is an epic and a martyr-dom. In Abbotsford, which he built as his darling retreat from the world, he found the rack on which his mighty in-tellect was tortured to death.

The day on which he died was still and warm. All the windows of Abbotsford House were open. They took his bed into the dining-room. Those who knelt around it could hear the Tweed running over its pebbles :

' God bless you all,' were his last words.

And the man who had written himself to death breathed his last breath. . . .

I must give you some idea of the study in which Scott's great fight took place. It is a small room lined with books from floor to ceiling. Ten steps lead up to a gallery that runs round the room and gives access to the upper shelves. There is a small door in a turret, and a winding stair that goes up to his bedroom. Often in the early morning he would come down that stair and, sitting at his desk, begin the day's work.

There is a window that looks out over green grass and shrubs to a yew hedge. The fire in the grate is laid ready to be lit, just as it was in Scott's time, for he, the earliest riser in Abbotsford, often lit it himself before he began his morning task.

The chair in which I have been sitting is an ancient high-backed chair whose black padded leather is here and there worn grey by Scott as he moved his body or lay back to think. No one has worked in this room for a hundred years. Yet it is like the room of a living man. I keep looking towards the stairs, where it seems that at any moment the tall figure of Sir Walter might descend and take possession of this desk and this chair.

Over twenty thousand people are shown this room every year. It is one of the best-known rooms in the world. But there are things about it that no one knows, because the desk is kept locked.

Major-General Sir Walter Maxwell Scott, the great-great-grandson of the novelist and the present laird of Abbotsford, unlocked it for me. When the desk is opened it seems impossible that Walter Scott has been dead for a hundred years. I looked into it and marvelled. If Scott could look now into this drawer he would find the little intimate things he knew so well, lying there just as he left them in September, 1832.

In a drawer on the right is a little pouch containing locks of his children's hair. They are wrapped up in spills of paper, each one labelled.

' My dearest Anne,' I read on one.

There is a bunch of his quill pens, the pens he had never used, the pens ready in his desk for the carrying on of his life's mission, cut and ready for his next novel.

One of them only has been dipped in ink. It was used many years ago when Queen Victoria visited Abbotsford, and it was used more recently by the present King and Queen.

There is Walter Scott's blotting-pad. It is a large folio book containing hundreds of pages of blotting-paper. If you held them up to a mirror you could read his writing, although this has not yet been done. There are his account books going back over many years.

Scott kept accounts that look exactly like a bank pass-book. In the year 1799, before he was famous—the year, in fact, in which he began to collect Border ballads—he put down every penny spent. ' Mrs. Scott. Housekeeping, £10 '; ' Labourer 2s. 6d.'   Those are the homely entries. There are three pairs of spectacles in leather cases. The desk is just as he left it a hundred years ago.

How is it, you will ask, that a man's room can survive a century? The next generation always alters and 'improves'. Why is it that the visitor to Abbotsford finds Sir Walter Scott's study untouched by change? I will tell you. Scott was so famous during his lifetime that Abbotsford became a ' sight ' long before his death. In the year 1833—the year after his death—the first Visitors' Book was opened. The advance guard of that great army of Scott pilgrims had begun. I have seen this interesting book. The first name is that of Mrs. Russell Eliott, of Chiefswood, under the date February 5, 1833. On the first page is the name of the first American visitor to Abbotsford. He is George C. Thorburn, who signs himself ' New York, North America '.

So it is clear that no sooner was Walter Scott dead than his family was made to realize that his study belonged not to them but to the world.

Abbotsford to-day is a happy country house lying in an exquisite curve of the Tweed. No writer ever designed a more beautiful home for himself. The world thinks of Walter Scott as the author of the Waverley Novels ; Walter Scott thought of himself as the author of Abbotsford House. He bought the land when there was not one stone upon another. He built the baronial castle, bit by bit, as his royalties came in, living and working in a humble dwelling in his own grounds, watching all the time how his towers and turrets arose, the hammers of his carpenters and the chisels of his stonemasons drowning the scratchings of the splendid pen which paid them. He adored this dream of Abbotsford.

A very different type of Scotsman, Thomas Carlyle, hit out at him, charging him with ' ambition ', for ' fast as the new gold came in for a new Waverley novel, or even faster, it changed itself into moory acres, into stone, and hewn or planted wood '. Carlyle considered this to be ' delirium of a kind '.

Scott would rather have been a soldier than a writer. He would rather have been a Border laird than the most famous novelist of his time. The world is full of fine men who succeed in the things that are not those things nearest to their hearts. And Scott was one of them. Fame and money came to him. He used them to make Abbotsford.

This house, and the establishment of his family in it, meant more to him than the applause of Europe. He adored the Borderland, and, like a tree, he had to strike his roots down into the very soil of it, or die.

If Walter Scott could come back he would feel less pride in wreaths and orations than in the fact that another Sir Walter Scott still lives in Abbotsford.

General Sir Walter Maxwell Scott is descended from Sophia, who married Lockhart, the famous biographer. If Sir Walter Scott could have visualized anyone so far ahead as his great-great-grandson, he would have been content. General Scott is a distinguished soldier whose career would have delighted his great-great-grandfather. He also possesses the outward form and the inward vision that would have appealed to the first Sir Walter.

A man may be accounted fortunate if his children do not disappoint him, but if his great-great-grandchildren—those mythical creatures—are made in his pattern, surely posterity has been more than generous!

The present Sir Walter Scott treasures every memory of his great ancestor. He knows every stone of Abbotsford and its story. A hundred years fall away when he shows one over Abbotsford, and so intimate is his knowledge and so deep his affection that one expects to see a door open in the library and to find oneself face to face with the founder of the house.

' I suppose Sir Walter Scott used to write by candle-light,' I said.

' Oh, no,' said Sir Walter. ' He was one of the first enthusiasts for gas in Scotland. He used to make gas at Abbotsford. It was made from oil, and the supply of gas often gave out at the most inconvenient moments. Lady Scott and the daughters hated it! The smell at times was said to be awful.'

Sir Walter knows the bewildering history of all the relics and treasures which his ancestor collected in such profusion.

' That stone plinth in the lawn,' he said, as we were walking round the garden, ' is the base of the old Mercat Cross in Edinburgh. The fountains of that cross ran with wine the day James V married Mary of Lorraine.'

We went into a walled garden. In the wall are set various stones, inscriptions, coats-of-arms and such like.

'Many of these,' said Sir Walter, 'came from the old Tolbooth in Edinburgh. Sir Walter Scott picked them up from a rubbish heap. The central stone shows the pre-Reformation version of Edinburgh's coat-of-arms. In the old days, as you see, the supporter of the arms to the left was a monk with a cord round his waist. After the Reformation they changed him into a maiden!'

And we came to the door which Sir Walter Scott used. A deer-hound carved in stone sits beside it. Two little steps lead up to his back. It is a mounting block, or a 'louping-on stane'. Scott, because of his lameness, always used one when he mounted a horse.

Beneath this stone is buried Scott's famous hound Maida, the dog that was so often painted with his master that he used to show his teeth and growl at sight of an easel! Scott —who was one of the greatest dog lovers of his time— considered Maida to be 'the noblest dog ever seen on the Border'. He was something between wolf and deer-hound, six feet long from nose to tail and so tall that he could clean a plate on a table without lifting a paw. Now he sleeps beneath this stone on which Scott wrote:

> *Beneath the sculptured form which late you wore,*
> *Sleep soundly, Maida, at your master's door.*

It was of Maida and his approaching death that Scott wrote, in a letter to Maria Edgeworth, a touching tribute to dogs and the love we can feel for them:

'I have sometimes thought of the final cause of dogs having such short lives,' wrote Scott, 'and I am satisfied it is in compassion to the human race; for if we suffer so much in losing a dog after an acquaintance of ten or twelve years, what would it be if they were to live double that time?'

In the hall are all the relics and the armour which Scott delighted to collect. He was one of the first civilians to visit Waterloo after the battle. Mementoes of his visit are the uniforms of a French cuirassier and of a member of Napoleon's Old Guard. Perhaps the most touching relics in this hall are the last garments worn by Scott, including a tall, light-coloured beaver hat and a pair of black square-toed shoes, with the heel of the right shoe built up to counteract the wearer's lameness.

No home, I am sure, in which a great man has lived, preserves his memory more vividly and more lovingly than Abbotsford preserves the memory of its founder.

Sitting here in his study, it is difficult to think of Scott's place in literature. It is of the man I think, the man whose character was pure gold. It is a commonplace that we who come after must forgive many a man for his sins because he was a great artist. Scott needs no forgiveness. He was a perfect man.

If you asked me what I consider to be the most remarkable thing in Abbotsford, I would tell you to look at something that every one of the twenty thousand yearly visitors may see. In the library—which is the next room to the study—is Chantrey's famous bust of Walter Scott. It was considered by his family as the best and most characteristic likeness of him.

It was made in the year 1820, when Scott was at the height of his fame. He was the foremost novelist of his time ; he was rich ; he had just been knighted by George IV ; and he was, above all, laird of Abbotsford.

You see a contented, happy man in the late forties, but he looks much younger. He looks, as Chantrey himself said, ' as if he were about to break out into some sly, funny old story'. Now walk a few yards into this little study. There is a kind of alcove in a corner, in which is exposed the death mask of Sir Walter Scott. It was made a hundred years ago, and twelve years after the Chantrey bust. You see a man bowed down by work and worry. His cheeks have sunk. Sad lines have etched themselves beneath his eyes and at the corners of his mouth. Sorrow and disappointment and self-denial are engraved on that face.

It is so sad, so tired and so over-burdened that, looking at it, you will sigh with relief to know that death came to release a proud spirit from its prison. How incredible it seems that twelve years can work such a change in a man.

That is the drama of Abbotsford and of Walter Scott. In one room is the proud ' Wizard of the North '; in another room is the tired, worn-out ' Slave of the Lamp '.

We who have felt our imaginations kindle at the fire of his mind should think of this when we pay tribute to his genius ; we should pay homage to a man who, with a courage more magnificent than that of any hero in fiction, flung himself into a fight for honour's sake and—wrote himself to death. . . .

I go from this quiet unchanged room, with the feeling that if the spirit of Scott came back to earth you would meet him in this study, sitting in this chair, perhaps prowling round these well-filled shelves, pleased and surprised, perhaps, that nothing has changed since September, 1832.

§ 14

Snow, they said, had fallen in the north. The Borders, in the grip of the first frost, waited for winter as men might wait an army marching south. Its spies were everywhere. The pale sun shone on hedges touched with rime, and every heel-mark in the fields was lidded with white ice.

This was a new Scotland, so different from the land which I had entered months before in the warmth of an autumn afternoon : a Scotland brilliant in winter sun and very still under snow-laden skies. It seemed to me that the approach of winter accentuated those human things about Scotland that I love so much : the warmth of firesides, the splendour of high tea, the pointfulness of liquor, and the friendliness of talk. And so I lingered in the hope that I might see the Borders sheeted with the first snow ; but, as day followed day and the outposts of winter lingered stubbornly round Blairgowrie, I began to get anxious, because I had duties in the south.

Never shall I forget those frosty morning walks, the red sunrise over Melrose, the headstones rising from white grass, the sharp morning air into which man and beast breathed a little mist of steam, and all day long from dawn until dusk the world alight, as with a million little stars, with the robin's plaintive song.

One day I climbed the Eildons and, looking down on hard fields and woodlands bare as beggars, saw the Tweed as dark as Acheron moving eastward through the frosty land to its meeting with the Teviot. How strangely a man sees a country through his own moods and through the prism of his imagination, and how generously a country responds to surrender. So I thought, as I looked down on this Lowland valley, feeling sad that my journey was over. A man meets many travellers bearing their arrogance about the world and finding nothing in foreign places but their own pride of mind. From such men all countries hide. If you would see a country, you must look for the good things and the kind things ; and they will come to you. How easy is this search in Scotland.

The snow held off, so that one day I took the road from Jedburgh to Carter Bar. Pausing on the crest, where two posts stand in the moorland wind, 'Scotland' on one, 'England' on the other, I looked back to a land that lay still and blue to the northern sky.

'Good-bye, and thank you for all the good and kindly things, for friendship, for humour, for beauty. . . .'

Then I went down the hill into England over miles of dead heather and burnt-out bracken.

INDEX

Stevenson, Robert Louis, 51, 344
Stewart, James, of Appin, 171, 172, 173-8
Stewartry, the, 22-3
Stirling, 145, 354, 355, 360
Stornoway, 196
Stranraer, 117,
Strathspey, 211
Sutherland, 262
  clearances in, 278-9
Sweetenham, Captain, 192, 218
Sweetheart Abbey, Galloway, 90, 91

Tarf, falls of, 309
Tartan, hand-woven, Kilbarchan, 133-5
Telford, Thomas, 14
Thistle, as national emblem, 127-9
Thurso, 262, 269, 279, 288-9
Tibbie Shiel, 398-9, 400
Tobermory Bay, 155, 159
  Spanish treasure galleon in, 162-5, 171
Tolbooth, Kirkcudbright, 55, 73
Tongue, 289
Tudor, Margaret, 129
Tullibardine, Marquis of, 192
Trawler fishing, North Sea, 314-33

Twizel Bridge, 388

Urr, Galloway, 112
Urr, the Mote of, 37, 38-40

Vikings, Caithness, 287-8

Wade, Field-Marshal George, 129, 212-14, 215
Wallace, William, 27, 105, 356
  Memorial, Dryburgh, 102-3
  Memorial, Stirling, 355-7
Walpole, Horace, 185, 193
Western Isles, 154, 156, 161, 165
Westminster Abbey, 155
White, Rev. Hugh, of Irvine, 28, 29, 30, 31, 33
Whithorn, 24, 115, 116, 117
Wick, 262, 279, 280
Wigtown, 50, 114-15
Wigtown Martyrs, 49-50, 115
William III, 257
William IV, 352
Wilson, Agnes, 49-50
Wilson, Margaret, the Wigtown Martyr, 49-50
Wishart, George, 345, 346, 347
Wolf, the last Scottish, 277-8

Yarrow Water, 390-400

Printed in Great Britain by
Butler & Tanner Ltd.,
Frome and London